A: 20/24 ART £3.50

THE BUILDINGS OF ENGLAND

CUMBERLAND AND WESTMORLAND

NIKOLAUS PEVSNER

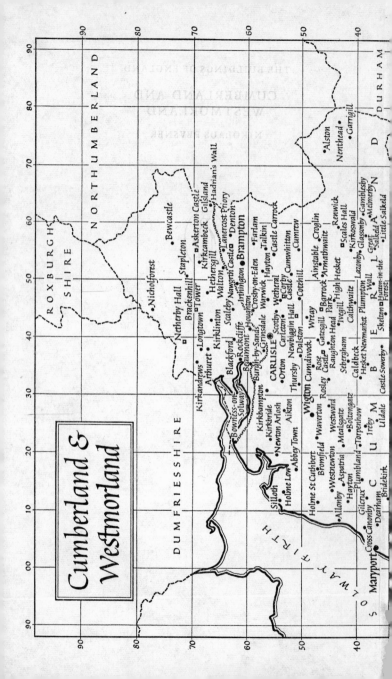

Cumberland &
Westmorland

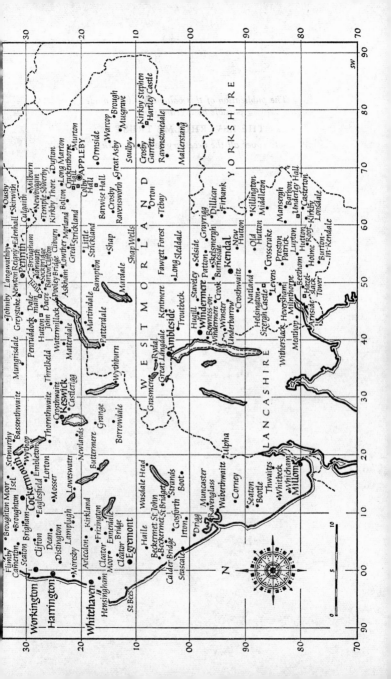

The publication of this volume has been made possible by a grant from

THE LEVERHULME TRUST

to cover all the necessary research work

THE BUILDINGS OF ENGLAND

Cumberland and Westmorland

BY

NIKOLAUS PEVSNER

★

PENGUIN BOOKS

Penguin Books Ltd, Harmondsworth, Middlesex, England
Penguin Books Inc., 7110 Ambassador Road, Baltimore, Maryland 21207, U.S.A.
Penguin Books Australia Ltd, Ringwood, Victoria, Australia

—

First published 1967
Reprinted 1973

—

ISBN 0 14 071033 7

—

Copyright © Nikolaus Pevsner, 1967

—

Made and printed in Great Britain
by William Clowes & Sons, Limited, London, Beccles and Colchester
Photogravure plates by D. H. Greaves Ltd, Scarborough
Set in Monotype Plantin

FOR
FLORENCE AND DIETER

CONTENTS

Map References

★

The numbers printed in italic type in the margin
against the place names in the gazetteer of the
book indicate the position of the place in question
on the index map (pages 2–3), which is divided
into sections by the 10-kilometre reference lines
of the National Grid. The reference given here
omits the two initial letters (formerly numbers)
which in a full grid reference refer to the 100-
kilometre squares into which the country is divided.
The first two numbers indicate the *western* boundary, and the last two the *southern* boundary, of the
10-kilometre square in which the place in question
is situated. For example Dacre (reference 4020)
will be found in the 10-kilometre square bounded
by grid lines 40 and 50 on the *west* and 20 and 30
on the *south*: Appleby (reference 6020) in the
square bounded by grid lines 60 and 70 on the
west and 20 and 30 on the *south*.

The map contains all those places, whether
towns, villages or isolated buildings, which are
the subject of separate entries in the text.

FOREWORD

This foreword must begin with apologies. One ought not to publish a volume on Cumberland and Westmorland without the Furness part of Lancashire. I had to do it, simply because preparation of Lancashire had not proceeded far enough for me to travel when the Cumberland and Westmorland travels took place. Yet one should not describe the W without the E bank of Windermere, or Carlisle, Lanercost, St Bees, Calder, and so on without Furness and Cartmel. In fact we actually did go to Cartmel for a quick check – we, i.e. Mr Neil Stratford, who drove me, and myself. Mr Stratford was a good companion, unbowed by culinary deprivations, and a very positive help on matters Norman.

The published research which had to be absorbed is very uneven in the case of this volume. For Westmorland we have the work of the Royal Commission on Historic Monuments (RCHM), i.e. complete coverage up to 1714 but not beyond. For Cumberland there is nothing comparable. One uses the volumes of the Transactions of the Cumberland and Westmorland Antiquarian and Archaeological Society, the old county histories, some articles contributed by Mr C. G. Bulman to the Carlisle Gazette, *and of course the lists of the Ministry of Housing and Local Government. They were to me a great blessing, in a county where all the available information on a church might occasionally be 'Kelly: small but ancient'. But in Westmorland, unfortunately, the whole N half was only ready to be issued to me when my volume was already in proof, and in Cumberland the same was true of the important rural district of Penrith. The rural district of Millom is not available yet at all. These were serious handicaps. On the whole there is a great difference between what has been published on Westmorland and on Cumberland. It was brought out very strikingly two years ago, when Margaret Wood's* The English Medieval House *came out. This comprehensive textbook contains references to ten houses in Westmorland, one in Cumberland.*

With research what it was, I had to rely doubly on information personally asked for and personally obtained. My secretary Miss Wendy Martin had to bear the brunt of that extensive correspondence. Miss Dorothy Dorn once again succeeded in converting my miserable handwriting into a neat typescript, and Mrs Nairn that typescript with all the odds and ends corrected and tacked on into suitable 'copy' for the printer. My thanks are also due, as always, to the Ministry of Housing and Local Government (here abbreviated MHLG) for allowing me the full use of their lists of buildings of architectural or historical interest, to the National Monuments Record (NMR), to Mr Peter Ferriday (PF), who placed his index of Victorian church restorations on permanent loan in my office, and to Sir Thomas Kendrick for allowing me the use of his index of Victorian stained glass (TK). I also made use of the late H. S. Goodhart-Rendel's card index of Victorian churches (GR).

In addition I had the benefit of the special knowledge of Professor Terence Miller, Mr Alec Clifton-Taylor, Mr Derek Simpson, and Professor Barry Cunliffe, who provided me with special introductions on geology, building materials, prehistory, and Roman remains respectively, and the latter two also with the gazetteer entries on their subjects. Their contributions seem to me a great asset to this volume.

And how much less useful would the volume be without the help I received from Mr Kenneth Smith, the indefatigable City Librarian of Carlisle, Mr D. F. James, the Librarian of the Kendal and Westmorland Library Service, Mr Daniel Hay, Librarian of the Public Library at Whitehaven, Mr H. J. Chandler, Librarian of the Public Library at Workington, and Mrs Russell Davies, Investigator for the Ministry of Housing and Local Government. Mr J. T. Smith of the Royal Commission on Historic Monuments and Mr R. W. Brunskill of Manchester University kindly put at my disposal some of their research on farmhouses in the North (which unfortunately the limited scale of this volume crowded out). Mr C. G. Bulman helped out with his great knowledge of Cumberland churches, Mr W. Carrick answered queries on Wigton, Mr M. R. Holmes on Appleby, Mr A. C. Taylor contributed on Webster of Kendal, and Miss Helen Kapp of Abbott Hall, Kendal and Mr H. Butler of Huyton Hill School, Ambleside offered Mr Stratford and myself welcome hospitality when we were in their neighbourhood. Owners or occupiers of houses were invariably generous and helpful, and I feel it my duty to single out among them Mr and Mrs R. Bagot, the Earl of Carlisle, Mr J. Coney, Mr and Mrs E. Curwen, Lord Henley, Lt.-Col. Hugh Levin, Col. Horneyold Strickland, and Mr I. J. Wall.

Inclusion in the gazetteer or exclusion from it are determined by the principles followed in The Buildings of England *throughout the years. I have myself seen everything that I describe. Where this is not the case, the information obtained by other means is placed in brackets. Information ought to be as complete as the space of the volume permits for churches prior to c.1830 and all town houses, manor houses, and country houses of more than purely local interest. On small manor houses and farmhouses this ideal could obviously not be attained in Cumberland. I must have overlooked much. Movable furnishings are not included in secular buildings, though they are in churches. Exceptions to the latter rule are bells, hatchments, chests, chairs, plain fonts, and altar tables. Royal arms, coffin lids with foliate crosses, and even with swords or shears, as they occur in Cumberland and Westmorland, and brasses of post-Reformation date are mentioned occasionally, church plate of after 1830 only rarely. Village crosses are omitted where only a plain base and a stump of the shaft survives. As for churches and chapels of after 1830, I had to make a selection, and this is dictated by architectural value or by significance otherwise in the light of architectural history. The same applies to secular buildings of the C19 and C20.*

Finally, as in all previous volumes, it is necessary to end the foreword to this with an appeal to all users to draw my attention to errors and omissions.

INTRODUCTION*

THE BUILDINGS OF
CUMBERLAND AND WESTMORLAND

BY NIKOLAUS PEVSNER

8, 9, p. 67

ART in Cumberland started its course through history at its climax. It never reached higher than with the Bewcastle Cross. The CROSSES of Bewcastle and of Ruthwell in Dumfriesshire, only 30 miles w of Bewcastle, are the greatest achievement of their date in the whole of Europe, their date being the late C7. This date, whatever doubts the most recent research has pronounced, is determined by the inscription on the Bewcastle Cross which refers to Alcfrith, son of King Oswi of Northumbria, and cannot reasonably be assumed to have been applied later than 709. Moreover, for reasons of style, Ruthwell must precede Bewcastle. On the Ruthwell Cross there are figures and scenes and scrolls of foliage with birds and beasts more completely Mediterranean–Early-Christian than anything was to be north of the Alps for many centuries to come. The figure style, even in a state of surface that does not allow the finer features to be recognizable any longer, is amazingly Roman and relaxed; iconography has been traced to Coptic, that is Egyptian, Early Christian sources – and Egypt was the country of origin of that branch of monasticism which via the south of France extended into Ireland and from there to Scotland and North England – and the style of ornament derives from the Eastern Mediterranean, e.g. such works as the Throne of Maximian at Ravenna, which is believed to be an Egyptian or a Syrian work of the C4 or C5. The Bewcastle Cross shares all these sources, but has lost some of the purity of the Mediterranean South which renders Ruthwell unique in the North. On the Bewcastle Cross there are less figures, and the ornament has side by side with the 'inhabited scrolls' the kind of close interlace which was to dominate later crosses and which occurs in Early Christian Rome (*cancelli* of S. Clemente) and in both Nordic (Sutton Hoo) and Celtic material. The technical mastery is as amazing as at

* Places in Westmorland are marked (W) in this introduction, as in the indexes of plates and places.

Ruthwell. How can it have been possible, in stone, and at so early a date ? Perhaps one ought to take into consideration that preceding stages may not be preserved – after all, the vast majority of early stone carving must have perished – and that England in the age of Bede and in the decades only just preceding Alcuin was infinitely more civilized than the rest of Northern Europe. Even so, and even if one draws into the comparison the immense artistry of the Lindisfarne Gospels, also of about 700, the fullness and ease of the Ruthwell and Bewcastle figures and foliage remain miraculous, as does the perfectly controlled composition of the beasts and birds in the scrolls. There is nothing barbaric here, as there is in the contemporary and also Northumbrian Franks Casket and the Coffin of St Cuthbert, and as there was going to be more and more the later the crosses were produced. Between Bewcastle and the c9 shafts of Irton, Heversham (W), and Dacre a hardening of the vine scrolls is noticeable, and at Irton geometric patterns, steps, frets, and symmetrical curly patterns set in circles dominate. Anglo-Saxon becomes Anglo-Danish or Anglo-Viking in the c10. The crosses multiplied, but most of them are rightly called by Professor Stone 'dreary and shoddy'. They are characterized by irregular interlace, by big animals entwined in scrolls, and by doll-like human figures. In Cumberland is one of the best of them all: the Gosforth Cross of the later c10, nearly 15 ft high, elegantly slender, with a square shaft merging by vertical lobes into a round base, much as block capitals at the same time do in the Rhineland and Saxony to mediate between square abacus and column below. The Gosforth Cross has a wheel-head such as they had apparently been introduced in the c9. The style at Gosforth is a mixture. Single-strand close interlace corresponds to monuments on the Isle of Man,* but the shape with the round upper part and the lobes is centred in the Peak District (e.g. Leek, Staffs.). The figures at Gosforth are mostly pagan, but there is side by side with them the Crucifixion with Longinus and Stephaton. The Gosforth type is also represented by crosses at Beckermet St Bridget (two) and Penrith (two). Cumberland is full of crosses and cross-fragments of the later c10 and the c11.‡ The only ones that can be singled out here are those with human figures. It is not always possible to say what they represent, but Christ, the Virgin, and St John are on the

74, p. 144 [margin note]

10, p. 129 [margin note]

---

* And, according to Kendrick, occurs on seven crosses in Cumberland.
‡ The gazetteer cannot describe them all; Calverley and Collingwood's book of 1899 is still indispensable.

Burton-in-Kendale Cross (W), at Kirkby Stephen (W) is the so-called Bound Devil, at Gosforth a boat with men – and an unusually big beast,* at Dearham three figures under arches and, on another fragment, a horse, a man, and a bird, and at Dacre some thin-limbed, untidy men and animals. Relations with the styles of Viking art, first Jellinge, then Urnes, are to be found at Gosforth, Kirkby Stephen (W; Bound Devil), and Cross Canonby – all these with Jellinge – and on the Saint's 11 Tomb at Gosforth with Urnes.

But the Saint's Tomb is a tomb, and on funerary MONU- MENTS nothing has as yet been said. Of course crosses could commemorate people, and one of the Beckermet St Bridget crosses perhaps does commemorate 'Edith, little maid'. But the usual form of tombstone in our counties was the hogback, and hogbacks can be seen at Appleby St Michael (W), Aspatria, Cross Canonby,‡ Gosforth, Kirkby Stephen (W), Lowther (W), 12 Penrith, and Plumbland. The Lowther hogback has human figures, and one of the Gosforth ones Christ, the other two armies meeting. An exception is the pedimental lintel at St Bees with St Michael and the Dragon, no doubt later CII, but Anglo- Danish in style.

Considering this glut of Anglo-Saxon and Anglo-Danish sculpture, it is bewildering indeed that so little should be left us of ANGLO-SAXON ARCHITECTURE. What there is without exception late, i.e. of the CII and possibly even of after 1066, and it is also without exception hardly worth including in this summary; the w tower of Morland (W) and some narrow door- ways such as those of Long Marton (W) and Ormside (W). At Long Marton a problem of tympana is involved, with one tympanum looking strangely pre-Conquest – as does that now 76 separated from the church building at St Bees – but the other quite emphatically Norman.§

So to NORMAN ARCHITECTURE. Here the great impetus in the north was monastic. MONASTIC HOUSES were founded as follows, including the part of Lancashire on the peninsula. Benedictines from St Mary York started Wetheral c.1110 and St Bees c.1120, and granges of St Mary York were at Kirkby Lonsdale (W) and Kirkby Stephen (W). Benedictine nunneries

* Cf. for such beasts Cross Canonby.

‡ At Cross Canonby is also the St Laurence Slab, and this is a coffin lid with tapering sides and more likely Norman than Anglo-Danish.

§ Tympana, even Norman, are a great rarity in Cumberland and Westmor- land. Apart from those already referred to, there are only Bridekirk and two at Kirkbampton, one of them with weird, bold, geometrical plaques.

existed at Armathwaite and Seaton near Bootle, both established
*c.*1190, and perhaps near Kirkoswald. There were no Cluniacs
in the area. The principal Cistercian house was of course Furness in Lancashire with between *c.*20 and *c.*40 monks. Its
origins go back to 1123, and it belonged to the Order of Savigny
then. From Furness Calder was colonized in 1134, from Melrose
in Scotland Holme Cultram (Abbey Town) in 1150. Holme
Cultram had between *c.*15 and *c.*25 monks. Hawkshead in
Lancashire was a grange of Furness. The chief Augustinian
houses were Carlisle, before it became a cathedral in 1133,
Lanercost, founded *c.*1166, and Cartmel in Lancashire, founded
*c.*1190. Conishead (post-1154) in Lancashire was a smaller
Augustinian house. The Premonstratensian Canons had their
establishment at Shap (W) from *c.*1200 onwards, having
migrated there from Preston Patrick, which they had reached
*c.*1190. Shap had up to *c.*20 canons and is the only major
monastery in Westmorland: Ravenstonedale was only a grange
(of the Gilbertine Watton in Yorkshire). This leaves the friars.
The Dominicans and the Franciscans were only at Carlisle (both
from 1233), the Carmelites at Appleby (W., *c.*1281), and the
Austin Friars at Penrith (late C13). It shows how un-urban the
whole peninsula was.

Of all these monastic establishments what survives in Cumberland and Westmorland is the following: nothing of the friars,
only excavated foundations of the Gilbertines at Ravenstonedale (W), at Carlisle the area of crossing and transepts in a
powerful Mid-Norman of *c.*1120–60 of which more will be said,
at Lanercost a part round the S transept and S aisle of about
1170–5 and more of the C13, in the other places nothing before
the late C12.*

The late C12 and early C13 are indeed the climax of ecclesiastical architecture in Cumberland and Westmorland. There is
only one monument of the early C12 which would have to form
part of any more than regional survey: the W part of the N
75 arcade of Kirkby Lonsdale (W), with its mighty piers directly

---

* To be a little more explicit, about later periods as well, the survivals are,
20 in alphabetical order: Calder church of the late C12 to C13 and the C14
[14] gatehouse; Carlisle E end and stump of the nave, and refectory and prior's
lodging; Holme Cultram (Abbey Town) nave; Kirkoswald The Nunnery
one doorway (if this was a nunnery); Lanercost church almost complete
(W range, undercroft of the S range, traces of the E range); St Bees church
only; Seaton near Bootle chancel E wall only; Shap (W) early C16 w tower
and sufficient traces of the rest of the church and of the monastic quarters;
Wetheral gatehouse only.

inspired by Durham. 1115 might be the approximate date of this. The same date can be suggested for the remarkable relief of two knights at Bolton (W). Its style is entirely Norman, 77 whereas, as we have seen, one of the two tympana at Long Marton (W) is still in the Anglo-Danish tradition. A little later, say c.1125–35, are the parts round crossing and transepts at Carlisle. Other work which appears primeval can in fact not be so early – e.g. the fleshy flat capitals at Lowther (W) and Crosby Garrett (W). At Lowther two hands can be distinguished, those of an older and a younger master, but both must have worked at the same time, and that time must be c.1170. About that time the flood was rising, and it did not recede during the TRANSI-TIONAL decades and into the C13. Ornate doorways are preserved at Brough (W), Burgh-by-Sands, Great Salkeld, Kirkby Lonsdale (W), Lanercost (pointed!), St Bees, and 13 Torpenhow, ornate chancel arches at Irthington, Kirkbampton, and Torpenhow. Torpenhow is the most impressive, strong and barbaric, yet again hardly possible before 1170. Beakhead under West Riding influence occurs at Brough (W), Caldbeck, and St Bees, an abstracticized beakhead at Burgh-by-Sands, zigzag in most places, waterleaf frequently too, and occasionally trumpet-scallops. The order of events, nowhere provable, how-ever, in exactly this sequence, is round piers with square abaci, then for a brief moment with octagonal abaci, and then with round abaci; round arches with rolls or steps, then with slight chamfers, then with full chamfers, but the latter nearly always only after they have become pointed; capitals with waterleaf or trumpets and then crockets and early stiff-leaf or broad, simple, large moulded shapes. The major monuments are Kirkby Lonsdale (W), Holme Cultram Abbey (Abbey Town), and St 16 Bees. Arcades are preserved in many places, and often the course of the development can be followed neatly. The most beautiful of all capitals is one lying loose at Kirkby Stephen (W). Of special features few deserve notice: the high, narrow blank arches all round the apse of Warwick, inspired probably by 15 Normandy, the inner wall arcading with columns round the E windows at Beaumont and Ireby, the central tower at Barton (W), and the tunnel-vaulting of its lowest stage and also that of the W towers at Brigham and Dearham, datable to about 1200 and introducing a theme which was to become a *Leitmotiv* of Cumberland and Westmorland architecture.

The late C12 impetus carried building enthusiasm well into the C13, and the transition from Late Norman to EARLY

ENGLISH is gradual in the monastic churches of Calder,
Lanercost, St Bees, and Shap (W). Calder, Lanercost, and Shap
incidentally have transepts with an E aisle. At Lanercost the top
of the W front was only reached after 1250, as the style of a too
little known statue of the Magdalen proves. Of the same date
was the chapter house of Calder. Its E window had geometrical
tracery. Characteristic of the C13 in Cumberland and Westmorland are piers of four or eight shafts, with or without fillets
(Calder, St Bees, and – in Westmorland – Shap). This motif
carries on to the end of the century and beyond.

At Carlisle a fire in 1292 destroyed the newly built E end,
except for the outer walls with their lancet windows, and rebuilding was done with piers of the same type. The capitals have
delicious bossy foliage, entirely DECORATED in style now, with
little people acting the labours of the months. Appleby (W) also
built Dec and with such piers. The end of the rebuilding at
Carlisle was the grand E window, a nine-light affair with the
most resourceful flowing tracery. Otherwise flowing tracery is
rare, as indeed Dec building is rare. The most attractive individual motif is the almond-shaped W window of the Hudleston
Aisle at Millom. The same motif occurs in the W window of the
S aisle at Brigham, which was a gift of 1323. An E window with
flowing tracery and a tomb recess with pierced mouchette
tracery go with it. A very different aspect of the C14 is the
fortified, or rather defendable, W towers of Newton Arlosh,
shortly after 1304, Burgh-by-Sands,* and Great Salkeld. They
are a second reminder (after the vaulted Norman towers) of the
necessity of strength and massive solidity in this part of
England.

The theme recurs in the later Middle Ages and the regional
PERPENDICULAR. There is a little more to note here than in
the Dec, though little of course also, when one thinks in terms of
East Anglia or Somerset or Gloucestershire. Even so, wool-
wealth made itself felt in towns like Kendal (W). The church
here received double aisles, and Kirkby Lonsdale (W) also
added an outer N aisle. Another prosperous-looking town church
is that of Appleby (W). What characterizes Perp North Country
churches is the broad, rather squat W towers and long, low
naves, often with chancel and chancel aisles continuing the nave
and aisles line without a break. Equally characteristic are
straight-headed windows. They usually have cusped ogee-arched

---

* The tower at Burgh has its original YATT, that is its strong iron gate.
Another is in the pele-tower of Dalston Hall, a third at Naworth Castle.

lights in the C14, normal cusped pointed arches to the lights in the C15, and then, in the early C16, turn to depressed-arched lights, cusped, and then uncusped, and finally – the typical Henry VIII form – uncusped round arches. Kirkoswald, e.g., of *c.*1523, has three-light windows with round-arched lights in the sides, and a five-light window of the same type in the E wall. The type was continued or revived in the C17, and it is not always certain what is 1520 and what Stuart. Greystoke is a case in point. The abbeys by the way kept up some architectural initiative to the end, as witnessed by the splendid W tower of Shap (W) of *c.*1510–20 and the W porch of Holme Cultram (Abbey Town) of 1507. On the latter dog-tooth appears, and one may well have to consider whether this is not an early case of revival rather than simply survival. We shall have to revert to this problem when dealing with the C17.

One more Perp church in Cumberland must be introduced, by far the most interesting one in either county: Boltongate, 33 which was built apparently from the late C15 to the early C16 and has its nave covered by a pointed tunnel-vault and its transeptal chapels by buttressing half-tunnels. The stone roof-covering lies (or lay) immediately on the vaults. This is not English at all; it is Scottish, and ultimately derives from Southern France. The use of this powerful vaulting is no doubt once again due to the needs of defence.*

So it is high time now that we turned to the principal subject of this introduction, the MILITARY ARCHITECTURE of Cumberland and Westmorland. Throughout the Middle Ages, and especially from the late C13 onwards, the North of England was in permanent danger of Scottish invasion,‡ or at least of cattle-stealing expeditions. The climax of the wars was the time from John Baliol to Robert Bruce. But after these heroic decades no quiet ensued in the C14 and C15, and there was in fact no peace until the Union of 1604. In Cumberland and Westmorland military architecture ranges from the large castle with outer and inner bailey to the stone-house, as it was locally called, i.e. the tower-like house suited for defence when need arose. Counting them all, I have noted 32 in Westmorland and 58 in Cumberland, and I may well have overlooked some.

The major castles are not different from those in other parts

* Cf. in Northumberland the tunnel-vaulted C13 chancel and transept of Kirknewton and the C14 aisles with half-tunnel vaults at Elsdon, also tunnel-vaulted W towers such as the C13 Embledon in Northumberland and the later Askrigg and Spennithorne in the North Riding.

‡ But in the C12 our two counties were Scottish.

of England. There are a number of Norman KEEPS of the familiar type, all apparently of the time of Henry II. They are in 78 the castles of Appleby (W), Brough (W), Brougham (W), and Carlisle. The keeps of Appleby, Brough, and Brougham were all heightened by one floor shortly after they were built. Norman also are certain other parts of the big castles: the late C11 herringbone walling at Brough (W), the herringbone walling and the gatehouse at Egremont.*

But whereas the keep in these castles was only the climax of a more complete system of defences, the keep in isolation, i.e. the PELE TOWER, as they are called in the North, also began already in the C12, and two specimens at least survive, Pendragon Castle, Mallerstang (W) and Dovenby Hall, Bridekirk, in which latter a small Norman ground-floor window is proof of the date. The tower is tunnel-vaulted in its ground stage, and this, which we have already seen applied to church towers about 1200, became the standard motif of pele towers for centuries to come. In church towers again we have had confirmation of this, at least down to the C14; for Boltongate, while vaulted throughout, has no tower.

The large castles went on developing. Of the C13 for instance there is a mighty rounded tower at Appleby (W) and there was such a one also at Brough (W). At Brough in addition a C13 hall was built of which hardly anything remains. But the hall at Egremont is C13 too, and still has enough left to convey an impression. Pele towers datable to the C13 are absent. Most of them are of the C14 and C15, for obvious enough reasons, and a decision between the two centuries, on grounds of masonry and details, is often impossible.‡ What they all have in common is the tunnel-vaulted ground stage and a spiral staircase. The tunnel-vault is very occasionally strengthened by broad transverse ribs (Greystoke Castle, licence to crenellate 1353, and Deanery, Carlisle c.1510–20), and just once these ribs run diagonally (Naworth Castle, Lord William Howard's Tower, c.1520). As a rule one vault covers the whole length and width, but there is one small group where the area is divided, not only by a wall, but by a cross corridor (Burneside Hall, Preston Patrick Hall, Lammerside Castle, Mallerstang; all Westmorland and all C14). A pele tower could, as we have seen, stand on its own, but

---

* The gatehouse has a domical rib-vault, a very rare thing.

‡ Certain details tend to be discarded late. Doorways with shouldered lintels e.g. occur much later than their normal period, which is the late C13.

mostly a hall range was added to it for comfort's sake, from the beginning or later. This pele-and-hall-range arrangement is the most frequent one, and such famous castles as Sizergh (W), Isel Hall, and Yanwath Hall (W) have it. At Johnby Castle and Scaleby Castle the hall range is tunnel-vaulted too. In some cases the hall range, at least in its present form, is post-medieval. At Hutton John e.g. it is Elizabethan, at Skelsmergh (W) Jacobean, at Lorton it is even as late as 1663, and very occasion- 45 ally the pele tower itself was converted in the late C17 or C18 into a house of three storeys with a normal front (Drawdykes Castle, Houghton 1676; Askham, Westmorland, c.1685-90; 81 Armathwaite, early C18). Sometimes the hall range is found to be flanked on both sides by towers (Bewley Castle, Bolton, Westmorland; Blencow Hall, Greystoke, Hutton-in-the-Forest, and Askerton Castle,* where the towers are later than the hall, and perhaps Levens (W)). If the towers project and are more or less identical, the plan becomes that of the normal hall house with solar wing and service wing. This is so at Howgill Castle, Milburn (W), where both wings are tunnel-vaulted, perhaps at Stonegarthside Hall, Nicholforest, and in a number of other castles. So here is a transition from the fortified to the un-fortified house. The latter type is well illustrated at Castle Dairy, Kendal (W) of the C14. The usual three doorways from hall to kitchen and offices remain at Levens (W), Middleton (W), and Preston Patrick (W). A desire for a more spacious hall after about 1300 is very noticeable in the major castles. At Brougham (W), Brough (W), Cockermouth, Middleton Hall (W), and Millom they belong – what is left of them – to the C14,‡ and at Carlisle, where the hall range has long been replaced, there is a staircase tower of the same century with ornate blank decoration. More of this is on the contemporary gatehouse. At Brougham (W), where the gatehouses are also early C14, they are arranged very oddly in relation to the keep. They skirt it in such a way that the small courtyard between outer and inner gate is flanked on one side by the sheer wall of the keep. The gatehouse at Cockermouth Castle of c.1360-70 has a charming rib pattern at the top of the staircase, and in other parts of the castle there are similarly charming and unusual touches: the stepping-down

* A very remarkable thing at Askerton is that the hall timbers have pre-served their C15 numbering applied in the timberyard to secure accurate assembly on the site.

‡ Licence at Millom was granted in 1335, and the plan here is un-commonly closely packed.

tunnel-vault of another staircase, and a small room between hall and kitchen with a tiny foiled oculus window and a vault of trefoil section. A similar attitude is apparent in the small
79 oratory on the top floor of the Brougham (W) keep which belongs to the additions of c.1300.

There has been no space in this survey to mention minor pele towers, but a few of them must find a place for the reason that they were built by men in vocations we would not connect with such structures. There are vicars' peles at Croglin, Great Asby (W), and probably Upper Denton; the college of priests established at Kirkoswald had their pele, and the priors of Lanercost and of Carlisle had theirs. The latter is now the deanery, and the pele with its two big oriel windows and its splendid ceiling*
dates from c.1510–20. So pele-building did not cease with the
31 C16. In fact the peles of Kirkandrews and Brackenhill close to the Scottish border are of the first half of the C16 and of 1586 respectively. It was only the union of Scotland with England which brought peace at last.

There are only two postscripts needed to this survey of castles. One refers to exceptional types of plan, the other to specially splendid details. The plan-type of Bolton Castle in the North Riding and Bodiam in Sussex which is of four regular ranges round a courtyard exists in our counties only once: at Penrith, where licence to crenellate was given to Bishop Strickland in 1397 and 1399. At Bolton and Bodiam there are four corner towers. Penrith has only two, and not in symmetrical positions. At Carlisle, in addition to the castle, Henry VIII built the citadel with two enormous round towers still in existence though converted. That was about 1540, and as the citadel was built for cannon and no longer for archers, it takes us out of the Middle Ages. To the years of Henry VIII, however, also belong those grand features of older castles which must now be referred to, because they are still entirely Perp. They are the large
40 hall and chapel windows of about 1520 at Naworth, very much like those of Kirkoswald church, and the two yet larger transomed windows of the Great Kitchen at Wharton Hall, Kirkby Stephen (W) of c.1540. The kitchen stood on a tunnel-vaulted basement. Adjoining it was the new great hall, also of c.1540, and adjoining that the tunnel-vaulted wing of the former, C15, hall. So here once more, as late as this, was the composition of

* But not as splendid as that from Kirkoswald Castle transferred to
32 Naworth and dating from the mid C14.

hall and two vaulted wings. The need for, and the skill in, stone vaulting held out long.*

What this survey of medieval architecture will have brought out is that these northern counties devoted their efforts more to security and solidity than to display. A room as ornate as that of Prior Salkeld in the Deanery at Carlisle is an exception. This being so, it is not surprising to find that the counties are poor in church furnishings and in funerary monuments. Of MONU-MENTS in Westmorland there is not one worthy of this intro-duction, and while there are a few in Cumberland, they also, nationally speaking, do not rank high. In Westmorland the most interesting monuments are some coffin lids with foliated crosses, such as those at Kendal, Morland, Musgrave, and Warcop. In p. Cumberland, for age and rarity the first is that runic inscription at Beckermet St Bridget which may (or may not) record 'Edith, little maid', and may (or may not) have the date 1103. This incidentally is a late date for runic script, but the runic inscrip-tion of the Kilroy-was-here type in the w wall of the s transept of Carlisle Cathedral is yet later, as it must be of c.1130–40. Next in order of time comes the outstandingly fine Purbeck-marble 21 effigy of a bishop of Carlisle which can be dated c.1250 and must be compared to two Purbeck effigies of the 1250s at Ely. Another Purbeck bishop at Carlisle is of the early C14, a little heavier, less elegantly stylized, but also of high quality. Of the same early C14 is the excellent wooden effigy of a Knight at Ousby and the effigy of Thomas de Caldebec, priest, at Great Salkeld. The alabaster effigy of a Knight of the mid C14 at Greystoke keeps up the quality, but after that there is nothing as good. The heraldic slab at Corby Castle to Thomas Mowbray 34 Duke of Norfolk who died in Venice in 1399 remains a mystery. It is said to have been brought from St Mark's, but it is neither Italian in design or workmanship nor English. The last medieval monument is that, only partially preserved, to Abbot Chamber of Holme Cultram (Abbey Town) † 1518 or 1519. Against the tomb-chest were the seated figure of the abbot and a number of kneeling figures as well. More decorative pieces from the abbey are preserved at Raby Cote, Abbey Town. We don't know their context.

---

* Perhaps in connexion with this vaulting skill a word may be added on Cumberland and Westmorland BRIDGES. A few only are medieval, among them foremost the Devil's Bridge at Kirkby Lonsdale (W) and the bridge 73 at Lanercost. But many are good to look at, right down to the early C19 Eden Bridge at Carlisle by *Smirke*.

Now the tally of CHURCH FURNISHINGS. To start with stone is to start with the oldest pieces and the best; the Norman 17 FONTS of Bridekirk, and then, less generously decorated, of 18, Dearham and of Bowness-on-Solway. The Bridekirk font inci- 19 dentally has an inscription referring to Richard as the maker of the font and even a small self-portrait of Richard chiselling away. The finest C13 fonts are a pair, probably by the same hand, at Aspatria and Cross Canonby, square, with thick leaves in scrolls or volutes. Second metal. But of PLATE there is singularly little: one engraved chalice of *c.*1500 at Old Hutton (W) and – not plate strictly – the C15 *cuir bouilli* case for a chalice at Uldale. That is all. Thirdly STAINED GLASS. Here two windows 36 are noteworthy: the stories of St Andrew at Greystoke, and 32 the Crucifixion with large assistant figures at Bowness-on- Windermere (W), probably originally at Furness or Cartmel in Lancashire. Both are C15 work. PAINTING, apart from the 38 three panels of 1514 at Naworth Castle which are German, is confined to the backs of the stalls in Carlisle Cathedral, covered about 1500, very poorly, with scenes from the lives of saints. 37 The STALLS themselves, on the contrary, are excellent, with their soaring tabernacles of the early C15. The seats have a series of entertaining MISERICORDS. A few misericords are at Grey- stoke too. SCREENS yield nothing, until one reaches in time the Salkeld Screen in Carlisle Cathedral.

39   The Salkeld Screen is of after 1541 – the date is certain – and decorated entirely in the new RENAISSANCE manner, with leafy curves and roundels with heads. The same foliage style may date the organ case in Appleby church (W) which comes from Carlisle Cathedral and may well have been decorated by the same craftsman. For the middle and the third quarter of the century evidence is confined to PLATE: an ornamental foreign Chalice of 1550–1 at Bridekirk, and then pieces at Boltongate, Cliburn (W), Hayton near Brampton, and Ireby (all *c.*1565), Crosthwaite (W; 1567), Great Salkeld (1567), Newton Reigny (1568), and a good many more of the years 1570–5, when in all England plate was replenished after the crises of the Reforma- tion (20; of which 9 were made in London in 1571–2). Arch- bishop Grindal of York in 1571 insisted that the parish clergy should minister 'in no chalice nor in any profane cup . . . but in a Communion Cup of Silver . . . with a cover of Silver'.

To get a fuller view of the ELIZABETHAN AGE IN ARCHI- TECTURE one must turn to the castles and houses and watch how the dourness of the North gives way to sumptuous display.

Sizergh (W) is the house to go to first of all. Hardly anywhere in England can we see so clearly what happened in the ten or fifteen Early Elizabethan years. The series starts with a number of benches, the earliest of them (with little Gothic buttress-shafts side by side with Early Renaissance bits) hardly later than 1530.* But the others are after 1560, and between 1563 and 1575 Sizergh received a number of gorgeous chimneypieces 84 and of quite restrained ceilings with wooden ribs. The ceiling patterns are simple, and only the plaster ceiling of c.1575 is of the richness one expects in an Elizabethan mansion and indeed finds at Levens Hall (W), where work started a few years after it had ended at Sizergh. The Sizergh chimneypieces still – except for the last one of 1575 – have fat big balusters in the Early Renaissance manner and lusty little boys playing in lush foliage, and pediments with a head or a bust – all Early rather than High Renaissance in derivation. The craftsmanship is splendid, and the taste subtler than in the bigger, richer, coarser chimney-pieces of 1586 and 1595 at Levens. These two are the *loci* 85 *classici* of Elizabethan decoration in the county. But there is more: plaster ceilings e.g. at Dalemain, the Two Lions Inn at Penrith (1585), Low Hall at Little Strickland (W), Calgarth Hall Windermere (W), Burneside Hall (W), and – the finest of all – Blease Hall Old Hutton (W), and chimneypieces at Casterton 86 Old Hall (W) of c.1530–40, Middleton Hall (W) of the mid c16, and Muncaster Castle.

One would expect CHURCH FURNISHINGS to keep pace with such wooden pieces of secular purpose, but, apart from the sumptuous PULPIT in Carlisle Cathedral, there is nothing dated which would be earlier than 1619. Then, in connexion with the Laudian Movement, replacements of older or lost pieces become a little more frequent. 1619 is the date on the pulpit at Kirkby Lonsdale (W), and that at Kirkby Thore (W) is dated 1631. The FONT at Harrington has the date 1634. It has intersecting arches, and one wonders whether that – like the dog-tooth of 1507 at Holme Cultram Abbey (Abbey Town) – is a sign of a revivalist attitude. At any rate it is worth referring in this context also to Johnby Hall, where in 1583 a spiral staircase has at the top radial ribs with fillets. The same date as that of the Harrington font is inscribed on the wooden Martindale lectern (W), and of 1636 is the font cover at Beetham (W). After that time the attitude and also often the style change.

* There is also some linenfold PANELLING, and that cannot be later either. More linenfold at Isel Hall.

This is also true of DOMESTIC ARCHITECTURE. The exteriors of houses like Levens (W) and Sizergh (W) have the mullioned and transomed windows one expects, and compositionally they are both entirely informal. Mullioned and transomed windows replace those of the Henry VIII type late, or at least there are two dated examples of the round-arched lights of straight-headed windows still as late as 1563 (a house at Penrith) 83 and 1567 (Cliburn Hall, W). More formal or ornamental plans are extremely rare. No E-plans, no H-plans, just one long oblong with four round corner towers, Scottish, i.e. French, rather than English (Smardale Hall Kirkby Stephen, W, undated; cf. Azay-le-Rideau, Gençay, and in North England Allerdale Hall) and one square with two projecting porches and two projecting staircases in the middles of the four sides (Gaythorne Hall Great Asby, W), a type which has its occasional parallel in counties further s.

In these years at last the CHURCHES also re-appeared as patrons of architecture. The story of the YEARS FROM 1600 TO 1670 in church building in Westmorland and Cumberland is one of special interest; for it is a Gothic Revival story throughout. At its beginning the problem whether revival or survival may be insoluble, at the end the existence of a romantic revival 42 is beyond doubt. The start is the E window of the nave of Holme Cultram Abbey (Abbey Town), put in after the E end had been burnt in 1604. Repairs went on during the years 1604–6; so that must be the date of this window, which continues the style and details of Henry VIII such as we have noticed them at Kirk- 41 oswald. Next follows Arthuret, begun in 1609. The same is true 43 here, except that the grand E window, now at Whoof House, Warwick, has a large oval in the tracery, and that can hardly be earlier than 1650. So the rebuilding of this quite large church took forty or fifty years. A third case is still in doubt: Greystoke, assigned by the RCHM and Mr Bulman to the time of Henry VIII. But there is a date 1645 on the chancel, and the similarity with Holme Cultram is great.* In 1649 Lady Anne Clifford, Countess of Pembroke and the last of the Clifford family, settled at last on her estates in the North. She was nearly seventy then, but had another seventeen years to live. Her estates were Appleby (W), Brougham (W), and Brough Castle (W), besides Skipton and Bardon in the West Riding of Yorkshire. She had

* A minor church of these years is at Martindale (W): 1633. Also C17 is the amazing transformation of Grasmere church (W) by a segment-headed 87 upper arcade separating the two naves and by a brilliant roof construction.

a strong family pride and a sense of tradition, and she set all her energy on re-instating the castles, restoring them, making them habitable, and indeed living in them rather than in up-to-date houses of the type which, as we shall see, entered the North in just those years, the type which her son-in-law was to apply at Appleby after her death. The inscriptions she placed on everything she built show her feeling for history, as do the terms she invented for the three Norman keeps of her Westmorland castles: Roman Tower at Brough, Pagan Tower at Brougham, Caesar's Tower at Appleby. Brough had been in ruins since 1521, Appleby since 1569, Brougham since the Civil War. The Lady Anne mended everywhere, sometimes considerably, and sometimes she even rebuilt almost from scratch (the round tower at Brough). Pendragon Castle, Mallerstang also was hers, and she restored it.

Now the Lady Anne built, rebuilt, or remodelled churches too. They are the parish church of Brougham (Ninekirk), St Wilfrid's Chapel nearer Brougham Castle, and Mallerstang (all W). They are perfectly plain, not at all showy, and have single-light windows, round-headed or pointed. The furnishings of the two Brougham churches also largely go back to the Lady Anne, though at St Wilfrid the issue is confused by much woodwork brought in by Lord Brougham and Vaux in the 1840s. However, the screen is more likely to be English C17 Gothic Revival than real French Late Gothic. The benches are set college-wise, and the pulpit is of c.1660 too. At Ninekirk screen, family pew, pews, communion rail, and font are all of Lady Anne's time. The font is dated 1662.* The style favoured by the Lady Anne is archaistic in most of her furnishings as well.

This archaism is a phenomenon which we had already observed before, in the dog-tooth of the porch of 1507 at Holme Cultram Abbey (Abbey Town) and the fillets on the ribs of 1583 at Johnby Hall. Now we find a broad surround of the Norman billet motif at Crakeplace Hall, Ullock, Dean in 1612, and we find dog-tooth framing a memorial † 1648 at Westward and a monument † 1653 at Ponsonby, Calder Bridge. Moreover, the kind of plain revival as in the Lady Anne's churches appealed to others as well: to Sir Philip Musgrave, who

---

* Other FONTS dated 1662 are at Crosby Ravensworth, Morland, and Orton (all W), the last-named decorated in a way typical of fonts of c.1661-2 with simple stylized geometrical motifs, including the head of a blank Perp window.

built the small church of Soulby (W) in 1662–3, and to John Barwick, Dean of St Paul's, and his brother who built the church of St Paul at Witherslack (W) *c*. 1669. Here again are the straight-headed windows with round-arched lights in the Henry VIII tradition, and the E window is a group of five stepped lights of the same type.* All this evidence put together amounts to a massive profession of faith in the past. The Lady Anne was no doubt its centre. What could be more characteristic of her mentality than the Countess Pillar outside Brougham (W) erected in 1656 to commemorate her last farewell from her mother forty years before. In shape it is much like market crosses such as they survive at Carlisle (1682), Appleby (W; C 17 and C 18), Kirkby Lonsdale (W), Ireby, and Alston (probably an C 18 copy of a C 17 cross).

The FUNERARY MONUMENTS also owe their existence to the Lady Anne, that of her mother and her own, both in Appleby church. Neither has anything to do with medievalism. That of 88 her mother, the Countess of Cumberland, erected in 1617, is the standard effigy on tomb-chest of the Jacobean decades, black marble and alabaster, with the mantle draped much as in the effigy of Queen Elizabeth and a number of Elizabethan monuments. Of equally high quality and also of alabaster is Sir Richard Lowther † 1608 at Lowther (W). The type of the Countess of Cumberland with the ample, generously spreading mantle extends into the middle of the century and is represented by examples at Penrith († 1637) and at Kendal (W; † 1656; the effigy under a table-top-like slab carried by four Tuscan columns). The Lady Anne's own monument belongs to a different age. It has no effigies and instead a display of her family tree in terms of coats of arms set inside a kind of reredos with Doric pilasters and a broken segmental pediment. So here the CLASSICAL STYLE has arrived. It was taken up at once in terms of sculpture as well in two Lowther monuments at Lowther (W), one of *c*.1675 with two free-standing busts on a fluted sarcophagus with fluted edge and, above, flower garlands 92 of Grinling Gibbons type, the other † 1700 (by *William Stanton*) with a comfortably semi-reclining figure in front of a reredos, again with Doric pilasters, and with a wide open segmental pediment. That takes us to 1700.

We must now find out how the classical style established itself in the DOMESTIC ARCHITECTURE of the decades between about 1640 and 1700. First a distinction must be made between

* Armathwaite chapel of *c*.1665 is extremely simple.

major and minor building. In minor building the TUDOR VERNACULAR came through unchanged or with only small changes into the C18. To the features in Westmorland belong round or oval chimneys, as they had e.g. been used early in the C16 at Nether Levens (W), and inside the houses plaster panels above the fireplaces and large cupboards. Both can be very handsome. The cupboards are not included in the gazetteer of this volume. Among the plaster panels the finest are at Strawberry Bank New Hutton (W), Borrowdale Head Fawcett Forest (W), and as late as 1687 at Hollins, Strickland Ketel, Burneside (W) and 1693 at South House, Pool Bank, Crosthwaite (W). Westmorland has in common with the adjoining parts of Yorkshire the use of door lintels for some decorative display, mostly of geometrical shapes, segments or semicircles, merlons, printer's brackets lying on their side, etc. It is not known when they started. In the West Riding they appear about 1630 and culminate in the last third of the century. So the date 1579 applied by the RCHM to the lintel of Barwise Hall (W) is unlikely. There is in fact another date: 1676. On the other hand 1602 for the crenellation motif at Hornby Hall, Brougham (W), is possible, and so is 1610 for the pair of segmental arches at Maulds Meaburn Hall, Crosby Ravensworth (W).* Among the lintels the best is perhaps that of South House, Pool Bank, Crosthwaite (W) of 1693. In the West Riding this desire for something a little more fanciful at the entrance occasionally conquers the whole doorway (The Folly, Settle). This also is matched in Westmorland, in the crazy doorways of Low Hall, Hallbeck, Killington of 1684 and Tearnside Hall, Kirkby Lonsdale of 1686. Windows in all these houses remained of the mullioned Elizabethan type and are only rarely disposed in any axiality. A relatively early case of axial mullioned and transomed windows is Gosforth Hall of c.1658. The efforts to make the façades into something more coherent begin by running the hood-moulds on so that they form a continuous string-course rising for every hood-mould. This is done e.g. in Tarn House, Ravenstonedale (W) in 1664, in Robinson's School at Penrith in 1670 and at Scallow, Arlecdon in 1687. At Beartree House, Mealsgate in 1686, the course rises only above the doorway, and at Low Hollins, Buttermere in 1687 it has become an entirely horizontal course. The next step is to apply a classical moulding

---

* In this context a chimneypiece in a minor room at Levens Hall (W) must be referred to. It is dated 1586 and has motifs similar to those of the lintels.

to the string-course. That is the case at Low Brownrigg, Caldbeck in 1695. The windows here are of two lights consistently, a
motif we shall find presently in the major buildings as well.*

At the beginning of the MAJOR BUILDINGS of these decades
stands the long gallery wing of Hutton-in-the-Forest, dateable
to the early forties. It has still got mullioned and transomed
windows, but a symmetrical composition. The ground floor is
open. Inside are niches flanked by bulgy Tuscan columns, but
the piers which support the shallow arches are without any doubt
in imitation of the C13. They are quatrefoil and have unmistakable C13 capitals. So here is yet one more instance of the
passionate archaism of the C17 North. Mullioned and transomed windows still go on in 1662 at Hutton John. They appear
here incidentally in conjunction with small heart-shaped windows, a Catholic demonstration of Andrew Hudleston who built
45 this range. 1663 is the year of Lorton Hall, and there we are
firmly on the road to the classical style. The range is of seven
bays, with upright three-light windows, carrying pediments on
the upper floor. But that was precocious indeed. More typical
of Cumberland in those years are such wild fantasies as Catterlen
44 Hall, Newton Reigny of c.1655, where the doorway jambs are
crossed by raised bands held down, as it were, by stone pegs and
where – yet once again – the arch has dog-tooth. The same
jamb-motif is found at Moresby Hall, no doubt somewhat later.
49 Here the whole seven-bay front is rusticated – quite an out-
landish effect – and the windows have a cross of mullion and
transom below, but two transoms above with pediments alternating between triangular and segmental. The regularly set cross
windows and the alternating pediments, though nationally
speaking no innovation, in Cumberland and Westmorland belong to the late C17. The record is as follows. Two-light mullioned windows but with a straight piece of entablature at
Orthwaite Hall, Bassenthwaite in 1675. Here the doorway has a
nearly semicircular pediment. Cross windows with pediments
alternatingly triangular and segmental, but each starting and
ending with a straight horizontal piece, at Branthwaite Hall,
Dean and with a date 1676 at Drawdykes Castle, Houghton.
Cross windows also were used by Col. Graham at Levens (W)
c.1700.‡ The staircase by the way which he put in has twisted

---

* But one major building, Colby Hall (W), still carries on with three-light
mullioned windows and even a hall doorway not in the centre as late as 1685.

‡ It was he who started the famous TOPIARY in the garden of Levens
Hall.

balusters, and this form of balusters is indeed – up here as in all England – typical of the late C17. It comes at Appleby Castle (W; 1686–8), at Askham Hall (W; c.1685–90), at Tullie House, Carlisle (1689) and at The College, Kirkoswald (1696). Only Hutton-in-the-Forest is an exception. Here about 1680 there is one of the gorgeous staircases with openwork acanthus panels. They also were a fashion of these very years all over England. The time-lag between South and North was shortening. At Hutton-in-the-Forest the façade which goes with this stair- 47 case is dramatically compressed. The window above the doorway has Corinthian pilasters and garlands, and the other windows have alternating pediments. So have those at Tullie House, so has the doorway at Askham (W), and 48 so had Corby Castle, in a three-storey range since pulled down. Appleby (W) differs from the others in that it has 91 two tiers of flat pilasters to articulate the façade, a motif in the South of 1650–60 rather than 1680–90. The door pediment of Appleby is of the open curly type first encountered here in the same years at the Mansion House, Eamont Bridge, Brougham (W) of 1686, a house with windows originally of the cross-type and yet another staircase with twisted balusters. It was also chosen at the Episcopal Registry at Carlisle in 1699 and at The College, Kirkoswald in 1696. This is really a completely classical house, and it has sash-windows which look original. This was the greatest innovation. In London it comes in the eighties; so, once more, the North was no longer backward. The same must be said of a house, ten years earlier, in Westmorland: Crackenthorpe Hall of 1685. It still has cross windows, it is true, but the composition with a three-bay pediment and a pediment over the doorway is entirely that of the home counties at the same moment.*

One year after Crackenthorpe Hall the great re-modelling of Lowther church (W) at the hands of Sir John Lowther († 1700) took place. The medieval church emerged with square-headed side windows and one tall round-headed W and one E window and a lantern and a dome – the latter two alas replaced by something in the C19 which seemed then more respectable.

This Sir John Lowther must not be confused with Sir John Lowther († 1706), his father's cousin, who was also responsible

---

* This whole account of the development from 1650 to 1700 leaves out Dalston Hall which, with its boxed-out windows and chunky gargoyles, is 46 more Scottish than English. In Cumberland anyway it is entirely odd-man-out.

for work of great interest, including a TOWN PLANNING job
which has little to emulate it in the C17 in England. It is the
laying out of Whitehaven in the 1680s as port for the shipping
of coal from Sir John's mines. The plan is a grid with one of the
oblong blocks left free for the church. Town planning on the
smallest scale had occurred once or twice in the Middle Ages in
Westmorland: New Appleby of the early C12, as one wide
straight street from the church up to the castle, rather like the
wide streets in the Bishop of Winchester's new towns about
1200, and Church Brough as just one oblong space with houses
on two sides. The grid pattern of Whitehaven was imitated
about 1750 at Maryport. Workington also has a quarter laid out
rectangularly with a square, Portland Square, in the middle.
That dates from *c.*1775. Longtown, laid out by Dr Graham of
Netherby Hall in the third quarter of the C18, is just a square of
four streets. At Lowther in the 1760s James, Earl of Lonsdale,
successor to both the Lowther and the Whitehaven estates, laid
out a so-called village, really a group of two closes and a crescent
built, it is said, for soldiers. The crescent was intended to be one
half of a circus. Bath must have been in the Earl's mind.

These remarks on town planning may be followed by a first
list of PUBLIC BUILDINGS. Cumberland and Westmorland
have not much to show: St Bees School, i.e. its first building of
1587, Lady Anne Clifford's St Anne's Hospital at Appleby (W)
of 1651–3, the Carlisle Town Hall of 1717 (and later), low and
quite homely, and so on to the Kirkby Stephen Cloisters of
1810 (W), *Smirke*'s Screen at the bottom of Boroughgate,
Appleby (W) of 1811, the Keswick Town Hall of 1813, and the
Brampton Moot Hall of 1817. That, with some exceptions,
covers the Georgian century, and on this we must now focus
attention.

The order in which the GEORGIAN AGE is to be summarized
is churches, church furnishings, church monuments, houses.
On CHURCHES we can be brief. Very many were built, but few
with any ambition. Of the smaller ones the majority were replaced in the C19, and others were made churchy by altering
their windows and removing their fitments. Among the larger
churches the seminal building was Holy Trinity Whitehaven,
built in 1693 and not preserved. It had a w tower, three galleries inside, and two tiers of oblong windows. Whitehaven was
followed by Penrith in 1720–2. The two tiers of windows are
arched now, and the E window is of the Venetian type. The two
tiers of arched windows were soon taken up at Holme Cultram

Abbey (Abbey Town), the Venetian window quite soon, in 1743, at Hugill (W). After Penrith – to confine ourselves to the bigger buildings – comes Ravenstonedale (W) in 1744, and then the finest of them all, St James Whitehaven of 1752–3. The interior [52], with the three galleries is perfectly preserved. St Cuthbert [53] Carlisle of 1778 is similar; so is Wigton of 1788. The same type goes on at Moresby in 1822–3. Most of the other churches before 1825 need not be commented on.* The only exceptions are Culgaith of 1756 because of the screens of columns separating the transepts from the nave and Kirkandrews of 1776 because of size, ashlar-facing, tower with an open rotunda, and general amplitude.‡

Some of the CHURCH DECORATION in these Georgian churches is of the same date as the buildings. Thus in Penrith parish church large WALL PAINTINGS were done by a certain *Jacob Thompson*. Of FURNISHINGS not much more need be said. There are of course quite a number of baluster FONTS. There are sundry PULPITS, and among them that at Bampton (W), probably of 1726, represents a favoured type. It has angle colonnettes and blank arched panels, i.e. really a translation of Laudian into Georgian. The Penrith pulpit of the same time is the same. Ravenstonedale (W) c.1745–50 has a fine three-decker,§ St James Whitehaven c.1755–60 a high column as the support of the pulpit.

For CHURCH MONUMENTS up to 1830 a paragraph suffices. Affluent people were rarely buried in Cumberland and Westmorland churches, or they chose not to make a display. The only really ambitious piece is that by *Nollekens* at Wetheral to Lady [56] Maria Howard † 1789, a white-marble group. One tablet in Cumberland is by *Banks* (Carlisle Cathedral † 1787), two in

---

* Here are some names and dates: Langwathby 1718, Bampton (W) 1726, [98] Grinsdale 1740, Temple Sowerby (W) 1754, Culgaith 1758 (*see* below), Mun- [54] grisdale 1756, Raughton Head 1761, Threlkeld 1777, Hayton near Brampton 1780.

‡ These are also the years in which NONCONFORMIST CHAPELS make their *début*. The earliest preserved ones are the humble cottages used for Quaker meetings. The dates of surviving buildings are Brigflatts near Sedbergh in Yorkshire 1675, Colthouse near Hawkshead in Lancashire 1688, and then Preston Patrick (W) 1691, Whelpo (Caldbeck) 1698, Eaglesfield 1711(?), Wetheral 1718, Pardshaw Hall (Dean) 1720, Whitehaven 1722. The first larger one is Moorhouse (Burgh-by-Sands) of 1733, seven arched windows long, i.e. as the established church would have built with sufficient means at that moment. The earliest Congregational Chapel recorded is Redwing (Garrigill) 1757, the earliest Methodist Chapel recorded is Penrith of 1815, a substantial, pedimented 'preaching box'.

§ The three desks are pulpit, prayer desk, and clerk's desk.

Westmorland are by *Flaxman* (Kendal † 1787, Bowness-on-
Windermere † 1816), and one, again in Cumberland, is by
Chantrey (Dacre, 1830). Many in both counties are by local men
such as *Webster* of Kendal (*see below*), *Kirkbride* of Carlisle, and
Nixson of Carlisle, and among them there is one who occasionally did outstanding work. He is *Musgrave Lewthwaite Watson*,
born at Sebergham in 1804. He came on his father's side from
yeoman stock, on his mother's from Carlisle merchants, studied
law, but then turned to art, and stayed in Rome from 1825 to
1828. He was never successful and spent most of his life ghosting
in the studios of the famous sculptors – Chantrey, Westmacott,
Behnes, Baily, Coade's – and died young, in 1847. The monu-
57 ment to his father at Sebergham, signed with the addition *Rome*,
is one of the most effective monuments of the 1820s in all
England, even if all but copied from Fuseli. Equally fine is the
monument to his schoolmaster at Raughton Head of *c.*1828, a
pensive young clergyman, and the strange, tall, bare urn on a
monument of 1843 at Ainstable is hardly less impressive. Church
monuments after that date will be taken up in another context,
once DOMESTIC ARCHITECTURE has been followed that far.

Cumberland and Westmorland were not counties to build
mansions in. They were considered out of the way, until towards
the end of the century the picturesque interest gave them a new
lease of life. In local building, i.e. the Georgian VERNACULAR,
one can watch how the classical style, established at Kirkoswald and Crackenthorpe before 1700, filtered down. A few
examples are enough to illustrate the process. Rowrah Hall,
Arlecdon in 1722 and Street Gate, Lamplugh in 1733 still have
cross windows, two houses at Sebergham in 1730 and 1737 still
upright two-light windows. But another house at Sebergham
has sash windows and yet is dated 1715, and the same is true of
Scarness Dower House, Bassenthwaite of 1726. Old Manor,
Little Braithwaite, Thornthwaite of the same year is entirely
classical; and so is Hall Farm, Ousby of 1743. In contrast the
MANSIONS: The Nunnery near Kirkoswald, 1715 and nine bays
long, the pele-tower of Armathwaite Castle, converted into a
Vanbrughian North Country house probably in the 1720s,
Dallam Tower, Milnthorpe, of 1720–2 (W), large, noble, and
reticent, Highhead Castle, Ivegill of 1744–8 (alas gutted) with a
front eleven bays long, a range of 1746 at Warcop Hall (W) with
quite a splendid room with columns inside, a number of garden
temples and especially the dramatic Cascade House high above
the river Eden at Corby Castle, and – a town house, though with

a stable-yard and a spacious garden – Abbot Hall, Kendal (W)
by *John Carr*, built in 1759. Good mid-c18 town houses were
put up in the other towns as well, quite a number at Carlisle,
14 Scotch Street at Whitehaven, Wordsworth House at Cocker- 55
mouth, the Manor House at Penrith, and so on.

The Picturesque Discovery of the Lake District, due in the
first place to Gilpin, led to houses rather than mansions built to
enjoy picturesque sites and views. Gilpin's *Tour of the Northern
Counties* had been published in 1770, Nash's *Guide to the Lakes*
in 1778. Belle Isle, on its island in Windermere, opposite Bow- 95
ness (W), comes first. This domestic rotunda with its portico
was built in 1774 by *John Plaw*. Storrs Hall, Bowness is not much
later (*c.*1790), though what one admires now is mostly by *Gandy*
and of 1808–11. Belle Isle and Storrs Hall are classical houses in
picturesque settings, but Lyulf's Tower, Matterdale, on Ullswater, built as early as 1780, has gone picturesque itself. Its plan
is three sides of an octagon, and it has four castellated towers.
Actually the ROCOCO GOTHIC, following after the more
serious-minded Gothic Revival of the c18 and preceding the
picturesque, i.e. romantic revival, had made its mark already in
the fifties, with the White House at Appleby (W) of 1756. After 94
Lyulf's Tower follow Sebergham Castle late in the c18, a folly
house with ogee-headed windows and Chinesey roofs on the
wings, and three folly farms with curiously Vanbrughian details
near Greystoke Castle about 1790, i.e. really screens to hide, and
a spire to enhance, farmhouses.* Higham School, Setmurthy is
a different matter. Here Gothic is applied to a symmetrical
Georgian body of eleven bays. The picturesque enthusiasm was
over, and Gothic went sensible, just at the moment when the
Georgian Classical went GRECIAN.

Cumberland and Westmorland have quite a fine crop of
Greek Revival houses – houses, not churches, for the only
church to display, very impressively, the sense of weight and the
grandeur of Greece, has no Grecian forms: St John, Workington 61
of 1823 which is by *Thomas Hardwick* and modelled frankly on
Inigo Jones's St Paul Covent Garden, which Hardwick had rebuilt after a fire. But that means sturdy Tuscan columns, and
they, ever since French architects of the late c18 made them
their principal vehicle, have served the same emotional ends as

---

* Cumberland can boast a folly built as early as 1709: Fiddleback,
Thursby; for this farmhouse with a semicircular front and a smaller barn
attached to its back, also with a semicircular front cannot be defined as
anything else.

the Greek Doric columns. The first dated Greek Doric displays
are at Corby Castle by *Peter Nicholson*. The date is 1812–17, but
it is quite possible that one or another of the Grecian houses and
villas in the counties, and especially near Carlisle, are as early.
The following are worthy of special notice: Rickerby Hall,
Carlisle, with a gate lodge with tetrastyle porticoes front and
back, Eden Grove, Crosby-on-Eden, which is single-storeyed,
Steelfield House, Gosforth, where even the gatepiers are Doric
columns, the so-called Grecian Villa at Cockermouth, Rigmaden
Park, Mansergh (W), which is alas in ruins, and Castletown
House, Rockcliffe with some Soanian details. This dates from
1831.*

These are exactly the years when the Cumberland Infirmary
62 at Carlisle received its impressive building with a Greek Doric
portico. The architect was *Robert Tattersall* of Manchester
(c.1804–44). At least as impressive is another of the PUBLIC
59 BUILDINGS of the early C19 at Carlisle, the Assize Courts.
They were designed by *Robert Smirke* in 1810–11, or rather remodelled out of Henry VIII's Citadel. Their style is Gothic,
but a solid matter-of-fact Gothic, no longer of the lightness with
which the C18 treated the Gothic style. Smirke had this corner
of the North at his feet, as soon as people saw his grandiose
96 Lowther Castle (W) rise. This mighty pile, now a ruin, was
begun in 1806, when Smirke was only twenty-five, and completed in 1811. In 1809–11 Smirke added some rather unfortu-
nate fancy Gothic features to Crosby Ravensworth church (W),
in 1811 he provided the happy Gothic screen between the bottom end of the main street of Appleby (W) and the churchyard
(see above, p. 34), and also early he designed Edenhall, which
was Grecian, in 1824 he did Edmond Castle, Hayton, near
Brampton in a Tudor style which was emerging only then, and
in 1832 the church at Askham (W) in a depressing neo-Norman.‡
The other architect most successfully employed during these
years was *Thomas Rickman*. His style in the county was Gothic
60 consistently. His Holy Trinity, Carlisle of 1828–30 is Gothic in
the sense of the Commissioners' churches, i.e. aisleless, with
long, thin side windows, but much more substantial than they

* Only as an appendix some more early C19 houses can be given access to
this introduction: Casterton Hall (W), Heaves near Levens (W), Houghton
Hall near Carlisle, Waterfoot at Pooley Bridge (W).

‡ Soon after, in the whole of England, neo-Norman became the fashion.
Examples in Cumberland are Talkin 1842, St Paul Warwick Bridge by
Dobson 1845, the tower of Aspatria by *Travis & Mangnall* 1846–8, Christ
Church Whitehaven 1847.

are. Of the run-of-the-mill Commissioners' stuff the county is full. In fact, remarkably many churches were rebuilt or built between 1820 and 1850. The gazetteer counts fifteen of them in Westmorland and thirty-six in Cumberland. While Rickman was busy at Holy Trinity, he also rebuilt Brunstock, Houghton near Carlisle (1827–8), large parts of Rose Castle, the bishop of Carlisle's palace (1829–31), probably large parts of Scaleby Castle, and in addition what is now Barclays Bank, at Carlisle (1830–1). All these are Gothic.

With these buildings we are on the threshold of the VICTORIAN AGE, and from the thirties to the sixties a great deal was built in the two counties. In HOUSES the development simply continued without a break. We had e.g. already seen that, apart from Classical and Gothic, Tudor was used by architects (*Smirke*, 1829). *Webster* of Kendal, whom we have met earlier on as a sculptor, designed Underley Hall (W) in a full-blown 97 Jacobean as early as 1825, which is remarkable indeed.* Tudor again with mullioned and transomed windows is Whelprigg, Barbon (W) of 1834 and Flosh at Cleator of 1837 and Tudor, as gorgeous as it could be made, Holme Eden Hall, Warwick Bridge of 1837. This is probably by *Dobson* of Newcastle and was commissioned by Peter Dixon of Carlisle, the cotton manufacturer whose Dixon's Mill at Carlisle by *Tattersall* (1836) is supposed 63 to be the largest mill of its date in England. It is 225 ft long and has a chimney 300 ft high. The building is solid and utilitarian, but if any stylistic detail can be defined, one would probably call it Classical to Italianate. The same would be the definition for a early job by *Anthony Salvin*, the most successful restorer and purveyor of castles in the second third of the century. The building is Patterdale Hall (W) of 1845–50.‡ Salvin also did much to restore Naworth Castle (faithfully) after 1844 and to enhance the medieval glories of Greystoke Castle (1839–48 and later), Hutton-in-the-Forest (*c*.1830 and later), and Muncaster Castle (1862–6). Add to these one job by *William Burn*, the baronial Netherby Hall, not one of his convincing works (1833), and you have the list of the mansions before 1870 complete.

Concerning CHURCHES: we had abandoned them at the

* Just as remarkable is the Congregational Church at Carlisle which is of 1843 and Jacobean too, a style utterly uncommon in ecclesiastical architecture.

‡ His church at Patterdale is of little interest, but his Keswick church of 1838 is quite ambitious. Its detail is still pre-archeological.

moment of Rickman's Holy Trinity, i.e. in 1830. Another re-
markably substantial and archeologically accurate job is *Ignatius
Bonomi*'s Catholic Church at Wigton of 1837. Bonomi (*c.*1790–
1855) incidentally went into partnership with *John A. Cory*
(1819–87; Nenthead church is by Bonomi & Cory and of 1845).
Cory built Great Langdale (W) in 1857, in 1862 became County
Surveyor of Cumberland, and about 1868 began to work as a
private architect with *C. J. Ferguson* (Pooley Bridge (W) 1868;
Bridekirk 1868–70; Plumbland 1870–1; Cumdivock 1871;
Welton, Sebergham 1874). They practised from Carlisle.
Ferguson (*c.*1840–1904) had been a pupil of Scott, and as such
in 1865 won the competition for Silloth church, an excellent
building. He must have left Cory soon; for churches by him
alone are Gamblesby 1868 (can that be?), Middleton (W)
1878–9, Burneside (W) 1880–1, and so on to St Aidan Carlisle
1899–1902 and Penruddock 1902. Cory on the other hand did
Martindale alone in 1880–2. He died in 1887, Ferguson survived till 1904. It is useful to follow such a local firm in order
to remember that up to 1900 architecture was much more
regional than it became after. *Paley & Austin* of Lancaster are
another example. Their story starts with *Edmund Sharpe* (1809–
77; famous for his scholarly works on the Dec style). He was a
pupil of Rickman. He built at Wigan, Blackburn, and once also
at Coventry. In Cumberland he did the church of Calder Bridge
in 1842. In 1845 he was joined by *E. G. Paley* (1823–95), and
from 1851 Paley worked on his own (Thwaites 1854) until in
1868 he took *H. J. Austin* into partnership (Crosscrake (W) of
1875 and the new houses at Sedbergh School of *c.*1875 etc.
are by Paley & Austin). Paley died in 1895, and the firm thereupon became Austin & Paley. Cory & Ferguson could be as
good as a good London firm (Plumbland), and Paley & Austin,
as we shall see later, as good as the best.

Who are the best, or what is best in church architecture
during the years of Queen Victoria? The first building to call
out, one introduces with hesitation; for it is a crazy building
without any doubt, even if it is a most impressive and in some
ways amazingly forward-pointing building: the church at
Wreay which *Miss Sara Losh* designed *c.*1835 as a memorial to
her sister. It was consecrated in 1842. It is in the Early Christian
or rather Italian Romanesque style, the style then called Lombardic, and that in itself is very remarkable; for the principal
churches in that style in England – Wilton, Christ Church
Streatham, and Christ Church Watney Street – were all three

begun only in 1840. The fashion came from Munich and Berlin, i.e. from Klenze, whose Allerheiligen had been begun in 1827, and Schinkel, who at least did designs in a free Lombardic c.1828. But how could Sara Losh have known about them? It is true that she was extremely learned and well read and that she had travelled in Italy and through Germany, but that was in 1817. Hittorf's *L'architecture moderne en Sicile* came out in 1835 and contained e.g. Monreale and the Cappella Palatina in Palermo, but Wreay is less Byzantine than Lombardic. As it is even less neo-Norman, the beginnings of the Norman fashion (Robinson's Leamington of 1825 was specially impressive) could have had even less effect. So it remains likely that Miss Losh chose Lombardic independently. Her details are certainly highly independent. The enrichments of the façade e.g. are more reminiscent of the Arts and Crafts Byzantinism of about 1900 than of anything in 1840. Moreover the position of the altar so that the parson would face the congregation is prophetic of 1960 or, to be more realistic, a proof of Miss Losh being thoroughly aware of Early Christian ritual. Finally, the whole church and the furnishings are replete with symbolism. The furnishings incidentally include pulpit and lectern cut out of a tree trunk with the bark left on, and the stained glass is made up of broken bits obtained from the Archbishop's Palace at Sens. Somewhat later, in 1850, Miss Losh had a mausoleum erected to her sister, a strange building of roughly hewn blocks laid so as not to fit too smoothly. Inside is the statue of her sister, by *Dunbar* of Newcastle, who did some other monuments in Cumberland as well.*

Wreay remained – one need hardly say it – entirely solitary and unfollowed. The main direction of Victorian architecture was to be established in these very years, and Cumberland has one of the first documents of the new attitude, even if a minor one. It is *Pugin*'s Catholic church at Warwick Bridge. This was built in 1841 and represents respect for the English Gothic past and the will to revive it by means of accuracy of imitation. *Rickman*'s Holy Trinity of 1828–30 at Carlisle and even *Dobson*'s neo-Norman St Paul, also at Warwick, seem far behind. Once Pugin had made a start, others followed, *George Gilbert Scott* among the first. He, in 1850–4, built the ambitious parish church of Ambleside (W) with its dominating S E steeple. The other

* A second mausoleum of the mid-century is the Lowther Mausoleum of 1857 at Lowther (W) with the seated figure of the earl by *E. B. Stephens*, 1863.

major churches of the mid c19 are by lesser known architects. *Butterfield*, it is true, did Lamplugh church in 1870, and restored others, but they are nothing special, and *Knowles* of the Grosvenor Hotel in London did a fountain at Wigton which is 66 memorable rather for its marble reliefs by *Thomas Woolner*, a sculptor who had belonged to the Pre-Raphaelites at the beginning and was capable of occasional work of a high order.*

But the seventies suddenly threw Cumberland into the centre of architectural events in England. The occasion was the 67 Brampton parish church by *Philip Webb*, William Morris's friend and the architect of Morris's epoch-making Red House near London. Webb designed the church in 1874. It was commissioned by, or at the suggestion of, the Earl of Carlisle, for whom Webb had, six years previously, designed a house in London. The church has all the exciting merits and all the irritating faults of Webb. It is inventive, always unexpected, ruthless with motifs of the various styles of the past which are confronted with each other by an architect convinced that strong personality can unite them, whatever their original *habitat*. The church is impressive everywhere, moving in more than one place outside as well as inside, but it suffers from a surfeit of motifs. The interior has the great asset of beautiful *Morris* windows throughout, and the intensity of his STAINED GLASS succeeds in overcoming e.g. the ambiguity of the aisle roofs. Morris and his friends, i.e. chiefly *Burne-Jones*, did these windows in 1878–80. They already a few years earlier had worked for Kirkbampton, Troutbeck (W), Staveley (W), Lanercost, and Calder Bridge. Another of the best designers for stained glass, though patently a follower of Burne-Jones, was kept very busy in Cumberland and Westmorland: *Henry Holiday* (born in 1839), who appears at Calder Bridge already *c*.1877 and then received commissions for Muncaster, Keswick (among his best), Ambleside (W), Wythburn, Buttermere, and Casterton (W). At Casterton he also did large wall paintings in the chancel, in a style which owes as much to Lord Leighton as to the Pre-Raphaelites.‡ To return to Brampton and *Webb*, he also did two

---

* At Wigton also, in 1887, a rich manufacturer built the craziest Victorian building in either county: the excessively high tower behind the innocuous Georgian house called Highmoor. The style is not easily named. It is a mixed Renaissance with Baroque touches, and as 'rogue', to use Goodhart-Rendel's term, as anything anywhere.

‡ *Kempe* did comparatively little in our counties, and most of the other Victorian glass is indifferent or bad. But two more glass jobs must find a corner in this introduction: the stars of clear cut or moulded glass in the

private houses at Brampton, Green Lanes, with a remarkably wilful garden front, and Four Gables, a wholly successful, com- 68 pact house, with blunt detail and a great strength of conviction.

From Webb and Morris the road of architecture leads straight into the C20. We can see it in Cumberland and Westmorland by examining churches as well as houses. In churches the local firm *Paley & Austin* already mentioned illustrates the growing freedom taken with period precedent.* Webb had blazed the trail; now such churches as Barbon (W) of 1893 and Natland (W) of 1909–10 followed. Their *parti*, their elements, their details are all well chosen and sensitively handled. Among non-local architects the same stage of development is represented by *Caröe*'s Broughton Moor of 1905, small but personal, and by *Sir Robert Lorimer*'s Plumpton Wall of 1907.

Lorimer also designed, a few miles away, Brackenburgh 69 Tower. Again, the style is still Tudor, but the details betray the newly gained freedom. In one of *Baillie Scott*'s most important houses, Blackwell School, Bowness-on-Windermere (W) of 1900, the exterior is hardly freer, but the interior has all the pretty 99 Arts and Crafts motifs of which Baillie Scott was capable. It makes *Voysey*'s excellent, square Little Holme at Kendal (W) of 1908 look very rational – which would have pleased its architect. Voysey's most famous country houses, Broadleys and Moor Crag near Bowness, both of 1898, are outside the West-morland frontier by a few hundred feet.

To appreciate the style of the TWENTIETH CENTURY, as it began to settle down in England about 1930, one would naturally not go to the far north-west. Yet by now there are even here a few buildings which one should seek out. One is pioneer stuff: the house at Brampton by *Leslie Martin* (now Sir Leslie), designed for Alastair Morton in 1936, a cubic brick house, quite varied in its grouping. The other two are very recent: the large and indeed varied house at Matson Ground 100 near Bowness-on-Windermere (W) designed for Mr Peter Scott by *Basil Ward* (1961), and the quite exceptionally strong chapel for St Michael's College, Underley Hall (W), by *William White* of the *Building Design Partnership*, begun in 1964 and just being finished at the time of writing.

---

tracery of the windows of Crosby-on-Eden and a copy in stained glass of Leonardo da Vinci's *Last Supper* used as a retable behind the altar of Gilcrux church.

* Paley & Austin had already in 1875, at Crosscrake (W), chosen the style of 1200, an unexpected choice, and handled it with great feeling.

Further Reading

ROMAN ARCHAEOLOGY. J. Collingwood Bruce: *Handbook to the Roman Wall*, 12th ed. (revised by I. Richmond), 1966.

ANGLO-SAXON AND AFTER. For Westmorland up to 1714 the volume of the Royal Commission on Historic Monuments (1936) contains everything and is preceded by an excellent introduction written by the then secretary, Sir Alfred Clapham. Cumberland has nothing comparable, and the Victoria County History (1901–5) has only reached volume two, i.e. general accounts of the county's religious houses and industries. So the main source for medieval matters is the *Transactions of the Cumberland and Westmorland Archaeological and Historical Society*. For anything post-medieval one has to go to the old county histories and see what one can get. They are J. Nicolson and R. Burn: *The History and Antiquities of the Counties of Westmorland and Cumberland*, 2 vols (1777), W. Hutchinson: *The History of the County of Cumberland*, 2 vols (1794), D. and S. L. Lyons: *Magna Britannia*, vol. IV (1816), J. Hodgson: *Topography and History*, S. Jefferson: *The History and Antiquities of Cumberland*, 3 vols (1838–42), and W. Whellan: *The History and Topography of the Counties of Cumberland and Westmorland* (1860). In addition, on more specialized topics, there is M. Taylor: *Old Manorial Halls* (1892) and R. S. Ferguson: *Old Church Plate in the Diocese of Carlisle* (1882).

GEOLOGY

BY TERENCE MILLER

Cumberland and Westmorland form, with North-West Lancashire, a kind of 'knot' – in the carpenter's sense – of ancient rocks, set in an oval frame, almost complete, of much younger strata. The ancient hard knot of Ordovician and Silurian rocks is the central core of the Lake District. Here the oldest formation, the Skiddaw slate group, lies in a broad strip from Cockermouth across Crummock Water and Bassenthwaite Lake to Keswick, and thence further E until, on a line from Hutton Roof down to Troutbeck station, the rocks pass under the Carboniferous limestone of the rim. Although old, hard, and twisted, these lowest Ordovician rocks weather down fairly easily, and form, on the whole, a gradually rising, smooth-featured upland. Next above them, and forming the heart of the Lake District and the most dramatic scenery, are the rocks of the Borrowdale Volcanic group, mainly lava-flows and ash-beds ejected from ancient volcanoes long since eroded away and vanished without trace. Individual bands within the group stand out as particularly strong, jagged lines in the landscape. Others, of more regularly laminated or foliated rock, are worked for cladding and decorative slabs, and for roofing slate, known to the trade as Westmorland Stone. These old rocks are pierced in a few places – Eskdale, Ennerdale, and Shap – by masses of grey and red granite. The quarries at Shap are famous, and have provided many fine examples of ornamental and building stone.

SE of a line Broughton-in-Furness–Ambleside–Shap, down to Ulverston, Kendal, and almost as far as Ravenstonedale, the country is of Silurian siltstones and sandstones, often 'blocky' or 'flaggy', or smooth and cleavable for roofing slate, but not able to form any specially striking accent in the landscape. The typical Silurian ground is high and whale-backed, often well forested, but as often open and rather desolate upland of sheepruns, bracken, and heather.

Around this core of generally hard and contorted rocks lies the rim or frame of pale limestones and sandstones, followed by bright red and brown sandstones. These tend to dip radially outwards from the centre to which the Lake-fingers point. The limestone beds lie for the most part almost horizontally, in broken terraces sticking out from the hillsides which look in towards the mountains. The country of this Carboniferous rim is sometimes startlingly like that of the North Yorkshire dales.

The NW quadrant of the rim carries the Pennine comparison even farther, for here the limestone group is overlain by buff and grey sandstones, mudstones, and shale of the Coal Measures. This region stretches from St Bees Head round the coast to Maryport, and then inland as a narrow strip to the edge of Inglewood Forest, S of Carlisle. The coal seams, like those of Durham, on the other side of the Pennines, run out below the sea, as the rim rocks slant away from the Lakes.

The last or highest (youngest) rocks of the rim are the red Permo-Triassic sandstones of the W coast – Ravenglass to St Bees Head – the Carlisle 'basin', and the Vale of Eden. The fine reds and browns, and the occasional sparkling surfaces of these excellent building stones are one of the characteristic tones of towns and villages around the Lake District rim.

BUILDING MATERIALS

BY ALEC CLIFTON-TAYLOR

For house building, stone is unfortunately beyond many people's means to-day, even in the stone areas, and Cumberland and Westmorland are no exceptions. In the Lake District itself, where roofing slates are a local product, the roof of quite a small house will now cost, in slate, about £750. So other materials are increasingly in evidence. And at a few places, mainly on or near the Solway Firth, and in Carlisle, red brick was employed for some buildings from the Georgian period onwards. But until recent times stone was the natural and obvious building material in almost the whole of the two north-western counties, a fact to which visually they owe a great deal.

Nevertheless, the stone is not always visible, for a very large number of buildings in these two counties have been given a coat of roughcast or have been cement-rendered, to make them drier. At Grasmere the entire church wears an overcoat of drab-looking roughcast. In 1891 this was removed from the tower, and its unhewn 'beck cobbles' were duly pointed. The pointing proved incapable of resisting the rain, and after only twenty years the roughcast had to be reapplied. In some towns, Cocker-mouth for example, or Whitehaven, there is hardly a house in which the stone walls are exposed. The facing materials are not attractive in themselves, but the use of applied colour is a help; and if white is the favourite, and often the most telling, many other colours can also be seen, almost always muted, as befits the visual character of the region.

Where the building stones are left exposed to view, they display several marked characteristics. The texture is usually rough, sometimes very rough indeed, for with the exception of the friable Permian and Triassic sandstones these are very hard stones, intractable to handle. An ashlared face in this region of England is rare, and even the rubblestone is usually uncoursed. In the Lake District, where much of the stone is of volcanic origin, the lumps are so difficult to break that the majority were used unbroken and laid random. Many were retrieved from the beds of the becks or from adjoining fields or moors. These 'cobbles', with their surfaces smoothed by the mountain streams or by waters from melting glaciers – for up here the Ice Age came to an end only about ten thousand years ago – are still available in unlimited numbers. Unbroken cobbles were a great standby for the wallers. These rugged building materials suit the country perfectly, of course, being in fact part and parcel of it.

Nowhere in England, perhaps, can dry walling, walls, that is, in which the stones are laid without mortar, be seen to better advantage. This method of construction is normal in Cumberland and Westmorland for boundary walls, but was also widely used for barns, as also for some of the humbler cottages; it was, and indeed still is, a traditional skill. Every wall is a complicated jigsaw of stones of the most diverse shapes, sizes, and maybe colours too. On the older walls it is not unusual to see large stones projecting at intervals from the plane surface; these are what the builders call 'throughs' – stones large enough to extend through the thickness of the wall, helping to give it strength and to add still further textural interest. Sometimes the topmost stones of a field wall were selected to be laid not horizontally but diagonally or vertically, yielding a vigorously serrated edge. This not only looks well but has the practical advantage of deterring jumping sheep. So effective is the dry walling in this part of England that modern architects, especially in the Lake District National Park, often like to keep their mortar as far back as possible from the wall face in order to give the impression of dry walling.

As for colours, the building stones of the two north-western counties are unrivalled in England for diversity: red, pink, brown, yellow, buff, fawn, grey, blue, green, lilac, white, black – all these are to be found in abundance. Outside the Lake District Cumberland is predominantly a 'red' county. From Carlisle to Longtown near the Scots border, to Brampton and Lanercost by the Roman Wall, to Kirkoswald, Lazonby, and Penrith, to Wigton, Aspatria, and Maryport, nearly all the stone buildings are red or pink or brown; and so they are along the coastal strip stretching SE from St Bees. Some of the pinks are delightful, and the deep cocoa-powder-brown of the Bunter sandstone formerly quarried just to the north of Aspatria has a dark glow, but at Penrith it must be admitted that the similarly coloured Permian sandstone seems a little sombre despite its 'warmth'. These New Red sandstones are attractive to lichen, and some of the best colour effects, beyond the power of man to imitate, derive from the spottings and splashings of grey and grey-green on shell-pink stones.

In Cumberland even the Carboniferous rocks, which on the E side of the county are the usual light greys and buffs, change colour farther W. The presence of haematite ore has stained the narrow strip S of Cockermouth quite a deep red, while in the district N and E of the lower end of Ullswater ferric oxide from the formations which once covered the Carboniferous limestone and Calciferous sandstone has changed the stone colour to a delicious grey-pink, paler than anything to be seen in the New Red sandstone country. At Dalemain near Dacre can be enjoyed some of the most beautiful building stone in the north of England. It was quarried only a mile away.

Red and pink are also the principal colours of the Cumberland granites. Most of the granite buildings are to be found in the area centring upon Eskdale and running southwards to near Bootle. Although the field walls are grey with lichen, the buildings hereabouts are mostly pale pink. This stone is unhappily no longer worked, but visually it is perhaps the most attractive granite in England. A similar stone may be seen in the walls of the farmhouses around Ennerdale Water. Threlkeld granite, occurring to the E of Keswick, is mostly bluish-grey with some pink patches. Until three years ago this excellent stone was available for walling on demand, but today all that is quarried is crushed for road metal. The tower of the R. C. church of Our Lady of the Lakes and St Charles at Keswick, completed in 1965, is likely to be the last building in England of Threlkeld granite.

The principal areas of Cumberland in which the building stone is not red, pink, or brown comprise the w slopes of the Pennines, from Alston to Gilsland and Bewcastle (Carboniferous limestone: light grey and some buff); the coast from Whitehaven to Maryport and for a few miles inland (Millstone grit: pale brownish-grey); and the NW half of the Lake District. Here the hard rocks from the Early Ordovician series provide an uncompromising-looking building stone, often very dark and sombre in tone, as can be seen at Keswick; on the other hand the Borrowdale volcanic rocks yield one of the most delectable of all roofing materials, the green slates from the Honister Pass. Mention must also be made of the excellent barn and field walls of 'cobble-ducks' (water-washed cobbles), gathered from the adjacent beaches, that are to be seen at certain places along the w coast between Millom and St Bees, notably near Bootle. In the best of these walls the cobbles are of nearly uniform size, so could be coursed, sometimes with bands of roofing slates introduced at intervals as 'levellers'. Splashes of brilliant yellow lichen add the final touch.

Westmorland, in contrast to Cumberland, is decidedly a 'grey' county. Red brick and tiles are still, fortunately, very rare, and red stone occurs in a few places only: Permian and Triassic sandstones *à la* Cumberland in the upper Eden valley, a few miles above and below Appleby, and the far older Ordovician stone at the centre of the Lake District. Although low in tone, the colours of this volcanic stone can be rather rich. They range from grey through every shade of brown to dark red and deep purple, the two latter due to staining from oxides of iron or manganese. The stone formerly quarried on Helm Crag, above Grasmere, is all dark red. Shap, the granite of Westmorland, only began to be quarried about a hundred years ago, and in the county itself it would be difficult to find even one building constructed of it, outside the confines of the company's works. But in the later Victorian period there was a considerable vogue for it outside the county, especially in its polished form, which unhappily many people still choose for gravestones. The colour of this grey stone enlivened with high crystals of pink felspar might from a little way off be described, in its natural state, as 'dusty pink'.

For the rest, apart from a small area of buff-grey Millstone grit near Appleby (a useful sandstone for dressings and where ashlar was required), three kinds of stone, and three only, cover the whole area, while for roofing there was until comparatively recently but one: slate. The Westmorland roofs are beyond doubt among the most beautiful in England. Old slates are very heavy; the roof of even a modest house may weigh as much as ten tons. But fortunately a great many survive, equally satisfying alike for colour, for texture and for scale.

In much of sw Westmorland, including Staveley, Bowness, Windermere, and Ambleside, the sombre greys and blacks and browns of the local Silurian flagstone dominate the architectural scene. This stone was relatively cheap and accessible, for, occurring largely with shale, it could be dug from the floors of the valleys, and, although hard, it could be broken up fairly easily into rough blocks. For expensive buildings these could be carefully shaped, but most buildings in this material are very rough-textured. With its dour colouring this Silurian stone cannot truly be described as attractive.

Much more enjoyable is the so-called greenstone from the slate quarries, which belongs to the Ordovician period. This is really the wastage (not by any means always green: from the Kirkstone quarry it is grey with a bluish tinge) which is inevitable in the production of roofing slates and of panels or slabs for cladding. These pieces, lopped off in the trimming, are often rather small, but there is no reason for wasting them, since many, after further shaping performed on the site, are quite suitable for walling stone. In recent years greenstone has been enjoying considerable popularity in and around the Lake District.

Finally, there is the light grey Carboniferous limestone, which is the most extensive of the three. This covers the whole of the NE portion of the county apart from the Eden valley, as well as an area to the SE which includes Kendal and Kirkby Lonsdale. Ravenstonedale, a grey village in a leafy hollow, is typical. This stone could be used where some degree of dressing was required, as for quoins and lintels; but most walls are rubblestone and constructed of rather small pieces – sturdy walls, with a good deal of mortar. Both in towns such as Kendal and Kirkby Stephen and dotted about the countryside, limewash often serves to give it a still whiter appearance. The limewash is usually applied over roughcast or, one is sorry to have to add, pebbledash. Needless to say there are also many excellent drystone walls of Carboniferous limestone; yet for some the surprise will not be the quantity of Westmorland's walls but the profusion, even here, of excellent hedges.

PREHISTORY

BY DEREK SIMPSON

The area of Cumberland and Westmorland, with the rest of northern Britain, was covered by ice during the glacial periods when Europe was first colonized by man. It was only with the final retreat of the ice at the end of the last glaciation that the earliest settlers made their appearance. This initial penetration must have been slight; small bands of hunters following herds of game and making temporary encampments on the coast and on the shores of lakes and rivers. Their characteristic microlithic flint equipment has been found at several sites in Cumberland (e.g. Drigg and Eskmeals) unassociated with any more permanent structure. This primary and scanty Mesolithic settlement was followed at the end of the fourth millennium B.C. by the first farming communities. Judging by the number of their artefacts there was a considerable increase in population, although the principal evidence is provided not by archaeological finds but by the examination of pollen grains in peat deposits and lake sediments. The appearance of farmers clearing forests, planting crops, and allowing their herds to graze freely had a marked effect on the vegetation pattern, and this is reflected in a decline in tree pollen and the occurrence of cereal pollens and weeds of cultivation. Temporary encampments and flint-knapping sites are known (e.g. Drigg; Eskmeals) but the most important site is that at Ehenside Tarn (*see* Beckermet St John), revealed when the tarn was drained in the C19. On the shores of the tarn were found a series of hearths associated with occupation material including a dug-out canoe, fish-spears, and throwing-sticks of wood all preserved in the waterlogged conditions. The most interesting finds, however, were numerous axes of igneous rock from the axe factories of Great Langdale (W). The scree slopes of Great Gable, Scafell Pike, Pike of Stickle, and Harrison Stickle are littered with flakes and rough-outs of these axes. At Ehenside the axes survived in various stages of completion, from simple rough-outs to finely polished and finished forms, some of great size, and associated with them were sandstone rubbers and grinders used in their manufacture. Stray finds of similar Langdale axes are known from the area, and other finishing sites must exist in western coastal areas, e.g. Gosforth; Mossgarth; Portinscale (W). From Langdale the axes were traded all over England and Scotland, the most notable concentrations being in Wessex and the Upper Thames region. The sherds of plain, round-based vessels with rolled-over rims from Ehenside suggest links with Neolithic groups in Yorkshire, and it is probably significant that a considerable number of polished Langdale axes are found in north-east England. The long cairn of Sampson's Bratfull, Ennerdale (*see* Calder Bridge), although unexcavated, may be tentatively associated with these Neolithic groups, and is probably a stone version of the long barrows of southern and north-eastern England associated with the burials of the first farming communities in those areas. Traces of dry stone walling are however visible in the damaged mound, which might in fact cover a megalithic tomb such as those found in the coastal areas to the N and S of our region. The links with Yorkshire are more clearly expressed in the long barrow at Crosby Garrett (W), excavated in the C19. The mound here covered a series of burials which had been cremated *in situ* in a trench beneath the long axis of the mound. This specialized form of burial is found beneath both long and round barrows in north-east England. Other monuments which might be attributed to this period include two round barrows, again excavated in the C19, at Wiseber Hill, Kirkby Stephen (W), and Crosby Garrett (W).

The distribution of the products of the Langdale factory was continued by later Neolithic groups in whose flint and stone equipment one may detect Mesolithic traditions suggesting the acculturation of hunting and fishing aboriginals. To them one may attribute the ceremonial henge monuments of Mayburgh and King Arthur's Table, Yanwath (W), and a curious oval barrow near Sunbiggin Tarn, Orton (W), covering twelve inhumation and cremation burials accompanied by boars' tusks, bone pins, and a perforated antler mace-head. No settlement sites of the period are known, and their absence may be attributed to the semi-nomadic pastoralism practised by these communities.

From c. 2000 B.C. a final element in the pattern of Neolithic settlement in the area was provided by the appearance of the Beaker folk, whose characteristic drinking cups have been found in association with crouched inhumation burials beneath a number of round barrows and cairns (e.g. Clifton (W), Sizergh Fell (W), and Irton). Penetration of the area was by means of the Irthing and Eden valleys and the Stainmore Pass from the north-east of England. The settlement appears to have been numerically slight. Their flint work, including barbed and tanged arrowheads, is represented by a number of stray finds, and the concentration of material at Eskmeals indicates temporary encampments in this area.

From these disparate traditions at the end of the Neolithic period there emerged a series of distinctive Bronze Age societies representing a fusion of earlier cultural elements. In southern Britain, as a result of trade and perhaps stimulated by some new immigrants, the culture has a distinctive aristocratic and warlike character. In the north, including Cumberland and Westmorland, native traditions predominate, and here continuity from earlier times is more apparent. The majority of the numerous round cairns in the county must belong to this phase from c. 1650 B.C. Excavated examples have produced cremation burials contained in collared urns (e.g. Gaythorn Plain, Great Asby (W); Crosby Garrett (W); Barnscar, Muncaster) and inhumations and cremations with Food Vessels (Askham (W); Shield Knowe). Flat graves, unmarked by any covering mound, have also yielded urn and Food Vessel pottery (e.g. Springfield, Ainstable; Waterloo Hill sandpit, Aglionby). Both ceramic types represent a development from Neolithic potting traditions, and in the case of the latter appear to have been introduced from north-east England, again probably by the Irthing–Eden route. Collared urns have also been found in association with stone circles (Leacet Plantation, Brougham (W); Lacra, Millom). The stone

circle may be seen as a continuation of the circular, ceremonial 6
sites, and even the remarkable avenue at Shap (W), now largely
destroyed, can be paralleled among henge monuments. On the
other hand, a relationship with megalithic tombs is suggested by
the internal setting in the Keswick circle. The production and
distribution of metal objects, begun by the Beaker folk, saw a
considerable increase at this time, but the main centres of
manufacture and purchasing power lay outside our area. The
Eden valley, however, would have provided a suitable route for
merchants peddling the products of Irish smiths in north-east
England. Halberds of Irish type from Maryport and Haberwyn
Rigg, Crosby Ravensworth (W), and axes from Brough (W) and
Whittington (W) indicate that bronzes were traded across the
county, although the paucity of finds suggests that few were
purchased by the inhabitants.

This pattern is repeated in the Late Bronze Age. Stray finds
of bronze axes and spearheads do occur, but only a single metalwork hoard has been recorded from the two counties. It consisted of four rapiers and a socketed axe and spearhead, found in
a peat moss at Ambleside (W) in the c18 and since lost. The
continuing use of the Stainmore Pass is suggested by a small
concentration of socketed axes in the neighbourhood of Brough,
but the very rarity of Late Bronze Age metalwork implies a
somewhat impoverished and perhaps numerically slight population. No field monuments can confidently be ascribed to this
period. Many of the upland cairns and enclosures may be works
of Late Bronze Age groups, but this has yet to be demonstrated
by excavation. Indeed, the Late Bronze Age/Iron Age transition
in Cumberland and Westmorland is both ill-defined and difficult to date. For the Iron Age the evidence is again ambiguous.
A number of small hillforts – e.g. Castle Crag, Bampton (W);
Allen Knott, Windermere (W); Dunmallet, Pooley Bridge (W) –
may be tentatively ascribed to this period. Their size is a
reflection of the broken nature of the countryside and the small-
ness of the social unit in contrast with the great hillforts in the
more open lands of south Britain with their large tribal group-
ings. The 5-acre area of Carrock Fell fort, Mungrisdale, marks
out this site from the others and implies the corporate activity of
a comparatively large group for its construction. Literary evidence suggests that Cumberland and Westmorland formed a
peripheral part of the territory of the Brigantes, themselves
more reasonably interpreted as a loose confederation of localized
units rather than a single tribe. None of the forts have produced

datable material. The same is generally true of the numerous settlements found in upland areas and consisting of one or more enclosures with associated hut circles. Few have been excavated, and the general paucity of finds makes even these difficult to date. Some occur in the same areas as cairns which have produced Bronze Age material and might indeed be contemporary with them. Others again are found in the vicinity of Roman roads, and their proximity might imply a much later date. Most, however, are considered Iron Age, in character if not in date, a northern variant of the peasant economy better known in the south from sites such as Little Woodbury in Wiltshire (*see The Buildings of England: Wiltshire*). They continued to flourish after the Roman occupation. Paradoxically, it is only after this event that one can perceive native fashions in metalworking in the trinkets from sites such as Kirkby Thore (W), or in the magnificently decorated sword scabbard from Embleton, produced under the stimulus of new masters but perpetuating the artistic traditions of the pre-Roman Iron Age.

THE ROMAN OCCUPATION

BY BARRY CUNLIFFE

The difficult nature of the countryside and the uncooperative and relatively uncivilized population, together with the always present threat of attack from the aggressive tribesmen of the N, forced the Roman administration to include the area, now Cumberland and Westmorland, within the zone of military occupation. In practical terms this meant a changing pattern of forts and signalling stations linked by a grid of roads, along which the troops and imperial messengers could quickly pass. It is not surprising that in this oppressive landscape the growth of civilian life, as it was known in the south of the country, was stunted.

The first contacts with the Roman army came during the governorship of Petilius Cerialis (71–4). After successfully campaigning in the s part of the area occupied by the Brigantes, it seems that an expeditionary force of legionary strength was sent through the Stainmore Pass, camping temporarily at Crackenthorpe and Rey Cross on their way to Carlisle and beyond. It was probably early in the governorship of Julius Agricola (78–84) that this important line of communication was consolidated by means of a road, which from then on served as a major artery through the Pennines, joining the west coast command to the fortress at York. A second E–W route was also constructed between Carlisle and Corbridge, and it was from this consolidated base-line that the Agricolan conquest of Scotland was sprung.

The vaguely-recorded but serious troubles in the early years of the C2 brought the barbarians down to the Stanegate line again, emphasizing the need for a new, well-considered frontier policy. It was in response to this that Hadrian visited the north in 122 and immediately initiated, under the control of the governor Aulus Platorius Nepos, the construction of the massive and complex barrier now known as Hadrian's Wall.* Its function was simply 'to separate the Romans from the Barbarians', and to the tidy Roman mind it was planned to be as much a political and legal barrier as a military obstruction. The frontier system was practically completed within eight years. As originally planned, it was to consist of a wall, 10 ft thick, fronted by a deep ditch and broken at one-mile intervals by gates defended by small contingents quartered in fortlets, known as milecastles, built against the inner face of the wall astride the roads serving the gates. Between each pair of milecastles were two turrets, used principally as signalling stations. The system underwent a number of alterations during construction. In the W sector, for example, the wall and milecastles were built first of turf-work, only to be replaced later by stone; but more important was the change in garrisoning. Hitherto, the main fighting force had been stationed well behind the wall on Stanegate in forts such as Old Church Brampton, and Nether Denton, but violent and unexpected barbarian opposition to the frontier meant that the garrisons had to be brought up to the line and housed in forts built astride the wall (e.g. Birdoswald; *see* Walton). In the final stage the vallum, a ditch flanked by banks, was constructed to demarcate the rear of the military zone. But the total defensive system was more than a single fortified line. To the fore were outposts, at Bewcastle, Netherby, and Birrens, from which news of enemy concentration could be signalled back to the wall. Behind were the strongly defended communications.

The W part of the frontier, particularly the Solway Firth and the coastal plain on its N side, created a serious defensive problem; for the wall could have been outflanked by sea, and the

---

* Entries in the gazetteer concerning Hadrian's Wall will be found, travelling from NE to SW, under Walton, Brampton, Irthington, Crosby-on-Eden, Houghton, Carlisle (p. 88), Beaumont, Burgh-by-Sands, Drumburgh, Bowness-on-Solway; and also under Bewcastle and Netherby.

plain would have allowed enemy troops to amass. Moreover, hostile tribesmen in the Lake District would have been a constant threat to the rear. To overcome the first of these problems the Romans extended the system of forts, milecastles, and turrets around the Cumberland coast to beyond Beckfoot (*see* Silloth), and continued the defence even further by placing isolated forts at the strategic sites of Maryport, Burrow Walls, Moresby, and Ravenglass. The potential danger from the inhabitants of the Lake District was simply overcome by creating a line of forts across the s side of the massif from Ravenglass, through Hardknott (*see* Boot) and Ambleside, to Brougham on the York–Carlisle road, thus containing the lakes within a closely-defended ring of military works. The problem posed by the lowlands N of the Solway was solved partly by the placing of the outposts and partly by stationing a crack regiment of 1,000 cavalry, the *ala Petriana*, at Stanwix (Carlisle), whence this fast-moving unit could sally should enemy movements become evident.

Within the early years of the reign of Hadrian's successor, Antoninus Pius, a major advance was carried out resulting in the construction of a new wall between the Tyne and Forth, and the temporary abandonment of Hadrian's frontier. But after a number of Barbarian uprisings in 155–8, 162, 181, and 197, followed by a series of Roman counter-attacks and campaigns, Caracalla eventually decided to return to the old Hadrianic frontier which had been restored some years earlier by his father, Severus, and to make it the permanent N limit of the Province. It was to suffer destruction on two further occasions, in 296 and 367.

Considerable emphasis has been given to military matters; for it is this aspect of the occupation which has provided most of the Roman remains to be seen in the area. But civilian occupation was not entirely lacking: many peasant settlements are known, particularly in the countryside to the s of the wall, and around most of the forts well-defined civilian settlements grew up, in which the families of the soldiers lived alongside retired veterans, traders, and other camp-followers. The distinction between military and civil was eventually broken down after 367, when the great 'Barbarian conspiracy' caused destruction and chaos in much of the Province. After this, for safety, soldiers and settlers lived together in the forts, which were by now nothing more than fortified villages. The defence of the north therefore passed into the hands of a semi-civilian militia.

CUMBERLAND

★

ABALLAVA see BURGH-BY-SANDS

ABBEY TOWN

ST MARY. This is the major part of the nave, shorn of its aisles, of Holme Cultram Abbey, founded as a Cistercian house from Melrose by Henry, son of David King of Scotland, in 1150. When Henry II took Cumberland, he confirmed the possession of the abbey. The nave as it is belongs to the late C12. Excavations have shown the church to have had three more bays of nave and aisles, then a crossing, transepts with E aisles or chapels, and a straight-ended chancel. The remaining part of the nave is six bays long. The walls now taking the place of the arcade openings with their unmistakable two tiers of arched windows date from some time between 1727 and 1739.* The piers have eight strong shafts. The capitals are plain or of the waterleaf type, and one has decorated scallops of the trumpet variety. All this dates this part fairly firmly. The arches are pointed, with one chamfer, one step, and a second chamfer. One pair of piers lacks the shaft to the nave: this is where the pulpitum will have been. Of the same date also is the glorious W portal, with four orders of columns and en- 16 riched waterleaf capitals. The arch is round with manifold mouldings, one of them being keeled. The outermost has the Late Norman bobbin motif. The doorway was probably gabled originally. The upper wall as it is seems Georgian, but inside an original W balcony taken out of the thickness of the W wall runs from N to S with a small doorway on the S side, perhaps into a stair-turret. Of the aisle walls the foundations have been found. All that is upright is the two big side buttresses, which are part of the aisle W walls. From the S aisle to the W a blocked Norman doorway is visible. The original Norman buttresses between nave and aisles are broad and flat. Their decoration is later, the ornate niche probably C14, the arcading and other decoration more probably C16. But the W façade is dominated by the porch, built by Abbot

* Buck's engraving.

Chamber in 1507. There are inscriptions and shields on it, and it is worth recording that dog-tooth ornament is used in a revival spirit. The upper windows must be a yet later alteration. The main gable of the w front with a double bellcote simply pierced in is presumably Georgian. The only other interesting motif is the present E window with its uncusped tracery, all lights and panels ending in round arches. This cannot be real Perp, it must be survival, and the C17 seems the most likely date. Indeed the crossing tower fell in 1600, and what was repaired was destroyed by fire in 1604. Repairs then took from 1604 to 1606. The E end was finally demolished only after 1727, but the Perp-looking window can certainly not be Georgian. So we are justified in assuming that it is Early Jacobean.*

SCULPTURE. Many architectural and sculptural fragments in the porch, from coffin lids with foliated crosses to Flamboyant tracery. – Large fragment of a Virgin, outside; C15. – PLATE. Chalice, made in London 1571–2; Hanap and Steeple Cover, with repoussé decoration, made in London 1613–14, and very good.‡ – MONUMENTS. In the porch parts of the monument to Robert Chamber † 1518 or 1519. The abbot enthroned, many kneeling figures, and inscriptions. His punning rebus is a bear on a chain. – Joseph Saul † 1842. With oval profile medallion.

MILLGROVE HOUSE, 200 yards s of the church. 1664, with a two-storeyed bow – not bay – with mullioned windows.

MOTTE with ditch, but without bailey, N of the abbey (Curwen).

RABY COTE, 1 m. N. The base course of the front of the house has a long late medieval inscription, upside down. It comes from the abbey, as does the shield of Abbot Chamber held by an angel, and the fine relief panel with a seated Virgin with two kneeling figures, one an abbot. There is also tracery, including one piece with a mullion reaching up into the apex of an ogee arch (cf. the staircase tower of Carlisle Castle, a late C14 piece).

AIKTON

CHURCH. Narrow Norman chancel arch, the columns with scallop capitals, the arch single-stepped. In the chancel the top of a lancet window, i.e. E.E. work, visible in the vestry.

* The roof timbers of the nave are pre-Reformation; see *Trans. C. & W. A. & A. Soc.*, N.S. XIII, 1913.
‡ Cf. Westward and also Ambleside (W).

The steeply pointed, trefoiled PISCINA is E.E. too. The nave s doorway has three continuous hollows between ridges. Is that E.E. also? The Perp s aisle was added in 1869. Most of the windows are C19. – FONT. Square, with bevelled edges. The plain rounded and pointed trefoils suggest the C14.

AINSTABLE

St MICHAEL. 1872 by *G. Watson*. Lancets and plate tracery. NW tower. The church has a number of odd, personal features, e.g. the two triplets of very closely set lancets of even height as nave s windows, whereas the N wall, because of the tower, has no windows at all; and also the E fenestration. – PILLAR PISCINA. Norman, with decorated shaft. – PLATE. Cup, gilt inside, 1707–8. – MONUMENTS. Effigies of John Aglionby and his wife who died in 1428. He wears a beard. – Tablet to Francis Aglionby, very bare, with a tall, slim urn in a recess, all very intense. By *M. L. Watson*, London, 1843. Watson is the sculptor of the outstanding monuments at Sebergham and Raughton Head.

(TOWNHEAD, Newbiggin, 2½ m. NE. 1702. Close by a bastle-house, now used as a farm building. The bastle-house is of stone, two-storeyed, with the ground floor for cattle and the sparsely-windowed upper room for living.*)

ALLONBY

Allonby was said in 1748 to have had 'considerable concourse for bathing in the sea'. The first church was built in 1744, and *The Beauties of England and Wales* in 1802 called Allonby 'a neat well-built town resorted to in the summer season'. The only attempt at formality on the sea front is NORTH LODGE, at the N end, a terrace of seventeen bays. This sounds grander than it is. The centre is two-storeyed and has a Tuscan porch, but the six bays l. and the six bays r. are one-storeyed and consist of two three-bay cottages each. The parish church is at the s end.

CHRIST CHURCH. The present building is of 1845. The single windows are still of the arched, keyed-in Georgian type, but the three triple windows at the E end and the ends of the transepts are already Early Victorian Italianate, and the triple arch between nave and crossing with its excessively small side pieces is what one usually calls debased.

* Information kindly provided by Mr Robin McDowall.

Allonby has a cobbled main street along a stream. There are no houses of distinction, except for the former SEA WATER BATHS, with Ionic columns *in antis*. This dates from 1835.

ALSTON

ST AUGUSTINE. 1870 by *J. W. Walton*, the steeple completed (by *G. D. Oliver*) only in 1886. A large church of creamy stone with the steeple on the SW and used as a porch. Tympanum with Christ and angels. The windows lancets, or with plate and also (E) geometrical tracery. S arcade with polished granite piers and large, fancy leaf capitals. – STAINED GLASS. The E window, very light, by *Wooldridge* (made by *Powell*). – PLATE. Fluted Cup or Porringer 1729. – MONUMENTS. Tablets by *Regnart* of London † 1807, by *Davies* of Newcastle † 1850 and 1852, and an unsigned one † 1858 which is Quattrocento in style.

TOWN HALL. 1857 by *A. B. Higham* of Newcastle (GS). Gothic, asymmetrical, with a tower. Alston in the first half of the C19 was a prospering mining centre.

From the town hall, past the church, the little town rises steeply. The MARKET PLACE, with the MARKET CROSS, a reproduction of the former cross,* is also on the slope, and the main street goes on rising from there. Past Martins Bank is the humble FRIENDS' MEETING HOUSE of 1732 (Kelly: restored 1759).

From Alston SMEATON'S DRAINAGE LEVEL went on for five miles to Nenthead. It was completed *c*.1810 and was a navigable tunnel.

RANDALHOLM HALL, 1⅜ m. NW. A pele-tower with the usual vaulted basement and corner staircase. But the staircase goes only up to the first floor. It continues in a different corner, and from the second to the top floor runs up in the thickness of the wall. The tower windows are sashed. In the hall wing mullioned windows.

CLARGYLL HALL, 1⅞ m. NNE. The pele-tower was provided with its gross oriel and its stepped gables and the hall with Gothic windows by the Rev. *Octavius James*, rector of Kirkhaugh across the border in Northumberland. He designed it all himself. A window of 1679 is still mullioned.

* But are not the stubby Tuscan columns original? And if so, can they be of 1765 (Kelly), or must they not be C17?

ARLECDON

0010

ST MICHAEL, $\frac{1}{2}$ m. N of the village, and thus with a good view
to the N. Arlecdon itself is a mining village of no attraction.
The church is of 1829 – cf. the lancet nave – but was much remodelled in 1904. The W tower is of the latter date. Rock-
faced, with a polygonal baptistery attached to the S.

ROWRAH HALL, $\frac{3}{4}$ m. SE. Derelict. Façade of cross-windows
and doorway with a segmental pediment. This is of 1722, the
date on the lintel of the doorway of the extension on the l. Or
is it of 1705, the date on a barn?

SCALLOW, $1\frac{1}{4}$ m. E. Derelict at the time of writing. Dated 1687.
The windows have mullions, but the hood-moulds are all
connected by a course which always rises around them. Above
the doorway instead of a window a blank vertically placed oval.

ARMATHWAITE

5040

CHAPEL OF CHRIST AND MARY. 'Built before 1668' (will of
Richard Skelton). Small, of nave and chancel in one. Small
round-headed windows with one hollow chamfer. Tie-beam
roof with king-posts. – STAINED GLASS. The E window by
Morris & Co., *c.*1914, i.e. long after Morris and Burne-Jones
had died. – PLATE. Beaker, decorated, 1609–10.

CASTLE. In a highly romantic position immediately by the river
Eden. It is a pele-tower with a recent addition. The tower is
of four storeys, but its front is Early Georgian and hence of a
different disposition: service basement, two storeys, and attic
storey. The style of this façade is typically North Country,
reminiscent of Duncombe or Gilling and a little of Vanbrugh.
Broad rusticated door surround with straight entablature.
The same entablature for the ground-floor windows. Flat
raised window surrounds. A façade of few words and great
dignity.

ENGLETHWAITE HALL. By *G. H. Hunt*, 1880–2. Very picturesque with its many gables, dormers, veranda, and chimneys. The house is of stone, but the gables are half-timbered.

ARMATHWAITE HALL *see* BASSENTHWAITE

ARTHURET

3060

ST MICHAEL, $\frac{3}{4}$ m. S of Longtown. Begun to be rebuilt in 1609 41
with money collected throughout the country by permission

of James I. It is a stately church with a W tower and a long uninterrupted roof-line and battlements on both aisles and the clerestory. All windows are perfectly convincingly Perp, i.e. with four-centred arches to the heads of the lights. Three-light clerestory windows, three-light S aisle windows with a transom, two-light N aisle windows also with a transom. Only the E window indicates the real date; for in the original (now at Whoof House, Warwick, *see* p. 199) the top is not a circle (as in the church now) but a vertically placed oval – a typical C17 motif, and one indeed more typical of 1670 than 1610. Another sign of a post-medieval date is the great evenness throughout. The interior is, however, not so even. There must be some interference from the predecessor building, which was in decay when rebuilding started. There are five bays, and the W pier has a perfectly normal octagonal shape, but the following piers have canted projections to the nave which get smaller and flat higher up, and half-octagonal responds. The capitals are more similar to the C13 than to later centuries. The two-bay chancel chapels are the most medieval-looking elements. – PLATE. Cup of 1618. – MONUMENT. (Brass plate, $7\frac{1}{2}$ in. high, C14 or early C15. Two slim hands holding a heart. A cross *fleury* behind. It represents a heart burial, of course. Chancel N wall.) – Sir George Graham † 1657, small, with a curly pediment. – Dr Robert Graham † 1782 of Netherby. With an urn.

(CHURCHYARD CROSS with Maltese-cross head. Regarded as Norman by Collingwood – cf. e.g. Cumwhitton.)

ASHES *see* IVEGILL

ASHNESS BRIDGE *see* GRANGE-IN-
BORROWDALE

ASKERTON CASTLE
$\frac{3}{4}$ m. NE of Kirkcambeck

The S range is of the C15, and Thomas Lord Dacre about 1500–10 added a tower at each end. His initials are on the W tower. The original entrance from the E into the C15 house is now covered by the E tower. Somewhat later C16 masonry carries on along the W and N sides, but the ranges built against them are later and have windows all of the C20. The E connecting wall is also of that time. Inside, the timber roof of the hall survives, with tie-beams, kingposts with two-way struts, and raking queenposts. One interesting fact is the preservation of assembling marks for the timbers as they were prepared on the ground before assembly on the scaffolding.

ASPATRIA

St Kentigern. The doorway to the vestry has a re-used Norman arch with zigzag. It was originally part of the chancel arch. The arch is placed unhappily now on two big scalloped capitals. In the tympanum is a length of the former hood-mould with criss-cross decoration. This bit of evidence inspired *Travis & Mangnall*, who built the stately new church in 1846–8, to give their tower a Norman portal and a Norman arch towards the nave. Otherwise, their church is E.E., on a townish scale, with a tower accompanied by a higher stair-turret. Dull interior with six-bay arcades, and a small clerestory, but an impressively high chancel. – Font. Early or mid C13. Square bowl with, on the four sides, three patterns of big, coarse leaves, one of them based on a pair of large volutes (cf. Cross Canonby). – Sculpture. Many Anglo-Danish fragments, and a copy of the Gosforth Cross in the churchyard. Among the fragments is a 5 ft length of an Anglo-Danish cross-shaft with interlace, wild and irregular on the E face, and two smaller pieces of another. Also seven in the vestry and a small piece in the N wall outside. – Monuments. One uncommonly elaborate hogback coffin. – In the Musgrave Chapel Sir Richard † 1710 with an open curly pediment, volutes and garlands, all very naïve. – Another, with a draped urn, by *Nixson*, 1823.

Opposite the church a pair of houses with Greek Doric porches.

Beacon Hill School, at the w end of the town. 1963–5 by G. K. Seed.

Round Barrow, ⅓ m. w of the church. This small mound was excavated in the C18. It covered a stone cist containing an inhumation burial accompanied by a sword, dagger, axe, shield, and a gold brooch. The most remarkable feature of the burial, which is presumably that of a Viking, was the fact that one of the side slabs of the cist was decorated with cup and ring and other carvings more appropriate to the art of the Bronze Age. The stone is presumably one originally decorated by a Bronze Age craftsman and re-used some two thousand years later.

BANKS BURN see WALTON

BARNSCAR see MUNCASTER

BARN'S PIKE CAIRN see BEWCASTLE

4040
BARROCK PARK
1¾ m. NW of High Hesket

An early C17 nucleus. The main rooms of the N and E fronts were added by James Graham *c*.1780. Also some C19 work, notably a small addition at the S end of *c*.1815–20 and the big, good porch on the E front of 1862. The house has a five-bay front with broken pediment over the doorway. Fluted Corinthian columns carry the pediment. Round the corner a Venetian doorway and a very free Venetian upper window.

(In the grounds a C17 DOVECOTE and an ICE HOUSE.)

BARROCK FELL, 1 m. NE. The site of a ROMAN SIGNAL STATION, discovered by aerial photography, beside the main road. From here the forts of Carlisle to the N and Old Penrith to the S are clearly visible (pp. 88 and 178). In the centre of a double-ditched enclosure is the foundation for a masonry wall 6 ft thick. The finds from the excavation were exclusively C4.

BARROW HOUSE see GRANGE-IN-BORROWDALE

2030
BASSENTHWAITE

ST JOHN, on the A-road, ½ m. S of the village. 1878 by *D. Brade*. Rock-faced, pretentious, and E.E. With a SE spirelet and a polygonal apse. The windows are mostly lancets.

ST BEGA, 1⅞ m. S, by the lake. Unmoulded Norman chancel arch on the simplest imposts. One wide arch to the S aisle, one wide arch to the S chapel. They are depressed pointed and have one slight chamfer. Is that late C13? The exterior of the church mostly of the restoration of 1874. – SCULPTURE. Crucifix, in wild Late Gothic style. – HOURGLASS STAND. By the chancel arch. – MONUMENT. Walter Vane † 1814. By *Nixson* of Carlisle.

MIRE HOUSE, ¼ m. SE of the former. Late Georgian, with seven bays between two canted bay windows (perhaps later) and a porch of four Tuscan columns.

(SCARNESS DOWER HOUSE, 1 m. SW of the new church. 1726, with sash windows in moulded frames. MHLG)

ARMATHWAITE HALL, 1¾ m. NW of the new church. Castellated Victorian Tudor mansion, quite freely composed, and with a superb view S over the lake. 1881 by *Charles F. Ferguson.*

ORTHWAITE HALL, 2 m. NE. Dated 1675 and interesting for that reason; for the house has small two-light windows, each already with its own piece of entablature as a hood, a doorway with a segmental, nearly semicircular pediment, and moulded frames to doorway and windows.

WHITEFIELD HOUSE, 2 m. NNE, i.e. SW of Overwater. The house is castellated but has two ample bows and between them three bays with a loggia of two pairs of Roman Doric columns. The three-bay centre is flanked by giant pilasters. The windows are tripartite, and the upper middle window uses pilasters as partitions. One would date all this *c.*1820. In fact there is a date-stone 1840 at the back. The hall inside runs right through, across the house. Staircase with iron hand-rail.

BEAUMONT

3050

ST MARY. The Late Norman S doorway is a re-set arch, probably a chancel arch. The semicircular responds do not fit a doorway. Waterleaf capitals. The E wall has arcading which is too thickly whitewashed to recognize its date, but it is likely to be late C12 too. It is placed so as to enframe the E lancet windows. The shafts have steep bases, too steep really for a date to go with lancets, and very plain moulded capitals. Another strange feature is that the arcade returns by one bay on the N side, but stops short of the S end of the E wall. Externally the three lancets are not symmetrically placed. There is indeed more bare wall S than N of them.

HADRIAN'S WALL, at this point 9 ft wide, was sectioned when the churchyard was extended in 1928.

BECKERMET *see* CALDER BRIDGE

BECKERMET ST BRIDGET

0000

ST BRIDGET, the old church, is roughcast and consists of nave with bellcote and chancel. It has plain domestic windows. – PLATE. Cup 1779; Paten, a domestic tray, 1784; Flagon 1840. – In the churchyard a Saxon CROSS SHAFT, quite

unrecognizable in its details. It is, like the Gosforth Cross,
round below and square above, with semicircles like those of
block capitals mediating between the two parts. Next to this is
another, very similar shaft, but this has, apart from scrollwork, a runic inscription which has had many readings, the
prettiest of them referring to 'Edith, little maid' (Edih ginel
miec) and the date 1103.

St Bridget, the new church. *See* Calder Bridge.

BECKERMET ST JOHN

St John. 1878–9 by *J. Birtley* of Kendal (GS). Red sandstone.
Quite sizeable, with N aisle, SW turret with spirelet, and
geometrical tracery. – SCULPTURE. In the church and the
porch Anglo-Saxon fragments with interlace etc. All are
Anglo-Danish. One of them is half a socket stone, another a
cross-head. – Also many later coffin lids with crosses. –
PLATE. Cup *c.*1680.
(CAERNARVON CASTLE, ¾ m. N. A motte standing in the
middle of a bailey.)
(BRAYSTONE TOWER, ½ m. W. Built on a motte. There never
seems to have been a bailey.)
EHENSIDE TARN NEOLITHIC SETTLEMENT, ½ m. ESE of
Nethertown. The site was discovered in the C19 in the course
of draining the tarn. On the edge of the lake were found a
series of hearths and associated occupation material. The
waterlogged conditions had favoured the survival of a considerable quantity of organic material, including a dug-out
canoe and paddle, fish-spears, and throwing-sticks. The most
important finds, however, were numerous stone axes of Great
Langdale origin, some roughly flaked, others partially or
completely polished. The sandstone rubbers and grinders
used in the finishing of the roughouts from the axe factory
were also found in the settlement. The site appears to have
been occupied from *c.*3000 B.C.

BECKFOOT *see* SILLOTH

BEWCASTLE

St Cuthbert. The E wall with three stepped lancet windows
seems original work of *c.*1200. Georgian W tower with the windows set oddly out of axis. The rest is in the lancet style of
the Commissioners, with thin buttresses along the S side but

Bewcastle Cross, late seventh century

no windows at all on the N side – no wonder, considering the exposed site among the border fells. – PLATE. Cup and Paten Cover 1630.

BEWCASTLE CROSS. In spite of recent denials, the late C7 is still the most probable date of the Bewcastle Cross, and indeed a date more securely established than most in the Early Middle Ages. The cross bears an inscription in runes commemorating Alcfrith, once King, son of Oswi. The latter, we know, died in 670. The Bewcastle Cross has lost its crosshead. As it is, it is 14 ft 6 in. high above the pedestal. What distinguishes it from all the other crosses of Cumberland and Westmorland is the sacred figures on it. This, on the other hand, ties it to the Ruthwell Cross the other side of the Scottish border. The w side of the Bewcastle Cross has at the bottom in a shallow arched recess St John the Evangelist, then the inscription, then in another such recess Christ stepping on the lion and the adder and holding a scroll in one hand, while the other is raised in blessing, and then, in a rectangular recess, St John the Baptist with the Agnus Dei. The s side has from bottom to top a panel of close symmetrical knotwork, a length of symmetrical vine scroll, a looser knot panel, also symmetrical, a large s-curve of vine scroll, and finally at the top a small knot panel. On the E face is one great vine scroll inhabited by beasts and birds. On the N face at the bottom another vine scroll, then a knot panel, then a large panel of chequer pattern, above this knot-work once more, and, at the top, yet one more vine scroll.

The quality throughout is amazingly high, even though not quite as high as in the Ruthwell Cross. There is nothing as perfect as these two crosses and of a comparable date in the whole of Europe. The figures are amply modelled, the gestures are at once convincing, the rendering of the Evangelist in profile held no problem. The scrolls are lush yet orderly. Indeed the composition of the large scroll on the E face is highly sophisticated – more so than any ornamental sequence for seven or eight hundred years. It ought to be observed closely how (from top to bottom) the first animal turns l., the first bird r., the second bird is frontal, and the three more animals are again turned in alternating directions. Equally sophisticated is the diminishing size of the runes in accordance with visibility and legibility.

Where do the origins of this accomplished art lie? For the iconography (Christ on the beasts, also motifs at Ruthwell)

Coptic inspiration has been proved. There is no surprise in this. Monasticism started in Egypt, and Irish monasticism is derived from Egyptian via Lérins in the south of France. Indeed the Book of Durrow is even more thoroughly Coptic than the crosses. The vine scrolls are Eastern Mediterranean too. A particularly close parallel is the ornament of the ivory Throne of Maximian at Ravenna, dating from the C5 or C6 and either an Egyptian or more probably a Syrian product. That leaves the knots. They strike us as barbaric, i.e. un-antique, and were taken up in late Anglo-Saxon art more and more, in preference to the more natural vine scrolls. They are absent in the Ruthwell Cross, but present very prominently in the Book of Durrow and the Lindisfarne Gospels, both of before or about 700. Their absence in the Ruthwell Cross makes this appear more purely Antique, or Early Christian, and in any case Mediterranean, than any other Northumbrian monument. Yet the knots are Antique and Mediterranean too, though they occur of course in Kentish and East Anglian pagan jewellery also. Mediterranean examples are the *cancelli*, i.e. the low choir screens, of S. Sabina and S. Clemente in Rome, both of the C6.

So the stylistic origins of the two crosses, though varied, all lie in the same area. But how was it possible for this highly accomplished art to be practised about 680 in the North of England and in Scotland? To this question we have no answer. We know of course that Bede's Northumbria was a spot of high civilization, that Bede's writing is as fresh as anything in the crosses, that churchmen visited Rome freely, that Benedict Biscop, when he built the sister monasteries of Monkwearmouth and Jarrow, brought over masons from Gaul to build for him *more Romanorum*. But this stone carving is a matter of skill, and such skill in naturalistic carving, as far as we know, did not exist at that time either in Gaul or in Italy. How can it have existed in England? Are all the more tentative forerunners lost? It is not likely, as so much of Anglo-Saxon crosses after Ruthwell and Bewcastle is preserved.

Finally one more question without an answer. How can the Bewcastle shaft, exposed to the trying weather of the North for nearly thirteen hundred years, be so excellently preserved?

(CASTLE. Square, *c.*90 by 90 ft. No angle towers, but one square tower on the W side. The S wall stands 30 ft high, and the N wall also mostly stands. The gatehouse is not bonded in. M. Taylor: *Old Manorial Halls.*)

ROMAN FORT. The fort occupies the entire area of an irregular 6-acre hexagonal plateau. The castle, church, rectory, and a farm all lie within the Roman fortifications. The fort was designed as an outpost to HADRIAN'S WALL and was linked to it by a road leading to the wall-fort of Birdoswald (*see* Walton, p. 196). Excavations within the defences, in 1937, revealed several masonry buildings. One, the headquarters building, contained a well-preserved basement store room built into the rear of the *sacellum*; among the rubbish filling it were found an altar, a statue base, and a group of silver plaques – all evidently fittings from the sanctuary above, which had fallen into the basement at the time of a violent destruction soon after 297. After this there is evidence of reconstruction. Next to the headquarters, part of the commandant's house was uncovered.

(Of PELE TOWERS near Bewcastle the following are still in existence: CREW CASTLE, 2⅛ m. N, with walls up to 9 ft in Curwen's time; HIGH GRAINS, 1½ m. E, with the base of the tower; LOW GRAINS, ¾ m. NE, with walls up to 3 ft; and WOODHEAD, 1 m. SE, dated by Curwen C15–16.)

BARN'S PIKE CAIRN, ¾ m. E of High Grains. The cairn is surrounded by a ditch 80 ft in diameter and 3 ft wide. There is an entrance causeway on the SW.

LONG CAIRN, in Kershope Forest. *See* Nicholforest.

BIGRIGG *see* EGREMONT

BIRDOSWALD *see* WALTON

BIRKBY LODGE *see* CROSS CANONBY

3060

BLACKFORD

ST JOHN BAPTIST, on the A7. 1870 by *Borough* of Carlisle. Nave and chancel and a bell-turret with thin spire.

BLENCOW HALL *see* GREYSTOKE

BLENNERHASSET *see* MEALSGATE

2040

BOLTONGATE

ALL SAINTS. The church is one of the architectural sensations of Cumberland, quite apart from offering a beautiful view of
3 Skiddaw. Externally all one sees is a Perp church. The chancel

side windows are of two lights, cusped with a little panel tracery, the E window has three lights. The nave windows are uncusped and have panel tracery as well. Only the upper W window is cusped again.* There are, in addition to nave and chancel, two transeptal chapels, a N porch, and a NE vestry, and they all have stone lean-to roofs. Moreover there is the bellcote, oddly set back so as to allow one to walk in front of it and behind the embattled parapet, and there is an irregularly polygonal little rood-stair turret to finish the unusual picture. But the sensation is inside. One is at once transported to Scot-33 land; for the nave is covered by a steeply pointed stone tunnel-vault on which originally the stone roofing lay without timber intervening. Moreover, the transeptal chapels have half-tunnels, and there the stone roof is still immediately on them. The arches into the chapels (two chamfers, dying into the imposts) cut into the nave vault. In Scotland pointed tunnel-vaults for churches had occurred in the late C14 (Bothwell) and became an accepted motif after 1450. The source for Scotland must initially have been the south of France. Only the half-tunnels of the transepts are not a Scottish custom, but they (for aisles rather than transepts) are South French too.‡ That much by way of a historical explanation. It does not reduce one's thrill at Boltongate to speculate on its validity. A final question is the function of the corbels in the nave vault and at the foot of the transept vaults. Are they a later insertion, proving that the building at some stage was divided horizontally by a timber floor? The W corbels are more easily explained. They carry the bellcote, which, as has been observed, is set back from the W gable. – FONT. Plain, octagonal, but on four primitive heads. – PLATE. Cup of c.1565 with band ornament.

RECTORY, S of the church. A pele is attached to it. Traces of the corner staircase remain, and also one narrow slit-window.

BOOT 1000

ST CATHERINE. The typical dale chapel. Low; nave and chancel in one. Bellcote. The E window of three lights Dec. The top of the jambs shows that it originally had a pointed

---

* And in the vestry is a two-light window with ogee-headed lights, and that is probably *ex situ*.

‡ At Elsdon in Northumberland they occur in the aisles, and are there convincingly assigned to the C14.

arch. One s window is c17: two lights separated by a mullion. – FONT. Octagonal, with four rosettes and four flowing tracery patterns. Is it of the 1660s? – PLATE. Cup of 1634.

GATE HOUSE, 1¾ m. W. 1896–1901, by *A. Huddart* of Whitehaven. Red granite and red sandstone. Tudor, with mullioned and mullioned-and-transomed windows. The slightly later broad angle tower is by another architect.

DALEGARTH HALL, ⅝ m. W. Farmhouse with the round chimneys more typical of Westmorland than of Cumberland. (C. Parker mentions a plaster ceiling of 1599.)

(BROTHERILKELD. Typical low, long c17 farmhouse with well preserved interior. Mrs Davies)

STONE CIRCLES, on Eskdale Moor, 1¼ m. N. There are five circles in this group, the largest over 100 ft in diameter. All the circles enclose low cairns. Excavation in the c19 revealed a number of cremation burials in cists beneath these cairns.

STONE CIRCLE, 1¾ m. N and 1 m. W of the Whillan Beck. This circle of forty-one standing stones encloses five small round cairns 15–20 ft in diameter. All were excavated in the c19, without result. 100 yds W are two smaller STONE CIRCLES, each 50 ft in diameter, enclosing cairns. ¼ m. NNW are two more STONE CIRCLES, one 50 ft in diameter enclosing a single cairn, the second 75 ft in diameter enclosing two cairns.

HARDKNOTT CASTLE, 2½ m. E. This is a ROMAN FORT sited in a dramatic position on a spur projecting SW from the mountain of Hard Knott, between the valleys of Eskdale and Hardknott Gill. The fort, covering an area of about 3 acres, is almost square, with gates in the centre of each of its four stone walls. The W, S, and E gates were double-portalled, the N single. Internally, the plans of the *principia*, the commandant's house, and the pair of granaries have been recovered by excavation. To the S of the fort is a small bath block, consisting of a *frigidarium* with a cold plunge, a *tepidarium*, and a *caldarium* arranged laterally; the *laconicum* is detached. NE of the fort is a levelled area, 3 acres in extent, joined to the fort by a road. It is evidently the parade-ground. Its *tribunal* is sited on a mound midway along the N side.

BOOTHBY CASTLE HILL *see* WALTON

1080

BOOTLE

ST MICHAEL. Cruciform with lancets. 'Ancient', but the transepts of 1837 and the substantial W tower of c.1860–80. The

division of the entry to the transepts into two bays was probably made then. – FONT. Inscribed R.B. and, in shields: In
nomine Patris, Filii et Spiritus Sancti. The inscription is in
black letter. When was this done? The arms are those of the
Hudleston family. Does this refer to *c.*1535 (rector R. Brown),
or could it be self-conscious historicism of the early C19? –
STAINED GLASS. The E window seems to be by *Hardman,* the
chancel N window by *Holiday* († 1899). The terrible transept
windows are signed by *Ward & Hughes.* – PLATE. Cup and
Paten on foot 1716; Flagon 1742. – MONUMENT. Brass to Sir
Hugh Askew † 1562.

By the churchyard the VILLAGE CROSS, by *Paley & Austin,*
1897.

SETTLEMENT AREA. *See* Waberthwaite.

BORROWDALE   2010

CHURCH. A white dale church with bellcote. Early C19, the
   lower chancel and the tracery of 1873. – PULPIT. Late
   Georgian, with pretty panels.
HILLFORT, ¼ m. E of the path from Thwaite House to Watendlath. This tiny fort, ¼ acre in area, is defended by three lines of
   ramparts. The site is unexcavated, but is presumably of the
   Iron Age.

BOWNESS-ON-SOLWAY   2060

ST MICHAEL. Late Norman N and s doorways, both with one
   order of columns. The s doorway has a single-chamfered arch,
   the N doorway a continuous inner roll up the jambs and round
   the arch, and fine mouldings in the arch. One capital with nice
   leaves off stems. One Norman N window in the chancel. The
   outer masonry of the church shows the use of Roman stones
   from the Wall. The chancel arch and N transept arch are probably of the restoration of 1891. What may be the date of the
   bellcote? It is plain, oblong, with an oblong pyramid roof and
   arched double openings, and stands on a broad buttress. –
   FONT. Norman and excellent. Square, but octagonal at the 19
   bottom of the bowl. Leaf-decoration, the stems beaded.
   Also a trellis of beaded strips. – PLATE. Paten 1697; Cup
   1724.
The modern village lies above the westernmost fort on
   HADRIAN'S WALL. Practically nothing is known of the
   Roman structure.

PORT CARLISLE, 1 m. E. The harbour was built by the Earl of
Lonsdale in 1819 and the canal to Carlisle made in 1823. The
harbour did not flourish, and so all there is as the architectural
expression of the new status of the place is a terrace of cottages with a detached five-bay house with a Tuscan porch
somewhere near the middle. The cottages are of three or two
bays.

DRUMBURGH CASTLE, 3¾ m. SE of Bowness. The end wall of
the house is the fine, if badly preserved, wall of the castle,
built of Roman stones by Thomas Lord Dacre early in the
C16. Leland calls it 'a pretty pyle for defens of the contery'.
For the preceding tower licence to crenellate had been granted
in 1307. The upper doorway of the house once had a date
1518.

DRUMBURGH HOUSE, NW of the castle. Close to the house is a
small tower, only about 8 by 8 ft. Was it an C18 look-out?

On top of the hill at Drumburgh is a ROMAN FORT of unknown
size, partly excavated in 1947. A stretch of HADRIAN'S WALL
of intermediate gauge runs along its N side.

EASTON FARM, ¾ m. SE of Drumburgh. 1724. Five bays, the
doorway with pilasters of the oddest section, a round arch,
and above it a curly open pediment.

BOWSTEAD HILL see BURGH-BY-SANDS

BRACKENBURGH TOWER see PLUMPTON WALL

BRACKENFELL see BRAMPTON

4060   BRACKENHILL TOWER
                      4¼ m. E of Longtown

By the river Lyne. Built by Richard Graham and dated 1586,
yet still a pele tower of medieval type, with the vaulted
ground-stage and the spiral stair in the corner. Corbelled-out
battlements and a pitched roof with stepped gables – Scottish
rather than North English.

BRACKENTHWAITE see BUTTERMERE

5060   BRAMPTON

67 ST MARTIN. 1874–8 by *Philip Webb*. His only church, built
here because the Howards, Earls of Carlisle, of Naworth were

faithful clients of his. It is a very remarkable building –
no one would question that. But it is not a building that has
any of the blissful beauties of a church of the same date by
Pearson or Bodley. A fairly detailed description will explain
the meaning of this criticism. The main side is to the N. There
are here the W tower serving as a porch, the prominent two-
light aisle windows, gabled and embattled, with the merlons
climbing up and having sloping tops, and then a vestry with
bare wall below, windows high up, and a consciously over-
stressed chimney. The porch arch has a small fragmentary
gable. The w side of the tower has a giant niche with a large
window (cf. Cowthorpe, West Riding) and below two very
small two-light windows for the baptistery. The bell-openings
are in the style of *c*.1200 to E and W, but quite different and
deeply recessed to N and S. The recession is carried between
the two bell-openings by a pier which at the top curves forward as if it now chose to be a corbel. Similarly the little lead
spire has extensions to N and S with pitched lead roofs. To
continue, the S aisle W window is round with tracery, the S
aisle S side has a pattern of alternating small rectangular
windows and bare gabled stretches. Only the last window to
the E is larger, Perp, of three lights. One roof slopes up from
the aisle eaves to the nave ridge. The E view is a large five-light
window, flowing tracery, partly, and – it seems – quite
arbitrarily, blank. It is framed by the bare projecting walls of
the vestries.

The interior confirms the impression of the exterior. Here
was a man inventive in the extreme, sometimes to the verge of
what we now call the gimmicky, a man of character and
imagination and one who in order to free himself from the
fetters of historicism fiercely mixed his styles. The interior is
reached by a low room and two arches. Above there is tracery
and clear glazing to show a light upper room, lit by the big W
window. Then there are the four-bay arcades, wide, with the
conventional octagonal piers and no chancel arch. The N aisle
has wooden transverse tunnel-vaults, the S aisle a wooden
lean-to-roof with dormers and a tie-beam on a coving. But
the nave ceiling is flat and has a kind of fan coving. All these
wooden parts are painted pale green. – STAINED GLASS. All
by *Morris & Co.*, designed by *Morris* and *Burne-Jones*, and
made in 1878–80. The E window is glowing with gem-stone
colours. In the centre light at the top is the Good Shepherd,
and in the l. and r. lights are angels. Then there is a tier of

angels only, and below are Saints and in the middle the Pelican, an intricate composition, proving how near Morris and his circle could get to the forms and rhythms of Art Nouveau. In the N aisle windows are large figures too, in the small s aisle windows small panels with stories. The three-light s window has Faith, Hope, and Charity, the s aisle w window angels. One need only for a moment remember Clayton & Bell, or Heaton, Butler & Bayne, or even early Kempe, as one sees them in other churches, to appreciate what a revolution Morris glass was, with its clarity and intensity. – PLATE. Late C17 Cup; Set of the 1870s. – MONUMENT. Rev. Thomas Ramshay † 1840, with a free-standing bust at the top.

ST MARTIN'S HALL, W of the church. Quite a large building, with broad, round-arched windows and in front of it a lower part, dated 1895, which has mullioned and transomed windows but a doorway with pilasters and pediment. The scale is a little too big for the church. This also is by *Webb*.

OLD CHURCH, I m. W. Only the chancel, with a Norman N window. The E half is a C19 lengthening. In the wall an outer tomb recess, and in the porch the front of a MONUMENT with quatrefoiled circles. – This is the site of a ROMAN FORT, lying 1½ m. S of HADRIAN'S WALL. The trial excavations of 1935 showed that it contained internal buildings of masonry.

E of the village is a MOTTE without a bailey. It is exceptionally large: height 136 ft above the surrounding level. About 40 ft down the slope is a ditch 20 ft wide. The outer rampart is 8 ft high. On it a STATUE of the seventh Earl of Carlisle, 1870 by *J. H. Foley*.

The little town is uncommonly attractive, with the main road running along close to and parallel to, but entirely separated from, the street which connects the church with the MARKET PLACE. The MOOT HALL is of 1817. It is octagonal, with an outer stair on the W side to the main upper entrance. Pointed windows and a square turret. S of it is an ambitious ashlar-faced five-bay house with a Tuscan porch carrying a segmental pediment. It is presumably of the same time as the Moot Hall. Also in the Market Place and side by side are the HOWARD ARMS and the EDEN HOTEL, both of three bays, with all windows tripartite – early C19 no doubt. N of the Moot Hall are recent shops and flats, 1964 by the County Architect, *D. W. Dickenson*, done with understanding of what the site allowed and demanded. In the main street are several pleasant houses with Georgian doorcases.

Philip Webb built two houses at Brampton, one major, one minor. The first is FOUR GABLES, on the A-road, 1 m. ENE. 68 This dates from 1876–8 and is square with four gables and a lower N attachment. The house, like the church, has many odd details, but they are here successfully integrated. Typical of Webb's faith in the elementary are the square eaves modillions, and even more the water-spouts, which look for all the world like a brutalist's design of 1960. Typical of the liberties Webb took with styles are the segmental pediments of the upper windows, which are not really pediments, because they have no foot-piece, and also the round-headed doorway of the porch under a gable, and the canted bay with its heavy diagonal fins. The house is crowned by a splendid oblong chimney assembling all the flues. GREEN LANES, ¾ m. SW, is on the A-road to Warwick Bridge. The chimneys and the bay window fins are of the same family as those of Four Gables. The garden façade is characteristic of Webb's passion for the unexpected in the breaking up of the symmetry of fenestration, e.g. by the one mullioned window.

BRACKENFELL, ¾ m. S, on a smaller road. Built in 1936 by (Sir) *Leslie Martin* and *Sadie Speight* for the late Alastair Morton. To the S a fairly even, not too eventful front, to the N mostly brick-faced, but with a concave porte cochère wall of local stone à la Le Corbusier and a large sloping studio-window.

On the Gelt, 1½ m. S, was the famous 'Written Rock' – a quarry bearing inscriptions cut by the Roman quarry workers for HADRIAN'S WALL. ½ m. up river was another quarry, at PIGEON CRAG.

BRANTHWAITE see DEAN

BRAYSTONE TOWER see BECKERMET ST JOHN

BRIDEKIRK

1030

ST BRIDE. 1868–70 by *Cory & Ferguson*. Neo-Norman, cruciform, with a crossing tower and an apse, all competently and dispassionately done. The architects incorporated parts of the old church, which had stood a little to the E, and whose chancel with a Late Perp E window was left standing. In the new church are two Norman doorways, both with one order of columns with scallop capitals and zigzag at r. angles to the wall in the arch. Both have billet hood-moulds too. One column of one doorway has a lozenge-pattern. The interior of the church is rather a shock, but it tells of some daring on the part of the architects. It is all brick-faced, with even the crossing-arches of brick. The crossing and the two-bay chancel are rib-vaulted, the cells being again of brick. – FONT. The Bridekirk font dates from the mid C12 and is one of the liveliest pieces of Norman sculpture in the county. It is oblong with tapering sides and has two broad bands of decoration. To the E the top band has two affronted dragons, and the bottom band is horizontally subdivided by a scroll with a Runic inscription. This reads: Rikarth he [has] me iwrokt [wrought] and this merthr gernr me brokte [to this glory* carefully brought me]. Above the scroll is ornamental foliage with a monster and a little man, below is foliage as well and *Rikart* working away with his hammer. To the S one band has grapes, the other affronted birds, the W one a centaur and a bird, the other a woman with a sword and a man and a woman kneeling by a tree. On the N side the top strip has a bird with two heads on excessively long, tail-like necks, the bottom strip the Baptism of Christ and a scrolly tree. The style is that of Yorkshire, the decoration has Italian touches. In Cumberland the piece is entirely exceptional. – PLATE. Chalice, 1550–1, attractively decorated; foreign.

VICARAGE, by the church. A pleasant Georgian house with moulded window-frames and a Tuscan porch.

TALLENTIRE HALL, 1¼ m. NW. Said to be of *c.*1770 and *c.*1850. Recessed centre with colonnade of unfluted Ionic columns.

DOVENBY HALL, 1½ m. WSW. The front is Georgian, of five bays with a porch of four unfluted Ionic columns, but behind and not at all noticeable from outside is a very early pele tower. Its ground stage is tunnel-vaulted and it has a window towards the present staircase which is unmistakably Norman. Outer moulding of two continuous chamfers. – (In front of the house a post-Conquest cross-head of the type of Arthuret, Cliburn (W), etc. *See* Calverley-Collingwood.)

BRIGHAM

ST BRIDGET. In the N aisle a blocked Norman doorway with a small window over. S arcade (three bays) Late Norman, cf. the square abaci on round piers and the waterleaf capitals. W tower probably begun only a little later. The responds of the

* I.e. this glorious place.

arch to the nave now have round abaci. Ground stage of the tower tunnel-vaulted, as if it were a pele tower. The w window is later (C14), but the bell-openings are typical early C13, with two pointed openings under a round arch. The s doorway has a re-used late C13 arch. In the early C14 the s aisle was rebuilt. It is known that in 1323 Thomas de Burgh, rector, founded a chantry in the chapel of St Mary. This no doubt is the present s aisle. It has a characteristic almond-shaped w window (cf. Millom), with a sunk-quadrant mould-ing and a slight ogee tip. In the aisle a tomb recess with open-work mouchette tracery and a gable and buttress-shafts. The gable has rather summary foliage. L. and r. of the E window are niches for images. The window itself and the s windows are of the restoration (1864–76) by *Butterfield*. Due to him also is the saddleback roof of the tower. In the chancel s wall and (re-set) in the vestry two Perp windows with ogee heads to the lights set under round arches. – FONT. Small, octagonal, pro-bably C17. – SCULPTURE. Anglo-Danish cross-socket with several beasts' heads. Several smaller fragments, also pre-Nor-man. – STAINED GLASS. The chancel E, s aisle E, and s aisle s windows look as though they might be by *Gibbs*, whom Butterfield liked. – PLATE. Cup 1661; medievalizing Set 1843–4.

OLD PARSONAGE, N of the church. One gable-end has two buttresses and between them a blocked two-light window with a circle over, i.e. the window of a later C13 upper hall.

BRIDGE, N of the church and parsonage. 1835. Three arches. Bulgy rustication, including the pilasters between the arches.

BROCKLEY MOOR see PLUMPTON WALL

BROMFIELD

ST MUNGO. The s doorway has a re-set Norman arch with zigzag. In the E wall of the nave, l. and r. of the present chancel arch, are short stretches of the Norman frieze of an aisleless nave. They are decorated with saltire crosses. The chancel arch itself seems bits and pieces. The responds have a broad fillet just like the three-bay arcade, where the piers are round and yet carry four such fillets. That arcade must be early C13, especially as it also has round arches with one step and one chamfer. But the chancel arch is of three proper chamfers and pointed, and the faces at its springing certainly do not look C13. The church had transepts, but they are E of the present chancel arch. The s transept s window has simple but curious bar tracery, a late C13 motif. The N transept has disappeared in so far as the N aisle is as wide as the transept was. Nearly all the windows of the church are Victorian. – SCULPTURE. Fragment of a cross-shaft with interlace, and a broad raised band round (cf. Rockcliffe). – PLATE. Small C17 Paten; Chalice 1759. – MONUMENTS. Many coffin lids with foliated crosses. – In the N aisle E wall a low recess with a large coffin lid, referred in the re-cut inscription to Adam of Crookdale, 1514 (Nicholson and Burn). – In the N wall of the chancel another tomb recess. In this a tomb-chest with an inscription about Richard Garth † 1673. The inscription is in typical Roman capitals.

HOLY WELL OF ST MUNGO. An insignificant little round building N of the church in the next field, half sunk and with a door.

(WINDMILL, Langrigg. A very rare survival; now a cottage. Three storeys and saddleback roof. Mrs Davies)

BROOMRIGG see CROGLIN

BROTHERILKELD see BOOT

BROUGHTON

3040

CHRIST CHURCH, Little Broughton. 1856. Nave with bellcote and chancel. Lancet windows. – PULPIT. A charming late C18 piece. – Art Nouveau STAINED GLASS with leaf motifs.

BROUGHTON MOOR

3040

ST COLUMBA. By *W. D. Caröe*, 1905, and at once recognizable as the work of an architect with an idiom of his own. Small, with a small, pretty N tower. The ground stage is open by a round arch as a porch. The bell-stage has four massive diagonal buttress-posts connected by segmental arches, and a spike on top. The church is rock-faced and has round-arched windows. Caröe has left C19 historicism far behind. He may not have been as refined as, say, Temple Moore, but he had the virtue of originality.

BRUNSTOCK see HOUGHTON

BUNKERSHILL see CARLISLE, p. 104

BURGH-BY-SANDS

ST MICHAEL. Built with stones from the Roman wall (*see* below). The broad tower, which is probably mid C14, was built with a view to defence. It has no doorway to the outside and only small windows (cf. Great Salkeld and Newton Arlosh). The ground floor is tunnel-vaulted. The top storey with its round-arched bell-openings is of different masonry and probably Georgian, as are the windows of the E end of the church. This, very strangely, is an addition E of the chancel. It may have been meant as a vestry from the beginning. The church which existed here before the tower was Norman, as is proved by the N doorway with its big stylized, i.e. abstracticized, beakhead and the remaining bits of the outer orders. But apart from this doorway all that is medieval is E.E., see the one chancel N lancet, the N aisle windows (a pair of lancets in the E wall, which is unusual), and the N arcade. It is of three bays with octagonal shafts (later substitutes) and interesting capitals with primitive stiff-leaf. – The small doorway from the nave to the tower has its original iron GATE, the yatt, as it is called in Cumberland (cf. Dalston Hall and Naworth). – PLATE. Cup of 1740. – MONUMENT. Charming large tablet of 1783 outside the church.

FULWOOD HOUSE, W of the church. Long Late Georgian front with two pediments and two doorways, one with an Ionic porch.

The site of the Roman fort of ABALLAVA, lying astride HADRIAN'S WALL, is now beneath the modern village: the church is almost in the middle of it.

MONUMENT TO EDWARD I, 1¼ m. NNW. Erected in 1685, rebuilt in 1803, restored in 1876. A square pillar, about 20 ft high with a cross at the top. Edward I died in camp on Burgh Marsh in 1307.

KERSHAW HOUSE, Bowstead Hill, 2¼ m. W. Late Georgian, of red and yellow chequer brick. The centre of three bays, and one-bay wings. Doorway with Greek Doric columns and a Doric entablature.

MOOR HALL, Moorhouse, 1½ m. SSE. Mid-Georgian, of five bays with a Venetian doorway and a Venetian window over.

METHODIST CHAPEL, Moorhouse, at the E end. Built in 1733 as a Quaker Meeting House, and no longer of the earliest and humblest cottage type. Seven bays, of which the fifth is the doorway, with a keyed-in round arch.

BUTTERMERE

CHURCH. 1841. Tiny, with a bellcote and a lower chancel. The position is superb. – STAINED GLASS. The E window by *Holiday*, 1893.

(LOW HOLLINS, Brackenthwaite. The house is dated 1687. It has some mullioned windows, and the continuous top moulding of the ground floor serves as hood-moulds to the windows as well, which is typical of the date. MHLG)

ENCLOSURE, Brackenthwaite, at the N end of Crummock Water and to the r. of the B5289. This is a small, roughly circular enclosure, 200 ft in diameter, with an entrance gap on the W. The bank is slight and nowhere more than 2 ft in height. Within the enclosure is a series of hut circles, and there are two subsidiary banks forming lesser enclosures on the E and S. The site is unexcavated and cannot be closely dated.

CAERMOTE *see* TORPENHOW

CAERNARVON CASTLE *see* BECKERMET ST JOHN

CALDBECK

ST KENTIGERN. The church poses a number of problems. There is first of all the W tower. The MHLG says 1727, but that cannot be. It is medieval, and the small unmoulded arch to the nave looks Norman. Some of the windows could be Norman too. The entrance to the modern S porch is as evidently Norman as it is *ex situ*. The arch has beakheads to the outside, and to the inside motifs like beakheads so stylized as to be abstract. It is suggested that they were the chancel arch – a very narrow one indeed. The doorway inside the porch is of the C13, with continuous mouldings. The N aisle windows and clerestory windows are Victorian. The problem inside is the chronology of the arcades. They are of six bays, with octagonal piers on the S, round piers on the N side. There is a marked difference between one to three from the W and the rest. On the S side the piers are slimmer and the arches change from slight to proper chamfers. That indicates W before E. The change of the boundary pier from being an E respond to being a pier is indeed evident. On the N side the change is less obvious, but the size of the capitals is also reduced, and the pier opposite the other shows the change, as one looks from the aisle. So a lengthening to the E seems indicated, and must have taken place as building went on. The only trouble is that in the chancel s wall a column has come to light, with a steep base and an elementary moulded capital, and this looks earlier than the arcades, i.e. would imply a chancel in a place to the E of the whole six-bay nave. Some alterations were made in 1512 by John de Wychdale, rector at the time, whose name occurs in an *Orate* inscription above the typical Latest Perp chancel E window (uncusped arches to the lights). – FONT. Big, octagonal, Perp, with a thickly moulded stem.

RECTORY. 1785. The front with a canted bay in the middle. In it the entrance. A screen of four Tuscan columns round the canted bay. Round the corner, facing the churchyard, are two delightful tripartite Gothic windows, the side parts with steep lancet arches, the centre with a broad ogee. Close Gothick glazing-bars. The archway to the churchyard has a re-used doorhead of the early C18.

WHELPO, 1⅛ m. W. Just E of the bridge is a plain, three-bay, single-storeyed cottage. This was built in 1698 as a FRIENDS' MEETING HOUSE.

(Another FRIENDS' MEETING HOUSE is at HOWBECK, just S of Upton. This is according to the MHLG C18.)

LOW BROWNRIGG, 1⅛ m. NW. Dated 1695. Mullioned windows of two lights in moulded frames. Between ground floor and first floor a moulded string-course. Above the doorway a round window. The inscription is worth reading:

> Grace brings salvation by an inward light
> Works reformation in a pious sight
> Then listen well unto Christs voice within
> And tender that which keeps us out of sin.

CAIRNS. *See* Mungrisdale.

CALDER ABBEY *see* CALDER BRIDGE

CALDER BRIDGE

ST BRIDGET, the parish church of Beckermet. Built in 1842 by *E. Sharpe*. Quite a stately building, red sandstone, cruciform, with a W tower, lancets, buttresses along the nave, clumsy pinnacles on the tower, and a short chancel – i.e. pre-Pugin or pre-Scott in archeological accuracy. – STAINED GLASS. E window, by *Holiday*, date of death commemorated 1877.

PONSONBY CHURCH, the parish church of Ponsonby, ¼ m. s. 1840 and 1874. Red sandstone. Low W tower with broach-spire. Lancet windows.* – STAINED GLASS. In the E window the glass is by *Morris & Co.*, second half of the seventies. Oblong sacred stories, clearly and simply told. The square foliage quarries charming as all Morris's are. – The W window is by *Holiday*, date of death commemorated 1893. – PLATE. Paten of 1802; Flagon of 1821. – MONUMENTS. Two coffin lids with cross, sword, and shears. – Thomas Curwen † 1653. Square tablet in a frame of dog-tooth (which is interesting). Two figures in relief l. and r. Very rustic.

PELHAM HOUSE, W of the former. Built *c.*1780, but the porch of four slim Greek Doric columns and the two LODGES with stubby Tuscan columns *in antis* are very unlikely before 1810. Fine semicircular staircase, the handrail of iron. On the upper floor pedimented doorways leading from the staircase to the rooms. Also chimneypieces of *c.*1780. The house was built for Edward Stanley.

SELLA PARK HOTEL, W of the former. All externally Victorian-Jacobean, but inside the walls of a pele tower and parts of the spiral staircase. The house then belonged to the Curwens. Parker also notes that part of the Jacobean work is original.

CALDER HALL and WINDSCALE, 1¾ m. SW. Built by the United Kingdom Atomic Energy Authority, which had been founded in 1946. Windscale is a plant producing plutonium, Calder Hall a power station producing electricity. Windscale was opened in 1951, Calder Hall in 1956. Calder Hall was the first full-scale nuclear power station in the world. Architec-turally the most prominent parts of Calder Hall are the two pairs of cooling towers – the noble shape of cooling towers can never fail to impress – and the three blocky reactor buildings, of Windscale the two reactors with their high, slim concrete towers and the globular Advanced Gas-cooled Reactor, put into operation in 1963. The buildings were designed in the Architects' Department of the Engineering Group of the U.K.A.E.A.

CALDER ABBEY, ¾ m. ENE. Founded in 1134 by William de Meschines for the order of Savigny. United with the Cister-cians in 1148. Nothing of the buildings is as old. The CHURCH was built in the late C12 and early C13. It lies by the river,

* The Rev. J. L. Johnson writes that the chancel arch comes from the preceding E.E. church, but was heightened in 1874.

as was a rule among the Cistercians. It has its cloister on the S
side, and part of the monastic buildings are now inside a Late
Georgian house. The oldest detail of the church is curiously
enough the W doorway. It has a round, moulded arch with an
outer rounded frieze of lobes and shafts with waterleaf capitals. Such capitals also appear in the outer shafting of the
transept E windows, and this must mean that the original
church was only completed in the waterleaf decades, i.e.
c.1170–90, and the re-building was begun at the E end immediately after the nave was finished. So c.1175 would serve
for the one, c.1190 for the other. The church as it is now has a
straight E end, only known from excavation, transepts with an
E aisle, and a nave with aisles, only five bays long. The chancel
is separated from the transept aisles by solid walls. These
chancel side walls, as far as they are preserved, had very tall
blank arcading, the slender shafts with several shaft-rings.
Curiously trefoiled SEDILIA. Of the E bay, which has disappeared, the W jambs of very high lancets are still recognizable.
The crossing carried a tower, and the four arches have all
survived to support at least a stump of it. The N and S arches
have canted responds, the E and W ones semicircular responds
resting on brackets, short in the E arch, somewhat longer in the
W arch. Of the transept E aisles only that on the S side exists.
The pier is quatrefoil with deep narrow hollows between the
foils. The foils carry fillets. Double-chamfered arches. The
aisle was rib-vaulted, and each of the two bays has two lancet
windows. Above the arcade is bold blank arcading, single-
chamfered with continuous mouldings, two lights for one
arch below, and with big blank quatrefoils in the spandrels.
The W wall has a tall clerestory of lancets (with later tracery)
and a wall-passage. In the S wall is the upper doorway which
connected the dormitory with the transept by means of the
night-stair. This also has continuous mouldings. The N
transept was probably the same or similar, but a modern
buttressing wall separates the transept itself from its aisle. A
small doorway leads out of the transept to the N. As regards
the nave, the S arcade has almost entirely gone, but the N
arcade remains complete. Only the arches from the aisles to
the transepts are both there. The arcade piers are alternatingly
quatrefoil (as in the S transept) and octagonal. The abacus of
one has a kind of zigzag of something like flat half-dogtooth.
An octagonal capital is a later replacement. Above the E
responds of both arcades are traces of the clerestory with

wall-passage. The foundation courses across the nave show
where the pulpitum was. – MONUMENTS. Three badly
preserved C14 effigies of Knights. – Head of an abbot under a
canopy.

Of the MONASTIC RANGES the W range has completely
gone. The S range has disappeared in the house (see below),
but of the E range much exists. There is first the usual
CHAPTER HOUSE entrance: a doorway with two window-like
openings l. and r. The details, especially the fine mouldings,
indicate a late C13 date. The E window indeed had geometrical
tracery. It must have been quite a spectacular piece. The
chapter house was vaulted in three bays. The E bay is preserved completely. The ribs were single-chamfered. The story
is complicated by the fact that the opening l. of the entrance
is not a window, like that on the r., but the opening into the
book cupboard or book closet. It is also rib-vaulted with
single-chamfered ribs. On this vault was a passage from the
doorway of the night stair to the DORMITORY. This has many
of its simple lancet windows preserved, to the W as well as the
E. It can only have started S of the chapter house, as the height
of the wall arches for the vaults of the chapter house proves.
Above the chapter house vault however was still a small room
(for the sacristan) reached by a narrow passage in the thickness
of the S gable wall and a small plain doorway. S of the chapter
house followed the SLYPE and then an UNDERCROFT under
part of the dormitory. This runs on into the house.

The HOUSE is supposed to be of c.1770. It has three bays l.
and three bays r. of a solid porch. The porch is pedimented
and has an entry with attached Tuscan columns. Above the
porch is a Venetian window. What of the walls of REFECTORY
(at r. angles to the cloister), WARMING HOUSE, and other
rooms (the arrangement was strangely enough two rooms
deep) survives in the basement of the house has no feature of
interest.

The GATEHOUSE seems to be of the C14. It has arches from
outside and inside the monastery which are double-chamfered.
The former has continuous mouldings, the latter responds
proper.*

SAMPSON'S BRATFULL LONG CAIRN, 4 m. NE, on Stockdale
Moor. The mound has an E–W orientation and a maximum
length of 96 ft. The E and broader end is 45 ft wide, and here

---

* A house in the street of Calder Bridge, dated 1727, has above the doorway a large quatrefoil from the abbey.

the mound still stands to a height of 6 ft. The site is unexcavated, although traces of dry stone walling can be seen at several points where the mound has been disturbed. The site may be a northern variant of the long barrows of South and North-East England. In the vicinity of the long cairn are numerous small ROUND CAIRNS.

CALDER HALL see CALDER BRIDGE

CALTHWAITE

4040

CHURCH. 1913.* Still Gothic, with lancets. – The PULPIT is a pretty conceit. It is a little like an opera box, set in the thickness of the wall, with a back window, and the body of the pulpit projecting polygonally.

SCALES HALL. See p. 186.

CAMBECKHILL see WALTON

CAMBOGLANNA see WALTON

CAMERTON

3040

ST PETER, by the river, away from the village, but also by a vast slag-heap. Small W tower of 1855 with polygonal top. Nave and chancel and S transept Dec. – PLATE. Chalice of 1571. – CURIOSA. Collecting-shovels (S transept). – MONUMENT. Blackened effigy of a Knight, early C16, known as Black Tom of the North or Black Tom Curwen (who was buried at Shap Abbey). On the tomb-chest shields in circles.

CAMERTON HALL, ½ m. NW. Late Georgian, with two big bows and a Tuscan porch. The LODGE to the grounds on the other hand has Gothic windows.

CARDEW HOUSE see DALSTON

THE CARLES see CASTLERIGG

CARLETON

4050

2½ m. SE of Carlisle

GARLANDS HOSPITAL, the Cumberland and Westmorland Mental Hospital. The style of the older buildings is broadly speaking Italianate. The designs were done by *Thomas*

* The name of the architect the vicar gave tentatively as E. Unwin. Is this (Sir) *Raymond Unwin*?

Worthington in 1856, and adapted for execution by *J. A. Cory* who was then County Architect. He also did the chapel in 1875 and many enlargements.

CARLETON HALL *see* DRIGG

4050

CARLISLE

Carlisle was a Roman civil settlement (LUGUVALIUM), which developed above a fort occupied from the Flavian period until its abandonment when Hadrian's Wall was built. The wall runs through the northern suburbs of the present town. In the C10 and C11 the town was Scottish. Rufus recaptured it in 1092. Henry I made it a bishop's see in 1133, and Henry II gave it its first charter in 1158. It was in the Anglo-Scottish battle line for nearly five hundred years and again in the '45. As a sign of medieval prosperity the settling of Greyfriars as well as Black-friars, both in 1233, can be quoted. Prosperity in the late C17 and the C18 was moderate, and is recognizable in the surviving houses and terraces.

THE CATHEDRAL

About the year 1102 Henry I granted a site at Carlisle for the foundation of a religious establishment. Building may not have been begun until Ranulph de Meschines had left Carlisle and Henry had taken over. He established Augustinian Canons. The church was under construction in 1130. Then, in 1133, Henry made the town the see of a bishop. These years probably are the time of intense building. For the chancel all we have is 1246 as the date for a gift of 20 Marks by Henry III to the building work. Then follows the fire of 1292, which made much rebuild-ing necessary. Work on this, according to gifts of money, still went on in 1354, 1356, and 1362. The principal restoration was undertaken by *Ewan Christian* in 1853–7.

The cathedral from its former Norman W façade to the E end was 315 ft long externally. It is built of red sandstone, except for the Norman parts, which are of dark grey stone, possibly re-used from the Roman wall.

EXTERIOR

It is at once evident that the nave survives only as a stump. It originally had eight bays; now there are only two. The rest was destroyed by the Scots between 1645 and 1652. On the N side the Norman aisle and Norman clerestory windows survive, shafted, with scallop capitals and decorated arches. On the S side only the clerestory windows are Norman, but on the other hand the transept has its E and W clerestory still Norman and a little on the S side at gable level too. Otherwise the S transept front is all of the 1850s. It must formerly have been quite different, as here the cloister adjoined. In the E bay of the aisle is still the blocked doorway into this. Long after the nave had been demolished, in 1870, a parish church of St Mary was built in its stead, but this in its turn was pulled down in 1954. At the time when this church was begun, the present W end of the stump of the nave was also built. It was designed by *Ewan Christian*. The N transept is largely a late medieval rebuilding. It is attributed to Bishop Strickland (1400–19), who also built the present crossing tower. The crossing tower has Perp bell-openings and battlements and a higher, square stair-turret. The odd wall extending N from its NE corner is explained by the fact that, when the chancel was rebuilt, it was decided to make it as wide as the Norman chancel and chancel aisle had been together and add a new N aisle. The irregularity that this leads to inside will be pointed out later. Strickland's work on the transept has neither a W nor an E clerestory. The N front has a large window in Early Dec forms but so handled that it may well be of after 1645. The same will thus apply to the round window over, with its seven circles.

The chancel is preserved in its full length and is quite a spectacular piece. It is confusing only at first that it patently belongs to two styles, E.E. and Dec. The N and S walls of the aisles are E.E. The system is pairs of lancets and blank arches l. and r., shafts with shaft-rings, and canted buttresses. But the W bay is different and has a two-light window with cusped and enriched Y-tracery. It is the same round the corner to the E, and the main E window is a gorgeous display of flowing tracery, 51 ft high, of nine lights, divided 4 – 1 – 4, with the middle light expanding into a bulbous shape with internal tracery and the side parts developing tracery of the type with leaves off a stem. Big buttresses l. and r. with statues in two tiers on its upper parts. Above the E window a window in the form of a spherical triangle with three spherical triangles set in and on the gable a display of pinnacles. This is from the restoration of the 1850s. The side walls of the aisles differ in so far as on the N side all is as described above, but on the S side work must have proceeded more slowly, and funds may have run out. So the shafting stops, and the fenestration is simply chamfered lancets in stepped groups of three. The remains of a vaulted building are those of a sacristy. The simplified type continues to the E chapel of the S transept, which was founded by a rich citizen, John de Capella. One would be inclined to date the shafted windows *c.*1220–50 and the simpler *c.*1250–80. On the N side there is no such chapel: instead there is a large, Perp four-light window. The chancel clerestory is again entirely Dec. The tracery patterns differ considerably, but reticulation occurs several times.

INTERIOR

For a reconstruction of the Norman cathedral we have not much to go by. Of the E end all that is known is a length of wall curving in the place where the Norman apse would have been, if the chancel was of two bays. Maybe there were side apses too, as at Durham. We are on safe ground only at the crossing. The W and E arches have no responds, but those of the N and S arches are triple and have scalloped capitals of a broad and elementary kind which suggests an early C12 date. The responds are not high and are continued by Perp responds, but it is likely that the capitals were originally high up and later re-set. The arches to the S chancel aisle and to the N and S aisles have the same responds and similar capitals. But it is very noticeable that the face towards the aisles themselves has smaller scallops, a little more decorated, a sign that the nave was built after the E parts. Of the Norman transepts little else appears on the N side, more on the S. In the E wall, to the r. of the arch into the chancel aisle, remains the arch into a former Norman E chapel. The chapel which is there now is, as has already been said, of the late C13. It has a rib-vault of elegantly thin ribs, standing on corbels. Three of these have stiff-leaf, one a human demi-figure. One corbel starts with a roguish knot. In the N transept of the E chapel only the blocked arch survives. It has, like that of the S transept, an outer band of zigzag. The opening into the chancel, which – as will be remembered – is wider than the Norman chancel had been, is pushed to the N. The S transept W wall is Norman throughout. It has plain windows and a clerestory with the stepped tripartite arrangement so typical of the Norman style. In the S wall something similar must have been done, but only the easternmost and westernmost shafts remain. The upper part of the crossing has leaf capitals, many-moulded arches, and, set in the N arch, a Perp traceried strainer arch. Tierceron-star vault.

Of the nave there are only two bays. They have enormous, 14 but not high, round piers, about 6 ft 6 in. in diameter, and round arches of two slight chamfers, a late C12 characteristic. The capitals are round and many-scalloped on the S side, plain on the N side. In the aisles are triple responds. But no cross arches are preserved. The gallery has un-subdivided plain single-step openings, the clerestory the tripartite arrangement as in the transept. Shafts, starting above the arcade capitals, led up to the principal roof-beams, but are now truncated.

That the chancel belongs to two periods is as obvious 26 inside as outside. Of c.1220-50 are the blank arcading of the aisle walls, cinquefoiled with small dog-tooth on the N but not the S, and the shafted lancets. However, the E bay does not partake of this arrangement. The bay is narrower, and the blank arcading has thick Dec capitals. So one must assume that this bay is a C14 addition, and Mr Bulman has made the convincing suggestion that the masonry of the lower courses of the E wall is E.E. and that it represented a chancel project-ing a little beyond the chancel aisles. That would explain the narrowness of the bay. The arcade piers are all of after the fire, and so are the vaults of the aisles, though they still look C13.

The Dec piers have eight strong shafts, the diagonal ones keeled, or rather filleted. There are deep continuous hollows between the shafts. The capitals are bands of nobbly leaves, and in them are small figures illustrating the labours of the 27 months: January as Janus with two heads feasting, February warming himself by a fire, March digging, April pruning, May offering a branch, June hawking, July mowing, August work-ing in the fields, September reaping, October harvesting grapes, November sowing, December killing an ox. All this is of delightful workmanship. Arches of many mouldings with prominent dog-tooth. Hood-mould with small nailhead. That gives a date not later than the early C14. The arch into the N transept from the aisle is of the same kind, and to its N, visible from the aisle, is the springing of a second such arch, proof that at that time the plan was to scrap the existing transept and build a new one with an E aisle. This was not done, and so, as we have seen, it was in the end left to Bishop

Strickland to build a very simple transept. To go back to the chancel 'nave', the gallery has three small two-light openings per bay with reticulation units. The clerestory is still tripartite, but very bare. The semicircular chancel ceiling of timber dates from *c*.1530. It was first intended to be a hammerbeam roof, and the beams were left when the plan was altered. The present decoration was designed by *Owen Jones* in the 1850s. It is stars on a blue sky.*

FURNISHINGS

From E to W. STAINED GLASS in the E window, by *Hardman*, 1861, but at the very top some of the original C14 glass, especially a seated Christ. – PULPIT. 1559. From St Andrew at Antwerp, but bought for Carlisle from Cockayne Hatley in Bedfordshire. Very rich foot with brackets ending in claws. Brackets for the pulpit proper too. They are human figures enclosed in strapwork. Fluted angle colonnettes and little pedimented aedicules with the statuettes of the four Evangelists. – BISHOP'S THRONE. By *Street*, *c*.1880. – By the same, at the same time, the REREDOS, now hidden. – STALLS. Of

37   *c*.1400, but the canopies said to be by Prior Haythwaite, i.e. after 1430. High canopies originally with many statuettes, the arms of the stalls with figure and leaf work, the ends with blank tracery and poppyheads. A delightful variety of MISERICORDS, including on the N side monsters, birds, the Coronation of the Virgin, angels making music, and on the S side angels, monsters, a boar killing a man, a mermaid. They are all full of life, even if they are not high art. – On the stall backs are PAINTINGS, rows of stories from the life of St Augustine (S) and St Cuthbert and St Anthony (N) and also the twelve Apostles (N). They are all of *c*.1500‡ and all bad, considering what the Netherlands or France or Germany did in that line of work. The Cuthbert stories are directly derived from a Durham manuscript in the British Museum (Add. 39943). – The DOORS to the Bishop's and Dean's Stalls are of *c*.1765 and were designed by *Thomas Pitt, Lord Camelford* for his uncle Bishop Lyttleton.§ – SCREEN. To the N aisle. Given

28   * At the top of the NE spiral staircase is a pretty vault with radial ribs and a rib-ring.

‡ A monogram of Prior Gondiber means any time between 1484 and 1507.

§ By *Thomas Pitt* also the upper part of the ORGAN GALLERY and the PANELLING on the N wall of the N transept. I owe this information to Mr S. E. Dykes Bower.

by Prior Salkeld after he had become dean in 1541. This is an 39
uncommonly complete example of English Early Renaissance
decoration, with all the typical motifs, profile heads in medallions and lozenges, dolphins, and also balusters instead of mullions. – SCREENS to the E chapel of the S transept. With close
panels of Flamboyant tracery, inspired by French and Scottish
rather than English work. Similar to the Aberdeen and
Hexham screens. The date is c.1500.* – SCULPTURE. In this
chapel a Nottingham alabaster panel of the Crucifixion. – In
the N transept FONT. 1890 by *Sir Arthur Blomfield*. Gothic,
with a boldly ogee-curved outline and three seated bronze
figures. – STAINED GLASS. In the N transept N window of
c. (†) 1858. – In the W window of *c*. (†) 1870. – PLATE. Silver-
gilt Set of 1679.

MONUMENTS

From E to W. In the bay E of the altar: Bishop Law † 1787. By
Thomas Banks. Faith resting. Her hand on the mitre. Fluted
obelisk behind.

NORTH CHANCEL AISLE. Purbeck marble effigy of a
bishop; early C14 and very good. It cannot be Bishop Barrow,
who died in 1429. The effigy lies on a plain Purbeck tomb-
chest with thinly outlined large quatrefoils. – Double tomb
recess with a segmental arch starting on short vertical pieces.
The arch aggressively decorated with thorns or short branch
stumps in three orders and two different directions. One recess is empty; under the other an excellent Purbeck marble
effigy of a bishop, mid-C13, the same type as those at Ely of 21
the 1250s. Pointed trefoiled canopy and originally shafts l.
and r. One stiff-leaf capital survives.

SOUTH CHANCEL AISLE. Bishop John Wareing Bardsley.
By *Andrea Carlo Lucchesi*, 1906. Strange bronze tablet, the
forms as if cut out in leather. Similar to Gilbert, but all is
broader and balder. – Bishop Waldegrave, by *John Adams-
Acton*, 1872. White and asleep. – Bishop Robinson † 1616.
Brass tablet with kneeling figure and many inscriptions, as it
was often done in those years, e.g. Deadly feude extinct. Also
one Greek inscription. – Dean Close. By *Armstead*, 1885.
White, under a wooden canopy. – Bishop Goodwin † 1891.
Bronze effigy by *Hamo Thornycroft*.

NORTH TRANSEPT. Prior Senhouse, c.1510–20. Plain black

* Here again are Gondiber's initials.

slab on a tomb-chest with shields in quatrefoils. – J. R. Graham † 1830. Standing mourning female figure bent over an urn. – Hugh James † 1817. By *Regnart*, and exceptionally busy. Two small allegorical figures l. and r. of a short sarcophagus. Urn on the top.

SOUTH TRANSEPT. In the W wall a stone block has a runic inscription: Tolfihu wrote these runes on this stone – a very remarkable proof of how long runes were still current; for the wall is of course C12. – Thomas Sheffield. Roundel by *George Nelson*, 1856. Seated figure, reading – a Flaxman motif. – Robert Anderson † 1833. With profile portrait. By *Dunbar*.

THE CLOISTER

Not much is left, but a certain amount can be pieced together. S of the S transept is a path with a low wall on the E, a high wall on the W. This path represents the E range of the cloister, i.e. the UNDERCROFT of the dormitory. This was vaulted, as the springers show. The ribs were single-chamfered. The doorways in the W and, in line, in the E wall are of the mid or later C13 and led one into the chapter house vestibule, the other into the CHAPTER HOUSE itself. This was, as the start of the wall N of the doorway proves, octagonal. The vestibule doorway has a *trumeau*, and the twin arches sit in a super-arch in the way Y-tracery is formed. The chapter-house doorway is single. The upper storey of the E range contained the DORMITORY, but that is gone, except for one small lancet now appearing in the E wall of the refectory (*see* below). The refectory, as usual, was in the S range. It also lay on the first floor. On the ground floor in the SE corner is the doorway to a passage leading S out of the cloister, and to its l., the doorway to the dormitory day-stair. The S view of the refectory range here is quite irregular and picturesque with a small turret. The REFECTORY stands to its full height. It was built in the early C14 and remodelled by Prior Gondiber, i.e. *c*.1500. The corbels to the N show where the cloister roof was. The refectory undercroft is vaulted, and dates from the early C14 entirely. It is a beautiful room, only very recently cleared of rubbish and restored to its full dignity. It has a row of very low octagonal piers along its longitudinal axis and vaults with hollow-chamfered ribs. The difference in moulding marks the difference between the C13 and the late C15. The refectory itself, now the library, has to the W a large Perp window, to the S also large Perp windows, but their tracery all Victorian, and to the N small two-light windows entirely Dec (one reticulation unit). In the S wall of the refectory is the reading pulpit, a delightful piece with original Perp tracery to the S (a window, smaller than the others) and to the N as well. In the W wall are two hatches, no doubt to the former kitchen. From the corner of the refectory the walls of the W range can just be seen for a few inches. The rest is missing. The porch is Victorian.

THE ABBEY

This is the customary name for the cathedral precinct, which, with so little of the claustral part preserved, merges with it. The precinct is entered from the E through a GATEHOUSE of 1527 (inscription of Prior Slee). This has to E and W a triple-chamfered round arch and midway between the two a division between pedestrian and carriage entrance. Both parts of the gatehouse are tunnel-vaulted. Above the E arch is a typical early C16 window with uncusped lights. As one enters, to the S is the REGISTRY, a pretty, single-storey, three-bay building dated 1699. Doorway with open curly pediment, moulded surrounds to doorway and windows. Opposite is No. 2 CANONRY, Early Georgian, of five bays, with broad rustication round the doorway. What does the framing round the staircase window at the back signify? A mullioned and transomed window? It can of course not be earlier than the demolition of the nave.

Next follows the DEANERY, again on the S side, and with its back towards West Walls. It was originally the Prior's Lodging and consists of a pele tower of c.1510–20, a hall range on the W, and another addition on the E. The tower has a basement, tunnel-vaulted and provided with five mighty, single-chamfered, closely set transverse arches. The room above has an oriel to the N and one to the S. Both have charming moulded transverse arches inside. The ceiling has splendid moulded beams, in one direction very prettily arched. It is here that Prior Senhouse recorded himself as the builder: 'Simon Senhus sette thys roofe and scallope here'. The staircases are partly in the thickness of the wall and partly spiral. The range to the r. contained the hall, and the room following that must have been the kitchen. Its enormous fireplace is still there. The main staircase of the house now is of the later C17, with dumb-bell balusters used upside down. The range has to the outside a blank, vertically placed oval with a coat of arms. This shape goes with a later C17 date. The l. range has an Early Georgian front, with a doorway with segmental pediment.

The THIRD CANONRY is s of the E end of the cathedral, placed at an angle. It is of c.1700, seven bays, with segment-headed windows. String-course with bricks sticking out triangularly. Jacobean staircase, i.e. from another house.

The great GATES by the E end of the cathedral are of 1930, by *John F. Matthew*.

CHURCHES

ST AIDAN, Warwick Road. 1899–1902 by *C. J. Ferguson*, late in life. Large, Dec, with low aisles and clerestory. Double bell-cote. Interior with six-bay arcades, i.e. no chancel arch. Low w baptistery with a pointed tunnel-vault with closely set chamfered cross-arches – a Cumberland pele-tower motif. Well grouped parochial buildings to the NE.

ST BEDE (R.C.), Wigton Road. 1959 by *W. Mangan* of Preston. Brick, Early Christian, with narthex and campanile.

ST CUTHBERT, St Cuthbert's Lane, off the Market Place. The principal parish church of Carlisle. 1778. Red and grey stone. w tower, nave of eight bays, and short, low chancel. In the chancel a Venetian window. The body of the church has two tiers of windows with raised flat frames. In bays one and eight are doorways. w tower embraced by the two staircases to the gallery. The gallery is on Tuscan columns, and on it is an upper tier of Tuscan columns again, but each carrying its bit of entablature with triglyphs. Flat ceiling. – PULPIT. A very big piece of c.1900 ready in the wings, as it were, to be rolled on rails into a position w of the chancel.* – STAINED GLASS. In a N window a C14 figure under a fine canopy and some C15 fragments. – PLATE. Cup and Cover Paten, 1642; Cup to match, early C19. – MONUMENTS. William Giles † 1797 and his wife † 1814. By *Paul Nixson*. Urn in an aedicule with Roman Doric columns. – Elizabeth Connell † 1825. By *Dunbar*. Big cherub with a torch, by an urn. – The Rev. John Fawcett † 1851. By *W. Jackson*. Marble bust in front of drapery.

ST JAMES, St James Road. 1865–7 by *Andrews & Pepper* of Bradford. The church of a well-off suburb. Quite large, with an apse and a sw steeple with broach-spire. Geometrical

* Mr I. Hall tells me that the same odd arrangement exists at Sacred Trinity, Salford. Another case I have come across is St Paul at Cheltenham. Yet another is St Andrew, Glasgow.

tracery. Short round piers with thick leaf-crocket capitals of an entirely Victorian type.

St John Evangelist, London Road. 1867 by *R. Clarke* of Nottingham. Dark grey stone. No tower. Lancets, shafted, some stiff-leaf capitals. Thin square turret by the E end of the nave.

St John, Upperby. 1840. Of the Commissioners' type, with lancets and W tower. The bell-openings have Y-tracery.

Our Lady and St Joseph (R.C.), Warwick Square. By *Dunn, Hansom & Dunn* of Newcastle, 1891–3. Short W tower, nave with clerestory and aisles. The E window modelled on the Bishop's Eye at Lincoln, i.e. flowing tracery. The W porch cusped and subcusped. The aisle windows have two-centred arches set under straight heads.

St Michael, Church Street, Stanwix. 1841, the apse of 1893. The original architect was *J. Hodgson*. Cruciform, of the Commissioners' type, with lancets. The polygonal buttresses of the W tower derive from Rickman's Holy Trinity. – MONU-MENTS. Robert Ferguson † 1816. By *Kirkbride* of Carlisle. With a figure of Faith. – Richard Ferguson † 1860 is almost a copy, i.e. entirely Georgian still. – Capt. Hugh Patrickson † 1821. By *Nixson*. Profile in relief, rather Neronic for an army captain. Military still life at the top.

St Paul, Lonsdale Street. 1868–75 by *Habershon & Brock*. No tower. Busy geometrical tracery, dull interior. – PLATE (from St Mary). Cup and Cover Paten 1635; Credence Paten 1639.

Holy Trinity, Wigton Road. 1828–30 by *Rickman &* 60 *Hutchinson*. The cost was £6,894. This was a real Commis-sioners' church, i.e. built under the One Million Pound Act. It is an excellent example of the type. Beige stone. The W tower has polygonal buttresses (familiar to Rickman from Great St Mary at Cambridge). The usual high and slender windows between thin buttresses have Perp tracery with a transom, which was less usual than lancets. Very short chancel with a quite convincing seven-light E window. Deep W gallery. Flat ceiling. – STAINED GLASS. Signed by *Wille-ment* and dated 1845. In the centre a large Crucifixion, still in the German Romantic way. Four small stories on the l., four on the r.

Church of Scotland Chapel, Chapel Street. 1834; classical. Three broad bays with a pediment across. Arched windows.

CONGREGATIONAL CHURCH, Lowther Street. 1843 by a Mr *Nichol* of Edinburgh. A very unusual façade for the time. Jacobean in a free treatment and simply one of a terrace of houses, i.e. neither religiously nor stylistically in conformity.

PRESBYTERIAN CHURCH, Fisher Street. 1854 by *James Stewart*. Geometrical tracery and a flèche.

PUBLIC BUILDINGS

CASTLE. Carlisle Castle guarded the W end of the Scottish border. It is splendidly sited on the highest point along the Eden, with one small tributary supporting the defence. A Norman castle was first put up here by Rufus in 1092, probably of wood, but then the Scots were in charge from 1135. In 1157 they handed it back to Henry II, and this is the time when the keep and curtain wall were built. The keep is in fine condition, but all other parts of the castle have been repaired, remodelled, and rebuilt many a time. This is proof of how essential a strong castle in this place was throughout the Middle Ages. Robert Bruce's siege in 1315 is reported to us in much detail. Even under Henry VIII the castle was very much a going concern. He modernized certain parts of it for artillery (and built the mighty citadel – *see* p. 101).

The castle was divided from the town by two ditches, the inner placed some distance from the outer. Walls connected the two on the E as well as the W. In the W wall is the Tile Tower, C15 in its upper parts. The OUTER GATEHOUSE is preceded by a barbican. The corbels were for a wooden gallery. The portcullis groove, as one enters the gatehouse proper, will be noticed. The outer arch is segmental, the inner pointed. The area within is tunnel-vaulted. There are also three vaulted rooms of the C13.

In the OUTER BAILEY are BARRACKS, built in 1819 and later. Especially noteworthy is Alma, like a big Nonconformist chapel. A further ditch separated the outer from the INNER BAILEY. The gatehouse is known as CAPTAIN'S TOWER. It dates from the C14 and is three storeys high. The passage has a pointed tunnel-vault. There are holes in it to pour down boiling oil or whatever else was chosen for the purpose. A small doorway to the S leads into a vaulted chamber. To the inside above the arch is a frill of little blank pointed trefoils. The window above is early C16, and so is the high arch in front of all this. It is connected with the remodelling of the castle about 1540.

The inner bailey itself is triangular in shape. The keep stands in the SW corner. Along the NW side were the principal domestic apartments; but they have long been replaced. The KEEP is of the standard Norman shape, with very broad, shallow buttresses. It is 60 by 67 ft in size. The forebuilding stood against the E wall. Its foundation has been excavated. In it a staircase ran up to the principal entrance, which was on the first floor near the S end of the E wall. The ramp along the N side is interpreted as a Henrician addition for the conveying of cannon to upper positions.

The basement vaults are obviously a later insertion. The Ministry guidebook attributes them to *c.*1580. Of the same date would be the partition walls of the upper floors. The spiral staircase is in the NW corner. The fireplace on the first floor still shows signs of nailhead, i.e. a late C12 motif. There are small wall cabinets. On the first floor are two S windows in their original state, on the second floor to the W is one original one. In the E wall a window embrasure has the often illustrated prisoners' carvings. They date from the C14 and C15 and are of delightful naivety of execution and include dragons and mermaids, coats of arms, the Crucifixion and the Virgin, Justice and the Wheel of Fortune, and stags and the fox preaching to the geese. The vaults on the top floor are again a later, i.e. C16, insertion.

Queen Elizabeth did indeed do quite a number of things to the castle. She built a whole range to connect the keep with the NW range. The remaining stump is dated 1577. This had started at its SE end with a major GATEHOUSE of which only traces remain. It dates from *c.*1330 and was still fairly complete early in the C19. The very handsome tower which is preserved is of the late C14 and contained a staircase serving no doubt also the C14 domestic range. It has polygonal buttress-shafts, two of them on head corbels, and blank tracery of an odd kind: two lights with a reticulation motif, cut by the upper continuation of a shaft which is the mullion of the two lights.

The wall running from the E gatehouse towards the town is not part of the castle, but of the city walls.

CITY WALLS. Not much survives, the best stretches by the W end of Heads Lane, i.e. close to the Tithe Barn (*see* p. 102), between Elim Hall in West Walls and Town Dyke Orchard, and between the SE corner of the castle and West Tower Street.

TOWN HALL. Built in 1717, but much altered at various dates later. Original the general outline, low, of two storeys, with a kind of pedimented dormer over the middle and stairs up to the upper floor entrance. The sturdy bollards of course are later (1799? 1834?). Round the corner a five-bay front with cupola. It has a date 1849, but is earlier.*

GUILDHALL, just NW of the town hall. Now with shops on the ground floor. The upper floors are timber-framed, the second-floor overhang on two brackets. To Fisher Street two Perp windows.

MARKET CROSS. In front of the town hall. 1682. Unfluted Ionic column on a square base. On top a sundial with balls at the four top and four bottom corners and on it a lion.

CIVIC CENTRE, Rickergate and Lowther Street, with a view N across the bridge. 1956–64 by *Charles B. Pearson & Partners*. An excellent composition of an eleven-storey office block, the top storey a pergola by means of the framework of the building being exposed without any infilling of walls, a two-storey Civic Suite, and the octagonal Council Chamber largely on stilts and with the peripheral posts sticking up above the roof.

EDEN BRIDGE HOUSE, opposite the Civic Centre, in Lowther Street, was designed by the *Ministry of Public Building and Works (E. H. Banks)*, 1963–4. A straightforward curtain-wall job.

LIBRARY AND MUSEUM, towards Abbey Street. This includes
48 TULLIE HOUSE, the most ambitious house in Carlisle. It was built in 1689 and uses the classical apparatus with ease and yet a certain provincial licence. Seven bays, two storeys, all windows and the doorway pedimented. The pediments are triangular and segmental and all a little open at the top. All windows are sashes. Were they so from the start? Doorway with bolection moulding. Good staircase with twisted balusters. The new buildings with a façade to Castle Street are of 1892–3 by *C. J. Ferguson* in a free C16 to C17 style, with a tower, pilasters in tiers, and Henry VIII as well as Eliza-

* INSIGNIA. Seal, early C14; three Maces, their silver worn off, probably Elizabethan; State Sword, the blade dated 1509, the sword bought in 1635; three Maces, one inscribed 1660; Tankard, London, 1675; Great Mace, given in 1685–6; Loving Cup, London, 1701; Salver, London, 1709; Tankard, Newcastle, 1729; Mayor's Seal, inscribed 1731.

bethan windows. The Library itself is by the City Surveyor, *W. Howard-Smith*.*

MARKET, Fisher Street. 1887–9 by *Cawston & Graham* of London. With glass and iron vaults inside. The façades free-classical, undisciplined.

ASSIZE COURTS, Court Square. By *Smirke*, 1810–11.‡ Locally 59 known as the CITADEL, and indeed on the site and with the outline of Henry VIII's citadel, which had the two round towers and a courtyard between. It was conceived in 1539 and built under the German engineer, *Stefan von Haschenperg*, in 1541–3. Where the wide road now is, was a square tower in the wall. The road was formed in 1804. Smirke created two large round court rooms in the towers and gave them Gothic two-light windows. Along the road, facing one another, two plain façades of six bays of Gothic windows. All embattled. The road is flanked at its SE end by two pedestrian archways. It is a handsome composition, worthy of the architect of Lowther Castle, though rather out of scale with the rest of Carlisle. In front the STATUE of the Earl of Lonsdale by *Musgrave L. Watson*, 1845.§

STATION. 1847–8 by *Sir William Tite*. Tudor, with mullioned and transomed windows, a porte-cochère, and a clock-tower. Enlarged in 1873–6. Next to the station the COUNTY HOTEL, 1856–7 by *Salvin*. Quiet five-bay house, white, the centre with a segmental pediment. Mansard roof and dormers. One could call the style a mild Italianate or a Classical no longer tied to rules. To the l. a much higher part with a French pavilion roof.

G.P.O. WIRELESS TRANSMITTER, London Road, at the corner of Hillcrest Avenue. 264 ft high, the highest object in the Carlisle sky. It is quite thrilling to look at, a steel skeleton in tiers of diminishing size, with a touch of Blackpool, and a touch of oil-drilling.

CITY GENERAL HOSPITAL, Fusehill Street. Built as the Workhouse. By *Lockwood & Mawson*, 1864. The cost was £11,195 15s. Long, even front with all the main windows

* In the garden is an iron GATE, signed in large letters: *Thos. Telford*, Eng., 1820. It comes from the old Esk Bridge.

‡ But Mr Colvin says: begun by *Telford* and *Chisholm* and continued in 1808 by *Peter Nicholson* and only completed by Smirke, though to his designs.

§ By the same, inside the Court House, a statue of Major Aglionby, also 1845.

arched. Pedimented centre flanked by two towers with French pavilion roofs.

62 CUMBERLAND INFIRMARY, Newtown Road. The original building, by *Robert Tattersall*, 1830–2, is extremely impressive, grand and restrained. Ashlar-faced front of eleven bays, with in the middle a giant tetrastyle portico of Greek Doric columns carrying a pediment. Wreaths in the frieze. This front was extended by one-storey links with pilasters and angle pavilions and a big W wing in the same style, added, all by *Ferguson*, in 1870–3.

PERAMBULATION

Starting from the cathedral, one is between the two most interesting Georgian streets of Carlisle. In ABBEY STREET No. 38 is of ashlar, in a decidedly debased Classical with odd variations on the motif of the tripartite window. No. 32 is of five bays, also ashlar-faced, and has a doorway with a blank basket-arch on slender Tuscan columns. No. 28 is specially pretty, with Ionic columns and a broken pediment for the doorway and elegant detail. Immediately behind Abbey Street is WEST WALLS, where one can see the city wall (*see* p. 99), and also the TITHE BARN by St Cuthbert. This is red sandstone, C15, with, in one gable, a two-light window with cusped lights.

In CASTLE STREET No. 19, ashlar-faced, three bays, two and a half storeys, with pink pilasters on the ground floor and large arches probably for former Venetian windows and doorway. Nos 26–30 are ashlar too, early C19, with porches of unfluted Ionic columns. No. 3 has a three-bay Grecian front with pilasters to the doorway. FISHER STREET runs just behind and nearly parallel with Castle Street. It starts at the castle end with a nine-bay front in chequer brick. Nice lacy overthrows. On the other side a pair distinguished by the charming way in which the eaves gently curve forward and backward to take in two bay windows. No. 34, again on the S side, is Grecian, with giant pilasters above and a doorway with Greek Doric columns below.

At the S end of Castle Street and Fisher Street is the MARKET PLACE, with a STATUE of James Steel, 1846. In SCOTCH STREET, running N, the BLUE BELL INN, a fine Georgian façade with a segment-headed archway and a Venetian window with pilasters over. From the Market Place SE ENGLISH

STREET leads to the Assize Courts. Near that end the remarkable BARCLAYS BANK by *Rickman*, 1830–1, built as Subscription News Room and Library, and Gothic in so easy and competent and yet un-historicist a way that one may mistake it for 1900. To the w is a four-light window with two-centred arch between two turrets, to Devonshire Street a longer front with an ogee-gabled window in the middle and the rest again roughly symmetrical.

To the N is LOWTHER STREET. This was laid out *c*.1824. The buildings here and in the streets around are of the 1830s. The first notable one is the SAVINGS BANK, former Athenaeum, excellent, with giant Corinthian pilasters. Then on the opposite side the LIBERAL CLUB, with two bow windows and a doorway with short Tuscan columns *in antis*. The same entrance motif in the next two houses. Again on the other side, No. 22 is Gothic of 1872, but Nos. 24–6 have Greek Doric porches. Round LONSDALE STREET more Tuscan porches. In VICTORIA PLACE, facing one another, two identical terraces, ashlar-faced, with unfluted Ionic columns to the porches. The first house on either side is of five bays, the rest are of three and have double porches of four columns. In CHAPEL STREET the DISPENSARY, dated 1857, yet still in the same classical tradition. Ashlar, four bays, the doorway and ground-floor windows with pediment. Next to it the Scottish Chapel of 1834 (*see* p. 97).

From the N end of Lowther Street the EDEN BRIDGE leads to Stanwix. The bridge is of 1815 and by *Smirke*. Five long segmental arches. The width was doubled in 1932. Up STANWIX BANK on the w side two terraces of brick houses with porches of unfluted Ionic columns, DEVONSHIRE TERRACE and EDEN MOUNT. They are of the 1850s and 1840 respectively and look older.

This completes the Perambulation. Only a few separate items need be added. First DIXON'S MILLS (now the Shaddon 63 Works) in JUNCTION STREET, built by *Tattersall* in 1836, a seven-storey block of twenty-two bays, of unrelieved evenness, yet undeniably monumental with its 225 ft length and its 300 ft chimney of strongly tapering outline. The mills were the largest cotton-mills of the moment in England. The windows have raised flat frames and completely unmoulded horizontal architraves. The interior has iron beams and columns and shallow brick vaults and tile floors and was designed by *Fairbairn*, the great engineer. Only a few minutes from here in St James Road, at the corner of Empire Road, is Tue Thur, by *Lorimer*, 1923, Voyseyish in style and quite modest in size. *Lorimer* also built a factory building for Morton Sundour's in Milbourne Crescent. It is L-shaped and remarkably straightforward, with large windows, a totally unadorned but well proportioned grid.

Rickerby House (Eden School), Stanwix, 1¼ m. NE of the cathedral. This fine building looks *c.*1820. It is ashlar-faced and has to the entrance a porte-cochère of four Greek Doric columns, to the garden a porch of six. The entrance side is of five, the garden side of nine bays. The staircase with a heavy, scrolly iron balustrade lies immediately behind the porte-cochère.* The STABLES are quite different, of brick, Gothic, castellated and with a tower with stepped gables. The LODGE on the other hand is again pure and ambitious Grecian. It has a Doric temple-front of four columns on both ends.‡

Bunkershill, 2 m. SW. Large, white Late Georgian house. In the garden a re-erected two-light window in the Dec style. Mr Bulman thinks this may come from the abbey buildings.

Morton Manor, 1½ m. S. Early C19, of two storeys and five broad bays. Good staircase with metal railing.

CARROCK FELL *see* MUNGRISDALE

₅₀₅₀ ## CASTLE CARROCK

St Peter. Built in 1828. Thin w tower. The church was violently normanized inside in 1888. It has no separate chancel. – STAINED GLASS. The E window by *E. R. Suffling & Co.* of Edgware Road, 1888. Bad. – PLATE. Cup inscribed 1691.

Tarn Lodge. 1807. Seven bays, with doorway with broken pediment and set in front of it a convex porch of four Tuscan columns. Triglyph frieze. (A small BELVEDERE or folly on the hill. MHLG)

₂₀₂₀ ## CASTLERIGG

St John, 2½ m. ESE of Keswick, on the saddle between High Rigg and Low Rigg. Small, low, chancel and nave in one and

---

* Mr Kenneth Smith, however, says the house must have been built between 1793 and 1811.

‡ Beneath Stanwix church and house is the site of a ROMAN FORT, lying immediately behind HADRIAN's WALL. The fort, 9¼ acres in extent, is evidently the base of the *ala Petriana*. Several buildings, including a granary, have been partly excavated.

a tiny w tower. Built in 1845 and restored in 1893. – COM-MUNION TABLE. Designed by *G. G. Scott* in 1848 for Crosthwaite.

THE CARLES, on the path between Goosewell and Castlerigg, 2 m. E of Keswick. This is an oval setting of standing stones with a maximum diameter of 110 ft. Within and abutting on this oval is a rectangular stone setting. A gap exists in the spacing of the stones of the oval on the N.

THRELKELD KNOTT SETTLEMENT. *See* Threlkeld.

SHOULTHWAITE FORT, to the SW. A small univallate fort, ½ acre in area, provided with a second, slight rampart on the E. The site is roughly circular in plan.

CASTLE SOWERBY   3030

1½ m. NE of Hutton Roof

ST KENTIGERN. White and low, with a good view to the w. S doorway with a roll-moulding, probably *c.*1200. Of about the same time the chancel with its lancets. C13 S arcade, or rather w and E responds; for the octagonal piers are more probably replacements of a later time, and who could say what time? The porch entrance is medieval too, presumably C14 or C15. The double bellcote looks as if it might be late C16 or C17. – PLATE. Cup and Cover Paten 1737.

CASTLESTEADS *see* WALTON

CASTLETOWN HOUSE *see* ROCKCLIFFE

CATTERLEN HALL *see* NEWTON REIGNY

CLARGYLL HALL *see* ALSTON

CLEATOR   0010

ST LEONARD. Off the main street of the mining village, in a street still of real village character. Red sandstone, 1841, but with the handsome N side added in 1900–4 by *J. H. Martin-dale* of Carlisle. It has N of the nave two recesses with seats, and the main entrance is placed in one of them. They have segmental arches. To their l. the domestic-looking vestries. Also of 1904 the w baptistery. However, the church is really much older in its masonry – cf. the one Norman chancel window, and one C15 window in the S wall. – FONT.

Octagonal, with rolls up the angles. It could be of the 1660s. – PLATE. Cup with band of ornament, 1617.

OUR LADY OF THE SACRED HEART (R.C.), at the N end of Cleator. 1856 by *E. W. Pugin*. Rock-faced, with lancets. The bellcote very fanciful in its details and therefore called by Kelly 'of exceeding beauty'. The s aisle also fanciful, but more successful, with two lancets per bay and between them a blank almond-shape. Very fanciful, very ornate, and exactly what one means by debased in descriptions of Victorian architecture is the interior. Rich capitals with foliation and volutes. Kelly's adjectives are 'exquisite', 'chaste', and 'elegant'.

FLOSH (Ennerdale Rural District). 1837, but the s front of 1866. Quite large, gabled, with mullioned and transomed windows protected by hood-moulds.

CLEATOR MOOR

ST JOHN EVANGELIST. By *George Ferguson*, 1870–2. Neo-Norman, with a starved W steeple. But the hills as a back-cloth help.

Cleator Moor is a mining village, drab undeniably, but it has at least made its effort. It has a large regular MARKET PLACE, and in the middle of this its public buildings. They are partly of 1877, partly of 1904. On the s side the Co-operative Society has its factory with a tower, on the W side the same has its shop with a long iron veranda.

CLIFTON

CHURCH, Little Clifton. 1858, but with a Norman s doorway. Single-chamfered arch. Hood-mould with billet and little flat triangles. – PLATE. Cup of 1574.

COAT HOUSE *see* WETHERAL

COCKERMOUTH

ALL SAINTS. By *Joseph Clarke* of London, 1852–4. A large church built of sandstone with a crossing tower carrying a recessed spire. The tracery is mostly geometrical. The arcades have capitals which are bands of nobbly foliage. The church replaced one of 1711. – STAINED GLASS. E window 1853 by *Hardman*; colourful. – W window by *Kempe*, c.1897. –

PLATE. Paten of 1736; Cup given in 1639 and remade in the C18; Cup and Paten, inscribed 1740; Flagon 1740; Christening Basin 1771.

CHRIST CHURCH, South Street. 1865 by *Bruce* of Whitehaven. An extraordinarily reactionary design, still with the features of the early C19, i.e. the plain tower with large pinnacles, the long nave windows, and the three galleries on iron columns inside. The plate tracery on the other hand is 1860s all right. – The adjoining SCHOOL is of 1884 and 1887.

ST JOSEPH (R.C.), Crown Street. 1856 by *T. G. Gibson* of Newcastle. Plain, with pointed-trefoiled windows, a bellcote, and an apse. Low interior with a hammerbeam roof.

CONGREGATIONAL CHAPEL, Main Street. 1856, and with a façade conservative for that date. Gothic, with pinnacles and three gables, the l. and the r. ones very steep.

CASTLE. Cockermouth Castle lies above the river Derwent at its confluence with the Cocker. It is thus protected by water to the S, W, and NW. The spur formed is occupied by the inner ward. The outer ward is without natural protection to the E. The castle was built by William de Fortibus in the mid C13, but little of that period survives: the basement of the rounded W tower at the far point of the spur, lower courses of masonry of the N and S curtain walls, and one jamb of the original gatehouse. The rest is essentially of *c.*1360–70.

The OUTER GATEHOUSE is on the E side. It has a barbican, i.e. side walls projecting to the E. The inner doorway is round-arched with one chamfer. Above it is a group of five shields under a hood-mould. Inside there are vaulting compartments of three different heights. The spiral staircase in the SW corner has at the top a handsome umbrella of eight ribs, then a ring, and outside that the continuation of the vault by sixteen radial ribs. The buildings of the OUTER WARD S of the gatehouse are Victorian, those along the N side Late Georgian, those of the S side a pretty Gothic of *c.*1800. Eight bays with pointed windows, the two middle ones raised into a tower. In the SE corner is the square FLAG TOWER, ending in a Scottish stepped gable.

In front of the range between outer and inner wards a broad DITCH was made in the later C14. This lay immediately E of the ditch of de Fortibus, and in that older ditch the range just referred to was built, using the depth of the ditch as a basement. The middle of the range is the INNER GATEHOUSE. It lies about six feet higher than the outer ward, and the drawbridge must thus have had quite a steep incline. The basement chambers to its l. and r. were rib-vaulted. The gatehouse has to the E an arch connecting the l. and r. parts high up and provided with machicolation. The gatehouse vault itself is ribbed also. Doors from it led into the rooms above the rib-vaulted basement chambers. The N room has a hooded fireplace. Small doors from the E projection of the gatehouse lead into small rooms, perhaps prisons, connected by trap-doors with lower prisons.

In the NE corner of the INNER WARD is the KITCHEN TOWER. Its basement is accessible by a staircase with a stepping-down tunnel-vault. The basement chamber has an octagonal pier in the centre with canted projections and single-chamfered ribs on wall responds. The kitchen has to the S two large fireplaces, to the E two 24-ft-high narrow windows, and to the N two mysterious high recesses separated by a rectangular projection. The two windows high up are later. The recesses are rib-vaulted. A wooden gallery originally ran in front of them and the projection along the N side of the kitchen.

W of the kitchen was the GREAT HALL. The big arch between the two rooms is of course not ancient. Next to it is a trefoil-headed recess, no doubt a cupboard, and next to that a spiral staircase up to a tiny room with a vault in trefoil section. It has a small window to the W with a cusped rose window over. The hall and adjoining chamber and solar were on a curved plan. Remains of the outer staircase to the hall are still visible, as is also one doorway jamb. The chamber and solar windows with mullion and transom crosses are later.

In the castle grounds is an octagonal early C18 brick building with stone dressings. Doorway with broken segmental pediment.

TOWN HALL, by the parish church. Built as a Methodist chapel in 1841. Three bays, with Greek Doric columns to the doorway.

DERWENT SECONDARY MODERN SCHOOL. Opened in 1958. A pleasant composition with a three-storeyed block whose inner court is accessible by one side of the block being on pilotis. Lower attachment. The school was designed by the County Architect's Department (architect *J. Haughan*).

A perambulation of Cockermouth is simple. It is virtually a walk along in one direction with a few sallies l. and r.

Starting from the Workington road there is first CROWN

STREET and then, opposite the long, low TROUT HOTEL with its porch of unfluted Ionic columns, follows one of the two best houses in the town. It is known as GRECIAN VILLA and must date from about 1830. It is of three bays, scanned by giant pilasters, and has tripartite windows and in the centre a loggia on both floors, unfluted Ionic below, of square pillars above. Then in the MAIN STREET the other best house, WORDSWORTH HOUSE, where the bard was born. It is quite a swagger house for such a town: standing on its own, nine windows wide and with moulded window frames and a porch with Tuscan columns. It is mid-C18, but the porch is of course later. No. 71 also has moulded window frames. It is five bays wide. What distinguishes the Main Street and gives it a very agreeable character is the two rows of trees. The houses are mostly unremarkable, two- or three-storeyed. Only the Victorian banks are more conspicuous. In the middle of the long street is the white STATUE of the sixth Earl of Mayo; 1875 by *W. & T. Wills* of London. Off the Main Street along Bridge Street to get a glimpse of the DERWENT MILLS, built in 1814 and later enlarged. The length is now nineteen bays.

Main Street is continued by the MARKET PLACE. No. 35 has a Greek Doric doorcase. Off the Market Place towards the castle is CASTLEGATE, with a group of good houses, ending in the detached CASTLEGATE HOUSE, Georgian, of three bays, with pedimented doorway on pilasters.

Finally off to the SW into KIRKGATE, which starts narrow and widens, again with trees. No. 47 has a standard late C18 doorway with fanlight and broken pediment.

HAMES HALL, ⅝ m. NW. Said to be by *Sir Robert Smirke*. Three bays, Tudor, with a centre with doorway, and oriel between turrets with arrow-slits. Embattled parapet.

On a hill above the village of Papcastle, 1 m. NW, lies the Roman fort of DERVENTIO. Between the fort and the river Derwent traces of an extensive civil settlement have been recorded. Although little is now visible, pottery recovered from limited excavations within the fort suggests that it was occupied from Flavian times to the end of the C4, with a possible break between 120 and 160.

COLD FELL *see* TALKIN

COOMBE CRAG *see* WALTON

CORBY CASTLE

Corby Castle started out as a pele tower, we do not know when. Some call it C13, some C14; it might be any date. It was probably built for the Salkeld family. All that is now visible of the tower is the thickness of the wall and the spiral staircase. To locate the tower one must look at the entrance side of the house and the two r. hand bays. They represent the tower. Then, as the property had passed to the Howards in 1611 and 1624, they added to the tower a long range, making the building L-shaped. We know from a drawing of 1793 that it was of three storeys with all windows pedimented, alternatingly triangular and segmental. That gives a date in the last third of the C17 (cf. Hutton-in-the-Forest, Tullie House Carlisle). This C17 range was placed steep above the river Eden, and this, the N, side of the house is irregular now, with windows of the early C18 and the early C19. The early C19 gave the house its present form. *Peter Nicholson* in 1812–17 filled in the space between the two ranges and made the whole a rectangle. He did this for Henry Howard.

The entrance side is of five bays, with the middle bay so wide that it has a porch of four Greek Doric columns – quite an early use of this order – a tripartite window with pilasters above, and a tripartite lunette above that. The other windows have finely moulded surrounds. To the w, with an even more spectacular view of the broad Eden, is a seven-bay front with a recessed centre filled in on the ground floor by a loggia of two pairs of Greek Doric Columns. The ENTRANCE HALL is unusually deep and decorated in a restrained classical way. It has in one of its long sides two niches. The rooms on the ground floor in Nicholson's part have minor plaster ceilings, but the STAIRCASE, except for the lantern, which is clearly Grecian, must date from *c.*1730, and the C17 range at the back, now subdivided, has stucco panelling and ceilings also of *c.*1730–40, and above them, on the first floor, are two quite spectacular ceilings of the same date. Nicholson partitioned a passage off one of them and re-set here two doorcases again of *c.*1730–40. Of work in the house at such a date nothing is recorded. In the entrance hall is a strange memorial, said to be the MONUMENT to Thomas Mowbray, Duke of Norfolk, who died in Venice in 1399 and received his memorial at St Mark's. It was saved from destruction in 1810 and brought here. It is an armorial plate entirely and must at least be re-tooled. It

also received a frame of egg and dart. In the CHAPEL the
ALTAR-REREDOS is said to be from Rome and to have been
once the property of Lord Stafford, who was executed in
1680. It is black and gold. Also excellent NEEDLEWORK.*

The grounds were laid out by Thomas Howard, who died in
1740. Several furnishings are worth seeking out. The GATE
LODGE has a Tuscan temple front with four columns on high
bases and deep eaves. In the pediment Apollo on his chariot,
done with some animation. Just sw of the house a SUNDIAL,
dated 1658 and with an inscription, the Instruments of the
Passion, and the Howard arms. The initials F. H. stand for
Sir Francis Howard, for whom his father, Lord William
Howard, bought Corby and built the new range. Farther
away to the sw another temple front, this one attached to the
dovecote of the farm. It is a memorial to an Italian lady who
died young and has, on the frieze, above the slender Tuscan
columns, the words 'A quella che [meglio ?] merita'. Above a
balcony. Top pediment. Then, ½ m. down, above the river,
the CASCADE, starting from a SUMMER HOUSE with a Venetian opening. On top mermaids. Inside against the back wall
two inept figures. The water would cascade down in four
leaps and end in a basin in which, incongruously, stands Lord
Nelson. But the cascade itself is most probably again of
c.1730–40. Finally, s of the Cascade House, on his own,
POLYPHEMUS with his reed-pipes, also wondrously badly
carved, but just for that reason very engaging. (At the end of
the river walk is yet another temple, this one with widely
spaced Tuscan columns up a wide staircase and again a pediment on top. Inside wall paintings by a Mr *Nutter* of Carlisle;
1832. *Country Life*) For the statue of St Constantine, ¾ m. s,
see Wetheral, p. 202.

In the village square a very odd EXEDRA, built in 1833 as a
blacksmith's shop with covered open space for shoeing. It is
a niche on short round piers with free capitals, and at the
back is a doorway, round-headed with one continuous roll-

* Mr G. F. Wingfield Digby listed this, and kindly communicated his
results to me. Chasuble, Stole, and Maniple, English, late C15. Cherry-red
velvet. – Two other Chasubles with Stole, Maniple, and Burse. One chasuble
is on purple velvet, the other on white satin. – Yet another Chasuble, on red
velvet. – C15 Orphrey on a C16 red velvet Chasuble. – C17 red satin Chasuble,
with Maniple, Stole, and Burse. – Mrs Canning's Chasuble, very elaborately
and beautifully embroidered. – C19 Cope with Elizabethan and C17 em-
broidery. – English C15 Cope. – C17 Veil. – Antependium on white satin. –
Several more Veils.

moulding, and this must be of *c*.1200 and taken from a church. The whole was meant to be like Vulcan's Forge.

RAILWAY BRIDGE. 1830–4. By *Francis Giles*. Five round arches.

1090 CORNEY

ST JOHN BAPTIST. Nave and chancel and bellcote. Most of the details of the restoration of 1882. Original the w nave and N chancel doorways. Kelly's comment is 'Ancient, mixed styles'. – MONUMENT. Joseph Benn, agent to the Earl of Lonsdale at Lowther, † 1860. By *Dunbar*.

4050 COTEHILL

ST JOHN EVANGELIST. By *Habershon & Brock*, 1868. Geometrical tracery, but a thin NE tower with an odd stupa-like top with pigeon-holes. Where did the architects get the idea from ? – STAINED GLASS. One two-light window, influenced by Morris and uncommonly good. It looks the work of *Powell's*.

HOLME HOUSE. *See* Cumwhitton.

CREW CASTLE *see* BEWCASTLE

CROFTON HALL *see* THURSBY

5040 CROGLIN

ST JOHN BAPTIST. 1878 by *J. Howison* of Edinburgh. Nave and chancel. Shafted neo-Norman windows with zigzag arches. Double bellcote. – STAINED GLASS. The E window by *Lavers & Westlake*. – COLOUR PRINTS of the *Fitzroy Picture Society*, e.g. the Annunciation. Late Pre-Raphaelite, on the way to the flat style of the C20 poster. The Fitzroy Picture Society had been founded by *A. H. Mackmurdo* to provide cheap pictures for schools. – MONUMENT. Completely defaced female effigy in the churchyard.

RECTORY PELE, opposite the church. The pele tower has a tunnel-vaulted ground stage. A recently discovered small window proves that the hall range l. of the tower was later than this. As it is now, it appears Georgian, except for the masonry.

BROOMRIGG STONE CIRCLES, ½ m. NE of Broomrigg and 1 m. S of the road from Ainstable to Newbiggin. This group consists of three circles of standing stones and two small circular settings of boulders, 12 ft in diameter, interpreted by the excavator as tent weights. In one of the stone circles was found a series of cremations, one contained in an Early Bronze Age collared urn.

CROSBY-ON-EDEN
4050

ST JOHN EVANGELIST. 1854 by *R. H. Billings*. A very inventive, rather naughty design. The body of the church is quite straightforward, though the chancel is still short, and flowing tracery is not what one expects in the fifties. It is the tower which floors one. Short, with a spire with colossal crockets up the edges, and nightmarishly long, tight lucarnes, and, inside, the side windows have segmental arches with lacy tracery pelmets of stone. What is the pattern for these? Also in the tracery heads themselves, instead of stained glass, there is cut (or moulded?) clear GLASS in the form of stars, a charming idea. The roof has arched braces forming big semi-circular hoops.

CROSBY HOUSE, ⅜ m. E. Five-bay brick house with a four-column porch of slender Greek Doric columns. In addition one-bay lower wings. Probably the house of a Carlisle merchant or manufacturer, built about 1830.

HIGH CROSBY FARMHOUSE, opposite. A three-bay façade of the late C18 with a prettily decorated frieze below the door pediment.

EDEN GROVE, ½ m. W. Three by two bays, and only of a basement and one storey, i.e. really a villa. Greek Doric portico of thin columns in two pairs, crowned by a pediment. This also will be a Carlisle man's house.

WALLHEAD, 1 m. NE, is the site of Milecastle 61 of HADRIAN'S WALL. A few hundred yards E, on White Moss, the vallum was constructed across marshy ground by delineating its sides with mounds, in addition to the usual two wider-spaced marginal mounds.

WALBY, 1¼ m. W of Wallhead. To the E is the site of Milecastle 62, to the W that of Milecastle 63.

CROSS CANONBY
3040

ST JOHN EVANGELIST. A Norman church. Witness are the doorway with blank tympanum, the S window now appearing inside above the arcade arch, the chancel arch, unmoulded,

on the simplest imposts,* and one chancel N window. The
arcade arch is depressed two-centred and has a single step
only, i.e. C13 presumably, But the responds were altered in
the C14, cf. the heads and more particularly the leaf motifs. –
FONT. Square, C13, on five supports. On each side are big-
scale heavy leaf motifs mostly in scroll or volute contexts (cf.
Aspatria). – SCULPTURE. Part of a C10 cross-shaft with,
on the front, dragons biting into themselves. The shaft is
exceptional in that the dragons are not interconnected by any
interlace, or indeed by their own tails. They are each an
individual representation. On one edge a more familiar dragon
in the Jellinge style. On the remaining two sides interlace. –
MONUMENTS. Coffin lid with a cross, zigzags l. and r. of it,
and on the l. lower down a human figure, 'an ungainly doll',
as Kendrick writes, who, however, adds that 'this lamentably
executed carving' is all the same 'entirely charming'. The lid
is called by Kendrick Anglo-Danish, but may well be Early
Norman. – Also Anglo-Danish is a hog-back tombstone outside the church. – STAINED GLASS. The E window signed
Carl Scott. – WOOD PANELS. On the parapet of the organ
gallery and two benches. They are dated 1730 and have quite
lush foliage patterns. Those of the benches, however, have
mainly military emblems. – PLATE. Cup, Cover Paten, and
Paten, 1720.

BIRKBY LODGE, ⅝ m. SW. A handsome late C18 house of three
bays with a porch of unfluted Ionic columns and the windows
l. and r. set in blank arched recesses.

CROSTHWAITE

ST KENTIGERN. A Late Perp church, except for the C14 N
chapel. The windows, mostly straight-topped, are of great
variety. They range from the C14 to well into the C16. The
latest are those of the S aisle (except W) and the clerestory
(except two SE) and the easternmost of the N aisle. The
arcades of standard elements run on for seven bays without
any articulation by a chancel arch. The W tower is as late as
c.1530–55. – FONT. Given between 1396 and 1400. The
square shaft has blank windows with tracery, mostly Dec in
pattern. The octagonal bowl has leaf and the Sign of the
Trinity. It looks Late Perp, and as the shaft is of different
stone, it may well be later. – STAINED GLASS. In a N aisle
window half a C15 figure. – The E window by *Kempe*, 1897. –

* This arch is considered to be Roman, re-set.

Several windows by *Wailes*. Which? – PLATE. Chalice of
*c.*1660. – MONUMENTS. Effigies of a Civilian and wife. Stone,
late C15. – Brasses to Sir John Ratcliff † 1527 and wife. On a
tomb-chest. The figures are 23½ in. long. He was responsible
for most of the building. – Many tablets, e.g. two by *Webster*
of Kendal (chancel N). – Robert Southey, the poet, 1846 by
Lough. Recumbent white marble figure, asleep, one hand on
his heart, the other holding a book. – Against the outer walls
of the church two large slate gravestones, obviously by the
same hand: Joseph Dover † 1810 with Hope at the top, and 58
Joseph Cherry † 1818 with Father Time. The stones are not
signed, but they are locally attributed with confidence to
William Bromley.

ORMATHWAITE HALL, 1 m. NE. A singular composition. Two
Georgian houses at r. angles to each other and facing a square
lawn. One is of seven bays with a doorway with Doric pilasters
and pediment, the other of five bays with a moulded door-
frame and a pediment over. The octagonal window can hardly
be original.*

UNDERSCAR, N of the former. A very characteristic Italianate
villa, the centre of three bays, with a centrally placed tower
with the typical low-pitched Italianate pyramid roof. The
house was built *c.*1856–63 for William Oxley of Liverpool.

CULGAITH

ALL SAINTS. Cruciform. Consecrated 1758, but all external
features Victorian. Inside, however, the transepts are separated from the nave by two responds and two columns. They
are long and have shapeless capitals, and instead of arches
they simply lead into the coving of the ceilings, but it is a
sign of some originality all the same. – PANELLING. Also of
*c.*1756. – PLATE. Plain Cup of 1731.

(MILLRIGG. With dates 1597 and 1696. The house has a two-
storeyed porch with an adjoining spiral-stair projection.
MHLG)

CUMDIVOCK
1¾ m. SW of Dalston

ST JOHN EVANGELIST. 1871 by *Cory & Ferguson*. Grey stone.
Nave and chancel. Perp details. The bellcote stands on two
little hanging arches.

* The turret on one of the farm buildings is dated 1769.

5050

CUMREW

ST MARY. 1890 by *George Dale Oliver*. It is bad architecture
with its busy rock-facing, its NW tower, and its C13 detail but
round-headed chancel arch. – PLATE. Cup of 1615. – MONU-
MENT. Defaced effigy of a Lady, early C14. A puppy by her
pillow.

CAIRN, on Cumrew Fell, 2 m. E of the B6413. This great cairn
is still some 70 ft in diameter and 8 ft high. It was partially
excavated in the C19, when a number of cremation burials in
urns were found.

5050

CUMWHITTON

ST MARY. Thin W tower, round-arched doorway, keyed-in
nave window to the S, smaller arched aisle windows to the N.
The chancel lancets are of course later. The inside reveals
quite a different story. The aisle E window, probably *ex situ*,
is Anglo-Saxon, small and double-splayed. In the S wall (outside) is a small length of Norman zigzag. The N arcade of
three bays is of *c.*1200: round piers and arches with one step
and one slight chamfer. – FONT. Plain octagonal bowl, dated
1662. – SCULPTURE. Part of a Maltese-cross-head, regarded
by Collingwood as Norman. – PLATE. Chalice, late C16 or
later.

HOLME HOUSE. 1778. The standard five-bay type with a pedimented doorway. But the graceful decoration of the frieze
below the pediment reveals the date.

4020

DACRE

ST ANDREW. Norman W tower, rebuilt in 1810. But the unmoulded arch to the nave must be genuine. Late C12 chancel
with doorway with thin shafts (one waterleaf and one crocket
capital) and long round-arched windows. Those of the E end
are C19. The aisles are Perp externally, but the arcades date
from the early C13. They differ from one another, and the N
arcade is earlier, because the arches here have slight chamfers,
while in the S arcade they have normal chamfers. The piers are
mostly round on the N, all octagonal on the S. But the responds are all four semicircular. – COMMUNION RAIL. Late
C17; with twisted balusters. – SOUTH DOOR. The lock and
key were given by Lady Anne Clifford; cf. the initials and the
date 1671. – SCULPTURE. Two parts of cross-shafts, one

with intricate trails with naturalistic detail and a human-faced quadruped. This appears to be c9. – The other is dated by Collingwood second quarter of the c10 and has from top to bottom a quadruped looking back, two figures hand in hand, another quadruped, and Adam and Eve with the tree. It is all very lively and not at all monumental. – PLATE. Cup and Cover Paten, formerly gilt, with a band of ornament, 1583;* Paten, 1674. – MONUMENTS. Effigy of a Knight, cross-legged. – Edward Hasell, 1708. Cartouche with putto heads in an architectural frame with segmental pediment. – Edward Hasell † 1825. By *Chantrey*, 1830. White marble. Kneeling female figure by an urn on a base. Relief. – CURIOSUM. The four corners of the original churchyard are marked by four bears, perhaps from the former gatehouse of Dacre Castle. On two of them squat lynxes.

DACRE CASTLE. An early c14 pele tower on its own with two 29 strong square and two more buttress-like diagonal angle projections. The SW buttress contains the garderobe. In the NW projection is the staircase. The large windows with their mullion and transom crosses are of *c.*1700. The battlements are unusually well preserved. The basement consists of two tunnel-vaulted chambers. On the main floor is the hall, with a pretty *lavatorium* with a trefoil-pointed arch and a twelve-petalled drain like that of a piscina. Above the hall is the solar, called the King's Chamber. In 1354 a licence for a chapel in the castle was granted.

(ROSE BANK. Partly 1689, partly 1773. MHLG)

DUNMALLET HILLFORT, *see* Pooley Bridge, Westmorland, p. 284.

DALEGARTH HALL *see* BOOT

DALEMAIN
1¼ m. E of Dacre

4020

Sir Edward Hasell, steward of Lady Anne Clifford, bought the estate in 1680. His son gave the house its exceedingly fine Georgian E front. The same family is still at Dalemain. The house is oblong and has a narrow inner courtyard. The E front and the sides are essentially of *c.*1740–50. They are faced with

* The Rev. K. H. Smith tells me that the cup originally belonged to George, third Earl of Cumberland, and was given to the church by Lady Anne Clifford.

50 pinkish-grey ashlar. The E front is of nine bays with the
middle five separated by rusticated quoins of even length. No
pediment. Moulded window surrounds. Doorway with ears
and a pediment on fluted Ionic pilasters. Inside are a spacious
C18 staircase and quite a number of very good wooden
chimneypieces, one in particular of exquisite Rococo openwork carving. Most of the W range is much older, probably
C15 or early C16. It consists of a former tower, only recognizable by a newel staircase in one corner, and the former hall.
This has a big fireplace, the chimneypiece made up of various
parts. In the former tower on the first floor is an Elizabethan
or Jacobean plaster ceiling with patterns of thin ribs. The
NW corner is an addition to the old house of c.1600. The
windows which are not sashed belong to that date.

3050   DALSTON

ST MICHAEL. The chancel is early C13. Lancet windows, still
with round rere-arches. The E wall has three stepped lancets.
The priest's doorway carries a little gable. The nave masonry
is partly medieval too, but the breadth of the present aisleless
interior and the PANELLING belong to the rebuilding of
1749. – SCULPTURE. In the porch a Norman capital, with
decorated scallops and flowers and leaves below. – PLATE.
Cup and Cover Paten, formerly gilt, 1661. – MONUMENT. The
Rev. Walter Fletcher † 1846. By *Watson*. Profile portrait head
and a broad tapering Grecian block above with acroteria.
The SQUARE in front of the church is not square. It has a
number of pleasant C18 houses, all small.
DALSTON HALL, 1¼ m. NE. The entrance side is almost entirely
46 of 1899 (*C. J. Ferguson*), but the garden side exposes a house
of considerable interest to the architectural historian. On the
r. is a pele tower with battlements and a higher stair-turret.
Coat of arms on this, and below the battlements an inscription: Iohn Dalston Elisabet mi wyf mad ys byldyng. This
points to c.1500. To the l. of the inscription a dog and a cat.
To the l. of the tower a stretch of wall, first broadly projecting,
then a little receding, and finally rising in a second higher and
slimmer tower. All this is C17 and probably not early, and it is
characterized by very curious motifs, otherwise lacking in
Cumberland. They are reminiscent of Scotland. Mullioned
windows, the mullions with fillets and the whole window with
its surround slightly pushed forward, almost as if it were a

timber oriel.* Water-spouts rather like decorated gun-barrels.
The tower has a round stair-turret starting on a corbel. Inside,
the original iron GATE or yatt (cf. Naworth and also Burgh-
by-Sands church and Cawdor Castle in Scotland) of the
entrance to the tower, but otherwise all 1899.

STONETHWAITE, 1½ m. WSW. 1724. Can this refer to the tripartite windows of the symmetrical three-bay façade? The
door surround is boldly moulded. The frames of the windows
have thin raised fillets along the outer and inner edges. The
same motifs are repeated at CARDEW HOUSE, ¼ m. SW, but
here the doorway and the whole middle bay have pediments.

HAWKSDALE HALL, 1¾ m. SE. Early Georgian. Of five bays in a
1–3–1 rhythm, two and a half storeys. Moulded surrounds of
windows and doorway. Older wing on the r.

HOLM HILL, 2 m. SE. A stately Early Victorian mansion of
three storeys, with the porch gable yet higher and a broad,
asymmetrically placed tower behind. But the two projecting
three-bay wings must be Georgian. They have Venetian
windows and tripartite lunette windows over.

DEAN

ST OSWALD. Low, of nave and chancel. Big double bellcote
over the nave E gable. It looks C17. In the chancel two-light
windows with the heads of the lights ogee, set in round arches.
This is Perp rather than Dec. Original gargoyles too, and
several original nave windows. Inside, the s arcade is older
than anything outside. Four bays, round piers, round, very
elementary moulded capitals, double-chamfered round
arches – i.e. c.1200.‡ In the s aisle wall a low, later tomb
recess. – FONT. Drum-shaped, Norman, with thin continuous
intersecting arches. – PLATE. Cup and Cover Paten, 1624;
Paten on feet, 1732.

FRIENDS' MEETING HOUSE, 2½ m. E, at Pardshaw Hall. 1720.
The white cottagey chapel is reached by a gateway through
the stabling.

BRANTHWAITE HALL, ⅜ m. W. An uncommonly interesting
house. It is an addition to a well-preserved pele tower with
a tunnel-vaulted basement, several original small blocked

* This can be compared with the boxed-out frames for shields at Glamis
Castle. They are there of 1606.

‡ The Rev. E. O. Bennett tells me of a window of this period which was
found in the W wall about ten years ago.

windows, battlements, and an angle spiral-stair ending in a turret with saddleback roof. The house has to the s mullioned windows with hood-moulds, and that work dates from 1604. But a projection on the same side has a c16 window with arched heads to the lights. So perhaps all this is in fact medieval in its masonry. The N façade was re-done about 1700, and this is quite a swagger, if rustic job. Five bays, two storeys. The ground-floor windows with diagonally fanning-out lintel-stones and straight entablatures, the first-floor windows with semicircular pediments continued straight to l. and r. as part of an entablature. Stone mullion-and-transom crosses and raised moulded frames to the windows.

FAR BRANTHWAITE EDGE, 1¼ m. SW. Dated 1683. Nearly symmetrical façade with two- and three-light transomed windows. Straight window entablatures.

CRAKEPLACE HALL, Ullock, 1 m. S. Inscribed as 'built anew' with the date 1612. The inscription re-set in a later porch has a billet frame, i.e. a Norman motif. Mullioned windows.

STONE CIRCLE, 4 m. SW, 400 yds N of the Greyhound Inn, Studfold Gate. The circle now consists of eight stones forming a setting 100 ft in diameter. A boundary dyke bisects the site.

3040

DEARHAM

ST MUNGO. A Norman church. In the chancel one Norman s and one low-side s and one N window, visible only inside. The s doorway to the nave is Norman too. It has very strange jamb mouldings and one order of columns. The abacus details are also very strange. One capital has waterleaf. So all this is c.1170–90. The arch with its strong and deep mouldings suits such a date. The unbuttressed w tower has a tunnel-vaulted ground-stage. That would go with c.1170–90 or may be a little later. The arch towards the nave is segmental, of two chamfers, quite probably a c13 form. Bell-openings of two ogee-headed lights. The N aisle is of 1882.* – FONT. A big Norman block capital with, on each lunette, a representation flanked by two spirals instead of volutes. On two sides are dragons, on the third are symmetrical scrolls, on the fourth a very curious pattern of a frieze of arched panels, a frieze of lozenges below, a frieze of rectangles below that. The style is

18

* By *Ferguson*.

connected with Yorkshire, e.g. Fishlake, which is of c.1170. –
SCULPTURE. A remarkable collection of Anglo-Danish fragments. The largest has a wheel-head and close interweaving
at the front and looser interlace at the back. A second, called
the Kenneth Cross, has a man on a horse, a bird facing a man,
and close wormy scrolls, plaiting, etc. A third has a runic
inscription at the top, then rosettes, then three standing
figures under arches, holding hands, then a quatrefoil, then
a cross like crossbones, and then a bearded head upside down
in a semicircle. Below that, also upside down, the word
Adam. – Also many COFFIN LIDS. – PLATE. Cup and Paten,
probably first half C18.

DENTON

5060

ST CUTHBERT, Nether Denton. 1868–70 by *Cory & Ferguson*.
Nave and chancel, bellcote, lancet windows. Well-built, with
an ashlar-faced interior. The church was paid for by the
Mounseys. – SCULPTURE. A fine, smallish Norman figure of a
King with sceptre(?) set against a cross with arms extending
Maltese-fashion beyond a small central circle. It must have
been a very good piece, and is reminiscent of the French mid
C12. – STAINED GLASS. The E window by *C. A. Gibbs* of 48
Marylebone Road.

VICARAGE, close by, on the hill. By *Salvin*; with bargeboarded
gables.*

CHURCH, Upper Denton. Built with Roman stones. Norman N
window, and Norman chancel arch of the most elementary
kind.‡ But the E quoins are of the Anglo-Saxon type with some
upright stones.

Opposite the E end a ruinous BARN, once probably a vicar's pele.

(TEMON, 1⅛ m. S. Bastle-house incorporated in the outbuildings. Two windows still have their original grilles.)

(DENTON HALL, 1½ m. E of Naworth, and DENTON FOOT
are two farms, both with remains of pele towers.§ Also,
Denton Hall has a MOTTE standing free in a bailey (Curwen).‖

* The ruined OLD VICARAGE was a bastle-house. For the Roman fort
lying beneath church and vicarage *see* Walton, p. 197.

‡ It is a reconstructed Roman arch, probably brought from Birdoswald
(*see* p. 196).

§ Information received from the Earl of Carlisle.

‖ Another MOTTE is noted by Curwen at Upper Denton on the S bank of
the Irthing.

DERVENTIO *see* COCKERMOUTH

DERWENTWATER *see* KESWICK

0020
DISTINGTON

HOLY SPIRIT. 1886 by *Hay & Henderson* of Edinburgh. E.E., with five stepped lancets at the end of the tall and noble chancel. Short SE tower. Lancet windows in other parts as well, and plate tracery. The clerestory with curious tracery of that type: three circles for each bay. Inside, arcade with Shap granite columns and stiff-leaf capitals. – The CHANCEL ARCH of the preceding church was re-erected in the churchyard. It has two continuous chamfers. – PLATE. Cup with banded ornament, clumsy, late C18.

HAYES CASTLE, ½ m. S. Just one wall stands up.

DOVENBY HALL *see* BRIDEKIRK

DRAWDYKES CASTLE *see* HOUGHTON

0090
DRIGG

ST PETER. 1850. Red sandstone. Nave and chancel in one; bell-cote, lancets. Also a N aisle. The nave has an impressively high single lancet in the W wall.

CARLETON HALL, 1 m. ESE. Late Georgian, of three bays and two storeys, with a porch of Tuscan columns. Low two-bay wings. The house is mentioned in 1802 (*B. of E. and W.*, III).

(DRIGG HALL. Late Georgian. Brick is used, as well as stone – which is rare in Cumberland. Pedimental centre and end wings. Mrs Davies)

FLINT WORKING AREA. On the boulder clay and gravels SW of Drigg, between the river Irt and the coast, are a number of flint-knapping sites. They have produced large quantities of waste flakes and tools, suggesting intermittent occupation by Mesolithic, Neolithic, and Bronze Age flint-workers.

DRUMBURGH *see* BOWNESS-ON-SOLWAY

DUDDON HALL *see* ULPHA

DUNMALLET HILLFORT *see*
POOLEY BRIDGE (W), p. 284

EAGLESFIELD

JOHN DALTON MEMORIAL CHURCH, 1 m. E. Really belonging to Mosser. By *C. F. Ferguson*, 1891. Nave with bellcote and chancel. No separation between them. Straight-headed windows, but geometrical tracery in the w window.

FRIENDS' MEETING HOUSE, at the NW end of the village. Dated 1693 over the doorway to the burial ground. The meeting house is dated by Kelly 1711. Humble, with two-light windows. Old benches.

EASTON FARM see BOWNESS-ON-SOLWAY

EDDERSIDE MANOR HOUSE see HOLME ST CUTHBERT

EDEN GROVE see CROSBY-ON-EDEN

EDENHALL

ST CUTHBERT. Low Perp w tower with projecting top and a small stone spire. w window with shields. In the nave one Norman and one Dec N window. The Norman chancel arch, however, is entirely Victorian, or rather of the restoration of 1834 etc. All the detail is of plaster. – STAINED GLASS. In the E window two early C14 figures and several Netherlandish roundels. – Also bits in the two s windows. – (STALLS. With linenfold panelling. – COMMUNION RAIL. C17.) – PLATE. Massive Cup and Paten, 1667; silver-gilt Cup and Paten, 1700. – MONUMENTS. Brass to William Stapildon † 1458 and wife. His a good 35 in. figure, hers is only 27 in. – Tablets to Musgraves of Edenhall, e.g. † 1735 and – Gothic and by *Webster* – † 1834.

EDENHALL. The mansion of the Musgraves, by *Smirke*, has been demolished. It was Grecian, with a portico. But the SOUTH LODGE with Roman Doric columns remains, and the three sets of GATEPIERS to l., middle, and r.

EDMOND CASTLE see HAYTON, p. 137

EGREMONT

ST MARY. By *T. Lewis Banks*, 1880–1. He made the church E.E. and re-used some genuine E.E. parts. They are to be found in the chancel side lancets and their inner shafting and in the transept arches. Also the W doorway was re-erected in the churchyard. It has shafts and a moulded arch.* Banks's church is large, with a NW tower placed outside the aisle, a W front with an apsidally projecting baptistery, and E.E. fenestration. The transept is two bays deep. The arcades have stiff-leaf capitals. – FONT. A kneeling life-size angel of metal. Given in 1883. – SCULPTURE. Carved fragments in the churchyard not far from the re-erected W doorway. – PLATE. Small Cup and Cover Paten, 1734; Paten, 1821.

ST JOHN, Bigrigg, 2⅛ m. NW, on the A-road. By *C. J. Ferguson*, 1878–80. Nave and chancel and a bellcote. Modest in size, Dec in style. – STAINED GLASS. The W and E windows by *Kempe*, c.1886 and c.1896.

CASTLE. N of the castle the mound of a yet older, Early Norman, castle of earth and palisading. On the mound later a round tower was built. It is visible in Buck's print. The castle itself was founded by William de Meschines c.1130–40. Of this period are the gatehouse and the adjoining curtain wall. They have very prominent herringbone masonry. The gatehouse was refaced to the outside in the C14, but has its Norman work largely preserved inside. It was vaulted by a domical rib-vault (not a normal rib-vault), it seems, resting on four columns. The curtain walling is irregular. The hall block stands in ruins, higher up to the N. It had the hall on the upper floor, and the large windows indicate a date in the first half of the C13 – see the motif like flat half-dogtooth which recurs in the nave of Calder Abbey. Two large windows, and on their l. the doorway covered originally by a porch with an outer staircase leading to it. The doorway has continuous double-chamfers. More domestic buildings along the E side.

The main street is wide, and the rows of houses are not parallel. It is quite a handsome sight for an industrial Cumberland town. The TOWN HALL, 1889–90, is architecturally of no value. Close to it the WYNDHAM SECONDARY SCHOOL, 1962–4 by the County Architect, *Douglas Dickenson*, with a five-storeyed main block, made more interesting by a few arbitrary motifs.

EHENSIDE TARN NEOLITHIC SETTLEMENT
see BECKERMET ST JOHN

* Excavations in 1881 showed that the original Norman church had its chancel s wall partly identical with the E.E. chancel s wall, and that the E.E. chancel was two-naved, as it were.

EMBLETON

ST CUTHBERT, ¾ m. SW of the village. 1806, remodelled 1884. The thin W tower is of the former, the plate tracery of the latter date. – PLATE. Chalice, Paten, and Flagon, 1790.

ENGLETHWAITE HALL *see* ARMATHWAITE

ENNERDALE BRIDGE

ST MARY. 1856–8 by *C. Eaglesfield*, enlarged 1885 (GR). Nave and chancel in one and apse. Norman features. To the SE a round bell-turret. Genuine Norman bits in the chancel arch (e.g. one scalloped capital) and the S doorway. – PLATE. Cup and Cover Paten given in 1680.

STONE CIRCLE, 2 m. SSW, ¼ m. W of the footpath between Ennerdale Bridge and Calder Bridge. This is a small circle, 30 ft in diameter, consisting of a dozen small stones each about 2 ft high.

SAMPSON'S BRATFULL LONG CAIRN. *See* Calder Bridge.

ESKDALE *see* BOOT

FARLAM

ST THOMAS A BECKET. By *Salvin*, 1860.* Nave with double bellcote, N aisle, and chancel. Lancet windows, and also simple plate tracery, e.g. under the cross-gables of the N side. Pretty entry to the PULPIT out of the wall by a doorway with shouldered lintel.

FLIMBY

ST NICHOLAS. Built in 1794, but nothing of that is visible. The features, such as bellcote and plate tracery, are of the restoration of 1862. – PLATE. Cup, Paten, and Flagon, 1806.

ALLANBY HOUSE, Wedgwood Road. 1731. Five bays, moulded frames to windows and doorway. Above the latter the date in a wreath. But can the oversized segmental pediment be Georgian? The pilasters certainly cannot.

FLIMBY HALL. Dated 1766. Also five bays, also raised frames. Above the first-floor windows straight entablature. Moulded top cornice.

* Cost £1570 (GS).

0010
FRIZINGTON

St Paul. 1867–8. Yet, with its wide nave (with a hammerbeam roof), its lancet windows, and its w gallery still derived from the Commissioners' type of the 1830s or 1840s. Only the exterior is typical sixties. Rock-faced, with a sw turret with a needle-spirelet.

Frizington is a depressing place, with, even in its main streets, no accents, nothing much but rows of two-storeyed cottages. (Rheda Lodge, ¾ m. wsw. Calverley and Collingwood report a post-Conquest cross-head on a garden wall.)

6030
GAMBLESBY

St John. 1868 by *C. J. Ferguson*. Nave and chancel in one, apse, and bell-turret. The style is late c13.

7040
GARRIGILL

St John. Nave and chancel in one. Built in 1790, but all the details of the restoration of the 1890s.
(Congregational Chapel, Redwing. 1757. Only four bays long. Round-arched windows with moulded surrounds. Inside original box pews and reading desk. mhlg)

GARTHSIDE see WALTON

GATE HOUSE see BOOT

3040
GATESGILL
1 m. ne of Raughton Head

Church. 1869. Nave and chancel, with a rose window in the w wall, filled with terrible plate tracery. Odd bellcote, placed asymmetrically and with a segmental pediment.*

1030
GILCRUX

St Mary. Nave and chancel and bellcote. Various windows, c12 to c19. The interior contains a Norman single-step chancel arch. The plain imposts do not repeat the step. Also Norman the remains of a chancel n window. Late c12 s arcade of two bays. Round pier, square abacus, arches of one step and one slight chamfer. The w respond was apparently free-standing,

---

* The church is to be demolished.

i.e. the arcade went, or was intended to go, further w. – FONT.
Like a big undecorated Norman block capital. – SCULPTURE.
Two parts of an Anglo-Danish cross. – STAINED GLASS.
Retable of the altar, a copy in glass of Leonardo da Vinci's
Last Supper. Made by *Chance Brothers* in 1865. – PLATE.
Cup, Paten, Flagon, 1818.

GILSLAND
6060

ST MARY MAGDALENE. 1852–4 by *James Stewart* of Carlisle
(GS). Nave and chancel. Lancets and pairs of lancets. Steep
bellcote. The church was paid for by G. G. Mounsey.
When, in the C19, chalybeate and sulphuric springs were dis-
covered at Gilsland, the village became a spa for a while, and
an ambitious SPA HOTEL, now Convalescent Home, was
built in 1865. It also was financed by G. G. Mounsey. It has a
wide, nine-bay front. The tripartite windows with arched
lights are typical mid-C19. The building is of yellow brick.
On the way from the church to the hotel is ORCHARD HOUSE.
Five-bay centre with lower four-bay wings, not quite regular.
The porches are recent.
Gilsland village is in Northumberland.
TRIERMAIN CASTLE, 2½ m. SW. Licensed in 1340. All that
stands upright is one high, dramatic fragment of a tower. The
castle was a quadrangle with square towers against the E and
W ends.

GLASSONBY
5030

ST MICHAEL. No dates seem recorded. The chancel windows
look C14 or C15, but a new church was built before 1704 as a
replacement of a medieval one swept away by the river Eden.
The nave s windows, whose arches are not original, could
well be late C17. – SCULPTURE. Two large pieces of a C9
CROSS with interlace and, on the short sides, vine scrolls (porch).
– Also, in the churchyard, a later, uncommonly large wheel-
head and top part of the shaft. Clumsy scrollwork on the
head. Probably C11. – STAINED GLASS. One s window by
Heaton, Butler & Bayne; bad. – PLATE. Cup and Cover
Paten inscribed 1612; Paten on foot, 1707–8. – MONUMENT.
A hogback coffin in the porch.
WHITE HOUSE FARM. A bastle-house of the early C17 (cf.
Wetheral, Ainstable, Naworth, Denton).*

* Information from Mr Robin McDowall.

LONG MEG AND HER DAUGHTERS. This is an oval setting of fifty-nine stones, each about 10 ft high, with a maximum diameter of 360 ft. 60 ft SW of this stone setting ('the daughters') is an outlying standing stone ('Long Meg'). A number of cup and ring carvings are visible on the latter stone. The oval setting is enclosed within an earth and stone bank, best preserved on the W.

LITTLE MEG, 700 yds NE. A circle of eleven standing stones, two bearing cup and ring and spiral carvings. The circle originally enclosed a barrow, beneath which was found a stone cist containing an urned cremation.

CAIRN, ¼ m. NW of Addingham church. The cairn, which appears to have spread considerably, is now 100 ft in diameter. Set in it is a circle of small upright stones, 49 ft in diameter, with a short cist towards the perimeter on the SE. The cist had been rifled prior to excavation, and the only find within the circle was a glass bead of Iron Age character. Outside the circle and beneath the cairn were two cremation burials, one contained in an Early Bronze Age collared urn.

_0000_

GOSFORTH

ST MARY. In the S wall a re-used simple Norman doorway with a continuous roll moulding. The chancel arch is probably of the C14, but stands on re-set Norman columns with figured capitals, on one a green-man's head, on the other three heads, originally with arms to carry the weight. But essentially the church is of 1896–9, by *Ferguson*. Red sandstone, nave and chancel and bellcote, Dec style, with, in the N arcade, nice capitals. – PLATE. Cup *temp.* Charles I, late C17, and 1784. – The church has the richest haul in the county of Anglo-Saxon and Anglo-Danish work, culminating of course in the

10   GOSFORTH CROSS. This is in the churchyard. It is about 15 ft high and can be dated to the later C10. It is second in importance only to the Bewcastle Cross, by three centuries its elder. It is characterized by extreme slenderness, a shaft starting round and turning square higher up, as if a tree trunk was squared off. The junction is hanging semicircles, just as in Early Norman block capitals. The figure representations are obscure. On the E face is Christ with outstretched arms, but not on the cross, and two men below, one with a lance. Two entwined busts in the semicircle below them, plaiting with a beast's head above Christ. On the S face is another such

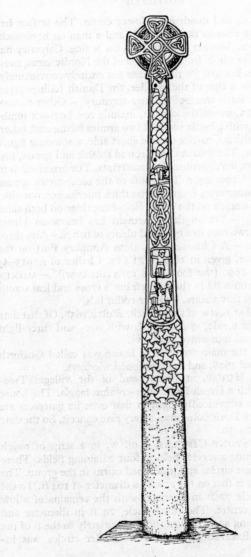

Gosforth Cross, later tenth century, east face

plaited beast, and quadrupeds lower down. The w face has two fighting men in the semicircle and a man on horseback, upside down. Another horseman on the N side. Calverley has explained the whole from the world of the Nordic sagas, most ingeniously, but just for that reason not entirely convincingly. Yet the style is that of the invader, the Danish Jellinge style, though Gosforth was not in their territory. – Other SAXON FRAGMENTS, inside the church, include two hogback tombstones, one with a battle scene of two armies facing each other, the other with a Crucifix on one short side, a standing figure on the other. The soldiers have round shields and spears, just as in Carolingian illuminated manuscripts. The ornament is in the wildest Urnes style. The roofs of the tombstones appear tiled. – Another cross fragment has thick interlace on one side, a big biting dragon on the other. Below the ridge on both sides a crocodile. – Yet another fragment has below an Urnes quadruped two men in a boat and plenty of fishes. – Also three cross-heads. – A Chinese BELL from Anunkry Fort on the Canton River, given in 1844. – PLATE. Chalice of c.1615–45 (the stem), 1690 (the foot), and 1784 (the bowl). – MONUMENTS. A coffin lid in the s porch has a cross and leaf scrolls l. and r. and tiny shears. – Other coffin lids.

GOSFORTH HALL, NW of the church. Built c.1658. Of that date probably the E side, symmetrical, with two- and three-light mullioned and transomed windows.

LIBRARY, in the main street. The house was called Gosforth Gate, is dated 1628, and has mullioned windows.

STEELFIELD HOUSE, at the w end of the village. Two-storeyed, with a Greek Doric four-column loggia. The house is indeed so convincingly Grecian that even its gatepiers are sturdy Greek Doric columns – a very rare conceit. So the date will be c.1820–30.

GRETIGATE STONE CIRCLES, ¾ m. W, in a strip of rough ground forming a service field to four adjoining fields. There are three stone circles and nine small cairns in the group. The largest circle is that on the s, with a diameter of 104 ft. To the NW is a circle 72 ft in diameter with the remains of a low cairn at its centre. The third circle, 24 ft in diameter and again enclosing a small cairn, lies immediately to the N of the latter site. Excavation of the two smaller circles was inconclusive.

STANDING STONE. See Seascale.

GRANGE-IN-BORROWDALE

HOLY TRINITY. Built in 1860. Nave and chancel in one and bellcote. Round-arched windows, the voussoir-stones of the arch cut so that each ends in a triangle or spike towards the opening. The beams of the tunnel-shaped roof also treated in this way. The architect must have been an aggressive man.

(GRANGE BRIDGE. Of two segmental arches with a grassy island between. MHLG)

BARROW HOUSE, 2 m. NNE. Early C19, with a centre with two canted bay windows close together and wings with a stepped tripartite window.

(ASHNESS BRIDGE, ½ m. SE of Barrow House, on the Watendlath Road. A famous packhorse bridge of one single small arch.)

(WATENDLATH, even more famous, and listed grade II by the MHLG in its totality.)

GREAT CROSTHWAITE see CROSTHWAITE

GREAT MELL FELL see MATTERDALE

GREAT ORTON see ORTON

GREAT SALKELD

ST CUTHBERT. Broad, late C14 W tower, with only small windows and even the bell-openings only of one light. The lowest stage of the tower is tunnel-vaulted. It was no doubt meant as a protection against the Scots (cf. Burgh-by-Sands and Newton Arlosh). On the first floor of the tower is a fireplace. The nave has a very sumptuous and barbaric Norman S doorway with three orders of columns, capitals with beasts, human heads, and disorderly trail work which even invades the abaci. Zigzag arches. The Norman nave windows are all Victorian (restoration 1866). The chancel windows must be C17. – ARMOUR. C17. – PLATE. Chalice and Cover Paten, York, 1567. – MONUMENT. Effigy of Thomas de Caldebec, priest, † 1320. With inscription. Good, broad treatment.

NUNWICK HALL. 1892 by *Ferguson*. Red sandstone, Tudor-style, with gables and mullioned windows with arched lights.

GREENTHWAITE HALL see GREYSTOKE

GRETIGATE STONE CIRCLES *see* GOSFORTH

GREY CROFT STONE CIRCLE *see* SEASCALE

4030   GREYSTOKE

St ANDREW. The church poses one major problem. It is built essentially in one style. Is this Late Perp? Let it be described first. The chancel has large three-light windows under two-centred arches, and in the s aisle the same are used. But the rest is all either straight-headed or with segmental arches. The tracery in all these is of round-headed lights without cusps, double in number and halved in size in the heads. Moreover, halfway down the s side is a projection of two storeys, and this has two such windows on the upper floor into the aisle. Above the s porch is a straight-headed three-light window. Finally the arcades. They are of six bays. The sixth was clearly once the entry to a transept, see the keeled E responds. They represent an early C13 date. The chancel arch also has C13 responds. But bays one to five have round piers with shapeless round capitals, and even if the arches they carry (two slight chamfers) may well be early C13 again, the piers can neither be that nor surely be early C16.* In fact, looking at the *ensemble* unbiasedly one is led to believe a C17 date, and this belief is confirmed by the similar E window of Holme Cultram Abbey, which must date from *c*.1605. On the chancel of Greystoke is indeed an inscription saying: 'This chancel was repaired 1645 by Thomas Howard of Greystoke Earl of Arundel and Surrey and William Morland Rector.' But the broad W tower looks medieval, and its bell-openings look Dec. However it is said (Bulmer) that it was wholly rebuilt in 1848. – SCREEN. One-light divisions. The top rail and the dainty tracery are Perp. – STALLS. Some have MISERICORDS, e.g. St Michael and the Dragon, two youths and a donkey, a man mounting a 36 horse. – STAINED GLASS. The E window has largely original C15 glass telling the story of St Andrew. It was assembled in 1848 and is mixed up with other fragments. The quality can never have been high, but it gives a sense of completeness which one does not often get. – N aisle NE by *Kempe*, 1901. – PLATE. A Recusant Chalice, dated 1690; Cup and Paten on pedestal, 1714; two Flagons, 1790; Almsdish, 1795. – MONU-MENTS. Alabaster effigy of a Knight, *c*.1360. Angels by his

* The piers were heightened *c*.1818 (Jefferson).

pillow; a canopy over his head. – Alabaster effigy of John Lord
Greystoke † 1436 (will). One side of the tomb-chest is preserved, with two saints still in the style of the C14, which
remained so long in England, and otherwise standard angels
holding shields. – Brasses of John de Whelpdale, priest,
† 1526 (bust, 7 in. long), Margaret Moresby † 1528 (13 in.),
Winifred Newport † 1547 (11 in.), Richard Newport † 1551
(11 in.).

GREYSTOKE CASTLE. As one approaches one looks at an ambitious and correct neo-Elizabethan mansion by *Salvin*. He did
this front (and more) in 1839–48, and worked again at Greystoke Castle after a fire of 1868 in 1875–8. The interior of the
hall e.g. is of the later date. The front has a porch, to its l. two
tall hall windows with four transoms, then the hall bay with
five transoms, and then chamber and solar – all as it ought to
be. But round the corner is medieval masonry, and at the back
there sticks out of Salvin's display, set diagonally, the mighty
original pele tower for which William Lord Greystoke was
given licence to crenellate in 1353. The basement is tunnel-
vaulted, with five broad flat transverse arches like hoops, and
two slit windows. Salvin's façade replaces one of *c*.1675, built
for Henry Charles Howard, which is known from old illustra-
tions and still stood after 1800. The alterations by the
eleventh Duke of Norfolk in 1789 appear now only in the
fanciful walling next to the tower and a thin tower at the end
of that walling. The quoins, roundels, and flat blank arches at
the top of the tower are typically Georgian and really
reminiscent of Vanbrugh. In one room a fine white classical
Georgian fireplace.

(GREYSTOKE CASTLE FARMHOUSE. 1836 by *John Barker*.
Two-storeyed, with three-storey wings and a large courtyard. MHLG)

The eleventh Duke of Norfolk, no doubt also about 1789, built
three folly farms w of Greystoke. The first from the castle is
FORT PUTNAM. The details are similar to those of the tower
at the castle. The whole is really a screen round a farm.
Battlements, a turret, a large church window, and then a
blank wall with arches, and round buttresses topped by
coronets of stiff petals.* The second is BUNKERS HILL, a
three-sided screen with a broad polygonal tower. The third is

---

* (Near Fort Putnam, in a field, is the GREYSTOKE PILLAR, an obelisk.
MHLG)

SPIRE HOUSE. Here a polygonal tower carries a recessed spire. Again the details have the Vanbrughian ring of the tower at the Castle.

HOUSE, W of the church. Five bays, doorway with segmental pediment, but the windows still upright, of two lights, i.e. in Cumberland early C18.

BLENCOW HALL, 1¼ m. NE. A hall range between two low towers. The N tower has a spiral staircase in one corner and is probably early C16. Some of the battlements are left. The S tower is later. It also has some of its battlements. The centre of the house has a date 1590 over the door. Mullioned windows; no display. In the courtyard a window with Y-tracery, belonging to the former chapel.

(GREENTHWAITE HALL. With mullioned windows, diagonally-set chimneys, and a three-storeyed porch dated 1650. M. Taylor)

BLENCOW BANK CAIRN. The cairn was excavated in the C18, when two urns containing cremations were found.

LOADEN HOWE, ¾ m. W of Laithes House. The cairn was excavated in the C18, when two urns, one containing a cremation, were found in a stone cist.

CAIRN, Great Mell Fell. See Matterdale.

GRINSDALE

3050

ST KENTIGERN. Immediately above the wide Eden river. Built in 1740. Thin W tower, nave of only three and chancel of two bays. Arched windows. – MONUMENT to Mrs Clara Steel. Tall, very unadorned urn in an equally deliberately bare recess. Signed by *Nelson* of Carlisle. It is evidently inspired by Watson's monument at Ainstable.

HADRIAN'S WALL, see p. 55n

HAILE

0000

CHURCH, NW of the village. It must be Georgian, see the plain arched windows. The W porch probably by *Ferguson*, 1882. – SCULPTURE. Part of an Anglo-Saxon cross-shaft with scrolls used as a nave SE quoin. – PLATE. Cup with band of ornament, 1570; large Cup and Paten, 1772. – MONUMENT. John Ponsonby † 1670 (W wall, outside). The inscription reads (in capital letters typical of the date):

Learn Reader Under This Stone
Doth Lye
A Rare Example Cald John Ponsonbye.
If I Said Ylese I am Sur I lyd
He was a Faithful Freind And Soe
He Dyd November 25 in the
    Year 1670.

HAILE HALL. One date-stone says 1591; another 1625. The front with the irregular mullioned and mullioned-and-transomed windows probably belongs to the former date. Another front is of five bays and two and a half storeys with a moulded string-course above the ground-floor windows. That is probably early C18. The Venetian window round the corner is yet later.

YEORTON HALL, ¾ m. S. One C18 façade of seven (1 + 5 + 1) windows and a doorway with a broken pediment.

HAMES HALL see COCKERMOUTH

HARBYBROW TOWER see MEALSGATE

HARDKNOTT CASTLE see BOOT

HARDRIGG HALL see SKELTON

HARRINGTON

9020

ST MARY. Rock-faced. The W tower is of 1905–7, the rest is supposed to be of 1885, but as a church was built here in 1811, one ought to consider whether the wide, aisleless nave and the side windows with Y-tracery are not of that date. Odd chancel, in one with the nave, but with narrow aisles. The W doorway between tower and nave with its basket arch must be C17. – FONT. High octagonal bowl with intersecting arches on thin colonnettes. Dated 1634, but probably medieval. – SCULPTURE. Norman capital with small figures (porch). – Part of an Anglo-Danish cross with disorderly entanglements.

ST MARY (R.C.), Church Road. By *Charles Walker*, 1893. Barn-like interior and a Nonconformist-looking façade.

BROOKLANDS, SSE of the church, below the playing field. Five bays, with a pedimented doorway. Georgian.

HARROW'S SCAR see WALTON

HAWKRIGG HOUSE see WAVERTON

HAWKSDALE HALL see DALSTON

HAYES CASTLE see DISTINGTON

1040

HAYTON

2 m. SE of Allonby

ST JAMES. 1868 by *Travers* of Manchester. Nave with bellcote and chancel. The church lies by the green, or rather one of those long, wide street-greens typical of Yorkshire. – Nice iron ROOD SCREEN, probably of *c.*1870.

HAYTON CASTLE. This is still a mystery house. It is at present simply a rectangle, and windows are of three periods, small and probably of the C15, Elizabethan with mullions and mullions and transoms, and Georgian. The W façade has the latter on the r. in a composition trying to make the whole as near symmetrical as could be, and the Elizabethan ones in the l. third. On the opposite side the whole of the third floor has C18 windows under gables. That side is also propped by two enormous buttresses. But there are walls of such thickness at the NW and SW corners and also at one place in the middle of the house (which is two rooms deep) that the C15 seems certain. Also in the basement is some tunnel-vaulting. A puzzling fact is two straight joints in the buttressed side, and, corresponding to one of them, two mullioned windows now inside the building. Again along in the same wall is a spiral staircase. So all this was outer wall still in the C16. The only known dates are a plaque of 1609 on the stairs, and 1719 in a window on the top floor. In addition it is recorded that *c.*1665 much rebuilding was done. 1609 would suit the Elizabethan windows better than 1665, 1719 only just the Georgian ones, which look rather later. A detailed examination of the house is very desirable.

CASTLE HILL. A motte, just N of the village, 270 ft high, with double rampart and ditch (Curwen).

1050

HAYTON

2½ m. SW of Brampton

ST MARY MAGDALENE. 1780. Thin W tower, nave of five bays with arched, keyed-in windows. On the N side an addition containing the raised family pew of the Grahams of Edmond Castle. It has its own W doorway. Chancel of two bays 1842, but the Venetian window apparently re-set. – PLATE. Chalice, rather coarse, of *c*.1565. – MONUMENTS. Tablets to Grahams, e.g. Thomas † 1807, with a draped urn.

EDMOND CASTLE, 1 m. NW. By *Smirke*, though older parts survive. Smirke's work was begun in 1824 and is dated 1829. It is a Tudor job, ashlar-faced. Three-bay entrance side with Tudor porch of three narrow bays and two shaped gables. Round the corner a larger front with two bay windows and also shaped gables. The SW GATE has a tall two-centred arch and lodges l. and r. Straight, embattled top.

RAILWAY VIADUCT. 1842. Three skew arches. By *Francis Giles*. The MHLG points out that it is a very early example of skew-arching.

HENSINGHAM   9010

ST JOHN EVANGELIST. 1911–13 by *J. Slack*. Rock-faced red sandstone, with a NE tower. The forms used are E.E., Dec, and Perp – the fag-end of historicism in church architecture. – PLATE. Cup, Paten, and Flagon, 1808. – MONUMENT. Tablet to John Steward † 1848 by *Kirkbride* of Carlisle.

WEST CUMBERLAND HOSPITAL, ½ m. SE. Good, large, recent buildings. By *C. B. Pearson, Son & Partners*.

INGMELL, 1¼ m. SE. Five bays, two storeys, with one-storey wings and a porch of two pairs of Greek Doric columns – i.e. early C19.

NETHER END, 1¼ m. ESE. Dated 1624. With mullioned windows on the ground floor and mullioned and transomed windows on the upper floor, not quite symmetrically arranged. On the doorway fanciful head, lintel, and finial.

HESKET NEWMARKET   3030

The village has a fine, wide main street, of the type of North Riding greens, and plenty of attractive houses, mostly of the C18. The MARKET CROSS is C18 too. It consists of four round pillars carrying a pyramid roof with a ball finial.

HESKET HALL. A square house with gabled wings. The centre has a pyramid roof with a big central chimney. Over the main doorway is a horizontally placed oval window with a square hood-mould. That points to the later C17. So do some cross-windows, and especially the staircase window in one of the wings. This has three lights and two transoms. (The house was built by Sir Wilfrid Lawson after 1630. MHLG) Lysons describes it as 'with twelve angles and a circular roof, so contrived that the shadows give the hours of the day'.

4060
HETHERSGILL

ST MARY. 1876 by *Brock* of London. Rock-faced. Nave with bellcote and chancel. Really of no interest.

HEWTHWAITE HALL *see* ISEL

HIGHAM SCHOOL *see* SETMURTHY

HIGHBRIDGE *see* IVEGILL

HIGH GRAINS *see* BEWCASTLE

HIGHHEAD CASTLE *see* IVEGILL

4040
HIGH HESKET

ST MARY. Fine view to the E. The chancel arch is medieval. Two chamfers dying into the imposts. Sturdy double bellcote, probably C17. C18 W porch. The nave with its keyed-in arched windows is of 1720. The chancel E window and the N aisle are Victorian. – PLATE. Cup of 1632; Flagon of 1806. – MONUMENTS. Bernard Kirkbride † 1677. Rustically classical, with a very curly wide-open pediment. – Gothic early C19 Mausoleum of the Parker family.

THIEFSIDE HILL, 1½ m. S. On the NW slope, near Petteril Green Farm, is the site of a ROMAN CAMP, nearly 2 acres in extent, discovered by aerial photography. This is one of the series along the road from York to Carlisle.

HIGH HOUSE *see* WALTON

HOLME CULTRAM *see* ABBEY TOWN

1050
HOLME LOW

ST PAUL. 1845 by *William Armstrong*. Nave with bellcote and chancel. Lancet style, the E triplet shafted inside.

1040
HOLME ST CUTHBERT

ST CUTHBERT. The church lies E of Mawbray and is sometimes called St Cuthbert, Mawbray. It is by *William Armstrong* and dates from 1845. Nave and chancel. N and S lancets. The low W tower with square higher stair-turret is of 1924. Typical

interior of 1845, but just a little out of the ordinary run. –
MONUMENT. Effigy in two pieces, badly defaced. It repre-
sents a Knight, probably cross-legged, and seems early C14.
N of Mawbray the sea has swallowed two churches.

(EDDERSIDE MANOR HOUSE. Dated 1739 and 1785, and the
two periods clearly distinguishable. Mrs Davies)

HOLM HILL see DALSTON

HOUGHTON

4050

ST JOHN EVANGELIST. 1840. Cream-coloured stone. W tower,
nave with lancet windows, short chancel. The bell-openings
have Y-tracery. – TABLET. John Dixon of Knells † 1857. By
Nelsons, Carlisle.

HOUGHTON HALL, to the NE. Five bays, with a porch of two
pairs of Greek Doric pillars and columns.

KNELLS, ¾ m. NE. Built in 1824. Three-bay front with a porch
of two pairs of unfluted Ionic columns and tripartite windows,
their entablature on big brackets.

BRUNSTOCK, ¾ m. ESE. 1827–8 by *Rickman*.* Thoroughly
Gothic, but with bargeboarded gables. Gothic porches to the
entrance and the garden. Also a Gothic conservatory. Even
the GATEPIERS on the road are castellated. The LODGE has
bargeboards and a Gothic oriel too. The house was built for
George Saul.

DRAWDYKES CASTLE, 1⅛ m. SE, on the B road. A complete
pele tower, but provided in 1676 with a three-storey, three-
bay front. The ground-floor and first-floor windows have
pediments, alternatingly segmental and triangular, and all
starting and ending with a little of straight entablature. The
doorway has a heavily moulded surround. Parapet with two
inept busts. The house was built for John Aglionby.‡

LINSTOCK CASTLE, 1⅝ m. SE. A pele tower and a range next to
it. The latter has two mullioned windows left, the former has a
tunnel-vaulted ground floor and a single-chamfered doorway
into this as well as a blocked one on the first floor. The tower
was originally one storey higher. Linstock Castle was in the
C12 and part of the C13 the only residence of the bishops of
Carlisle.

* Jefferson has the date 1833.
‡ Drawdykes is the site of Milecastle 64 of HADRIAN'S WALL. TARRABY,
¼ m. SW, is the site of Milecastle 65.

HOWBECK *see* CALDBECK

HUDDLESCOUGH HALL *see* RENWICK

4030   HUTTON-IN-THE-FOREST

The absorbing historical interest of the house lies in its two C17 contributions. They are an object lesson in how the century moved from the Jacobean to the Baroque without seriously going classical. But the story of the house begins in the Middle Ages. The N part of the main block is a pele tower, vaulted on the ground level and with a spiral staircase in the SE corner. This may date from the time of Thomas de Hoton, who died in 1362. Added to this was the hall range, running N–S, and now medieval only in the masonry of the fireplace wall. But the S tower, now entirely Early Victorian, stands* on a vaulted basement which extends S beyond the Victorian S wall, i.e. would probably also be medieval.‡ As it is, the whole of that S side is now *Salvin*'s, who worked on the house from about 1830 and again in the 1860s to 80s.

Some time between 1641 and 1645 Sir Henry Fletcher built the long gallery. The Fletchers, rich men of Cockermouth, had bought the estate in 1606. The long gallery runs E from the pele tower and is a most curious building. It has a central canted bay projection with a porch, one mullioned and transomed window l. and one r. of the porch on the upper floor, and three to the back. The ground floor was originally entirely open to the front. The arches are depressed segmental and the columns or clusters of columns without any doubt intended to look E.E. The capitals in particular are quite unmistakable. This as a case of medieval revival is most noteworthy. Inside, the ground floor has at the back three flat recesses with segmental arches on over-swelling Tuscan columns. In Kip's engraving of *c.*1705 the gallery wing is matched by a wing to the E from the S end. This was never built, and so the centre piece of the E front does not get the support it should. It was built by Sir Henry Fletcher's son Sir George, and is a dramatic five-bay composition of about 1680 with all the features pressed into too narrow a compass. The doorway has a broad rusticated surround, the window

47

* So Lady Inglewood told me.
‡ Blencow Hall also has two towers, *see* p. 134.

above it Corinthian pilasters, a frieze with two garlands, and a bulgy entablature, the windows l. and r. of this alternatingly open triangular and open segmental pediments. The attic storey has in the middle, instead of a window, drapery and a shield. To this centre piece belongs a gorgeous staircase, not *in situ*. It has thick pierced acanthus scrolls and chubby rustic cherubs. In one upper room is a mid-C18 plaster ceiling with Cupid in the middle.

St James, ½ m. N. Built originally in 1714, but wholly re-modelled, if not rebuilt. The chancel with imitation C15, the nave with imitation early C16 windows. – COMMUNION RAIL. C17. – (SCULPTURE. 18 in. fragment of a cross-shaft with interlace. Calverley-Collingwood) – PLATE. Cup, Flagon, and Salver, *c.*1822. – TABLETS to two Fletchers † 1700 and † 1761.

BLENCOW BANK CAIRN. *See* Greystoke.

HUTTON JOHN

4020

The house started from a pele tower, now in the SE corner. It has a tunnel-vaulted ground stage, a spiral staircase in the NW corner, and on the ground stage a small fireplace with a smoke-hole in the wall. The upper windows are sashed.* To this tower on the W side a hall range was added. Its present S windows are replacements of 1830, when also the third floor was put on. This received the original S windows. After the S range followed a larger range to the N of the tower. This has a date 1662, but its mullioned and transomed windows are still entirely in the Jacobean tradition. The most interesting feature is the small heart-shaped windows on the ground floor and the one at the top of the N wall. The latter carries a cross. Andrew Hudleston, who built this, was a Catholic, and the symbolism is much like that of Sir Thomas Tresham's build-ings in Northamptonshire a hundred years earlier. The C18 is represented by a doorway of 1739 (date on the door-lock) with moulded frame and open segmental pediment and by a plaster ceiling in the part of 1662 and the staircase in the same part which has three balusters to the tread and carved tread-ends. Finally in 1866 *George Ledwell Taylor* made a new entrance hall and library. High Victorian Gothic chimney-pieces. Taylor was related by marriage to the Hudlestons

* Taylor adds to this a sleeping cell and a garderobe on the first floor, a similar arrangement on the second floor, and on the same floor a round-arched window.

(who still own the house). – In the garden wall, between s wing and dovecote, is a re-set doorway with a steep gable. This belongs to the work of 1662.

INGMELL see HENSINGHAM

IREBY

ST JAMES. 1847. Nave with bellcote and chancel. Lancet windows.

MOOT HALL. In the middle of the village. Centre and two wings. Doorway with segmental pediment. – PLATE. Cup of c.1565.

BUTTER CROSS. Octagonal shaft with a square block on top which has enriched crosses carved on.

OLD CHURCH, 1 m. w. Late Norman. In the E wall three round-headed windows of equal height and one above. The lower windows are separated inside by detached columns with waterleaf capitals. In the s wall traces of two Norman windows.

IRTHINGTON

ST KENTIGERN. 1849–53 and *Bloxham* of Rugby as the consultant are perfectly convincing, as long as one stays outside. Lancets and a clerestory with windows in the form of spherical triangles. The NW tower outside the N aisle is later – of 1897. But the chancel masonry is evidently medieval. And so the surprise starts. The chancel arch is early C13. It has two orders of columns with spurs and crocket capitals. The innermost order is a continuous roll, and the arch has rolls as well and dogtooth. The arcades are yet older, say of c.1170. They have round piers and still square abaci, and the arches are round, with one step and one slight chamfer. The capitals are uncommonly interesting – all broad, flat, fleshy leaves of various forms and various degrees of stylization. Most of them are carved only towards the nave. – PLATE. Cup of 1615.

(MOTTE. Perhaps of the time of Robert de Vallibus. C. Bulman)

WHITEFLAT, ½ m. NE, is the site of Milecastle 58 of HADRIAN'S WALL.

OLD WALL, ½ m. w. The site of Milecastle 59 lies to the E, that of Milecastle 60 to the w.

WATCHCROSS, 1 m. s of Old Wall, is the site of a Roman temporary CAMP connected with the wall. It occupies 1½ acres.

IRTON

ST PAUL. 1856–7 by *Miles Thompson* of Kendal. Fine view towards Wasdale Head. Nave and chancel (enlarged 1873) and W tower. Perp style. – SCULPTURE. The C9 CROSS-SHAFT in the churchyard is one of the most important ones in Cumberland. It is 10 ft long and has its head preserved. On the edges still vine-scrolls, but on the face and back, apart from interlace, close patterning of steps and fret and also rosettes, all of Irish derivation. The handling is convinced and barbaric.

IRTON HALL, 1 m. E. By *Grayson*, 1874. Of sandstone, in the Elizabethan style, irregular in plan. Only the clock tower is frankly nothing but Victorian. However, the house incorporates a high, well preserved C14 pele tower. The ground level is tunnel vaulted as usual. Part of a two-light window with uncusped heads to the lights survives. The work of 1874 was done for J. L. Burns Lindow.

ROUND CAIRN, ½ m. NW of the road between Eskdale Green and Santon Bridge. The cairn is 30 ft in diameter and 3 ft high. The stone kerb serving as a revetment to the mound is still visible. Excavations failed to produce any evidence of burials, although a single sherd of cord-impressed Beaker pottery was found during the investigation.

ISEL

ST MICHAEL. A Norman church of *c.*1130, as proved by the two small N windows, the S doorway with one order of columns with scalloped capitals and zigzag in the arch, one S window, externally of the C18, the simple priest's doorway, and one chancel N window now giving on to the vestry. The chancel arch is of the same date too, see its moulding of a half-roll and two quarter-hollows. – SCULPTURE. Small part of an Anglo-Danish cross-shaft with a rounded swastika, a similar triskele, and another similar motif. – PLATE. Cup and Cover Paten, 1570, the cup with a band of ornament.

ISEL HALL. Quite a spectacular building, with a glorious view to the S. The oldest part is the pele tower, still partly vaulted at ground level and with a few original slit windows. On the top floor is a two-light window of the period of Henry VIII. On the first floor an original fireplace is preserved. To this tower, but not in axis, a domestic range was added, it is said,

Irton Cross, ninth century, east face

also at the time of Henry VIII. Of this there are no windows, but the buttressed masonry to the s, and the moulded beams inside. It was a hall range. The mighty fireplace stands against the former screens passage. A second fireplace was nearer the high-table end on the N side. In the hall excellent linenfold panelling, and also Elizabethan panelling with painting in imitation of tarsia. More such panelling in other rooms. In the room above the hall, re-used, simpler early C16 panelling with plain muntins. The C16 range was continued later in the same century to the W, and is three-storeyed with three-light windows arranged fairly regularly. A painting of the early C16 in the house shows this extension only two-storeyed, but the masonry hardly bears that out.

HEWTHWAITE HALL, ¾ m. SW. The house has a three-bay front with an inscription of 1581 (ano rae 23) above the lintel of the doorway. The lintel has shields and two small standing figures. The inscription is also flanked by such figures. It is all very unusual. The doorway is set between two windows with plain, round-arched lights. Above are cross-windows, and at the back is a window with an embattled transom and cinquefoiled lights. Which windows are of 1581? Most probably the cross-windows. The others must be older, say Henry VIII or c.1500.

ISLEKIRK HALL see WIGTON

IVEGILL

CHRIST CHURCH. By *R. J. Withers & Putney*, 1868. Polygonal bell-turret on a mid-buttress. Nave and chancel. Plate tracery. – The STAINED GLASS all by *O'Connor* and all of 1868. – PLATE. Cup of 1679.

HIGHHEAD CASTLE, 1½ m. W. The mansion itself was almost totally gutted by fire in 1956. The façade stands, of 1744–8, eleven bays long, with a pedimented three-bay centre, a doorway with rustication of alternating sizes and a pediment, and a walled front garden with coupled Ionic columns. The work of 1744–8 was done for H. Richmond Brougham. The only still inhabited part of the house is the W side, and this is much older, probably of the second third of the C16, with the unmistakable straight-headed windows with round-arched lights. Fine STABLE quadrangle, the front with windows and archway all heavily rusticated. Steep pedimental gable and cupola.

(Near Highhead Castle is a CHAPEL in a field, dated 1682. It has pointed-arched windows and one mullioned window. Mrs Davies)

SCALES HALL. *See* p. 186.

(THISTLEWOOD, Highbridge, 1½ m. W of Ivegill. Pele tower with C16 additions. The tower has mullioned windows. MHLG)

(ASHES, 1⅛ m. WSW of Ivegill. C17. The front to the farmyard is original. Five bays. MHLG)

4030

JOHNBY

JOHNBY HALL. One short range with a staircase projection to the S at the E end. Over the door to the staircase an inscription and the date 1583 in a very curious framework. Mouldings rise l. and r. ogee-wise above the door and then separate again to frame the inscription. The pattern is more late C17 than late C16 in character, and the doorway has indeed a bolection moulding. The W part of the range was the pele tower. Its ground level is tunnel-vaulted, and the rest of the range also has tunnel-vaults. In the tower NE corner is a staircase from the first floor up. The top of the main spiral stair, the one of 1583, has radial ribs, and they and the top of the newel post have fillets, an interesting Gothic survival, or more probably revival.

2020

KESWICK

ST JOHN EVANGELIST. 1838 by *Salvin*, but, according to Kelly, the aisles added in 1862 and 1882 and the chancel lengthened in 1889. Salvin's windows etc. must have been faithfully re-used. The whole church with its commanding W tower with recessed spire is entirely of a piece and in style still without archeological ambitions. In the E wall e.g. are three stepped pairs of lancets, a successful motif, but one without authority. Otherwise simple geometrical tracery. Wide nave, arcades of low round piers. The church was built by a famous Leeds manufacturer, John Marshall, who had bought the estate in 1832. – STAINED GLASS. By *Holiday* the E windows, 1888–9, among his best; also the chancel side windows, of the same date, and one S aisle window.

The MAIN STREET is made memorable by the TOWN HALL on its island site. It dates from 1813 and has a tower in one end wall like a church (pretty concave-sided pyramid roof) and then the body of three formerly open arches below and arched windows above. Rendered and whitewashed, with black trim. It is an exceedingly pretty sight.

On Derwentwater three islands, Lord's, Vicar's, and St Herbert's. On Lord's Island excavations have shown remains of medieval settlement, on Vicar's Island was a mansion, on St Herbert's a Gothic hermitage.

GRETA HALL (part of Keswick School). The house looks later C18. It has three bays, with a doorway whose pediment stands on fluted Ionic columns.

(DERWENTWATER TENANTS ESTATE, next to Greta Hall. Begun 1909. One of the earliest Co-Partnership estates in the country. Twenty-seven cottages on 2 acres. The architect was *N. W. Hodgson* of Winchester.*)

KIRKANDREWS 3060

ST ANDREW. Built in 1776, and not at all a villagey job. Ashlar-faced, with a w tower crowned by an open rotunda of columns at the bell-stage and a stone cap. Widely spaced arched windows, only three along the nave. The W wall has a Tuscan doorway with pediment and a large top pediment, the E wall a large window and two niches. – SCREEN and REREDOS, green and gold. Italian in style, rather Comperish. It is by *Temple Moore*, who was so sensitive at Gothic. The work at Kirkandrews was done in 1893. – PLATE. Cup and Cover Paten 1640; Paten early C18; Flagon 1740.

KIRKANDREWS TOWER. Built by the Grahams, in the first 31 half of the C16. Of a decidedly Scottish type, i.e. with a plain parapet on corbels and a pitched roof. The ground-floor vaulting and corner staircases are standard elements. The farm has a castellated wall no doubt of the C19.

SUSPENSION BRIDGE. *See* Netherby Hall, p. 169.

LIDDEL STRENGTH, ½ m. NNE on the river Esk, i.e. the Scottish border. Outer bailey, inner bailey, and motte in the E corner. The whole is about 4 acres in size.

KIRKBAMPTON 3050

ST PETER. A Norman church of interesting details. The N doorway has one order of columns. In the tympanum in one corner a small figure of an abbot or bishop is preserved. More

* Information received from Miss Margaret Tims.

may have been chiselled off. The arch has flat zigzag, the hood-mould grotesquely big billets. The details of the s doorway are almost unrecognizable, but in the chancel is another doorway, too close to the w end of the chancel to be a priest's doorway, and that has a very remarkable tympanum consisting of three horizontal bands each consisting of squares set lozenge-wise and connected with one another by pairs of stones one on top of the other. In the bottom row the squares are cream-coloured and the connecting stones red, in the next the colours are reversed, in the top row they are again as in the first. The chancel arch is Norman too. The responds have one a capital of big scallops, the other smaller scallops. Fish-scale pattern in the abaci. The arch has one roll and one step. All this is not later probably than *c.*1150. In the chancel s wall one small window, the arch of one stone and with incised lines. A second such window is re-set in the organ chamber. – STAINED GLASS. The E window must be by *Morris & Co.*, although it is badly preserved. Eight angels with musical instruments and a beautiful figure of Christ: just compare this – commemorative date 1871 – with the insufferable neighbouring window of 1885 (by *E. R. Suffling* of Edgware Road). – PLATE. Cup 1702.

KIRKBRIDE

2050

ST BRIDE, N of the village. Nave and bellcote and chancel. The church is essentially Norman. It has a plain s doorway and a plainer blocked N doorway. This latter has a straight top and is quite exceptionally narrow. Norman also the unmoulded chancel arch on the plainest imposts, one nave N window, one chancel N window, and – probably a little later – the chancel s doorway, round-arched, with a continuous chamfer. – FONTS. One small, square, with rounded corners, a lamb and cross, and some dog-tooth and fleurons down the edges. – The other square, larger and Perp, with nobbly leaf around the underside and against the sides circles, trefoiled and quatrefoiled. – SCULPTURE. Excellent small (*c.*10 by 8 in.) Italian panel of the Entombment, approximately late C16. It is of plaster and may be a cast. – PLATE. Cup 1649.

KIRKCAMBECK

5060

ST KENTIGERN. 1885. E of it an arch built of materials of the old church.

KIRKLAND   *0010*

St LAWRENCE. The church seems 'ancient', as Kelly would
call it, i.e. the masonry is medieval, the pointed-trefoiled
PISCINA E.E., and the triple-chamfered chancel arch partly
dying into the imposts could be called late C13 or C14. The
rest is of the rebuilding of 1880. – PLATE. Cup and Paten,
1637; Paten, 1687. – MONUMENT. Effigy of a Knight; C13. –
(CHURCHYARD CROSS, over 8 ft high, the head free-armed,
but round holes between the arms. Collingwood)

KIRKLINTON   *4060*

St CUTHBERT. Built in 1845, but incorporating a few fragments of a Norman arch made up into the finished article as
the arch from the tower to the nave.* It is noble of the unknown architect not thereupon to have fallen into the fashion-
able neo-Norman but to have stuck to the lancet style. W
tower with corbelled-out top. Thin buttresses between the
lancets. – PLATE. Cup and Paten Cover, 1732. – MONU-
MENTS. Edward and Dorothy Appleby, both † 1698. Two
coats of arms with two inscriptions. – Joseph Dacre Appleby
† 1729. Standing monument with fluted pilasters and open
segmental pediment, quite metropolitan. – Joseph Dacre
Appleby † 1738. Tablet with Ionic columns and an open curly
pediment.
(FRIENDS' MEETING HOUSE, Sikeside, ½ m. SE. 1736. Dis-
used. Small, but with arched windows. MHLG)
KIRKLINTON HALL. An indifferent Georgian five-bay centre
and large Jacobean additions of 1875, all rather bleak. Two
big gabled pavilions l. and r. of the old front and a whole new
wing.

KIRKOSWALD   *5040*

St OSWALD. The church looks blunt as one approaches it,
without even a bellcote. The campanile in fact stands at the
top of the hill into which the church is almost built. It is like
the top of a Gothic tower, with higher stair-turret taken off
and re-erected. It dates from 1897 and replaces a charming
wooden structure of 1747. The exterior of the church has a
blocked mid C13 doorway with thin roll-mouldings, a N

* The Rev. R. H. C. Hall writes that parts of other ancient arches are
built into the ringing chamber of the tower.

window with odd late C15 tracery, and a chancel consistently and very regularly built when Thomas Lord Dacre founded a college of six priests about 1523. The E window is of five lights, the side windows are two on either side, of three lights and quite long, all straight-headed, with uncusped round arches to the lights. Heavy timbers of the former S porch. The interior has aisles of three bays. The E two are older than the rest of the church, the W bays are a lengthening. The S arcade comes first. It must be of the late C12, except for the pier shafts, which are later replacement. But the capitals and the single-step arches are in order. The N arcade also has round arches, but one has two slight chamfers, the other two normal chamfers. The W bays, according to the faces on the W responds, must be C14 or even C15. The aisles were continued by chapels whose W arches remain. They die into the imposts and were probably C14 work. They must have disappeared when the chancel was built. The chancel arch now is wide, high, and shapeless, but its bases are the oldest feature in the church. Their mouldings show them to be Norman. – COMMUNION RAIL. C18. – PLATE. Silver-gilt Chalice and Paten, 1641. – MONUMENTS. Many coffin lids with foliated crosses outside the church. – Small roundel of alabaster put up in 1609 (Browgham and Bertram). Kneeling figures and symbols of death. – Many tablets of Fetherstonehaughs of The College.

CASTLE. To study the plan of the castle on paper is more profitable than to walk in its ditch and nettles. What remains is one monumental tower on the N side pointing triangularly outward. In it is a spiral staircase. It is assumed that it stood at the NE corner of the hall. The castle was oblong, with two tunnel-vaulted angle towers on the S side (of both substantial chunks remain) and the gatehouse in the W side. Much of the moat is preserved.

THE COLLEGE. The beautiful entrance side is entirely of 1696 and very progressive for Cumberland. It could be anywhere in the Home Counties. Five-bay centre and two-bay short wings, two storeys, hipped roof. The doorway has an open curly pediment on brackets and a pulvinated surround. The windows are sashed. At the back, i.e. towards the garden, is much older work. The place where now a canted bay window of the early C17 projects was a pele tower. The staircase in one corner is still there. Adjoining it inside are parts of walls probably of the original college. N of the tower is also old walling, and the gable here has a small round-headed window. This stretch of wall seems to be Elizabethan or Jacobean. Inside, the hall has beams decorated with egg and dart and panels with wreaths, and the fine staircase has twisted balusters and the stair-ends still hidden by a string. Older elements are the panelling of one room dated 1619 and the wooden chimney-piece in the same room dated 1644, with very crude caryatids in the overmantel.

SHEFFIELD HALL. 1848. Red sandstone, Tudor, with a castellated tower.

THE NUNNERY, 1⅝ m. NW. Built in 1715 by Henry Aglionby (Jefferson, I, 245). Fine front of nine bays and two storeys. The doorway is the only ornament. It has Doric pilasters, a metope frieze, and a segmental pediment. The windows have flat raised frames. The back of the house goes back to the Benedictine nunnery which is said to have existed here about 1200.* Only recently a doorway of the mid C13 was found in the back wall. It has a segmental head and dog-tooth. Other walling also belongs to the nunnery. The staircase of the house is again mid C18. Three balusters to the step, and modestly carved tread-ends.

KNELLS see HOUGHTON

LACRA see MILLOM

LAMPLUGH

ST MICHAEL. 1870 by *Butterfield*. The wilful details of the big double-bellcote, the prominent chimney on the N side, and the handsomely traceried large opening in the E wall of the nave into the chancel betray the architect. Old parts were re-used, such as the chancel N doorway with continuous mouldings and a Perp one-light window and the doorway of the vestry. One can perhaps assume that Butterfield had more evidence to choose Perp fenestration, which he would otherwise hardly have done in 1870. – STAINED GLASS. By *Kempe* chancel N and S windows and also the W window. They are of 1891, 1901, 1910, showing in that order no signature, the wheatsheaf signature, and the wheatsheaf with the tower (for *Tower*, Kempe's later partner). – PLATE. Clumsy Cup and Cover Paten, late C17.

* Not in Knowles and Hadcock.

GATEWAY, SE of the church. Reputed to date from 1595 (but
the date-stone is new). Low-pitched two-centred arch,
continuous mouldings, and stepped gable. It looks *c.*1900
rather than *c.*1600.

STREET GATE, 1⅛ m. NW, W of the A-road. Dated 1733 and
still with cross-windows.

SCALLOW. *See* Arlecdon.

5060

LANERCOST PRIORY

Lanercost Priory was founded about 1166 by Robert de
Vallibus (de Vaux) for Augustinian Canons. A first consecration took place probably in 1169. Not much can have been built
by then, but it is likely that it included some housing for the high
altar. We know little else of dates: damage from Scotch wars and
raids in 1296, 1297, and 1346, evidence of poverty in 1409, the
Dissolution in 1536, and the transfer of the buildings to Sir
Thomas Dacre of Naworth.

The priory lies beautifully secluded on the river Irthing. Of
its buildings the church is exceptionally well preserved. The
nave is now the parish church, and the E parts also stand without
exception to eaves level. The monastic ranges have fared less
well.

EXTERIOR. We start from the E. The chancel is four bays long
and ends straight. The E wall has three lancet windows of even
height and three stepped ones above. There is a change in
masonry between lower and upper half, and this continues
round the corner. To the N and S the chancel has first two
lancets, and then chapels attached to it, merging with the E
aisles of the transepts. The N chapel has an E lancet and a Perp
N window, followed by an identical one as the N window of
the transept aisle. The S chapel windows have three lancet
lights under one arch, a sign of the late C13. The clerestory
has lancets with hood-moulds. There is a corbel-table of three
small hanging arches between every two corbels. The N
transept N wall has the aisle window already mentioned and
the 'nave' flanked by polygonal turrets. The fenestration is
again tall lancets, two below, three stepped ones above. The
crossing tower is perfectly plain and evidently later. The S
transept has the clerestory windows to the E connected by a
horizontal course from hood-mould to hood-mould – a
change from the chancel. The S wall shows the roof-line of
the E range round the cloisters, and above three lancets of

even height. The W side has of course windows only above the former cloister roof. They are lancets, in two tiers, and not in axis. The upper windows have their hood-moulds again connected by a course.

But there is evidence in this place of an earlier stage in the architectural history of the building. The S transept has to the W a broad, flat, i.e. typically Norman buttress. It also has a doorway into the cloister which has a round arch with two slight chamfers and columns with waterleaf capitals. That, in terms of Cumberland, might be as late as 1190, but in terms of an Augustinian priory may well be 1175 or 1180. So here we would have part of the original buildings, and the chancel as it is now would be a replacement of c.1220–30. As one carries on along the S side of the nave the earliest phase clearly continues. The buttresses show that at once, the E nave doorway into the cloister, though pointed, again has waterleaf capitals, and the W nave doorway into the cloister is round-arched with two slight chamfers and has the same capitals. Higher up the windows are again lancets, and the eight clerestory windows are lancets too. Except for the first they have big nailhead along the continuous string-course, rising, as it did before, around the windows. The masonry is red throughout, i.e. the change in the upper parts does not continue. All this is the same on the N side, except that the church has a N, but no S, aisle. There is a N doorway with two orders of columns, some small nailhead enrichment, and a fillet along one of the arch rolls. The aisle corbel-table has two of the little hanging arches, the clerestory (as from the beginning) three.*

The W front is not quite even, and this is due to one of the early, broad, flat buttresses remaining at the S end of the nave, whereas the aisle side is different and of course later. In the middle of the nave part is a sumptuous portal of four orders of columns, their moulded capitals with small nailhead. The arch is pointed and richly moulded. The four rolls all have fillets. At their start l. and r. they have odd sockets. Dog-tooth in the hood-mould, the first we see in the building, but not the first chronologically. Above the portal is a frieze of small pointed-trefoiled arcading, and above that a group of three tall stepped lancets connected by a shafted arcade with shaft-rings. In the gable is a niche with the statue of St Mary

* But the last six of the units in the aisle turn to three hanging arches.

Magdalen, a genuine C13 piece, with the mantle raised over one arm so that the hems fall down like a cascade. It is a favourite motif of *c.*1250–75 (cf. e.g. the Wise and Foolish Virgins in the Angel Choir portal at Lincoln).

INTERIOR. We can now perhaps deviate from the topographical order and start with the oldest parts, i.e., as we have seen, the S transept. Here there is first of all clearly a difference in masonry between lower and upper parts which continues into the E bay of the nave (outside). Then there is a keeled string-course in the S and W walls of the transept. This incidentally also occurs in a confusing place in the N transept, the place where the E end of the aisle meets it. Is the explanation that at first no N aisle was planned? Once again, whether this earliest preserved part of the church was indeed the earliest part built, we do not know; for we do not know what the original chancel was like. At any rate the whole rest of the church seems of a piece – with one more exception – and of the first third of the C13. The chancel came before the nave; that is – for reasons which will be shown – as much as we can surmise.

So now we can return to the E end. The chancel E wall is a beautiful composition. The dado is bare, except for a segment-headed niche in the middle. Above are the tall lancets, shafted, and with shaft-rings and then a wall-passage which was to continue throughout the building. It is articulated by clusters of four shafts. The exception referred to in the uniformity of the interior is the chancel N and S walls. The chancel itself projects by two bays. The two W bays have chapels. This is where the diversity lies. The S side probably came earlier. The aisle windows here have shouldered rere-arches which are absent on the N side. The arcade responds and piers are slender, semi-octagonal and round. In the aisle a ceiling was put in – cf. the corbels – but that was an after-thought. The chapels are rib-vaulted, the ribs single-chamfered. There is no evidence of any vaulting of the major spaces, i.e. the chancel 'nave' or the transept. A straight joint in the N arcade wall immediately E of the NE crossing pier shows that the N side of the chancel was intended to be like the S side. Then, however, and no doubt very soon, the plan was altered and the N side was given a full-grown gallery. It has round arches subdivided into two pointed openings by two colonnettes set in depth and with a blank quatrefoil in the spandrel. The arcade below has details like those of the S side, but responds and pier are shorter. The arches are triple-chamfered. The clerestory continues the wall-passage on the quadruple shafts. Each bay has a small pointed transverse tunnel-vault. The wall-passage in the E wall is made to harmonize precisely, by shaft-rings corresponding to the capitals. The S clerestory is of the same design as the N clerestory.

In the N transept E wall the gallery continues (without the quatrefoils in the spandrels), and the rest continues too. In the S transept E wall also nothing changes. Of the crossing piers only one, the SW one, is part of the earliest work. It is triple, with the main shaft keeled. The E arch is on short keeled corbels. The N arch and SE respond are semi-octagonal and probably a later remodelling. The muddle in the N transept W wall, where the aisle opens into it, has already been re-marked on. In the aisle is a blocked doorway now which can-not be *in situ*. Also there are two arches, one above the other, visible from the transept. In the S transept S wall is an upper doorway. This must have been the night exit from the dormi-tory with wooden stairs down into the transept. The upper windows are shafted with shaft-rings, as are those in the N wall of the N transept. The S transept W wall has windows with oddly rounded trefoiled rere-arches. These arches also indicate an early stage. It can be seen to continue round the corner in the nave.

The nave is a fine and harmonious room, although its S side differs entirely from the N side. The S side, there being no aisle, and there being a cloister, has a high, completely bare wall, and only above that windows and the clerestory with its wall-passage. Of the main windows, to repeat it, the first has the rere-arch as in the transept, the others have them no longer. On the N side the arcade consists of an E arch separated from the others by a piece of wall, where no doubt once the pulpitum stood, and then three bays with standard octagonal piers and triple-chamfered arches. The E respond has stiff-leaf, the first we come across. The clerestory wall-passage gives some indication of the details of building pro-gress. On the S side the first three bays from the E have no adornment, then dog-tooth starts in the arch, then nailhead in the abacus, and finally dog-tooth in the abacus as well. One capital and one only, the tenth of the sixteen (from the E), has stiff-leaf, and quite lively though not very thick stiff-leaf. On the N side there is no such hesitation. There are four bays without dog-tooth, and then arch and abacus take them on together. Another small alteration concerns the clerestory windows proper. They have single-chamfered reveals but turn to a hollow chamfer on N and S in the same place, one bay away from the E. The W wall has shafted windows. When these final parts of the church were erected, we can only guess. It must be remembered, however, that the statue in the gable can hardly be earlier than 1260.

FURNISHINGS. STAINED GLASS. By *Morris & Co.*: N aisle NW, St Luke, date commemorated 1875. – N aisle W, date commemorated 1890. – N aisle N, one-light window, c.1896. – SCULPTURE. In the N aisle fragment of a shaft with an inscription in Roman lettering and dog-tooth down the edges. The shaft belonged to a cross outside and N of the nave. – PLATE. Cup of 1637; Set of 1875. – MONUMENTS. At the E end a plain tomb-chest (chancel N). – Another with three big coats of arms, Perp, under a canopy with a segmental head with dog-tooth. – Yet another (S transept E aisle) with two angels and a coat of arms. The inscription refers to Lord Dacre. – In the N transept N, recess with a tomb-chest with five quatrefoiled circles. – Also in the N transept Lady Elizabeth Dacre Howard † 1883. By *Sir E. Boehm*. Terracotta model of a sleeping baby. – Charles Howard † 1879 and wife, excellent bronze tablet with two profile medallions and underneath the Nativity and the Entombment. The portraits are by *Sir E. Boehm*; the scenes, in an Italian Renaissance relief style, were designed by *Burne-Jones*.

THE MONASTIC QUARTERS. Round the cloister things are not well preserved. Of the E range only the walls are set out in the ground. They show an earlier and a later state of the chapter house and the room between it and the S transept. The later stage, from the remaining fragment of the jamb moulding of the chapter-house entrance, is C13; so the earlier is presumably C12. Of the S range the undercroft survives, nine bays long with a difference in the forms between the six E and the three W bays. Octagonal piers, single-hollow-chamfered ribs. The W bays have thinner piers and two large windows to the W. On the upper floor was, as usual, the refectory. The wall recess at ground level was the lavatorium, handsomely decorated with dog-tooth. From the W bay of the undercroft a small doorway with shouldered lintel led into a two-bay rib-vaulted room in the W range.

The WEST RANGE is in perfect working order, but that is

due to Sir Thomas Dacre, who made this part his house. Hence the C16 windows, straight-headed, with pointed lights. The roof is preserved too, with tie-beams, kingposts, two-way struts, and raking queenposts, all rather rough. To the S, from the W end of the S range, projects a PELE TOWER. This was the prior's lodging. It has a spiral staircase to the first floor in the NW corner, from the first to the second in the NE corner. The windows are partly like those of the W range, but mostly straightforward Elizabethan with mullions and transoms. On the first floor was the kitchen, as shown by the fireplaces and the oven.

VICARAGE. Opposite the W range. To it belongs another, earlier pele tower, called King Edward's Tower, but, on the evidence of the dog-tooth frieze below the battlements, of the C13.

GATEWAY. Only the inner (E) arch stands. On the W side the springers of the vault are preserved. Hollow-chamfered ribs. Triple-chamfered arch.

LANERCOST BRIDGE. A beautiful medieval bridge of two elliptical arches, slightly humped, and with a triangular cutwater.

HADRIAN'S WALL. *See* Walton, p. 197.

LANGRIGG see BROMFIELD

LANGWATHBY   5030

ST PETER. Built in 1718. Nave of five bays and chancel of two. Long, thin, round-arched windows, quoins. The porch is of 1836, and the chancel E window probably yet later. But inside is a medieval N arcade of three bays. The piers are replacements, but the capitals are clearly E.E. So are the double-chamfered arches. – ARMOUR. C17. – PLATE. Cup and Cover Paten, 1760.

LAZONBY   5030

ST NICHOLAS. 1863 by *Anthony Salvin*. Quite large. W tower with higher stair-turret. The tracery partly in the style of 1300, partly with ogees. – PLATE. Chalice of 1571 with ornamental band; Paten, 1718. – (CHURCHYARD CROSS. Over six foot high, unornamented, late. Collingwood).

LIDDEL STRENGTH see KIRKANDREWS

LINSTOCK CASTLE see HOUGHTON

LITTLE BRAITHWAITE *see* THORNTHWAITE

LITTLE BROUGHTON *see* BROUGHTON

LITTLE CLIFTON *see* CLIFTON

LITTLE MEG *see* GLASSONBY

5030   # LITTLE SALKELD

SALKELD HALL. The front is of shortly after 1790. Five bays, two storeys, pedimented doorway, one-storeyed two-bay wings.

LOADEN HOWE *see* GREYSTOKE

LONG MEG AND HER DAUGHTERS
see GLASSONBY

3060   # LONGTOWN

This market town, as *The Beauties of England and Wales* call it in 1802, was planned as a square of four streets by Dr Robert Graham of Netherby, two miles away, i.e. in the later C18. He also built a small harbour at Sarkfoot. The houses are mostly of three bays with a middle entrance and not detached. Quite a number have archways as well. The GRAHAM ARMS is a stately inn with two canted bay windows and a Tuscan porch. Many of the inhabitants of Longtown in 1802 were home-weavers for Carlisle manufacturers.

ARTHURET church, *see* p. 61.
NETHERBY, *see* p. 169.
BRACKENHILL TOWER, *see* p. 74.

1020   # LORTON

ST CUTHBERT. Rendered. Apparently early C19, with an embraced w tower, small lancet windows, and a short chancel. Victorian Dec tracery. – STAINED GLASS. E window by *Mayer* of Munich, really indefensible.

45 LORTON HALL. Roughcast. A pele tower originally with tunnel-vaulting at ground level and a spiral staircase. Attached to it a living range dated 1663. This has seven bays of mullioned windows, higher than wide on the ground floor, pediments above the upper windows, and a pediment above the central

doorway. It is an impressively even display. A further addition, rather grander in style, dates from 1880.

LOW BROWNRIGG see CALDBECK

LOW CROSBY see CROSBY-ON-EDEN

LOWESWATER   1020

St Bartholomew. Built in 1827 and restored in 1884. All one sees now appears to be of 1884, except perhaps the nave lancets with Y-tracery. Typically Victorian polygonal apse, and geometrical tracery. – PLATE. Cup and Cover Paten of 1570.

LOW GRAINS see BEWCASTLE

LOW LORTON see LORTON

LOW WALL see WALTON

LUGUVALIUM see CARLISLE, p. 88

LYULF'S TOWER see MATTERDALE

MARYPORT   3040

Maryport existed before the mid C18, but it became Maryport only when Humphrey Senhouse, lord of the manor, named the village after his wife and decided to develop it as a coal port. That was in 1748–9. The place was laid out as a grid like Whitehaven, but it never developed so satisfactorily. In fact it has little to show now. The first chapel of ease was built in 1760. It was rebuilt in 1847. The railway came in 1840, the lighthouse was built in 1846.

St Mary. The church of 1847 was rebuilt in 1890–2 by *J. H. Martindale*. Only the w tower, with its high pinnacles and its bell-openings as three stepped lancets, is of 1847. Red sandstone. Geometrical tracery. – FONT. A square baluster; dated 1764. – PLATE. Cup, Paten, and Cover Paten, 1768; Cup and Spoon, 1808.

The only street with houses of any note is HIGH STREET. No. 11 has attached Greek Doric columns l. and r. of the doorway. No. 35 was the Athenaeum. It was built in 1855 and is of five bays, with arched windows and an Ionic porch. At the corner of Senhouse Street is a former bank, four bays, in a cheerfully ignorant Italianate, with alternatingly blocked columns. The most enjoyable bit of Maryport is by the QUAY, where all is humble and villagey. Down there is the other church of the town.

CHRISTCHURCH. 1872 by *Eaglesfield*. E.E., with a round apse and a NE steeple. – PLATE. Spoon, *temp*. George III.

NETHERHALL. The mansion of the Senhouses. Derelict at the time of writing. The house incorporates a pele tower, but is mostly Victorian.

(CASTLE HILL, at the S end of the town. A motte. Curwen)

On high ground to the N overlooking the Irish Sea lies a 4½-acre ROMAN FORT defended by a double ditch and a stone wall. The positions of the four gates can be seen. To the S of the fort lay a levelled parade-ground with a tribunal immediately adjacent (known as Pudding Pie Hill). Outside was an extensive civil settlement, of which a number of strip-houses, serving as shops, workshops, taverns, etc., have been found.

4020 MATTERDALE

CHURCH. Nave and chancel in one, domestic windows. Can that be of the time when the church was licensed, i.e. 1573 ? Or is it of 1686, the date of an inscription, where *G. S.* is mentioned as the mason ? The latter is more probable. The nicely primeval W tower of slate was built in 1848, but looks a C20 interpretation of ancientness. – PULPIT. C18, with tester. – BENCHES. Plain and pleasant, just with a knob on the corner of back and arm. – COMMUNION RAIL. C17, three-sided. – STAINED GLASS. By *Kempe*.

COCKLEY MOOR, I m. WSW, above Dockray. A cottage with some Victorian and post-Victorian additions and further additions made in 1938 by (Sir) *Leslie Martin* and *Sadie Speight*. An uncommonly sensitive blend of modern and old.

LYULF'S TOWER, 1¾ m. SE, above Ullswater. 1780, and said to be the first picturesque, medievalizing house in this area. Three sides of an octagon, like a fire-screen, with four hexagonal towers, castellated, but with round-arched windows. The house was built by the Duke of Norfolk and is still Howard property.

CAIRN, 2 m. N of the church, on the summit of Great Mell Fell, at a height of 1760 ft above sea level. The low cairn, *c.* 25 ft in diameter, is surrounded by a ditch 60 ft in diameter and 3 ft wide. The latter is broken by a causeway on the SW.

1 *Scenery :* Wastwater

2 (above) *Scenery* : Wetheral, the river Eden
3 (top right) *Scenery* : Skiddaw from Littletown near Keswick
4 (right) *Village* : Hesket Newmarket

5 (above) *Town :* Whitehaven, air view
6 (top right) *Prehistory :* Castlerigg, stone circle
7 (right) *Vernacular :* Orton, cruck barn

8 (far left) Bewcastle Cross, late seventh century, east face

9 (left) Bewcastle Cross, late seventh century, west face

10 (right) Gosforth Cross, later tenth century

11 (left) Cross Canonby church, cross shaft, tenth century

12 (below) Aspatria church, hogback coffin, probably eleventh century

13 (right) St Bees church, west doorway, c. 1160

14 (left) Carlisle Cathedral, nave arch, late twelfth century

15 (below) Warwick, St Leonard, apse, late twelfth century

16 Abbey Town, Holme Cultram Abbey, west doorway, late twelfth century

17 (left) Bridekirk church, font, mid twelfth century

18 (below) Dearham church, font, probably *c.* 1170

19 (right) Bowness-on-Solway church, font, Late Norman

20 (left) Calder Bridge, Calder Abbey, completed c. 1170–90

21 (below left) Carlisle Cathedral, effigy of a bishop, mid thirteenth century

22 (right) Lanercost Priory, St Mary Magdalen in the west gable, c. 1250–75

23 (bottom right) Lanercost Priory, founded c. 1166, west front finished c. 1250–75

24 (left) Lanercost Priory, founded c. 1166, chancel

25 (bottom left) St Bees church, chancel, late twelfth century

26 (right) Carlisle Cathedral, chancel, c. 1220–50 and early fourteenth century

27 (top) Carlisle Cathedral, chancel, capital showing the month of March, early fourteenth century
28 (bottom) Carlisle Cathedral, vault of spiral staircase in the chancel, early fourteenth century

29 (top) Dacre Castle, early fourteenth century
30 (bottom left) Newton Arlosh church, licensed 1304, west tower
31 (bottom right) Kirkandrews Tower, sixteenth century (first half)
(*Copyright Country Life*)

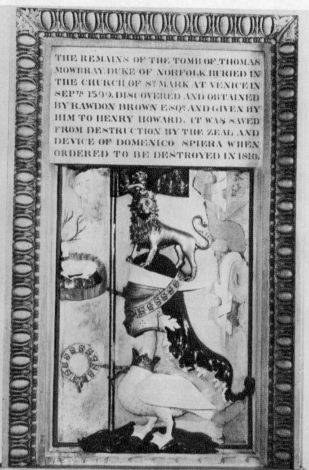

THE REMAINS OF THE TOMB OF THOMAS
MOWBRAY DUKE OF NORFOLK BURIED IN
THE CHURCH OF St MARK AT VENICE IN
SEPtr 1399, DISCOVERED AND OBTAINED
BY RAWDON BROWN ESQr AND GIVEN BY
HIM TO HENRY HOWARD. IT WAS SAVED
FROM DESTRUCTION BY THE ZEAL AND
DEVICE OF DOMENICO SPIERA WHEN
ORDERED TO BE DESTROYED IN 1810.

"MANY A TIME HATH BANISH'D NORFOLK FOUGHT
FOR JESU CHRIST, IN GLORIOUS CHRISTIAN FIELD -
STREAMING THE ENSIGN OF THE CHRISTIAN CROSS,
AGAINST BLACK PAGANS, TURKS AND SARACENS:
AND, TOIL'D WITH WORKS OF WAR, RETIR'D HIMSELF
TO ITALY: AND THERE, AT VENICE, GAVE
HIS BODY TO THAT PLEASANT COUNTRY'S EARTH."

34 (left) Corby Castle, monument to Thomas Mowbray, Duke of Norfolk, †1399 (*Copyright Country Life*)

35 (right) Carlisle Castle, prisoners' carvings, fourteenth and fifteenth centuries

36 (bottom right) Greystoke church, stained glass in the east window, fifteenth century

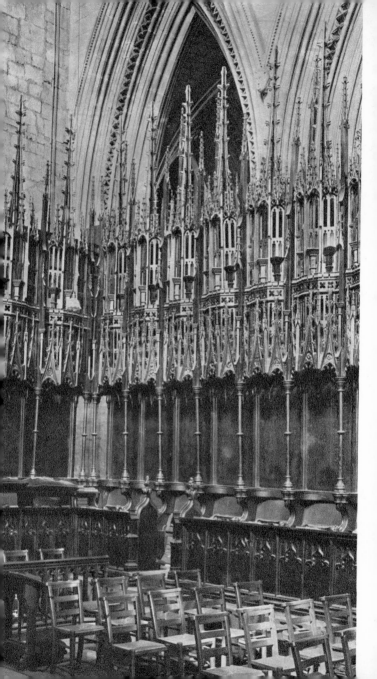

37 (left) Carlisle Cathedral, stalls, canopies after 1430
38 (below) Naworth Castle, Crucifixion, German, 1514
39 (bottom) Carlisle Cathedral, Prior Salkeld's screen, after 1541

40 (left) Naworth
Castle, courtyard,
c. 1520

41 (bottom left)
Arthuret church,
begun 1609

42 (right) Abbey
Town, Holme
Cultram Abbey,
east window,
c. 1605 (?)

43 (bottom right)
Warwick, Whoof
House, window from
Arthuret church,
c. 1650-75 (?)

44 (left) Newton Reigny, Catterlen Hall, doorway, c. 1650–60

45 (below) Lorton Hall, pele tower and range of 1663

46 (right) Dalston Hall, garden front, late (?) seventeenth century and c. 1500

47 (bottom right) Hutton-in-the-Forest, east front, gallery wing 1641/5, centrepiece c. 1680

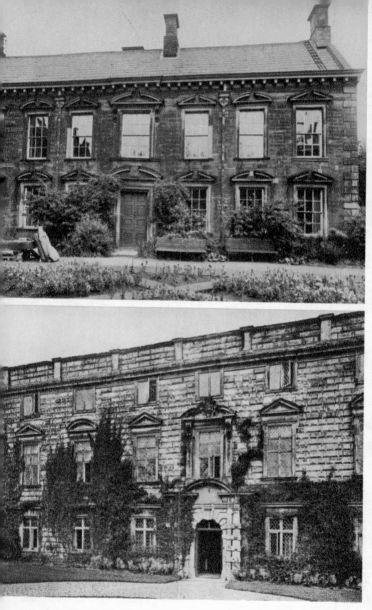

48 (top) Carlisle, Tullie House, 1689
49 (bottom) Moresby Hall, *c.* 1690–1700

50 (top) Dalemain, east front, *c.* 1740–50 (*Copyright Country Life*)
51 (bottom) Penrith church, 1720–2

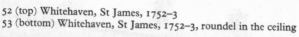

52 (top) Whitehaven, St James, 1752–3
53 (bottom) Whitehaven, St James, 1752–3, roundel in the ceiling

54 (top) Mungrisdale church, 1756
55 (bottom) Cockermouth, Wordsworth House, mid eighteenth century

56 (below) Wetheral church, monument to Lady Maria Howard † 1789 by Joseph Nollekens (*Copyright Country Life*)
57 (bottom) Sebergham church, relief from monument to Thomas Watson † 1823 by M. L. Watson
58 (right) Crosthwaite church, slate gravestone to Joseph Dover † 1810

Sacred to the Memory of

JOSEPH DOVER Woollen Manufacturer, KESWICK, WHO
died on the 24th of Sept.r 1810, aged 85 years.

Also of E S T H E R his Wife,
who died on the 21st of June 1797, aged 70 years.

Also of Sarah their Daughter, who died July the 18.th 1768,
AGED 17 YEARS,

Also of JOHN DOVER their Son, of FORGE NEAR Keswick
Who died on the 2.d of April 1839, aged 85 years.

Also of William Dover their Son, of Caldbeck in this County
who died on the 10.th of May 1797, aged 41 years.

Also of ANN their Daughter, who died 1762, aged 3 years,

Also of Dinah their Daughter, Wife of Christopher Hodgson of
Causewayfoot, who died Dec.r the 12th 1807, aged 46 years

Also of JOSEPH DOVER their Son, who died March 29.th 1765
AGED 1 YEAR,

Also of Esther their Daughter, Wife of William Christopherson
of Keswick, who died August the 8th 1823, aged 66 years.

Also of Mary Dover their Daughter who died
April 29th 1803, aged 34 years.

DANIEL DOVER of Skiddaw Bank their Youngest SON & only SURVIVER
caused this Stone to be Erected in gratefull remembrance, March 28.th 1840

WHO DEPARTED THIS LIFE APRIL 20TH 1842
IN THE 70TH YEAR OF HIS AGE.

Also of Martha his Wife, who died
August the 31st 1843, Aged 59 years.

59 (top left) Carlisle, Assize Courts, by Sir Robert Smirke, 1810–11
60 (left) Carlisle, Holy Trinity, by Rickman & Hutchinson, 1828–30
61 (above) Workington, St John, by Thomas Hardwick, 1823, tower 1846

62 (above) Carlisle, Cumberland Infirmary, by Robert Tattersall, 1830–2
63 (right) Carlisle, Dixon's Mills (Shaddon Works), by Robert Tattersall, 1836

64 (left) Wreay church, by Sara Losh, consecrated 1842
65 (bottom left) Wreay church, window
66 (below) Wigton, Market Place, fountain, relief by Thomas Woolner, 1871

67 (above) Brampton church, by Philip Webb, 1874–8
68 (top right) Brampton, Four Gables, by Philip Webb, 1876–8
69 (right) Plumpton Wall, Brackenburgh Tower, by Sir Robert Lorimer,
1903

70 *Scenery :* Ullswater, looking towards Patterdale
71 (above right) *Scenery :* Appleby, High Cup Nick
72 (below right) *Villagescape :* Bowness-on-Windermere, The Rectory

73 (left) *Scenery*:
Kirkby Lonsdale,
The Devil's Bridge,
fifteenth century

74 (top right)
Heversham church,
cross shaft, ninth
century

75 (bottom right)
Kirkby Lonsdale
church, north arcade,
c. 1115

76 (top left) Long
Marton church,
south doorway,
tympanum,
eleventh century (?)

77 (bottom left)
Bolton church, relief
of knights on horse-
back, Norman

78 (top right)
Brougham Castle,
keep, c. 1175

79 (bottom right)
Brougham Castle,
keep, chapel, c. 1300

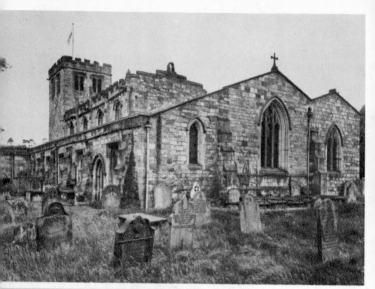

80 (top) Appleby church, early fourteenth century and later
81 (bottom) Askham Hall, tower wing, late fourteenth century and
c. 1685–90
82 (right) Bowness-on-Windermere church, stained glass, late fifteenth
century

83 (above) Cliburn Hall, 1567
84 (right) Sizergh Castle, Morning Room, chimneypiece, 1563

87 (top left) Grasmere church, roof, seventeenth century

88 (bottom left) Appleby church, monument of Margaret, Countess of Cumberland, 1617

89 (right) Ambleside church, Cup and Steeple Cover, 1618

90 (top left) Brougham, St Wilfrid's Chapel, screen, *c.* 1660 (?)
91 (bottom left) Appleby Castle, east range, 1686–8
92 (below) Lowther church, monument of John, Viscount Lonsdale,
† 1700 by William Stanton
93 (bottom) Lowther Village, by James Adam (?), begun *c.* 1765

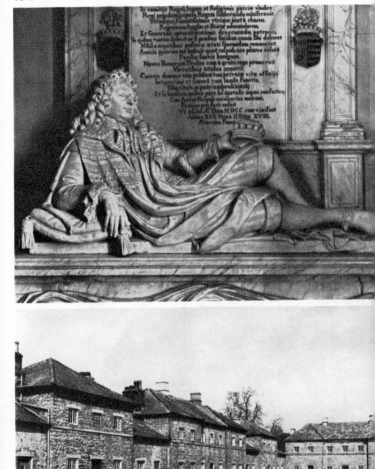

94 (left) Appleby, White House, 1756
95 (bottom left) Bowness-on-Windermere, Belle Isle, by John Plaw, 1774
96 (below) Lowther Castle, by Sir Robert Smirke, 1806–11

97 (above) Underley Hall, by G. Webster, 1825
98 (top right) Bampton church, columns 1726–8, the rest 1885
99 (bottom right) Bowness-on-Windermere, Blackwell, by M. H. Baillie
Scott, 1900, hall

100 Bowness-on-Windermere, Matson Ground, by Basil Ward, 1961

MAWBRAY see HOLME ST CUTHBERT

MEALSGATE
2040

OLD ALL HALLOWS, E of Whitehall (see below). Norman. The chancel only is preserved, including the chancel arch, which is now blocked and has set against it the plain Grecian MONUMENT to Thomas Moore † 1876 (by *John Adams-Acton*).

NEW ALL HALLOWS. 1896–9 by *Ferguson*. Nave and chancel and a low W tower. Some of the small details outside and inside tell of the sophistication with which the Gothic style was handled about 1900. Grouped lancets and single lancets; wide nave; no aisles. A satisfying, honest interior. – The BENCHES help much to achieve that effect.

HARBYBROW TOWER, ⅞ m. SSE of the new church. The MHLG refers to a former inscription of 1594, and the preserved inscription (in the farmhouse) referring to the prices of wheat, barley, and malt in a year when prices were very exceptional, and that year is 4th Edward VI. But the pele tower must be older, cf. the cusped lights of the two-light windows, i.e. a C15 motif. The ground level is vaulted as usual.

WHITEHALL, ¾ m. SE. By *Salvin*, 1861–2 for George Moore, but the pele tower is original. An inscription with 'hoc fieri fecit' refers to Laurence Salkeld and the year 1589. Even that was no doubt only a restoration. But in 1794 the house was called ruinous.

BEARTREE HOUSE, Blennerhasset Green. The house is dated 1686, and one motif points to that date. The hood-moulds of the two ground-floor windows form a continuous band which rises above the middle doorway.

MELMERBY
6030

ST JOHN BAPTIST. The position of tower and chancel show that the church must have had an aisle and arcade. The church looks in its present state mostly Victorian (1849 ? 1895 ?). The tower is entirely Victorian and has a higher stair-turret. In the N wall two late medieval windows and a blocked one in the S wall high up. In the short chancel to the N is a triple-chamfered arch dying into the imposts. What was its job ? – PLATE. Cup, 1742.*

(MELMERBY HALL. One wing early C17, another 1658. The latter has cross-windows. The front block is C18, of three storeys. MHLG)

1080

MILLOM

HOLY TRINITY, s of the castle. Red sandstone. A Late Norman church – cf. the N doorway with one order of (C19) shafts and a manifoldly moulded arch, one chancel N window,‡ and the plain s doorway. To this church a s aisle was added in the early C13 – see the two round piers with octagonal abaci. This aisle was rebuilt and probably enlarged in the early C14 – see the broad and somewhat bald flowing tracery of one s window, the almond-shaped w window (with C19 tracery; cf. Brigham), and the E pier and w respond of the arcade. Most of the detail of the church belongs to the Victorian restorations. But what does the wide blocked arch in the w wall of the nave stand for ? – Handsome WEST GALLERY of 1930. – COMMUNION RAIL. Partly of c. 1630. – BOX PEWS. – PLATE. Cup with band of ornament and Cover Paten of 1634; Paten of 1696; Cup given in 1710. – MONUMENTS. Alabaster effigies of Sir John Hudleston † 1494 and his wife. The tomb-chest has stiffly frontal angels under ogee canopies, a type familiar from many places. But at Millom on the long side at the feet of the angels kneel little daughters, on the one visible short side little sons. – Another tomb-chest, C16, with very coarse shields. – Sir Joseph Huddlestone † 1700 and his wife † 1714. Standing monument without figures. Pilasters and pediment.

CASTLE. The ruins of the castle now closely surround the farmhouse, which partly occupies the mighty pele tower. The castle has an oddly congested plan with a minimum of courtyard. E of this is the gatehouse, s the great chamber is assumed, N the kitchen, W of that the great hall, and s of the great hall and almost touching on the E side the great chamber is the pele. Licence to crenellate was given in 1335, and of that date are the hall and the supposed great chamber with the wall continuing it to the w just s of the pele, and probably also the gatehouse in the E wall. The kitchen is connected with the hall by two doorways. So this was services in general. Of the

---

* A Chalice and Paten 'of base metal' were found in a grave.

‡ In 1930 the chancel, except for the E wall, was pulled down and rebuilt 6 ft wider.

hall N windows one remains, with a two-centred arch. The great chamber was on the first floor. Its windows have round rere-arches, and it has a large fireplace. Below, on the ground floor, is a fireplace too, but this has its flue simply through the wall with a finial to the smoke-hole. The doorway from the courtyard has an ogee head. The pele tower is assigned to the C15 or C16. It is divided by a wall. The ground level is vaulted in two parallel tunnel-vaults. Four floors follow. The original entrance was on the first floor from the E. There were here three, not two rooms. The staircase in the NE corner starts from here. On the second floor were again two rooms only, and they seem to have been connected originally by a passage in the S wall accessible through two small doors.

The town of Millom developed S of the castle and church.

HOLY TRINITY. The new church built in 1874–7 by *Paley & Austin* is a sign of industrial prosperity. Large, of red sandstone, with a central tower with recessed spire. Geometrical tracery of varied patterns. The N transept is the organ chamber, and hence the N wall is blank. It has free tracery, including ogees. The nave has a N aisle and a wooden wagon roof.

The new Millom is laid out regularly. The MARKET PLACE in particular is evidently a piece of regular layout. In the middle of the side recessed from the street is the MARKET HOUSE, symmetrical, Tudor, with a domed porch. Kelly dates it 1879, but it looks rather 1890, and the three stately BANKS facing it also look about that date. One of them indeed carries the date 1892.

LACRA STONE CIRCLES, 2 m. NW, ¾ m. N of the A 5093 to Kirksanton and 300 yds SW of Lacra. The S site consists of three standing stones – all that remains of a former circle. 300 yds NE is an oval setting of stones, 60 ft in maximum diameter. An Early Bronze Age collared urn was found at the base of one of the stones. WSW of this site a scatter of half-buried boulders may indicate an avenue. To the W is a third circle, 48 ft in diameter, consisting of six stones. At the centre is a low cairn, 32 ft in diameter, beneath which was found a cremation burial without grave goods.

STONE CIRCLE, 5 m. N, 1 m. NW of Crag Hall and to the r. of the path to Swinside. The circle is composed of fifty-five stones and has a diameter of 90 ft. Two outlying stones form an entrance on the SE. The site was excavated in 1961, without significant results.

MILLRIGG *see* CULGAITH

MIRE HOUSE *see* BASSENTHWAITE

MOORHOUSE *see* BURGH-BY-SANDS

9020   MORESBY

ST BRIDGET. 1822–3 by *G. Crauford*. w tower with round bell-openings and nave of four bays. Two tiers of arched side windows. The chancel with its Venetian E window and pediment is of 1885, quite amazingly convincing. Fine w view to the sea. The interior all of 1885. – WEST GALLERY on cast-iron columns with Gothic spandrels. – PLATE. Cup and Cover Paten, 1774. – In the churchyard the CHANCEL ARCH of the former church, with semicircular responds.

The site of a 3½-acre ROMAN FORT exists on the plateau between the churchyard and the steep slope down to the sea. A Hadrianic inscription shows that the stone fort was built in, or very soon after, 128. An extensive civil settlement is known to the SE.

49 MORESBY HALL. An eminently interesting building with a splendid façade of *c.*1690–1700. It is all rusticated, as if it were in Bohemia. Seven bays, two and a half storeys. The doorway has pilasters crossed by bands, tied, as it were, to them by lozenge-shaped nails. Broken segmental pediment. The upper windows have alternatingly segmental and triangular pediments. The middle one is on brackets. The windows themselves still have stone crosses below and even two transoms above. Moulded window-frames. But behind all this lies an older building, a pele tower with its spiral staircase only just recognizable and a hall annex with mullioned and transomed windows. The two parts are separated by a courtyard made very narrow by the projecting staircase of the front range. The balusters are of dumb-bell type, inverted. The end of the hall range must have been the kitchen; for here is an enormous chimneybreast.

ROSEHILL, ¼ m. NE. Handsome late C18 house with a long garden front with two canted bay windows and a boldly forward-curving centre on the entrance side with Greek Doric columns *in antis*. The loggia thus formed is oval, and the entrance hall circular. A recent addition to the house, at a very small distance, is the THEATRE, weatherboarded and inside with the pedimented proscenium of the Music Hall of the

Royal Standard Inn at Whitehaven. In the parapet of the W gallery four painted panels. The interior of the theatre was designed by *Oliver Messel*.

MORTON MANOR *see* CARLISLE, p. 104

MOSSER

1020

ST MICHAEL. 1773. Small, of nave with bellcote and chancel. Plain oblong windows, plain oblong doorway. The type of the dale chapels preserved that late.

JOHN DALTON MEMORIAL CHURCH. *See* Eaglesfield.

MUNCASTER

1090

ST MICHAEL. Low, with a bellcote. Lower chancel. The chancel windows look Late Perp, the nave windows are plainly mullioned. *Salvin* in 1874 added the N transept and made the handsome Dec tracery partition between the annex E of it and the chancel. – STAINED GLASS. The chancel side windows and one S window by *Holiday*, 1882 and 1887. – SCULPTURE. In the churchyard a CROSS SHAFT with broad, flat, defaced plaiting. – Next to it a wheel-head. – PLATE. Cup and Paten Cover, 1680. – MONUMENTS. Brass Plates to ancestors in a fake ancient script, put up by the first Lord Muncaster († 1813) some time in the late C18.

MUNCASTER CASTLE. In a superb position and with beautifully landscaped gardens, including the famous Terrace Walk. One can say that the castle is by *Anthony Salvin* and was built in 1862–6 (DNB) for the fourth Lord Muncaster. (The Lords Muncaster are of the Pennington family.) In fact the castle incorporated parts of a medieval castle, including the pele tower. It was in an excellent strategic position on a spur in the Esk estuary. The tower is at the SW end and was matched by Salvin with a second, NW tower.

The original tower is tunnel-vaulted at ground level, and it has a spiral staircase in the NE corner (and another from the first to the ground floor in the SW corner). The entrance was by the NE staircase on the ground floor. On the top floor are remains of the tracery of the windows. The medieval walls of the house extended N from the NE corner of the tower, and it is not certain how much of them remains. There are in any case no features. The features are all Salvin's, except that the octagonal library E of the tower seems to be part of a remodelling in the late C18. But, as it is now, it is internally as well as externally by Salvin. He did a competent job all round, with towers, battlements, and mullioned and transomed windows. The main rooms are the Library with its ribbed ceiling and the handsome, perfectly simple brass railing of the gallery, the large Drawing Room with a coved ceiling, and the former Billiard Room with an oblong skylight. In the house are three sumptuous Elizabethan stone chimneypieces, said to come from somewhere else, a number of wooden Jacobean or Elizabethan chimneypieces, and a beautiful late C18 white-marble chimneypiece from Bulstrode. This has figures of Apollo and Diana and a lintel with Apollo and the Nine Muses. One of the Elizabethan pieces has two tiers of caryatids and atlantes, and all three have intricate strapwork.

The STABLES have a Gothick screen wall with blank quatrefoils and cross-slits.

The same style in a more Vanbrughian vein appears in the MONUMENT to the meeting of Henry VI with the shepherd in 1461. This lies $\frac{7}{8}$ m. NE and is a broad, three-storeyed tower on an octagonal plan with an octagonal spire. The top storey has lancets, the floor below cross-slits, the ground floor round openings high up. It is entered by a broad, pointed doorway and is domed inside. The date is most probably the late C18.

BARNSCAR CAIRNFIELD. On the S slope of Birkby Fell and extending for over $\frac{1}{2}$ m. are numerous small cairns, 15–25 ft in diameter, and a group of enclosures or large hut circles. A number of examples of each class have been excavated. In the C19, Early Bronze Age collared urns were found beneath some of the cairns. The excavation of ten further cairns in 1957–8 failed to produce evidence of burials, but indicated that they were built structures and not merely field clearance heaps.

CAIRNS. $2\frac{1}{2}$ m. NW of Ulpha and W of Devoke Water, in the area known as Birker Fell, are over one thousand small round cairns, occurring in groups of up to two hundred and fifty. Most of the sites occur between 750 and 850 ft. The majority have diameters between 12 and 20 ft. None have been excavated, and nothing is known of their date.

3030

MUNGRISDALE

54 ST KENTIGERN. 1756. Nave and chancel in one with arched windows with keystones. Bellcote. – PULPIT. A three-decker,

the lower panels C17 (one is dated 1679), but the pulpit itself no doubt of the time of the church. – Some BOX PEWS, also later C17. – PLATE. Cup and Cover Paten, 1600.

(THWAITE HALL. An inscription says: Rebuilt 1555, modernized 1870. Huge stone chimney and water spout, all in the C16 style. Mrs Davies)

CARROCK FELL HILLFORT, 1 m. NW of the path from Mosedale to High Row and over the boundary with Hesket Newmarket parish. The fort is univallate, and the rampart encloses a roughly oval area of five acres. The bank is stone-faced and survives to a height of 5 ft in some places. Traces of an inner face are visible, indicating an original width of 13 ft for the defences. Within the fort at the E summit of the enclosed area is an oval CAIRN, 50 ft in maximum diameter. The slabs of a stone cist are visible projecting from its centre.

CAIRNS, 1 m. S of Carrock Beck and W of the footpath from Mosedale to High Row. There are over two hundred small round cairns and ring cairns on the lower slopes of Carrock Fell. An example of each category has been excavated. The round cairn covered a central pit containing an unaccompanied cremation. Evidence of burning, but no burial, was found in the ring cairn.

NAWORTH CASTLE 5060

Ranulph of Dacre received licence to crenellate in 1335. The site was excellently chosen for defence, with a steep fall on three sides. About 1520 Thomas Lord Dacre altered and added. In 1604 Lord William Howard, third son of the Duke of Norfolk, came into possession, through his wife, who was a Dacre. The estates also included Henderskelf, the future Castle Howard. Lord William converted the castle into a mansion. Then nothing more was done, i.e. no Georgian interiors were created, until after a disastrous fire in 1844 *Salvin* got to work. He freshened up everything but seems to have added little of his own. Where drawings exist of before the fire, they show how faithful to the old Salvin was.

The castle had its outer GATEHOUSE S of the S front. It has the Dacre arms, but they and the whole building are much renewed. The so-called BOAT HOUSE to its E, projecting into the moat, has the Dacre initials in the top frieze. It is not known what purpose it served. The archway into the courtyard is from the W. It is curiously thin and undefended. The main fronts of the castle are as follows. The S side has the Dacre Tower with a higher stair-turret in the SW corner, and Lord William Howard's Tower, also of the Dacre time, in the SE corner. In the range between was the chapel (later library) and other rooms. The chapel windows to the courtyard are much larger than any of the others, except for the high-table bay window of the great hall. All these have close panel tracery. The hall is in the E range, N of Lord William Howard's Tower. Lord William's tower to this side has a strange mid-recess and corbelling out inside it. There is also a garderobe higher up. The top masonry of the tower is different and may be a renewal of Lord William's – cf. the interior. The tower which follows is Salvin's. The N range is of less interest. In the W range N of the archway is another garderobe projection.

The GREAT HALL is the largest in the county (78 by 24 ft). It has a large fireplace with segmental head. The oaken beasts are supposed to be of Dacre's time. The roof is Salvin's. At the foot of Dacre's Tower is that rare survival, a yatt, i.e. a door of iron bars (cf. Dalston Hall, Cawdor Castle, and Burgh-by-Sands church). In the LIBRARY is an overmantel with the Battle of Flodden Field in gesso. This was designed by *Burne-Jones*, modelled by *Sir E. Boehm*, and painted by Burne-Jones. The most interesting part of the castle is LORD WILLIAM HOWARD'S TOWER. Here, on the first floor, there is the most astonishing strengthening inside by big, broad ribs, square in section and set diagonally across. There is no parallel to this in England. In the room above is a Howard fireplace, and in the room on the third floor a marvellous timber ceiling from Kirkoswald Castle. It has richly moulded beams and bosses, and the panels have all got a blank window pattern with gorgeous flowing tracery. It cannot be later than c.1350. In the small ORATORY next to it is a German PAINTING dated 1514 and representing the Flagellation, the Crucifixion, and the Resurrection. How did it get here? – There are also parts of a very rich SCREEN from Lanercost with crocketed ogee panels.

(In the park THE STONE HOUSE, a ruined C16 bastle-house, i.e. a house with provision for cattle on the ground floor, and the living quarters with small barred windows on the upper floor.)*

* Information kindly given me by Mr Robin McDowall.

NENTHEAD

7040

ST JOHN. The polygonal bell-turret probably part of the original church of 1845 (by *Bonomi & Cory*), but the fenestration must be of a restoration, presumably that of 1907 (by *Hicks & Charlewood*). Dec tracery, also flowing.

FOUNTAIN, at the main crossing. With a dome and florid detail. 1877 by the *London Lead Company*. There was much mining around here, of which traces can be seen.

Nenthead was built in the early C19 as a model village.

NETHERBY HALL

3070

2 m. NE of Longtown

A curiously deceptive house. As one approaches it, it seems entirely Early Victorian, though surprisingly provided with reiterated Gibbs motifs. In fact the three plain l. and three plain r. bays might well be mid C18. The rest is baronial with some Jacobean touches, and the last thing one would expect is the real pele tower hiding behind the seemingly Victorian tower with its comical knight in a niche. For his work, *William Burn* took his cue not only from the existing C15 tower but also from the garden front, which, with its two broad bay windows and the three bays between, is indeed of the mid C18, except for the top frills. Burn's drawings at the RIBA are dated 1833, and some of the armorial GLASS in the hall was done by *Willement* in 1836.* All this is remarkably early for a façade which one would without hesitation date *c*.1850. The house was Graham property from the C16. Dr Robert Graham came into possession in 1757. Inside, on the garden side, of his time are one room with an excellent plaster ceiling, one rounded room with two niches, and one room with wall pilasters. The other rooms are mostly Victorian, especially the staircase. But the hall and the dining room have C17 panelling with many small religious scenes and also barley-sugar columns said to come from a Belgian abbey.

SUSPENSION BRIDGE to Kirkandrews. 1877, but looks earlier. It is a pedestrian bridge, only 4 ft wide.

Netherby is the site of a FORT serving as an outpost to HADRIAN'S WALL.

---

* Jefferson in 1838 includes the recent alterations.

NETHER DENTON *see* DENTON

NETHER END *see* HENSINGHAM

NETHERWASDALE *see* STRANDS

NEWBIGGIN *see* AINSTABLE

NEWBIGGIN HALL
3¾ m. SE of Carlisle

4050

This was a house of the priors of Carlisle and has a pele tower with basement vault and spiral staircase, even if all this is now hidden by a symmetrical seven-bay façade. The doorway has a curly open pediment, probably of *c.*1720. The same pediments over the tripartite side windows are probably echoes of a hundred years later, i.e. of the time when the staircase received its Gothick plaster rib-vault and its Grecian details, and when the end-gable was made stepped and a Gothick outbuilding erected. Close to this is an ICEHOUSE, just a grassy bump.

NEWLANDS

2020

CHURCH. 1843; restored 1885. Small, of nave and chancel in one, with round-headed windows.

NEWTON ARLOSH

1050

Newton is Newtown, the new town founded in 1305 by Holme Cultram Abbey after Skinburness, a town with a market in the C13, had been swept into the sea in 1301. As a new town, Arlosh is a disappointment. One ought not to think of Montpazier or even New Winchelsea. There is nothing planned about it.

30 ST JOHN BAPTIST. Licensed in 1304. The w tower was intended to be defensible, i.e. it has no outer doorway and only small windows, including a ground-level w slit. A doorway into the tower was from inside at first-floor level. The ground level is tunnel-vaulted.* At the top a turret projected on corbels. The s wall of the nave also exists, but in 1844, for parish purposes, the church was built from that wall northward with a chancel facing N. This addition, though made for Sara Losh (*see* Wreay), is in the usual lancet style. Moreover, in

---

* Cf. Burgh-by-Sands and Great Salkeld.

1894 an apse was added to the E of the parochial nave to re-establish orientation. – FONT. Octagonal, with crocketed gables. The bottom part is fragmentary. There was probably no stem. The most likely date is the C14.

NEWTON REIGNY
<small>4030</small>

ST JOHN. Nave with bellcote, aisles, and higher chancel, the latter 1876 by *Ewan Christian*. The interior is all late C12 to C13. First the S arcade: round piers, round abaci, and pointed arches of only slight double chamfers. Then the chancel arch, and then the N arcade with octagonal piers and normally double-chamfered arches. – PLATE. Cup with ornamental band and Cover Paten, 1568.

CATTERLEN HALL, ¼ m. N. An L-shaped building of considerable interest, consisting of a small pele tower at the N end, vaulted in the basement and with a spiral stair in the SW corner, then a hall range of 1577 S of it, still with the typical Henry VIII windows and a C17 spiral stair projection on the W side, and then the other arm of the L projecting to the E from the S end. This dates from *c.*1650–60 and has a large room on the upper floor reached by an outer staircase. The doorway is wild and gorgeous, with jambs with alternating raised bands fastened, as it were, by lozenge pegs (cf. Moresby Hall). The arch is even more fanciful. In the apex are corbel-like forms, and they include a bit of dog-tooth, surely a conscious archaism. The centre of the range is also stressed by a pedimental gable. The windows l. and r. and at the back are plainly mullioned. Inside two rich stone chimneypieces, the bigger one with enormous scroll supports. The detail of the lintels is much the same as that of a chimneypiece in the adjoining S corner room of the older range, and this is dated 1657. It has funny caryatids. To return to the pele tower, most of its windows are straight-headed with cusped arches, i.e. of the C15. There is also one larger and later window (uncusped arches). To the W at the top are corbels formerly carrying a wooden platform for defence.

NICHOLFOREST
<small>4070</small>

ST NICHOLAS. By *Alexander Graham*, 1866–7. Rock-faced; nave and chancel with apse. Funny wooden bell-turret with spire. Plate and bar tracery, e.g. a plate-tracery W rose window. The wooden porch is eminently Victorian.

(STONEHOUSE, 1¾ m. NNE. A pele tower in ruins. Parts of two walls stand up to *c*.12 ft. MHLG)

STONEGARTHSIDE HALL, 3 m. NE. An unusual and forbidding-looking three-storeyed house on an H-plan with four stepped gables. It carries a date 1682.

LONG CAIRN, 2½ m. NE of St Cuthbert's Hall, in Kershope Forest. The cairn is wedge-shaped in plan, 130 ft long and 70 ft wide at its broader, NW end. The mound has been considerably disturbed, and much of its material has been removed for building stone.

THE NUNNERY *see* KIRKOSWALD

NUNWICK HALL *see* GREAT SALKELD

OLD CARLISLE *see* WIGTON

OLD PENRITH *see* PENRITH

OLD WALL *see* IRTHINGTON

ORMATHWAITE HALL *see* CROSTHWAITE

ORTHWAITE HALL *see* BASSENTHWAITE

3050 ORTON

ST GILES. Nave with bellcote and chancel. In the chancel one Norman S and one Norman N window. Also on the N side a length of nailhead. Plain Georgian nave. – PULPIT and FONT COVER are neo-Norman. – PLATE. Cup and Paten Cover, probably 1570; specially good.

7 (CRUCK BARN. With crucks, as the name indicates. NMR)

ORTON PARK, 2 m. SE. An unusual Latest Georgian building. The garden side is of five bays and has giant pilasters throughout. On the entrance side the rhythm marked by giant pilasters is 2 – 3 – 2. Greek Doric porch of four columns. On the gate lodge is a date 1839.

6030 OUSBY

ST LUKE. Outside the village, to the E. Mostly of 1858, but one lancet window on the S side may be E.E., and so is what little is original of the SEDILIA and PISCINA. – PLATE. Cup of 1672; Paten of *c*.1700. – MONUMENT. Excellent, elegant oak effigy of a Knight with crossed legs; early C14.

HALL FARM, at the SW end of the village. Dated 1743 and entirely classical, which in other counties would be nothing remarkable. Five bays with sash windows and a segmental pediment over the doorway.

(RAYSON HALL, Townhead, ¾ m. SE. Doorway with carved label-stops and the date 1606. MHLG)

PAPCASTLE see COCKERMOUTH

PARDSHAW see DEAN

PELHAM HOUSE see CALDER BRIDGE

PENRITH

ST ANDREW. Built in 1720–2, and the stateliest church of its time in the county. Red sandstone. Only the W tower was kept of the preceding building. It has a minimum of small openings and only the bell-openings are larger: two pairs of straight-headed two-light openings with cusped arches for the lights. The doorway with Tuscan columns, triglyph frieze, and pediment is of course of 1720–2. The sides are of eight bays. Two tiers of round-arched windows separated vertically by very broad pilasters. At the angles they are rusticated. The chancel is of two bays, and the E window is of the Venetian type, very large, under one arch and with blunt details. Inside, the W tower has a handsome two-arm staircase up to a gallery. Three balusters to the tread. The chancel arch is of two chamfered orders and dies into the imposts. The body of the church has three galleries on Tuscan columns, with long, thin, quasi-Tuscan columns above. – FONT. Plain octagonal bowl, dated 1661. On the tower gallery. – PULPIT. Probably of c.1725. Fluted angle colonnettes; arched panels. – CHANDELIERS. Of brass, in a usual Baroque shape, given in 1745. – PAINTING. In the chancel Agony in the Garden and Angels appearing to the Shepherds. By *Jacob Thompson*. They are wall paintings, filling the side walls of the E end and running up into the vault. – STAINED GLASS. Many fragments of the C15 in a N aisle window. In a S aisle window (Neville window) just two heads. – SCULPTURE. In the churchyard the GIANT'S GRAVE and the GIANT'S THUMB, the former displayed as a group with the hogbacks (see below). The group stands N of the N wall of the church, the Thumb NW of the W tower. The Giant's Grave is two crosses, the Giant's Thumb one. They seem to date from c.1000. Kendrick calls the Giant's Grave crosses 'the Cumberland type proper' and derives them from the crosses of the Peak District. They are characterized by the shafts being round in their lower half and then turning square with four lunettes at the transition – cf. Gosforth and Beckermet St Bridget. Compared with Gosforth, they are a good deal coarser. In detail the W cross of the Giant's Grave is over 11 ft high and has much interlace and an unusually small cross-head. The arms of the cross are free. The E cross is 10 ft 6 in. high and has interlace too, but on one side a bound figure with a woman next to him, and a serpent above his head. Above the serpent is the Agnus Dei. The head of the cross is again free. The Giant's Thumb is shorter. Its head is of the wheel type, and it has on its sides interlace, but also a close scroll in the Anglian tradition. – PLATE. Pair of Chalices, 1678; Paten, 1706; silver-gilt Cup and Paten, 1740. – MONUMENTS. Four sides of hogback coffins in the churchyard, between the two crosses of the Giant's Grave. They are of red sandstone and have interlace of various kinds, except for one with a snake and a small figure standing on the head of the snake. The motif seems to be repeated. – In the tower hall the upper part of a specially good C13 coffin lid with foliated cross. – Anthony Hutton and wife † 1637 (tower gallery), two badly preserved stone effigies, broadly treated. – Robert Vertue † 1846. Odd Gothic mausoleum in the churchyard, or rather two piers with tracery between.

ST CATHERINE (R.C.), Drovers Lane, 1850 by *Atkinson* of Carlisle.* Cruciform, without a tower. The tracery geometrical to Dec. – STAINED GLASS by *Francis Barnett* of Edinburgh.

CHRIST CHURCH, Stricklandgate. 1850 by *Travis & Mangnall*.‡ Thin W bell-turret on a mid-buttress. Nave and aisles; dull. The Perp tracery is of plaster and looks later.

Some of the NONCONFORMIST CHAPELS are quite an object lesson: the FRIENDS in Meeting House Lane, just a plain C18 house, with two galleries inside; then the METHODISTS in Sandgate, 1815, large, of three by three bays with a three-bay pediment, a doorway with Tuscan columns and a broken

---

* J. Walker says: enlarged by *John Seed* in 1860.
‡ Tender £2500 (GS).

pediment, and arched windows in two tiers – the proper
spacious Late Georgian preaching box; but then the Methodists, again in Drovers Lane, 1872 and now a showy Italianate,
also large and also pedimented; and finally the CONGREGA-
TIONALS in Duke Street, 1866, all churchy, with an asymmetrically placed steeple and geometrical tracery.

CASTLE. Penrith Castle is very different from all other Cumberland castles. Licence to crenellate was given to William
Strickland, later Bishop of Carlisle and Archbishop of
Canterbury, in 1397 and 1399, and so he built one of those
massive, compact square structures with four ranges round a
courtyard. It is the type of Bolton Castle in the North Riding,
though without the regular angle towers. Penrith has instead
just one tower projecting on the E side and one projecting on
the N side close to the E corner. Next to this was the gateway
provided with forebuildings later in the C15, at the time of
Richard Duke of Gloucester, i.e. the 1470s. The hall range
was on the S, with the solar continuing the hall to the E, and
the kitchen was in the W range next to the hall. As one
examines the castle, the most impressive part is the S wall,
standing up to a considerable height. It is quite sheer, except
for a mid-buttress and a diagonal SW angle-buttress. The W
wall was treated in the same way. The S range has only a few
slits at ground-floor level, and only small windows for hall and
solar also – at least to the outside. Of the inside wall we know
nothing. The large clerestory windows with four-centred
heads are attributed to the 1470s. Several fireplaces are easily
recognized. High up also stands the E tower. Of the NE
tower one wall stands, and the tunnel-vault of the basement.
S of the E tower was a second, narrower, gateway. S of this, in
the SE angle, i.e. below the solar, an oven has been exposed.
Its smoke-hole is in the S wall.

TOWN HALL, Stricklandgate. 1905–6 by *J. J. Knewstubb*, a
local man. Converted out of two Adamish houses, of which
only two chimneypieces survive as features. The style is a
kind of Italianate, out-of-date by a whole generation after
1900.

GRAMMAR SCHOOL, Ullswater Road. Neo-Georgian, with
cupola and a doorway with curly pediment. By *Harrison &
Ash*, complete in 1915.

ROBINSON'S SCHOOL, Middlegate. Inscribed 1670, yet still
with mullioned windows. However, the way the hood-moulds
form a continuous frieze rising over each window is a sign of

lateness, and the two oval windows are of course entirely characteristic of *c*.1670.

PERAMBULATION. The centre of Penrith is intricate in its street pattern, and it is not easy to decide where to start and how to go. Moreover, the traffic on the A6 makes it almost impossible to see and to enjoy what one sees.

The main route coming from the S would be by KING STREET and on in that direction, with forays l. and r. In King Street, the MITRE HOTEL has a lintel of 1669 with an ogee motif, and the CROWN HOTEL a five-bay façade of 1794, red ashlar, three storeys, l. and r. bay windows with Tuscan columns, and a doorway with a pediment on columns with Adamish fluted capitals.

Up to the r. (NE) to BISHOP YARDS, by the church. Here first, SW of the church, a bay window dated 1563 and still with uncusped round-headed lights to the windows. After that a five-bay house with a doorway with broken pediment. Then the PARISH ROOMS, 1894 by *Watson & Son*, a big, red, gabled front with tiers of pilasters and a Baroque doorway. Then another five-bay house with the broken pediment over the doorway, and yet another with moulded window-frames and a doorway with a thin moulded surround. Opposite this, at an angle, the MANSION HOUSE, built in 1750, the grandest house in Penrith. Five bays, two and a half storeys, doorway with segmental pediment on brackets. The string course rises to the pediment. Projecting lower wings ending in Venetian windows. The arches of the windows have rustication of alternating sizes. The short links between wings and house must be later. They have Gothick motifs. As one continues in the direction of Bishop Yards, one joins FRIARGATE (named after the Austin Friars, who had a house at Penrith, founded in the C13, of which nothing remains), and at the N end of this is HUTTON HALL (Masonic Lodge), mid C18, with a red sandstone front of seven bays and a doorway with segmental pediment on brackets. (Inside, the original staircase and some plasterwork; MHLG. Also, according to Taylor, a Jacobean chimneypiece.) Attached also is a C15 pele tower with some later mullioned windows.

Back into King Street and on to the MARKET PLACE, an irregular area, with the utterly insignificant CLOCK TOWER of 1861, erected to commemorate Philip Musgrave of Edenhall who had died at the age of twenty-five. Off in ANGEL LANE a house dated 1763 on the double doorway, with moulded surround and one joint pediment, but with the fenestration of an extremely odd pattern. Ogee-headed windows l. and r. and a double-Venetian window in the middle, i.e. low, arched and high, arched and high, low. In the Market Place the GEORGE HOTEL; the well-done Georgian r. part is of 1924 and acts as a screen in front of the Market Hall. The middle part with tripartite windows, tripartite lunettes over, and a porch with Tuscan columns is also neo-Georgian, but the l. part is real Early Georgian, of six bays and three storeys, with a segmental pediment over the broad doorway. The Young Pretender had his headquarters here in 1745. Opposite the hotel a pretty double shop-front; late C18.

At its w end the Market Place is continued in an inarticulate way as Cornmarket and then merges into Great Dockray, another square of no determined shape. In the CORNMARKET, inside Messrs Pickering, is a fine staircase with twisted balusters. There are here two houses of interest. The GLOUCESTER ARMS* is said to date from c.1470 but has no feature older than the one Elizabethan cross window. There is a date 1580 on the house. (Inside is an overmantel with Elizabethan decoration. NMR) The TWO LIONS INN is of 1585 and has a plaster ceiling whose main motif is squares with lobes in the middle of each side. It was built for a Lowther.‡

Back to the Market Place and N, along Middlegate to CORNEY SQUARE. Off this, in HUNTER LANE, is CORNEY HOUSE. (This has one C13 impost to its archway, semi-octagonal, with nailhead decoration. NMR)

Houses a little further out must be taken singly. The order is by direction.

(COCKELL HOUSE, Drovers Lane. Partly c.1660, partly mid C18. Doorway with Doric columns. Staircase, etc., and also some windows C17. NMR) – CROZIER LODGE, Fell Lane, just opposite the Methodist Church of 1815. The house is of 1826. Ashlar, three bays, doorway with broken pediment, two low wings with a Venetian window each. – Opposite the far end of Fell Lane, i.e. proceeding to the NE, is CAROLINE COTTAGE, the lodge on the way to the Beacon Tower. This is Late Georgian, of three bays and castellated. The centre is of two

* Formerly DOCKRAY HALL.
‡ Taylor mentions the kitchen hatch with an ogee arch.

storeys, the side parts of one. – The BEACON TOWER was
built in 1719 and repaired in 1780. It is of red sandstone
ashlar, not high, square, with a pyramid roof. The windows
are round-arched.

s of the centre along the A6 is first TYNEFIELD HOUSE in
Bridge Lane, dated 1804. Three-bay ashlar front. The
ground-floor windows l. and r. tripartite under blank arches,
the doorway Venetian, also with a blank arch. Then a turn to
the NE and on the r. CARLETON HALL, with a fine Georgian
garden front. The six-bay centre seems older than the two
canted bay windows. Spacious staircase. In the rooms behind
them late C18 plaster ceilings in the Adam manner. The E
room is specially handsome: octagonal with two niches. A
little further NE on the same side CARLETON FARM, with a
later C17 façade of three bays, but the doorway enriched by a
Gibbs surround and a pediment. Finally, turning W from the
A6 by Eamont Bridge, ¾ m. W, is SKIRSGILL, built in 1795.
It has two wide bow windows and a central tripartite window
with a blank arch. Originally there were also one-storey
wings and a four-column porch or veranda (Neale II, 3). (For
the SKIRSGILL HILL SETTLEMENTS see Askham (W),
p. 223.)

OLD PENRITH. The 3-acre ROMAN FORT lies beside the main
Penrith–Carlisle road, 5 m. N of Penrith, on a platform above
the valley of the river Petteril. Nothing definite is known of its
internal buildings. A MARCHING CAMP is recorded to the
SW.

PENRUDDOCK

4020

ALL SAINTS. 1902 by *C. J. Ferguson*. Nave and chancel in one.
Roughcast. Late Perp windows.

PIGEON CRAG *see* BRAMPTON

PIKE HILL *see* WALTON

1030

PLUMBLAND

ST CUTHBERT. By *Cory & Ferguson*, 1870–1, and their best
work, strong and quite personal, with its N tower with four
gables and the three cross-gables of the N side of the clerestory.
They each have a group of three stepped lancets. On the S
side there is less display. The fenestration is mostly lancets,
and rere-arches are used inside. Looking at the church out-

side, one would regard it as entirely of 1870, if it were not for the plain Norman doorway re-set in the porch side wall and the lancet re-set in the vestry E wall. That promises surprises inside, and indeed, as one enters, while the arcade is of 1870, the chancel arch is a proud piece of about 1130 or 1140, high and wide, with tripartite responds, capitals of only a few big scallops, and an arch with an early moulding. The C13 is also represented, though only by the pointed-trefoiled PISCINA and the doorway into the vestry, whose mouldings are of a slightly later type. – PLATE. Cup and Cover, probably c.1600–10. – MONUMENTS. (Hogback tombstone in three fragments, one of them later, carved with some stiff-leaf. The hogback had Anglo-Danish dragons.) – Francheville Lawson Ballantine Dykes † 1866. By *J. Forsyth*, a Gothic tablet. More and earlier tablets with permutations of the same names.

PLUMPTON WALL

4030

ST JOHN EVANGELIST. 1907 by *Sir Robert Lorimer*. An excellent church which should be better known. The windows admittedly are conventional, but the S tower, with its very pronounced batter and its bell-openings as a stone screen of reticulation, the S porch, also with a batter, and the bare windowless E wall are features not easily forgotten. – FONT (outside). An octagonal baluster. – STAINED GLASS. One window by *Morris & Co.*, but after the deaths of both Morris and Burne-Jones. – PLATE. Cup and Paten, 1811.

BRACKENBURGH TOWER, 1½ m. NW. 1903, and also by *Lorimer*. Also excellent, although still in a Tudor tradition. But the garden side is splendidly composed, and there are here and there charming touches, betraying that historicism was no longer taken in deadly earnest, e.g. the oriel above the entrance. Behind the new house parts of one of 1852 (by *William Atkinson*), and this seems to incorporate a pele tower.

(IVY DENE, Brockley Moor, ½ m. W. Dated 1677. Mullioned windows with a continuous label-course. MHLG)

PONSONBY see CALDER BRIDGE

PORT CARLISLE see BOWNESS-ON-SOLWAY

RABY COTE see ABBEY TOWN

RADALHOLM HALL see ALSTON

RANDYLANDS *see* WALTON

3040
RAUGHTON HEAD

CHURCH. 1761. Very broad W tower, the upper part of 1881. As the tower and the nave as well have Georgian, keyed-in, round-headed windows, the style chosen for the top part of the tower was Norman. The semicircular stair-turret goes well with the general massiveness of the tower. The Venetian E window was altered in 1881. – PLATE. Cup, 1633; Flagon, 1682; Paten, 1819. – MONUMENT. The Rev. Robert Monkhouse † 1822, aged thirty. Signed *L. Watson*. He had been Watson's first schoolmaster and mentor. Watson was the most talented Cumberland sculptor of these years (cf. Sebergham). This was his first work in marble, and he seems to have done it in 1828. At the top of the tablet is the small, pensive seated figure of the deceased.

0090
RAVENGLASS

A wide street between two-storeyed cottages runs N–S to a bend in the estuary of the river Esk. Between the houses a small round-arched METHODIST CHAPEL of 1848.

The ESKDALE MINIATURE RAILWAY, from iron mines near Boot, was built in the 1870s. It now runs on a 15 in. gauge.

ROMAN FORT. The site of a 4-acre Roman fort, now cut through by the Furness railway, is known on the edge of the harbour just S of Ravenglass. Its site is bounded on the W by the cliffs and on the S and N by the valleys of the Mite and the Esk. Although there is little to be seen of the fort, parts of its external bath building, known as Walls Castle, are very well preserved. The actual walls, built of a coursed red freestone and rendered internally with pink mortar, stand to a height of more than $12\frac{1}{2}$ ft. Two doorways survive, each with a shallow relieving arch above the wooden lintel, and there are traces of five splayed windows. The wall of one of the rooms, possibly the entrance hall, contains a round-headed niche, semicircular in plan.

5040
RENWICK

ALL SAINTS. 1845 by the *Rev. J. Watson*(?), the replacement of a church of 1733. Nave, chancel, and bellcote in the Norman style. – PULPIT. Two-decker, probably of c.1735. Only the minimum Norman frill of c.1845. – HARMONIUM. An

ultra-Victorian piece, probably of the 1850s or 1860s. –
PLATE. Cup, 1711.
(HUDDLESCOUGH HALL, ¾ m. s. Date stones 1601 and 1617.
The latter date is on an ornamented lintel. MHLG)

RHEDA LODGE *see* FRIZINGTON

ROCKCLIFFE   *3060*

ST MARY. 1848 by *James Stewart* of Carlisle. Dec, with a later
(1881) s porch tower with broach-spire. Nave, chancel, and N
transept. Steep open roof. – CROSS in the churchyard. The
fragment has a solid wheel-head and along the shaft two broad
raised bands (cf. Bromfield). The decoration is of interlace
and also bands of dragons. – PLATE. Cup and Cover Paten,
early C17; Flagon with lid, 1639; Almsdish, 1705.

CASTLETOWN HOUSE, ⅞ m. ENE. Dated 1831. The fine, ashlar-
faced Grecian house of the Mounsey family. The entrance has
unfluted Ionic columns *in antis*, the garden side a four-pillar
portico with Soanian incised ornament and pedimented wings.
These and the centre have broad angle pilaster-strips, not
pilasters, and this refusal to have bases or capitals tells of the
wish for the elementary at that moment. The doorway behind
the portico is tripartite and has a segmental fanlight. (Good
interior, including plaster ceilings and screens of two columns,
in the entrance hall – Doric, and in the dining room – Ionic.
MHLG)

ROSE CASTLE   *3040*

Rose Castle has been the residence of the bishops of Carlisle
since the C13. It is curious that the bishops never had a palace
in the town. The present castle, beautifully placed, appears
essentially of the C19, and *Thomas Rickman* in fact did much
to unify a building considered much too disjointed. He worked
at Rose Castle in 1829–31. The medieval castle was of four
quite irregular ranges round a courtyard. A fire damaged it
about 1646, and after that, about 1665, Bishop Rainbow pulled
down the E and s ranges. So the castle now consists of a N and
a W range. The N range starts at the N end with the Strickland
Tower, a pele tower, vaulted as usual at ground level and provided by Rickman with a semicircular higher stair-turret.
The original entrance was on the first floor from the W by a
doorway with a shouldered lintel. The room here must have

been divided; for a pointed-trefoiled PISCINA shows that part
of the room was the chapel.* The forms of doorway and
piscina incidentally show that the tower was built *c.*1300 and
not in Strickland's time. w of the Strickland Tower is Bishop
Bell's Tower of *c.*1488. It has two-light windows, the lights
with two-centred uncusped arches. After that there is medieval
masonry, but the features from now begin to be all Rickman's.
Behind the blank walling lies the chapel, with its buttresses
and side windows to the s and a large window and open bell-
turret to the E. This chapel, originally Bishop Bell's of
1487–9, was rebuilt by Bishop Rainbow *c.*1665–70, but what
one sees now is all Rickman's, including the three tall w niches
inside.‡ Rickman also removed a third tower to build his
entrance and added on the w front Percy's Tower afresh,
thereby squeezing Bishop Kite's Tower of 1522–4 into in-
significance. Its two-light windows are like Bell's. Rickman
here is all Late Gothic, not what one usually calls Tudor. He
also provided the Gothic staircase, rather too close to the
entrance, and the large dining room and above it the equally
large drawing room, in the w range facing E. They share two
bay windows and have modest Gothic ceilings and more
sumptuous Gothic fireplaces.

The landscaping was done for Bishop Percy by *Paxton*.

(THACKWOOD PARK, 2 m. SE. Irregular front, but the upper
floor fenestration more or less symmetrical. A date stone says
1681. NMR)

(THISTLEWOOD TOWER, 2½ m. SE. Pele tower with mullioned
windows and adjoining house of five bays with two-light
windows. NMR)

ROSEHILL *see* MORESBY

3040

ROSLEY

HOLY TRINITY. 1840. Thin w tower with steep pyramid roof.
Wide lancets; no separate chancel. Low, flat ceiling. – BOX
PEWS, converted.

ROWRAH HALL *see* ARLECDON

* PLATE. Cup, Paten, and Flagon inscribed 1684; Paten, 1748.
‡ Some of the panelling is said to be medieval and to have come from
Lambeth Palace.

ST BEES

ST MARY AND ST BEGA. The church was the church of a
Benedictine nunnery founded about 650, destroyed by the
Danes, and re-founded by William de Meschines c.1120. The
nunnery quarters have all been destroyed, but the church is
gratifyingly complete. Its E end is a remodelling, as we shall
see presently, but the S transept has plain Norman windows,
and the nave and S aisle W wall are Late Norman. The doorway is the richest in the county, of three orders of columns, 13
with scrolly capitals including figure-work and much zigzag
and also some sparse beakhead in the arch. This one would
date c.1160. Inside, the crossing turns out to be Norman too,
with the simplest keeled demi-columns as responds. The
arches and the tripartite W responds are a later alteration, as
the way shows in which they jut against what was meant as the
corners of the tower. The W bay of the chancel has Victorian
C13 windows, but that on the N side has a round rere-arch
with continuous moulding, i.e. forms part of the Norman
chancel. Very soon after the completion of the church, if one
assumes that it was built in the customary way from E to W,
the first chancel was pulled down and replaced by an E.E.
one.* Very long side lancets, preserved on the N side, shafted
outside, still with waterleaf capitals, i.e. c.1190 at the latest,
and with a continuous roll inside. The E wall has three lancets
of the same height, and inside these are separated by two tiers 25
of tabernacles. Their capitals are singularly bad. The side
lancets are separated outside by shallow buttresses, and the
corbel-frieze is complete. The gable had a shafted window
and shafted niches, but the present low-pitched roof has
destroyed much of that. The crossing tower is imitation E.E.
and dates from *Butterfield*'s restoration of 1855–8. Due to
Butterfield also are the N transept front and the aisle windows.
The clerestory windows look Late Perp. Inside the nave however we go back to the genuine E.E. work. The arcades are of
six bays with alternatingly round and octagonal piers, the
capitals decorated with very small nailhead. Only one pier
has eight attached keeled shafts instead. The arches are simply
moulded, and the Perp clerestory windows stand above the
spandrels, not the arches. The responds are all keeled, and the
E responds have leaf capitals. Two label-stops have beasts'

* This is now part of the School.

heads, one of them a Norman piece without doubt. Butterfield separated the aisles from the transepts by walls with a large cinquefoil. The nave w wall has three stepped lancets and shallow buttresses later helped by bigger canted ones. In the late C13 or early C14 the chancel received a s aisle of four bays. The piers and the arches have a number of quarter-hollow mouldings. The same was true of the large E window, of which now only the N jamb survives. There is also a detached fragment of the s wall.

FURNISHINGS. SCREEN. The high wrought-iron screen between nave and present chancel is of 1886 and also by *Butterfield*. This is late for what it looks like; yet it is an outstandingly good piece. – SCULPTURE. W of the w end of the church above a gateway a Norman LINTEL with cambered top. It still has much of the Anglo-Danish tradition. A large dragon in the middle, close interlace on the r., wild Urnes interlace on the l. – (In the churchyard two fragmentary cross-shafts, one with interlace, the other with untidy spirals and scrolls. Calverley–Collingwood) – PLATE. Silver-gilt Cup, 1570; parcel-gilt Cup, 1570; Cup with complex ornament, 1570. All three are specially good. – MONUMENTS. Prior Cotyngham † 1300. Effigy in the New College Hall. – Incised effigy of Joan de Lucy † 1369 (N transept E). – Capt. Willcox † 1798. Tablet by *Bingley*, with the usual mourning female by an urn. – William Ainger † 1840. With a fully round bust. By *John G. Lough*. – Maria Claudine Lumb † 1865 aged four. Sleeping child in an elaborate gabled Gothic recess.

ST BEES SCHOOL. The centre of the school is the courtyard opposite the chancel of the church and open towards it. Its N side is the original schoolhouse of 1587. The school was founded by Archbishop Grindal in 1583. The w side with a gate tower and the s side and the larger s side of this s range, with its own central entrance tower, were built in 1842–4 by *Thomas Nelson*. Or was he only the contractor? They are in a restrained Tudor style. The chapel, the Headmaster's house, and the laboratories and library N of the chapel are by *Paley & Austin* of Lancaster and were built in 1907–10. By the same in 1885 School House, some distance to the NE, i.e. w of the Memorial Hall. The CHAPEL is in a free Perp, with a s tower with projecting top and saddleback roof. It is not large, and has inside low aisle-passages below a clerestory.

Nothing much of note in the town. Nos. 19–20 FINKLE STREET is probably Early Elizabethan. It has a round-headed doorway, one window with round arches to the lights, and two windows where these round arches are blank. Opposite is a neo-Tudor terrace, rendered, presumably of c.1840.

SALKELD HALL see LITTLE SALKELD

SAMPSON'S BRATFULL see CALDER BRIDGE

SARKFOOT see LONGTOWN

SCALEBY

4060

ALL SAINTS. E.E. throughout, and probably as early as the earliest C13 – cf. the round-headed S doorway with two continuous chamfers. The windows all lancets. The original chancel seems to have disappeared and been replaced by the present one. The main restoration took place in 1861. The W tower has lancets at its lowest stage too. The top is probably C17 work. – FONT. Dated 1707, yet still a plain octagonal bowl. Very short, thick columnar stem. – SCULPTURE. A baffling fragment of about 1200 with a bishop or abbot in relief on one side, and another on the adjoining side round the corner. The other two sides were bonded in. What can it have been? It is 33 in. high. – PLATE. Cup with vine decoration, 1600; Paten, 1777.

SCALEBY CASTLE.* The house was de Tilliol property when licence to crenellate was given in 1307. Of that date is much of the lower courses of masonry. This refers, to start on the N side, to the gatehouse, whose inner arch has a C14 moulding (sunk quadrant). The gateway has l. and r. vaulted porters' lodges, and the round outer arch may be a later thickening. The polygonal tower must be late C15 – cf. the ground-floor windows. The tower in the NE corner is now also assigned to the C15. It has the usual vault at ground level and the usual spiral staircase. The continuation of the pele on the E side is the hall, also tunnel-vaulted at ground level, which is very rare indeed in England but more common in Scotland. The room above it has late C17 windows. As for the S range, much of it is of c.1835–40 (Jefferson in 1838 says: at present being rebuilt), and Lord Henley's attribution to *Rickman* – cf. his work at Rose Castle – is perfectly convincing. What the architect worked on was a range built by Sir Edward Musgrave in

* The following remarks are based on Lord Henley's study of his house.

1596 upon 1307 courses. Of the early c17 e.g. the dormers of
the s front of the range and the windows of its N front.

SCALEBY HALL, ¼ m. E. 1834. Five-bay front with a porch of
unfluted Ionic columns and the l. gable-end treated as a
pediment. The comparative heaviness tells of the late date.

SCALES HALL

2¾ m. W of Calthwaite

(On one side mullioned windows with arched lights. On the
same side a four-light transomed window under a gable. On
another side two doorways with broad rusticated surrounds
and more mullioned and transomed windows (NMR). Mrs
Davies adds that it is on an L plan, with a former moat and a
gatehouse. Dated 1491, 158 ?, 1591, and 1724. The gatehouse
is of the 1580s, the outer courtyard beyond the moat of 1724.)

SCALLOW see ARLECDON

SCARNESS DOWER HOUSE see BASSENTHWAITE

SCOTBY

CHURCH. 1854 by *Salvin*. Not a small church. s tower, nave,
and chancel. Geometrical tracery. – STAINED GLASS. The E
window no doubt by *Powell*. The date is 1879.

ROSEHILL, on the A-road. The house must be of *c*.1820–30.
Three bays plus, at the angles, bay windows set diagonally.
Porch segmentally convex on four Roman Doric columns,
unfluted however in their lower parts. Wreaths in the frieze.

SEASCALE

On the sea front there is nothing to report.

ST CUTHBERT. 1890* by *C. J. Ferguson*. Long, of red sandstone.
Nave and chancel and bellcote. Dec in style, the s aisle with
the almond-shaped w window inspired by Millom.

SEASCALE HALL. Probably of *c*.1700, that is a symmetrical
five-bay façade, the doorway with a pulvinated frieze, but the
windows still with crosses and hood-moulds.‡

---

* Parker says 1879.
‡ In the back wall is a stone with the date 1606.

Much recent Calder Hall housing.

STANDING STONE. 300 yds SE of Seascale Mill is a single
standing stone, 4 ft high, which originally formed part of a
stone circle.

GRETIGATE STONE CIRCLES. *See* Gosforth.

GREY CROFT STONE CIRCLE, 1½ m. N of Seascale Railway
Station and 350 yds NW of Seascale Howe Farm. The present
circle of ten standing stones, with a diameter of 80 ft, represents restoration work carried out in 1949, when the stones
buried by a farmer in the C19 were located and re-erected.
There were originally twelve stones in the circle. At the
centre of the site is a low oval cairn, 22 ft long, beneath which
were found fragments of burnt bone and part of a small ring
of jet. A partially ground stone axe from the Great Langdale
factory was found beside one of the stones of the circle.

SEATON

1080

1 m. N of Bootle

NUNNERY. Benedictine, founded in the late C12. The only
remaining fragment, the E wall of the chancel, is E.E. Three
stepped lancets, shafted inside and with a little nailhead. In
the spandrels (re-set) trefoil and cinquefoil. Remains of blank
arcading(?) in the S wall. Next to the ruin a house which,
though all its details are Victorian, seems to be Elizabethan or
Jacobean, built probably with the materials of the nunnery.
The house was built by Sir Hugh Askew, who died in 1563.

SEATON

3040

2 m. NE of Workington

ST PAUL. 1883 by *George Watson* of Keswick. The cost was
£2,213 13s. 4d. Aisleless, with a thin NE tower and a polygonal apse. Plain geometrical tracery.

SEBERGHAM

3040

ST MARY. Short, thin W tower, built in 1825. Nave and chancel. In the nave one original lancet. In the chancel original
lancets too. But the grouped nave S lancets and the pretty
oriel from the tower into the nave belong to the restoration of
1905. – BENCHES. Also of *c.*1905. Nice curvy ends, rather like
North German Baroque. – PLATE. Very small Cup of 1728.

– MONUMENTS. Thomas Denton † 1616. Four shields and an inscription in distichs:

> Molliter ossa cubant, men aurea vivet Olimpo
> Vivet in eternum chara deo soboles Qth BE.

The inscription continues in Latin. – Daniel Watson † 1753 and his family down to 1795. Large tablet with an urn and the large words 'Virtus vivit'. Fan motif at the foot. – Thomas Watson † 1823. Black setting, and in it a white oval with the three Fates in profile, and three arms pointing forward. It is a sensational composition, copied from Fuseli's Three Witches (from Macbeth), shown at the Royal Academy in 1783. The tablet is signed *M. L. Watson* Rome. He was the son of Thomas Watson, and this is his most impressive work, up to the standard of the best that was done in these years in England.

ST JAMES, Welton, 2½ m. NW. By *Cory & Ferguson*, 1874. Nave and chancel in one, geometrical tracery. The bellcote is not on the apex of the W gable but by the NW corner.

On the way from the S end of the lane to the church towards the bridge two HOUSES on the N side, one dated 1730, the other 1737, and both still with vertical two-light mullioned windows. Across the bridge on the NW GREENFOOT, dated 1715 and already with a sashed five-bay front and an open segmental pediment.

SEBERGHAM CASTLE (pronounced incidentally Sebberam), 2⅜ m. NW. A late C18 folly front, i.e. all windows in ogee-headed pairs with Y-tracery, a centre raised and castellated and with an over-sized blank quatrefoil, castellated wings, and end pavilions with concave-sided gables – *Anglo-Chinois*, as the French said in the C18.

SELLA PARK see CALDER BRIDGE

1030

SETMURTHY

ST BARNABAS. 1794, restored 1870. Nave and chancel in one. Polygonal NW turret, polygonal SW baptistery. No features of 1794 left. – FONT. Small, with the date 1661, initials, and simple geometrical decoration.

HIGHAM SCHOOL, ½ m. S. Gothic, probably of *c.*1800, a rarity in the county. Symmetrical, of eleven bays, with two tower features with angle-turrets set symmetrically. Pointed windows. Earlier building remains behind.

HEWTHWAITE HALL. *See* Isel.

STONE CIRCLE, 1½ m. NE of Embleton and 200 yds NE of Elva Plain House. The circle consists of fifteen small stones, the largest 3 ft 6 in. high, forming a circle 100 ft in diameter. A single outlier on the SW.

SHANK CASTLE see STAPLETON

SHOULTHWAITE FORT see CASTLERIGG

SIKESIDE see KIRKLINTON

SILLOTH

1050

The development as a holiday resort and, less successfully, as a harbour and docks dates from 1857–8. The layout is by Messrs *Hay* of Liverpool (GS). It is a grid of streets and three terraces, mildly Italianate, two of them of one composition. In the middle between the two and the third a square was left free and the church placed in it as if it were an architectural model. The whole group does not actually border a sea promenade, but a large green, with a brake of pine trees between it and the sea and the marvellous view of the mountainous Scottish coastline.

CHRIST CHURCH. 1870–1 by *Cory & Ferguson,* but won in competition by Ferguson, when still a pupil of G. G. Scott. Quite an ambitious church, with nave and aisles, an apse, and a NW porch steeple with broach-spire. Plate tracery. Inside all is brick-faced, yellow bricks with red-brick trim and also bands of brick used in projection and recession. The capitals have been left uncarved.

SKINBURNESS. *See* Newton Arlosh.

BECKFOOT, 3 m. S. The site of a ROMAN FORT, about 3 acres in extent, with walls 6 ft thick backed by internal rectangular towers. Practically nothing is known of the internal buildings, but traces of the civil settlement lie to the SE.

SKELTON

4030

ST MICHAEL. The nave with thin round-arched windows is of 1794. Of 1879 such a feature as the tripartite Norman E window. It looks more like 1840. The W tower is medieval (C14?) – cf. the arch towards the nave dying into the imposts. – FONT. The former font is an octagonal baluster. – PULPIT.

Mid C18, with fluted angle colonnettes and arched panels. –
COMMUNION RAIL. C18. – PLATE. Cup and Paten, 1672.

HARDRIGG HALL, 1 m. NW. In ruins. One side and parts of
two more of a pele tower. The ground level was tunnel-
vaulted – see the springing. In one corner the spiral staircase
with doorways to the first and the second floors. Fireplaces on
both floors.

LOADEN HOWE. *See* Greystoke.

SKINBURNESS *see* NEWTON ARLOSH

SKIRSGILL *see* PENRITH, p. 178

6030
SKIRWITH

ST JOHN EVANGELIST. 1856 by Messrs *Francis* (GS). SW
tower with short spire, made to look busy by two tiers of
lucarnes. Dec tracery. – The STAINED GLASS is by *Wailes*
(TK). – CHANDELIER. A gorgeous, naturalistic Victorian
piece. Is it French? It comes from Brougham Hall.*

THE ABBEY. Called 'a modern built mansion' in 1802. Seven
bays, two storeys and basement offices. The three-bay middle
projection has a top balustrade and a doorway with a blank
arch. Parts of the house have an odd banded rustication with
V-joints. On the entrance side doorway with pediment, and, at
r. angles, two detached ranges of outbuildings.

STANWIX *see* CARLISLE, pp. 97, 103, 104

5070
STAPLETON

ST MARY. 1830. All alone, an unusual thing for a church of that
date. W tower with obelisk pinnacles. Wide nave with lancet
windows, short and narrow chancel with a three-light E
window with intersecting tracery. – PLATE. Bowl, inscribed
1638; Flagon, 1716.

(SHANK CASTLE, 2¼ m. WSW. Ruined pele tower. Several later
two-light mullioned windows; NMR. Taylor (1892) has a
more detailed description.)

STOCKDALE MOOR *see* CALDER BRIDGE

---

* A CUPBOARD with linenfold panels is said to be a specially early case of
this mode of decoration. – The REREDOS in the Lady Chapel is considered
to be medieval.

STONEGARTHSIDE HALL *see* NICHOLFOREST

STONEHOUSE *see* NICHOLFOREST

STONETHWAITE *see* DALSTON

STRANDS

1000

CHURCH. The parish church of Netherwasdale. A typical dale chapel. Low, nave and chancel in one, and a bellcote. Pebbledash. Some Georgian windows, including the arched E window. The ROYAL ARMS are those of George III from 1816 onwards. The white coved ceiling looks early C19 indeed. Alternatively, as a N aisle and vestry were added in 1830, the ceiling may be of that date. The PANELLING by the altar and the carvings of PULPIT and LECTERN are late C17. They come from York Minster. – PLATE. Cup, formerly gilt, probably 1597.

WASDALE HALL, 1¼ m. E of Strands. Not a large mansion, but one with a superb view towards the screes of Wastwater. The plan is of the hall-house type. The l. gable is stone, the r. gable half-timbered. Half-timbered also the porch. Mullioned and mullioned-and-transomed windows. The house is said to have been built in 1829, but if so there must have been later alterations.

STREET GATE *see* LAMPLUGH

STUDFOLD GATE *see* DEAN

TALKIN

5050

2½ m. E of Hayton

CHURCH. 1842; Norman. Nave and bellcote and chancel. – Even the PULPIT and the COMMUNION RAIL are Norman.

COLD FELL CAIRN, 4 m. SSE, on the summit of Cold Fell and on the boundary with Geltsdale parish. The cairn is oval in plan, with a maximum diameter of 50 ft, and stands 4 ft high. It lies in a curious circular depression. The site is unexcavated, and nothing is known of its date.

TALLENTIRE HALL *see* BRIDEKIRK

TARRABY *see* HOUGHTON

TEMON *see* DENTON

THACKWOOD PARK *see* ROSE CASTLE

THIEFSIDE HILL *see* HIGH HESKET

THISTLEWOOD TOWER *see* ROSE CASTLE

2020

THORNTHWAITE

St Mary. Originally built *c*.1760. Remodelled in 1831 and 1853. Cruciform, with a bellcote and lancet windows, i.e. in the early C19 tradition.

Vicarage, ⅝ m. s. By *Barry Parker*, *c*.1900 (between 1895 and 1903), for the Rev. William Unwin. Nothing special. Shallow bows with slate-faced dados.

Old Manor, Little Braithwaite, 1½ m. ssw. Dated 1726, and already wholly classical, i.e. with sash-windows with raised moulded frames and a doorway with Doric pilasters, a triglyph frieze, and a pediment.

3020

THRELKELD

St Mary. Built in 1777. Nave and chancel in one. Keyed-in round-arched windows. Porch entrance with broken pediment. The E window Venetian with a flat surround. The W tower, oblong, not square, and with primitive obelisks, looks C17. – Late Georgian Organ. – Monument. Rev. Thomas Edmondson † 1797 and his son, a merchant, who died at Baltimore in 1822. By *Webster* of Kendal, probably at the later date.

Settlement, ½ m. se of the Railway Station and s of the granite quarry. The settlement is defined by stone banks, forming a series of rectangular enclosures, with associated hut circles. The site is unexcavated, but presumably belongs to the pre-Roman Iron Age or was occupied by native farmers during the period of Roman rule.

Threlkeld Knott Settlement, 1 m. se of Birkett Mire Railway Station. There are four linked sub-rectangular enclosures and three hut circles in this group. Each hut is approximately 20 ft in diameter. A number of small, low cairns – possibly the result of field clearance – can be seen in the vicinity of the settlement. The site has been excavated, but nothing was found to throw light on its age.

THURSBY

ST ANDREW. Quite large; ashlar-faced. The church was built in 1846, but the plate tracery of the bell-openings and the Dec tracery of the side windows are likely to be of the restoration of 1878. Three stepped lancets in the E wall. Wide nave in the early C19 tradition. – PLATE. Cup, 1619. – TABLETS to members of the Brisco family of Crofton Hall, e.g. † 1741 (with an inscription worth reading), † 1760, and † 1805 (the latter by *Kirkbride* of Carlisle).

CROFTON HALL, 1 m. SW. The mansion has recently been demolished, but the gatehouse and stables remain. The GATEWAY has two pairs of fluted Ionic columns and a straight top, and the two LODGES have pilasters. That should be c.1820. The STABLES are dated 1826. They also are ashlar-faced, and they have seven bays with the middle bay singled out by fluted Ionic pilasters, a pediment, and a cupola.

GREENWAYS, a cottage NW of the Crofton Hall stables. The front is three sides of an octagon. The windows are pointed, with Y-tracery. That also is probably of the 1820s.

FIDDLEBACK, ¼ m. SW. Dated 1709. It is an early folly. The cottage has a front more than semicircular and is continued at the back in the semicircular front of the barn. The whole is indeed a fiddle shape.

THWAITE HALL see MUNGRISDALE

THWAITES

ST ANNE. 1854 by *E. G. Paley*.* With plate tracery. Nave with clerestory of pointed quatrefoils. Chancel with lancets. S aisle. – PLATE. Cup of 1739.

TORPENHOW

ST MICHAEL. Nave and aisles and C17-looking bellcote. The N transept N wall with three stepped lancet lights and the chancel E window with intersecting tracery must be late C13. But the chancel N windows are Norman, and there is a trace of a Norman E window as well, one apparently of two or three. And Norman also is the doorway in the S aisle, which in its upper parts with windows and battlements seems C17. The

---

* The tender was £1,500 (GS).

doorway has odd jamb mouldings and very crude capitals, one with heads. Arch with zigzag and rope, hood-mould with a reel motif. As one enters the church, the chancel arch reveals the same hand; it is crude, but in its barbarity impressive. The responds are triple, one capital with figures, the opposite one with heads coming out of the scallops. Decorated abaci, arch with zigzag. The chancel s wall has a blocked Norman window. The stylistic relations of this Norman work are with the West Riding of Yorkshire, and they suggest a date *c.*1170.* In the chancel s wall also a tomb recess with a double-chamfered arch. Now the arcades. They are of three bays and have single-step arches. The sw respond has scallops with little heads just like the chancel arch. The nw respond has plain scallops. Piers and abaci are round. – (The NAVE CEILING was given in 1689 by T. Addison, brother of the essayist. It is painted with cupids and garlands and is supposed to come from a London Livery Company's Hall.)‡ – FONT. Norman, round, with thin intersecting arches and loose knot or interlace on the underside. – PULPIT. Jacobean; simple. – PLATE. Cup and Paten of *c.*1670 (cf. Castle Carrock).

CAERMOTE, 1¾ m. s, is the site of a ROMAN FORT. The remains show two structural periods, a 3½-acre fort of turf and timber, probably of Flavian date, and a superimposed 1-acre fortlet, occupying the NE corner of the earlier fort, and probably belonging to the C2.

TOWNHEAD see OUSBY

TRIERMAIN CASTLE see GILSLAND

ULDALE

St JOHN EVANGELIST. Demolished.

St JAMES, 1 m. NW, at Uldale Mill. White. Nave and chancel and bellcote. The windows are arched with keystones. The w doorway has a moulded frame. All this is of 1730, but the N wall has medieval masonry, and the chancel was rebuilt in 1837. Inside, a depressed pointed chancel arch with two chamfers dying into the walls. It is probably early C16. –

---

* A water-colour of before the restoration shows an angle pier in the chancel NW corner as if for a vault. Or is it a bad rendering of the easternmost shaft of the triple respond?

‡ Information kindly given me by the Rev. W. F. G. Wittey.

PLATE. Chalice of 1571 with band of ornament in a *cuir bouilli* case which is certainly older. Can it be C14?

ULLOCK *see* DEAN

ULPHA

1090

ST JOHN. A dale chapel, low, of nave and chancel in one, with a bellcote. The E window probably C17, the other windows later and domestic. – WALL PAINTINGS. Discovered in 1934. C17 and C18, and including the ROYAL ARMS of Queen Anne.

PELE TOWER, in ruins, 1¼ m. SW. Late medieval. One wall and part of the opposite wall with the start of a projection survive, with indications of an oven at ground level.

(DUDDON HALL. Early C19. Doric details and a very ornate Composite TEMPLE in the garden. Mrs Davies)

CAIRNS. *See* Muncaster.

UNDERSCAR *see* CROSTHWAITE

UPPERBY *see* CARLISLE, p. 97

UPPER DENTON *see* DENTON

UXELLODUNUM *see* WALTON

WABERTHWAITE

1090

ST JOHN EVANGELIST. By the estuary of the Esk. The type of the dale chapels, low and white. Nave and chancel in one and bellcote.* Perp two-light W window. Other windows C16 or C17, two lights with uncusped round heads. A homely interior. – BOX PEWS, a little raised at the W end. – PULPIT dated 1630. – The FONT is mysterious, a square black block with broaches in the corners. – SCULPTURE. Fragment of a CROSS SHAFT in the churchyard, with interlace; decayed. Comparable with the Irton Cross. On three sides the interlace is quite orderly. On the fourth the upper panels are close, intricate, and confused, and an animal and two human figures seem to be entangled in it. – In the vestry fragments of another shaft. – PLATE. Cup and Paten, 1576. The paten has a band of ornament.

* The bellcote dates from 1796.

SETTLEMENT AREA. In the dunes W of Eskmeals Railway
Station numerous flint scrapers, knives, and arrowheads have
been found, indicating intermittent occupation of the area by
Neolithic and Bronze Age groups.

WALBY see CROSBY-ON-EDEN

WALL BOWERS see WALTON

WALLHEAD see CROSBY-ON-EDEN

5060

WALTON

ST MARY. 1869–70 by *Paley* of Lancaster. This is an early job,
and the front still has something of the bluntness of early
Bodley. NW tower with pyramid roof. The staircase tower
flat in front of it. The gable of the nave with lancets and a rose
window to the r. The S lancets are tall, the N aisle lancets
small, as the roof runs in one from the nave ridge to the aisle
eaves. – PLATE. Cup of 1627.

CASTLESTEADS, I m. SW. Late C18, of seven bays with a pedimented doorway and lower wings (with Victorian dormers).
The staircase projects apsidally at the back. (For the Roman
fort of Uxellodunum, *see* below.)

From the Northumberland boundary SW to Walton runs a
stretch of HADRIAN'S WALL, as follows. (For the remaining
stretch, *see* footnote on p. 55 of the Introduction.)

HARROW'S SCAR, 6 m. NE. The site of Milecastle 49. Between
the milecastle and Birdoswald is a well-preserved section of
wall.

CAMBOGLANNA (Birdoswald), ½ m. SW of the former, is a
5-acre Hadrianic FORT situated on a ridge overlooking the
gorge of the river Irthing. Extensive excavations have eluci-
dated the main structural development on the site, but most
of the details are no longer visible. However, substantial parts
of the wall with its gateways can now be seen. Particularly
well preserved is the NW angle-tower, surviving to a height of
fourteen courses. The wall at this point is butted on to the
curving outer corner. The main E and S gates, of double-
portalled type, are also exhibited, as is the W postern gate,
of which the threshold, scored by wheel-ruts, may still be
seen.* W of Birdoswald, the narrow-gauge wall continues and

---

* For a Roman arch probably from Birdoswald, *see* Denton.

can be seen to the S of the road as far as Turret 49b. S of the turret part of the original turf-wall is visible.

HIGH HOUSE is the site of Milecastle 50TW. The milecastle became famous when excavations there produced a small piece of a timber dedicatory inscription dated to the governorship of Aulus Platorius Nepos, thus proving that the turf-wall was of Hadrianic date. E of the milecastle the vallum runs so close to the turf-wall that its N mound is omitted, the S being twice the size. To the W both mounds, of normal size, are represented.

WALL BOWERS, W again, is the site of Milecastle 51, where the turf and stone walls converge. The milecastle contains two barracks and was surrounded by an unfinished ditch.

The site of a Roman FORT is now beneath the church of Nether Denton (see p. 121): the bath building lies below the vicarage. It was occupied from Flavian to Hadrianic times, when the Garrison was moved up to the wall. COOMBE CRAG was a QUARRY worked in Roman times, bearing names of Roman soldiers engaged in quarrying.

PIKE HILL. On the highest part, overlooking much of the surrounding area, is the site of a Roman signal-tower, 20 ft square and orientated askew to the wall, into which it was later incorporated. It was probably used for long-distance signalling. 150 yds to the W is Turret 52a, now exposed, adjoined by a well-preserved piece of the wall. 200 yds to the E was Milecastle 52, of which nothing can now be seen.

BANKS BURN, ¾ m. NE of Lanercost Priory, is the site of Milecastle 53. To the W is a piece of wall standing to a height of 10 ft but refaced in the C19. Included in its N face is a CENTURIAL STONE found near by, at Moneyholes.

BOOTHBY CASTLE HILL is the site of a Roman FORT occupied in the early Hadrianic period.

RANDYLANDS is the site of Milecastle 54. Excavations in 1934 showed that here a turf-wall milecastle lay below that belonging to the stone-wall.

GARTHSIDE, 1¼ m. E of Walton, is the site of Turrets 54a: two were found. The first, set within the turf-wall, had partly collapsed into the ditch and had been replaced by another immediately behind it. The stone-wall first ran up to the new turret; later (after 197) the wall was carried across it.

LOW WALL, ½ m. W of the former, is the site of Milecastle 55.

Now under the village of Walton itself is the site of Milecastle 56.

Castlesteads, 1 m. SW of the village, is the site of the small
Roman FORT of UXELLODUNUM, a little s of the wall, overlooking the Cambeck. A number of inscriptions have come to
light here.

CAMBECKHILL, NW of Castlesteads, is the site of Milecastle 57
of the wall.

4050   WARWICK

The BRIDGE, a fine job of 1837 by *Dobson* of Newcastle, with
three segmental arches, divides Warwick on the w from
Warwick Bridge on the E.

15 ST LEONARD, Warwick. This is the most memorable Norman
village church in Cumberland; for it has an apse decorated
outside by plain projecting pilaster-strips carrying small
arches. Each of the deep recesses is quite narrow – only about
18 in. wide. The motif is exceptional in England, but occurs
here and there in France (St Loup, Bayeux, tower; Jezeneuil,
Vienne; Thaon, chancel). As the former chancel arch, now
tower arch, with its mighty responds, its big scallop capitals
with small bits of decoration (including the corn-cob motif),
and especially its arch mouldings is entirely of the Carlisle
Cathedral type of about 1130, Mr Neil Stratford suggested
(verbally) to me that the composition of the apse may reflect
the original E end of the cathedral. The apse has only three
small windows. On one of the chancel buttresses appears the
rebus of Prior Thornton of Wetheral (thorn-tun) corresponding to an early C16 date. The church itself however is of
*c.*1870 (by *R. J. Withers*), with lancet windows and a bellcote
on machicoulis-like brackets.

ST PAUL, Warwick Bridge. 1845 by *John Dobson*. Neo-Norman,
with a w tower whose bell-openings are (correctly) a little
later in stylistic chronology than the rest. Broach-spire with
one tier of lucarnes. Polygonal apse with a tripartite E window.
The apse has a plaster rib-vault. The church was paid for by
Mr Dixon of Holme Eden Hall.

OUR LADY AND ST WILFRED (R.C.), Warwick Bridge. 1841
by *Pugin*. Although this is a small church which cost little
(£2,586), there is a world between it and Dobson's St Paul.
Dobson is still entirely naïve in the use he makes of Norman;
Pugin's Gothic is correct Gothic. It is here and more or less
precisely in 1841 that archeological accuracy begins in English
church design. Nave with bell-turret and chancel. The N
windows alternating lancets and two-light windows of the

cusped Y-type. W wall with three stepped lancets, W doorway with naturalistic leaf capitals. In the S porch also one stiff-leaf capital. In the chancel S wall SEDILIA and PISCINA as they ought to be (and who would occupy the three seats at Warwick Bridge?), in the N wall Easter-Sepulchre-like recess with the founder's tomb. Henry Howard (of Corby Castle) died in 1842. – STAINED GLASS. The side windows clearly by *Hardman*, who mostly worked to Pugin's designs, though these windows were done after Pugin's death (dates commemorated 1860, 1865, 1867).

Former METHODIST CHURCH, Warwick, on the way to St Leonard. A fine pedimented front with just a simple door surround and no front windows. The date 1847 is surprisingly late for so Georgian a design.

WARWICK HALL. Of *c*.1930, by *Guy Elwes*, neo-Georgian. The stables are real Georgian. The house preceding the present one was built in 1828.

HOLME EDEN HALL. *Dobson* in 1837 built this sumptuous Early Tudor mansion for Peter Dixon, one of the founders of the great cotton mills at Carlisle.* It bristles with ornamental chimneys, and has a porch-tower, bays, and mullioned windows. The skyline seen from a distance is superb.

WHOOF HOUSE, $1\frac{3}{4}$ m. W, on the A-road. In the garden stands the splendid six-light C17 Gothic-Revival E window of 43 Arthuret church. The composition is three plus three lights, each with a segmental arch and above intersecting tracery, and in the mid-spandrel an oval. Arthuret (*see* p. 61) was rebuilt from 1609 onwards. But such an oval looks 1650–75 rather than 1610.

WASDALE HALL *see* STRANDS

WASDALE HEAD   *1000*

CHURCH. Very small, of nave and chancel in one, with a bellcote. Plain mullioned windows. – Victorian IRON BRACKETS for oil lamps. – PLATE. Cup of 1565.

WASTWATER *see* WASDALE HEAD

WATENDLATH *see* GRANGE

WATERFOOT *see* POOLEY BRIDGE (W), p. 284

* But Manner and Whellan say 1833 by *James Stewart* of Carlisle.

WATERMILLOCK

ALL SAINTS. 1884 by *C. J. Ferguson*. Mauve slate and red sandstone; quite substantial, and a serious job. Short, broad w tower, wide nave and chancel. Lancet windows. – PLATE. Cup of 1581.

(WATERMILLOCK HOUSE. Dated 1689. Characteristic of that date the three-light mullioned windows all under one label-course and the oval windows in the gables. MHLG)

WAVERTON

CHRIST CHURCH, E of the village, at the crossroads. 1865. Nave with bellcote and chancel. Plate tracery.

HAWKRIGG HOUSE, I m. SE. 1821. Nicely placed on an eminence and agreeable to look at. Rendered white. Three-bay centre with lower pedimented wings. The windows in the latter and l. and r. of the doorway in the centre are of the Venetian type in which the side openings are continued blank as a band round the open arch in the centre.

WELTON *see* SEBERGHAM

WEST CURTHWAITE *see* WESTWARD

WESTNEWTON

ST MATTHEW. 1857 by *Hugall* of Cheltenham (GS), who also did the SCHOOL in 1858. Very thin w turret with spire. Nave and chancel; geometrical tracery.

WESTWARD

ST HILDA. Probably early C19.* Groups of three lancets of the same height. Pedimental E gable. Thin w tower with a pointed-arched w porch above which steps lead back to the tower. – PLATE. Silver-gilt Cup with steeple Cover, 1635 (cf. Abbey Town and Ambleside). – MONUMENTS. Pair of TABLETS to Richard Barnise † 1648 and a legacy of Francis Barnise. The interesting thing is that the paired frames have dog-tooth.

GREENHILL. Late Georgian, rendered, of seven bays. Porch of two pairs of Roman Doric columns. The staircase is apsed

* The neighbouring SCHOOL is dated 1828.

inside. R. and l. runs a corridor, and at its start are four pairs of tiny stucco caryatids and atlantes, two pairs l., two r. They are reminiscent of Michelangelo and – though earlier – of Alfred Stevens.

(MEADOW BANK FARM, West Curthwaite. Dated 1666, but inside cruck construction. MHLG)

WETHERAL

4050

HOLY TRINITY. Right above the river Eden. The exterior is₂ essentially early C16, with most of the windows of two or three lights with uncusped round arches to the lights. The w tower turns octagonal higher up and has a round-arched w doorway. The doorway is more probably of 1790 (the date when a tower was built) than of 1500–20, and the upper part belongs to the restoration of 1882. The chancel was largely rebuilt by *Withers* in 1872, but on the s side are two original *Orate* inscriptions for Prior William Thornton of Wetheral Priory and his successor (after 1530), Richard de Wetheral. In 1791 a mausoleum for the Howard family of Corby Castle was added. It is Gothic in the thin, brittle way of these years. Five bays of slim windows with slim buttresses and a large E window. Mullions and tracery are of cast iron. Inside plaster rib-vaults. But inside the church architectural evidence much earlier than the rest. The arcades (the s arcade much renewed) are of the C13. Four bays, round and octagonal piers, double-chamfered arches. – STAINED GLASS. The w window has two saints and kneeling donors; C15. – PLATE. C17 Chalice. – MONUMENTS. Two defaced effigies on a tomb-chest with shields in quatrefoils; *c*.1500. – Lady Maria Howard † 1789 ₅₆ at the age of twenty-three. By *Nollekens*. It cost £1,500. White marble group, free-standing. Young woman seated on the ground with a baby. Religion, generously draped, bends over her. It is one of Nollekens' major works, though it must be admitted that he was better at portrait than at life-size scenes. Fuseli was not of this opinion. He called the monument superior to anything by Canova.*

WETHERAL PRIORY, s of the church. It was a Benedictine priory, founded *c*.1100 by Ranulph de Meschines. Only the gatehouse is preserved, and this is of the C15. The entry arch dies into the imposts. Above a two-light window, and above

---

* Quoted from an unpublished entry in the Faringdon Diary by D. Irwin: *English Neo-Classical Art* (1966), p. 162.

that another; cusped lights. Tunnel-vaulted archway. To the inside the small doorway to the spiral staircase. The farmyard E of the gatehouse probably partly represents the priory cloister. Some medieval walling remains with a two-light window. This may be the E wall of the E range.

CAVES. About ¼ m. s are man-made caves in the rocky river bank. They are traditionally connected with St Constantine and known to have been in use in the C14. There are three, and they are 20 by 9 by 9 ft. On the opposite (Corby) side of the river a life-size STATUE of St Constantine, put up in 1843.

The former FRIENDS' MEETING HOUSE is dated 1718. It is a plain three-bay cottage.

VIADUCT. Of the Newcastle–Carlisle railway, 1830-4. Five 80-ft arches, 100 ft high. By *F. Giles*.

The village has a handsome GREEN, but on one side of it a grossly High Victorian villa. It is of yellow brick and has a tower, a half-hipped dormer, and Gothic detail. Close to the NE end is the CROWN HOTEL, seven irregularly spaced bays and a porch with Ionic columns, the capitals far better than the shafts.

(EDEN BANK. Built in 1834. Whellan)

(COAT HOUSE, 1½ m. SSE. A bastle-house incorporated into a modern farmhouse. The bastle-house is two-storeyed with accommodation for cattle below, for the farmer and his family above.*)

WHELPO see CALDBECK

WHICHAM

₁₀₈₀

ST MARY. The s doorway has a single-chamfered Norman arch. The E window is C17. The N transept dates from 1858, and the other windows were then also 'improved'. In 1902 the W window seems to have been done. Nave and chancel in one, and bellcote. – PLATE. Cup and Cover Paten, 1628.

WHITBECK

₁₀₈₀

ST MARY. Nave and chancel in one. Mostly of the restoration of 1883. The chancel seems to be partly genuine Perp. – PLATE. Cup, 1825. – MONUMENT. 6-ft effigy of a Lady, early C14, rather rubbed off.

---

* Mr Robin McDowall told me about this house.

STANDING STONE, 1½ m. NW, ¾ m. NNW of Gutterby. This isolated stone is all that remains of a stone circle which originally stood on this site.

WHITEFIELD HOUSE see BASSENTHWAITE

WHITEFLAT see IRTHINGTON

WHITEHALL see MEALSGATE

WHITEHAVEN

9010

Whitehaven in an engraving of 1642 was just a village with its village street. The estate then belonged to Sir Christopher Lowther. His son Sir John created the new Whitehaven about 1680 etc. as a port for coal. Defoe calls Whitehaven the most eminent coal port in England, except for Newcastle and Sunderland. Hutchinson in 1794 gives the population as 2,272 in 1693, 16,400 in 1785.* The layout of Whitehaven remains complete, the 5 earliest post-medieval planned town in England – preceded only by Londonderry as a town planned by the English. It is a simple grid of streets with one whole block left free for the church – just as it had been done in New Winchelsea at the end of the C13. To the E was the Lowther mansion, which is now part of the hospital, and to the S was the irregular old town with its market place and quay. Part of the OLD QUAY is indeed still of 1687. The old church was augmented in 1715 by Holy Trinity at the E end of Roper Street, destroyed only in the C20, and in 1752 by St James at the N end of Queen Street.

ST NICHOLAS. The old church was built in 1693. It was long and had windows in two tiers all along its sides. Its W doorway with Doric pilasters‡ is preserved inside the W porch of the new church, which was built in 1883 by *C. J. Ferguson* at the expense of Margaret Gibson in memory of her parents. It is a large church of red sandstone in a Dec to Perp style, with a W tower and a W transept – the *parti* of Ely. The W tower has detached buttress-shafts and pinnacles *à la* Somerset. East Anglian on the other hand is the doubling of clerestory windows as against arcade arches. – PAINTING. Last Supper by the local painter *Matthias Read*. – PLATE. Damaged Paten of

* The latter figure, Mr Hay points out, must include areas outside the township proper.

‡ And also two of the wooden gallery columns.

1602; Paten on foot of 1685; Flagon of 1690; Cup and Cover Paten of 1710; Cups of 1732 and 1805.

ST JAMES. Built in 1752–3, on the hill at the far end of Queen Street, facing it with its broad w tower. This is why above the pedimented doorway there is another larger pediment. Arched bell-openings, obelisk pinnacles. The tower is embraced by the aisles. The long sides, on the pattern of old St Nicholas, have windows in two tiers. They look entirely domestic, without any adornment. The thrill of the church is the interior, the finest Georgian church interior in the county. Under the tower a lobby with a staircase with thin turned balusters leading in two arms to the gallery doorways. The arrangement is the same as in the Penrith parish church of 1720–2. Between these a simply and beautifully carved MEMORIAL TABLET of 1785. The church has galleries round three sides supported on Tuscan columns and carrying unfluted Ionic ones. Flat ceiling, with two delightful stucco roundels, one with the Ascension and angels, the other with the Virgin and angels. The E end is an apse with Ionic pilasters. – The ALTARPIECE, a beautiful Transfiguration by *Giulio Cesare Procaccini* (from the Escorial, it is said, and given by the third Earl of Lonsdale), is also flanked by Ionic pilasters. They carry a pediment. – COMMUNION RAIL. Of Roman Doric balusters. – PULPIT. On a very high columnar support. The pulpit itself with fluted pilasters broken round the angles and arched panels with a little rocaille. It is probably to be dated *c.*1755–60 (cf. the pulpit in St Andrews, Glasgow, of 1739–56).

CHRIST CHURCH, Preston Street. 1847 by *William Waller*, neo-Norman with a broad, ill-composed E front with bellcote and an aisleless interior.

ST BEGH (R.C.), Coach Road. 1868 by *E. W. Pugin*. Dec.

FRIENDS' MEETING HOUSE, Sandhills Lane. 1722. A plain rectangle. The gallery is reached by an outer staircase.

SALVATION ARMY, Catherine Street. The former United Methodist Chapel of 1836. Three widely spaced bays and a pediment all across. Pointed windows, doorway with pilasters.

CONGREGATIONAL CHURCH, Scotch Street. 1874 by *T. L. Banks* (cost £10,500). Rock-faced, E.E., with a prominent NW tower with debased top.

WESLEYAN CHURCH, Lowther and Scotch Streets. Also E.E. (geometrical tracery), and also with a very prominent NW tower. Also by *T. L. Banks*. Built in 1877 (cost over £10,000).

TOWN HALL, Dale Street. On the site of the nine-bay Mansion House (or The Cupola), built in the late C17, and incorporating part of its masonry. The present building is of 1851. The architect was *William Barnes* of London. It is of five bays with a porch of four sturdy Tuscan columns, l. and r. Venetian windows, and the upper windows crowned by pediments on very demonstrative brackets. It is a typically Early Victorian job.

WHITEHAVEN HOSPITAL. This was built in 1769 by Sir John Lowther. It was also known as The Flat or Flatt Hall. Sir John Lowther had built his house on the same site before 1694. The present house is that rebuilt by Sir James Lowther, Earl of Lonsdale, in 1769. It is castellated.

MEADOW VIEW HOSPITAL, the former Workhouse, Low Road. Built in 1854, in a restrained classical style.

QUAYS. The OLD QUAY of 1687 has already been referred to. It was altered in 1792 and 1809. Its LIGHTHOUSE is round and dated 1730. The OLD NEW QUAY is of 1741 and was lengthened in 1767, the WEST PIER is by *Rennie* and dates from 1824–39. At its end is another lighthouse.

A PERAMBULATION is never easy in a town of a grid plan. Those who have tried it in New York or Philadelphia will agree. Whitehaven is smaller, and so retracing one's steps is not so painful. The two main E–W streets are Lowther Street and Duke Street. In LOWTHER STREET three good banks, the best the TRUSTEE SAVINGS BANK of 1833. Three bays, Greek Doric porch carrying a balcony with cast-iron railing. Pilasters above. The WESTMINSTER BANK of three by four bays is a good, restrained Italianate job.* To its r. the CLYDESDALE BANK, lower and in a simple Classical.

DUKE STREET has the town hall at its E end. Yet a little further E is SOMERSET HOUSE (now Civil Defence H.Q.), with a charming mid C18 Gothick porch with clustered shafts, reached by outer stairs. The building itself is quite severe, all with tripartite windows (of *c.*1830-40 ?). But the entrance hall is Gothick again. Further down on the same side more houses with nice pedimented doorways (e.g. No. 44). Round the corner between Duke Street and Lowther Street is No. 14 SCOTCH STREET, the finest house in Whitehaven, stone, of five bays with a centre emphasized by quoins of even length and with a top balustrade. Doorway with attached Ionic

* But Mr Hay tells me that the house itself was built in 1705.

columns, a pulvinated frieze, and a pediment. The date must be about the middle of the C18.

Pedimented doorways are features of the C18 and early C19 in many streets of Whitehaven. Scotch Street is continued in IRISH STREET. Near the corner of Scotch Street is a quite splendid Italian six-bay palazzo of three storeys. No. 7 has a good mid C18 doorway. At the end of Irish Street in HOW-GILL STREET is the former ASSEMBLY ROOMS of 1736. Four bays, doorway with Tuscan columns and pediment. Entirely run-of-the-mill. In Howgill Street also pedimented doorways. At its E end turn l. into CATHERINE STREET. Here is the factory of DOBSON & MUSGRAVE, once a militia barracks. It is four-storeyed, long, and with a three-bay pediment. According to Mr Daniel Hay it was most probably built between 1811 and 1829 as a linen mill.

More to be seen in ROPER STREET, which runs W from Irish Street to the quays. Also in Roper Street the former THEATRE, built in 1769. The interior was remodelled in 1909 but still maintains at least the mood of Georgian theatres in small towns.* By the quays turn l. to the former CUSTOM HOUSE, with a porch with thin Tuscan columns, and the ROYAL STANDARD INN, Early Victorian. The interior fittings of the Music Hall at its back have been partly re-used at Rosehill, Moresby (see p. 164). Back to the centre by Roper Street, and for a moment S into QUEEN STREET for No. 151, of five bays with a pretty doorway with fluted Ionic pilasters.

On the hill to the S of the town WELLINGTON PIT of 1840 etc., with a high chimney and castellated buildings.

WHOOF HOUSE see WARWICK

WIGTON

ST MARY. 1788 by *Nixson* and *Parkin*, masons. Almost a copy of St Cuthbert, Carlisle. W tower embraced by the two rooms housing the two arms of the staircase. Nave of eight bays with windows in two tiers. Doorways in the first and eighth bays. They and the W doorway with rustication of alternating sizes. Inside, three galleries on Tuscan columns, and with upper Tuscan columns, each carrying its own bit of entablature with a triglyph in the frieze. Flat ceiling very prettily decorated with stucco ornament in two roundels and an oval. Short

* Since this was written, the building has been pulled down.

chancel with a Venetian E window with fluted Ionic columns.
– PULPIT. Handsome, with swags. No doubt late C18. –
RETABLE of the N aisle altar, made up of C16 and C17
North German woodwork.* The panels with religious scenes.
– In the former graveyard S of the church a two-light window
from the preceding church. Cusped lights and a sexfoiled circle
over, i.e. late C13. – PLATE. Paten on foot, 1800; Cup,
1806.

ST CUTHBERT (R.C.). By *Bonomi*, 1837.‡ A remarkably
substantial building for its date and its denomination. Red
sandstone, with a façade with shafted lancet windows. The
side windows with Y-tracery, the E window five stepped
lancets. The ceiling is recent. – PULPIT. A fine Georgian
piece.

FRIENDS' MEETING HOUSE. 1830. A building of some size
and dignity. Ashlar-faced, with broad, rusticated angle-
pilasters and Grecian windows.

RURAL DISTRICT OFFICES, South End. 1964–5 by *Graham,
Roy & Nicholson*. A straightforward, honest job without
gimmicks.

NELSON TOMLINSON SCHOOL, South End. The l. building of
1807: five bays with a deep Tuscan porch and a tripartite
window over. The r. addition Victorian-Gothic.

FOUNTAIN, Market Place. 1871 by *J. T. Knowles Sen.* Square,
with a pyramid spire of leaves against a gold ground. Finial
at the top. On the sides four reliefs of Acts of Mercy by 66
Thomas Woolner, very good indeed, still with classical
discipline, but also with genuine feeling.

Wigton has no architectural surprises, but it is a pleasant little
town, and there are plenty of pleasant houses. The best street
is WEST STREET, with quite a number of attractive doorcases; No. 20, with a doorway displaying an open curly pediment above a round arch, is the earliest of them. Its nearest
parallel, Easton Farm near Bowness (p. 74), is dated 1724. Between them the former Mechanics' Institute with two Tuscan
columns *in antis* and a pediment with three carved figures. It
was built in 1851. The figures represent Wisdom receiving
homage from Knowledge and Learning – quite a bit of a
problem of characterization to make such closely related
allegories recognizable. The sculptor was *Irving Ray* of

* The Rev. Canon G. Winder tells me that it is said to come from Cleves.
‡ Enlarged in 1857, according to Mr Denis Evinson.

Wigton. At the end of the street is WIGTON HALL, ashlar-faced, of eight bays and neo-Tudor, i.e. with Georgian windows under hood-moulds and a porch with pointed arch under a straight hood-mould and crowned by a pedimental gable with a parapet decorated by quatrefoils.

Pleasant doorways also in the streets running E from the Market Place, i.e. King Street–East End–Bankfoot.

But the *clou* of Wigton is of course the crazy ashlar tower which Mr William Banks, exporter of factory-made clothing to Australia, added in 1887 to his house, HIGHMOOR. The house is a five-bay house of 1810 with a three-bay pediment, and it has additions on the l. of before 1878. But nothing could prepare one for this absurdly high tower (136 ft), lopsided in the staircase arrangement, and with open lantern and ogee cap on top. The style cannot be defined. It is what the decades themselves called the Mixed Renaissance. The architect may have been *James Henderson* of Wigton. Or was he only the builder?

(ISLEKIRK HALL, 2½ m. S. The house has some mullioned windows with arched lights. NMR)

ROMAN FORT. The site of the Roman fort of OLD CARLISLE lies 1½ m. SE, on the ridge between Old Carlisle Farmhouse and the Wizabeck. The prepared platform upon which it was constructed and traces of its ramparts can still be seen. A civil settlement lies to the NE and SE.

WINDSCALE *see* CALDER BRIDGE

WOODHEAD *see* BEWCASTLE

WORKINGTON

Workington grew as a coal and iron town. Coal was exploited already before 1650. The first ironworks were started in 1763 at Seaton. Now two companies employ 3,000 and 2,000. However the town felt the slump of the 1930s badly and is only now picking up. The town as a town has not got much of a face, but it has some major buildings and one small area of considerable charm. The main church is somewhat out of the way.

ST MICHAEL. Elevated and isolated. The church was built in 1770, but rebuilt after a fire in 1887–90 by *Bassett Smith & James Howes*. The two-tier arrangement of the windows along the long sides is a heritage of 1770. Short, broad W tower. N aisle under its own gable. The interior still has galleries as they were in 1770, but the thin Perp-looking piers are of 1887. The shortness of the chancel is Georgian too. Re-erected inside a Norman arch with a roll and a hollow. In the w porch also a huge Norman two-scallop capital. It must be late C11 or early C12, and where would it come from? – FONT. Octagonal, with panels semicircular at the foot. Probably Perp. – SCULPTURE. Several minor parts of Anglo-Danish cross-shafts with interlace. – PLATE. Paten on feet, 1732; Cup and Cover Paten, 1734; Cup of 1635 remade in 1745; deep Dish 1789. – MONUMENTS. Several coffin lids with cross and sword. – Tomb-chest with the effigies of a Knight and Lady, first half C15. Homespun but impressive. Two angels by her pillow, two puppies biting her skirt. Against the tomb-chest shields under ogee gables with very flat, summary leaves.

ST JOHN, Washington Street. 1823 by *Thomas Hardwick*. The mighty Tuscan portico is an enlarged copy of Inigo Jones's at 61 Covent Garden, rebuilt or repaired by Hardwick in 1795. The tower behind the portico was added in 1846. It has a square base and an octagonal top with diagonally-projecting pairs of pilasters and a stone cap. Long, arched side-windows. The interior has galleries on thin iron columns. Flat ceiling with a thin rib pattern and leaf motifs. No chancel at all. The organ is in the tower, and the opening is flanked by fluted Corinthian pilasters. – Gilt altar BALDACCHINO and FONT COVER by *Comper*, 1931, in his Italian mood.

OUR LADY STAR OF THE SEA (R.C.), Bank Road. 1876 by *E. W. Pugin*. Front with bellcote and geometrical tracery. Terribly debased, fussy interior.

METHODIST CHURCH, South William Street. 1890. In the showiest Italianate, with Venetian tracery and a prominent SW tower. By *Charles Bell*. The estimate was for £3,863 (GS).

WORKINGTON HALL. The chief Curwen mansion, but now the property of the town, which leaves it to decay. Yet it is one of Cumberland's most historic houses. It was built in the first place in 1379 (licence to crenellate). Of that time is the pele tower in the SE corner with its vaulted basement. The hall probably lay N of it and filled the E wing. The NE corner is medieval too, and so essentially is the gatehouse in the W range. The land falls steeply to the E. The buildings grew by two Late Elizabethan wings linking the E range with the gate-house and now appear quadrangular. The features are mostly of 1782–1828. Hutchinson gives *John Carr* as the architect. The pele tower and hall have large arched windows. The N side is a long, even twelve-bay front with raised, flat window-frames. The w side has, apart from the gatehouse, angle pavilions with round-arched windows with Y-tracery.

PARKEND HOUSE (Museum), Parkend. Georgian, of five bays with a doorway with fluted Ionic pilasters and pediment. Venetian window in the N gable.

THOMAS WILSON SCHOOL, Guard Street. 1831. Original the five l. bays, the pedimented centre with pilasters, and the two following bays. The rest a later alteration and addition.

MECHANICS' INSTITUTE (former), Pow Street.* Built c.1849. Three bays, stuccoed, with pediment all across. Pairs of angle pilasters and a porch of four thin unfluted Ionic columns. The details all very provincial. Opposite, the DISTRICT BANK, also three bays, but in a wild Italianate. It is of 1865, and by D. Birkett of Carlisle (GS).

The one area which can really be perambulated is the streets round PORTLAND SQUARE, laid out apparently c.1775.‡ The square itself is delightful, long and narrow, cobbled, and with two rows of trees. It is not at all like England. The streets surrounding it immediately form a grid. No houses deserve special mention, but many are pretty in a modest way.

(SCHOOSE FARM. Built by J. C. Curwen in 1800 as a model farm. Much remains, including the windmill tower.§)

WREAY

ST MARY. John Losh lived at Woodside, a house now mostly demolished. He came from an old Cumberland family (Arlosh), and had been to school at Sedbergh and then at Trinity Cambridge. He branched out into industry and founded alkali works at Walker near Newcastle. In 1809 he established the Walker Iron Works, which his brother William managed. William was a partner and friend of George Stephenson and also something of an inventor. John Losh had two daughters, Sara and Katherine. *Sara Losh* was an exceptionally talented girl. She knew French, Latin, and Greek and was good at mathematics. When she once translated pages from the Latin *ex tempore*, a visitor did not realize that she was not simply reading an English text. She was calm, dignified, and beautiful. Katherine was lively and hearty. The two sisters were the

---

* Demolished since this was written.
‡ Leases are recorded between 1780 and 1790.
§ I owe this reference to Mr H. J. Chandler.

closest of friends until Katherine died young, in 1835. Sara,
who was unmarried too, decided in her grief to dedicate a
memorial to her sister. She was passionately interested in
architecture and had travelled in Italy with Katherine. So she
conceived first of a church and then of a mausoleum, and of a
church reminiscent of their travels and beautified by symbolic
conceits. The church was consecrated in 1842. It cost £1,200.
It was intended to be a Roman basilica, and its apse marks it 64
at once as such for hyperboreans. But much else is Romanesque rather than Early Christian, and French rather than
Italian. Thus the w front has its gable enriched by rising little
blank arches – the dwarf gallery of Italian Romanesque
churches. But there are no aisles, and the apse is internally
provided with a close arcade of strong columns, both French
Romanesque motifs. Above the four side windows of the nave
is a clerestory of three dwarf openings for each bay, and that
is neither Early Christian nor Romanesque. In short, Miss
Losh was quite free in her interpretation, and quite original.
Her choice of what was soon to be known as the Lombardic
style was in all probability an original decision too; for though
the beginnings of the neo-Norman fashion of the forties date
back to the twenties (e.g. Robinson at Leamington, 1825),
Wreay has nothing to do with that brand of *Rundbogenstil*, and
as for the Italian Romanesque, the three principal English
examples – Wilton by Wyatt & Brandon, Christ Church
Streatham by Wild, and Christ Church Watney Street by
John Shaw – were all begun in 1840, i.e. just after Miss Losh's
design. It is true that the English versions were inspired by
the Munich ones of Klenze (Allerheiligen 1827–37) and
Gärtner (Ludwigskirche 1829–40), but these Miss Losh can
hardly have known. We do not know much of her travels; she
was, with Katherine and Uncle William, in Italy in 1817,
travelled through France in the same year, and apparently
saw something of Germany too. But that was long before
Klenze and Gärtner (and Schinkel) had begun their revival.
By the time when the church was started, on the other hand,
Moller e.g. was translated into English, and the principal
Romanesque buildings in the Rhineland, from Lorsch to
Gelnhausen, could be admired in his excellent plates. Moreover, Wreay has a solidity all of its own, and in any case its
symbolic carvings have no parallel at all. In fact one might
easily make the mistake of dating St Mary as one of the
examples of the Early Christian or Byzantine revival which

took place about 1900 and its carvings as Arts and Crafts. The latter is indeed almost unavoidable. Miss Losh, just as she had no architect, used as her sculptor simply a local boy, *William Hindson*. The W doorway and W windows have surrounds with vine, corn ears, water-lilies, roses, pine, monkey-puzzle, and also beetles, birds, and butterflies, all naturalistically but flatly carved, of a stylization which would be expected of 1900 but is unique in the forties. The gargoyles (needless to say not Romanesque at all) represent snakes, tortoises, an alligator, etc. Inside, the tiny E apse windows have metal grilles again of leaves, and this time with fossilized fern forms, etc. – ALTAR TABLE. Of green Italian marble, carried by two brass eagles and placed so that the parson faces the congregation, an arrangement familiar today from the recent Liturgical Movement, but again entirely unexpected in the forties. How did the church authorities react? Was this not popery? Perhaps they were not on their guard yet. – The altar CANDLESTICKS are of alabaster and represent lotus-flowers.* – FONT. Byzantino-naturalistic. Of local alabaster. The carving is partly by Sara herself, that of the cover by her cousin, *William S. Losh*. The motifs include Norman zigzag and Greek fluting, and also lily, butterfly, vine, and pome-granate. – To the l. and r. of the font, against the wall, are the TABLES OF THE LAW, one with a Jewish lamp in front, the other on a bracket with an owl and a cock – meaning vigilance.* – PULPIT. The stump of a hollowed oak, and in imitation of the calamites found in coal measures. – LECTERNS. Also naturalistic tree-work, one with an eagle, the other with a pelican. – SCULPTURE. L. and r. of the apse arch a wooden Annunciation. – STAINED GLASS. Non-figural, and partly made up of bits of ancient glass, bought after the revolution of 1830 by Sara Losh's cousin William from the ruins of the archbishop's palace in Paris. – MAUSOLEUM. The mausoleum for Katherine Losh is built of large blocks of stone, left quite accidental in shape and surface and laid deliberately in a cyclopean irregular way. Henry Lonsdale in 1873 called it 'Druidical' or 'Attic–Cyclopean'. Flat roof. Inside, the white seated marble figure of the girl, reading. By *Dunbar*, 1850, from a sketch made by Sara near Naples in 1817. – BEW-CASTLE CROSS. In front of the mausoleum, put up in honour of Miss Losh's parents. It was designed in or just before 1835,

* I am told that these have recently been removed. How can this have been done?

and an inscription says 'Hoc saxum poni duae filiae sibi posuerunt, una maestissima effecit'. The cross is usually called a copy, but it is not. The ornamental carving is made more realistic and again given that peculiar Arts and Crafts flavour, and the figure in profile of the Grecian stele type is of course not to be found in Anglian Northumbria. Sara Losh's attitude to decoration is as remarkable as her architectural choices. The decoration made use of by her includes fossil forms, Egyptian motifs (scarab w window, lotus), the Early Anglian of the Bewcastle Cross, a Jewish motif, and animals used symbolically (caterpillar–chrysalis–butterfly, w windows).

(In the churchyard also a copy of the early sanctuary of St Perran in the sands near Perranzabuloe in Cornwall, found in 1835. It is only 29 by 16½ ft in size, and has inside a rude altar and a palm tree.)

A ROMAN FORT lies ½ m. NE, to the w of the main York–Carlisle road.

WYTHBURN   *3010*

CHAPEL. Built in 1640 and restored in 1872. Low and white. The apse and w front clearly of 1872. The small, squarish side windows equally clearly of 1640. – In the apse one STAINED GLASS window by *Holiday*, 1892. – Wordsworth called the church (unavoidably) a 'modest house of prayer'.

WYTHOP   *1030*

ST MARGARET, 1¾ m. ENE of Embleton church. 1865–6 by *Bruce* of Whitehaven (GS). Nave with a fussy bellcote and chancel. Plate tracery. – STAINED GLASS. The w window († 1911) by *Kempe & Tower*.

CHAPEL, ¾ m. SE of the former, by Kelsick Farm. In ruins.

HILLFORT, ¼ m. SE of Bassenthwaite Railway Station. The fort is of multivallate construction, defended by four lines of ramparts on the w and by two on the E, where the steepness of the slope provides additional natural protection.

YEORTON HALL *see* HAILE

WESTMORLAND

*

ACORN BANK see TEMPLE SOWERBY

ALLEN KNOTT see WINDERMERE

AMBLESIDE

ST MARY. 1850–4 by *Sir G. G. Scott*, a prosperous and townish-looking church with a SE steeple. The spire has broaches. It is not at all a North Country type. The style is the Second Pointed, i.e. later C13 to 1300, which Scott favoured. – PAINTING. Mural by *Gordon Ransom*, 1944. It represents the traditional rush-bearing procession and was done while the Royal College of Art was evacuated to Ambleside during the war. – STAINED GLASS. N aisle NW and S aisle SW windows by *Holiday*, 1888–91. – The W, E, and other windows evidently of *c.*1855–60. – PLATE. Cup and Paten, London, 1571–2, the bowl probably a secular beaker; Cup and Steeple Cover, 89 1618; Set of 1843–5. – MONUMENTS. Jane Harden † 1829. Reading woman and standing angel. – Captain Lutwidge † 1861. With a very Gothic canopy. By *J. Chapman* of Frome.

ST ANNE, Chapel Hill. The old chapel, built in 1812. It is now de-consecrated. W tower, low entrance bays l. and r. The body of the church with lancets filled with Victorian tracery.

METHODIST CHURCH. 1898. The HALL attached to it is in the free Tudor of *c.*1900, with a Baroque doorway. It is indeed of 1903–7. The architect was *W. Mason*.

The little town of grey slate houses with grey slate roofs has no architecture of distinction. The MARKET HOUSE of 1863 is Gothic. BRIDGE HOUSE, one bay wide and one bay deep and sitting on a minute bridge, is a curiosity. The hotels range from the ROTHAY MANOR HOTEL, early C19 or Early Victorian, a former private house, white, of three bays with one-bay wings, a nice doorway, and a nice balcony railing, to the PRINCE OF WALES HOTEL, large, dark and gabled, of 1855.

(ROTHAY HOLME, now Lakes Urban District Council. By *Waterhouse*. Built in 1854; enlarged in 1890. Originally L-shaped. Large former dining room with a canted bay window. Steep-pitched roofs and three principal gables.*)

LOUGHRIGG BROW, ½ m. W. 1863 by *Ewan Christian*. In a rather drab Gothic, with dormers and wooden mullioned and mullioned-and-transomed windows. Over the entrance it says: God's Providence is my Inheritance.

CROFT HOTEL, Clappersgate, ¾ m. SW. Said to date from 1829. Front with two canted bay windows and between them a cast-iron veranda. Also gloriously elaborate cast-iron brackets to support the far-projecting eaves. On the entrance side a wide, tripartite Late-Perp–Tudor porch. Handsome entrance hall, also Gothic.

(MERZ BARN, Kurt Schwitters's barn, i.e. the barn in which he made up a large Merz mural in his last years, when he lived here. The mural was detached in 1965 and taken to King's College, Newcastle.)

ROMAN FORTS. About ½ m. S, on a promontory jutting out into the head of Windermere, two distinct forts have been recognized by excavation. The first, of late C1 date, was defended by a double-ditch system backed by a clay rampart; its internal buildings were of wood. The second, built in the Hadrianic period, lay across the earlier fort and was defended by a stone wall backed by a clay rampart and fronted by two ditches. Inside, the pair of granaries, the *principia*, and the commandant's house have been examined.

                              APPLEBY

80 ST LAWRENCE. Externally the Perp church of a prospering town, internally mostly Dec. Actually the bottom part of the W tower is Norman – cf. the window in the N wall – and the S porch entrance with its dog-tooth and hollow chamfers is a re-used C13 piece. The five-bay arcades determine the early C14 impression inside. They have quatrefoil piers, the foils more than semicircular and with fillets, and double-chamfered arches. The tower arch towards the nave is of the same type; so is the W bay of the S aisle half embracing the tower, and so are the chancel arch and the two-bay S chancel chapel. The N chapel is different. The flat, square capital on

---

* I owe this description to Mr Stuart Smith.

its octagonal pier is so unmedieval that one at once believes it to be part of the Lady Anne Clifford's family chapel, built in 1654-5. The Lady Anne lived in the castle. We are told that she 'caus'd a great part of Appleby Church to be taken down' and rebuilt. That is surely not so, but the chancel is hers. The Perp windows are alas not hers but Victorian. The Perp character of the exterior is most prominent in the upper part of the tower and in the clerestory with its three-light windows, its splendid gargoyles, and its battlements. The s aisle wall is Dec, though the windows are all Victorian replacements.* Finally the plastered ceiling, with its rather parsimonious Gothic panelling. This must be of the early C19. – SCREENS. C15 screens of one-light divisions between the chapels and the chancel. – ORGAN CASE. A nationally important piece. It comes from Carlisle Cathedral, where it replaced one broken up in the Civil War. However, it is said to contain older parts. It looks in fact c.1540, with its playful bits of Early Renaissance decoration. The composition is of three turrets. The lower part appears to be the base designed by *Thomas Machell* about 1836, but its woodwork is probably of the years after 1684, when the case was given to Appleby. – SWORD REST. Early C18, of iron. – PLATE. Cup and Cover Paten, 1630; Cup, Cover Paten, Paten on foot, Flagon, and Almsdish, 1694. – MONUMENTS. Effigy of a lady(?) praying. The lower half of her body is hidden by a foliated cross. Early C14. – Margaret, Countess of Cumberland, erected in 1617. Alabaster and touch. Recumbent effigy of excellent workmanship with a metal coronet. The trophies of death on the tomb-chest are equally well done. One panel of the inscription reads:

Who fayeth, love, mercy, noble constancie to God to virtue, to distress, to right, observd, exprest, shewd, held religiously hath here this monument thou seest in sight the cover of her earthly part. But passenger know heaven and fame contains the best of her.

The mantle of the Countess is draped in the same way as that of Queen Elizabeth in Westminster Abbey. The convention goes back to monuments of the fifteen-seventies and eighties. – Lady Anne Clifford, Countess of Pembroke, † 1676. Erected during her lifetime. Standing monument. Reredos background with a broken segmental pediment. No effigy, but a proud family tree of twenty-four shields.

* One original head is re-erected w of the church.

ST MICHAEL, Bongate. Again we read: 'Raised from its ruins by Lady Anne, and again that is a gross exaggeration. The N doorway is of Saxon proportions and has a Saxon hogback gravestone used as its lintel. The S doorway with dog-tooth and rolls with fillets is E.E. The S transept is Early Dec, and so is the S arcade of five bays. The piers are the same as in S Lawrence, but the capitals are polygonal. Lady Anne may be responsible for the ogee arch of the porch entrance. The W tower is an addition of 1885–6.* – In the chancel a CARTOUCHE with Lady Anne's initials A P set in strapwork. – PAINTINGS. The wall paintings on the W wall and the chancel N wall are of *c.*1900. They are said to be students' work. – STAINED GLASS. The E window by *Kempe*, 1889. – The transept windows by *Mayer* of Munich and London, 1893 (a diehard style). – PLATE. Steeple Cup of 1612; Cup, Newcastle, 1712; Cup, Newcastle, 1759; Paten, London, 1790. – MONUMENT. Effigy of a Lady, late C14, badly preserved and bad from the start. In a recess in the S wall. It has the arms of Roos and Vipont on mantle and pillow (*see* note on this page).

APPLEBY CASTLE. The castle belonged to the Viponts before it went to the Cliffords in the late C13. It remained Clifford property to the death of the Lady Anne. It then went to her son-in-law, the Earl of Thanet. It is a splendid castle, standing at the top of the town, up on the steep bank of the river Eden and surrounded by moats marking an inner and at least two outer baileys. The oldest stone building is the later C12 KEEP kept happily isolated from all else and happily finished off with four turrets with pretty lanterns, in all probability of 1784. The keep is of squarish silver-grey stones. The ground floor has a round-headed entrance, which is unusual. Another doorway is on the first floor. The partition walls on all floors are Lady Anne's. Large windows, their details all altered, are on the first as well as more customarily on the second floor. The keep was originally lower than it is now, as the former roof-lines indicate. The merlons of the battlements have slits. The CURTAIN WALLING is largely of the late C12, and the RCHM also ascribes to the late C12 the POSTERN in the middle of the principal domestic, i.e. the E, range. It has a round, single-chamfered arch and in front of it a giant blank arch. The portcullis groove is preserved. This range other-

* In the wall of the former Vicarage opposite the church are many fragments from the church, dating from the C14 and after, including fragments of a tomb canopy with the arms of Roos and Vipont (*see* below).

wise, with its N and S towers, is attributed to the C15, though not many features remain to demonstrate it. Most of the SE tower is of 1883, the angularly projecting part to the W of Lady Anne's time. Of the C15 the NE tower has a tunnel-vaulted sub-basement, a two-light window to the N, and a recently found doorway in the basement in the S wall. Another leads from the N to the E wing. On the first floor (the *piano nobile* of the E range) the former CHAPEL has its C15 PISCINA. The S wing close to the SE tower has a one-light window with a shouldered lintel inside. This must have belonged to a room not otherwise preserved and is probably earlier than the C15. The semicircular N TOWER attached to the N wing is the only C13 contribution. It has a garderobe projection high up on corbels.*

But the EAST RANGE is really remembered not as medieval, but as a stately piece of late C17 architecture. It was rebuilt by the Earl of Thanet in 1686–8 with stone from Brougham and Brough castles. Its W front is of six bays and two storeys and has stone cross windows and flat pilasters in two tiers. The doorway has an open curly pediment on brackets. The window above it has brackets too, and the top parapet in this place a length of balustrading. The N range was probably added in 1695. This is more utilitarian, with three storeys to the height of the two of the other wing. The windows are the same.

The HALL goes through the two storeys. It has a coved ceiling, its Gothic detail more probably early C19 than late C17 (cf. the parish church). The panelling however is certainly of c.1690. The STAIRCASE with its strong twisted balusters is also of that date. The N wing has a middle corridor all along its length, which deserves notice.

In the grounds is Lady Anne's BEE-HOUSE, square, with a pyramid roof. The STABLES are a large building with inner quadrangle, but modest in its details.

PERAMBULATION. Appleby consists of two parts, divided by the broad river Eden. In the C13 the area round St Michael was called Old Appleby, and the centre, i.e. Boroughgate, is indeed a New Appleby, founded as a self-conscious effort about 1110 by Ranulph de Meschines. The new town is just one uncommonly wide street, its name indicative of its status.

---

* In the NE tower wall is another garderobe, this complete with its stone seat.

It runs from the church up to the castle. Such single wide streets are e.g. the new towns planted by the Bishops of Winchester about 1200 (Alresford, Downton). This historical dichotomy is still expressed today. The A6 traffic races along the E bank of the river, the town that matters is on the W bank, connected by the BRIDGE of 1889 in the style of the late C18. It consists of two segmental arches with quatrefoiled Gothic circles in the spandrels. On the E side there is little to see: the POLICE STATION in THE SANDS, three bays, plain Georgian, with two low projecting one-bay wings, one of them with an archway in. Also an eight-bay r. attachment (what for ?). THE FRIARY at the N end of BATTLE BARROW has three bays with a porch of two pairs of thin Ionic columns. It commemorates the site of the house of the Whitefriars.

Over the bridge in BRIDGE STREET is the plain, wide-spaced five-bay, ashlar-faced KING'S HEAD; early C19. And so one turns into BOROUGHGATE. Boroughgate runs up to the castle gates and starts at the bottom with the SCREEN which *Smirke* set up in 1811 to terminate the street with. It consists of two two-storeyed end pavilions with corbelled parapets and seven pointed arches between. The beginning and end of the street were however marked earlier already by the LOW CROSS and the HIGH CROSS, two Tuscan columns with strong entasis, on square bases and carrying a square top. The High Cross has an inscription: 'Retain your loyalty Preserve your Rights', and dates from the C17, the Low Cross is supposed to be an C18 copy. Boroughgate is not dead straight, and it is also varied by the fact that the MOOT HALL of 1596, but with C18 windows, occupies an island site, closer to the W than the E frontages,* and that above it the street has grass and trees l. and r. The houses are not without interest either. The first from the N on the W side is the TUFTON ARMS of 1873, Gothic, with a gable, two dormers, and a half-hipped gable (maximum variety!), on the E side MARTINS BANK, more seriously Gothic and of three storeys. On the same side the first pre-C19 building of considerable interest is No. 11, later C17, with two gables with stepped three-light windows, the heads of the lights being semicircular. Then on the opposite side the CONSERVATIVE CLUB, Italianate of c.1850, and then the best group at Appleby: on the W side a three-bay

* Appleby possesses the following corporation PLATE prior to 1830: Sword of State, late C17; Loving Cup, London, 1705; Mace, London, 1733; Punch Bowl, London, 1784.

Georgian corner house of three storeys, with a semicircular hood over the door, and then the RED HOUSE, dated 1717, seven bays, two storeys, with a segmental pediment over the doorway, and opposite the WHITE HOUSE, dated 1756, all 94 Gothick, with every window ogee-headed, and even the doorway treated in that way. The pediment above the door consequently assumes an odd and graceful shape, two rising ogee curves and a semicircle at the top. Then a gabled Victorian Gothic house, dated 1851, and more houses with pleasing minor features: the MASONIC HALL, e.g., which is of five bays, has a central archway.

The only more telling building in this upper part of the town is ST ANNE'S HOSPITAL, founded by Lady Anne in 1651 and built in 1651–3. It is low and has seven excessively widely spaced windows to the street. The archway in the middle is plain, and the courtyard, with a gap just opposite the entrance, is humble too. The CHAPEL has an E window of two round-arched lights, a PULPIT with C17 panelling, and BENCHES with simply shaped ends.

ARNSIDE

4070

ST JAMES. 1866 (GR; Kelly: 1869) by *Miles Thompson* of Kendal. Enlarged 1905 and 1914. Plate tracery. – STAINED GLASS. E window by *Burrow*, 1880, old-fashioned.

ARNSIDE TOWER, 1 m. S. Large pele tower in a beautiful position. The size is *c.*48 by *c.*33 ft. It was probably built in the C15 and is oblong with a projecting NE tower. The tower was five storeys high, the rest four storeys. The building is ruined, the SE corner has collapsed, and there are no floors left. But a part of the corbelled parapet is still in position. Originally the building was divided by a cross-wall running W from the place in the E wall where the spiral staircase is. In the NE tower at the bottom is a vaulted oven. The hall was on the second upper floor.

ASHES *see* HUGILL

ASKHAM

5020

ST PETER. 1832 by *Robert Smirke*, who had built Lowther Castle twenty-five years before. He tried to be Norman here, and the result is rather depressing. NW tower, N aisle with bald Gothic arcade with four-centred arches. The windows

(except for one) all round-headed. – FONTS. One plain, and
dated 1661. – The other plainly panelled, with no separate
foot. Can this be *c.*1832? – PLATE. Flagon of 1711 (Newcastle); Cup of 1712 (Newcastle); Cover Paten probably
1712; Paten on foot, 1712 (London). – MONUMENTS. Elizabethan tomb-chest with simple geometrical pattern. Only
partly preserved. – Several tablets to the Sandfords of
Askham Hall.

ASKHAM HALL. A spacious, but not a grand house. It has three
irregular wings round an oblong courtyard, quite informal,
and not high, except for the mighty broad tower at the s end
of the E wing. This and the parts adjoining to the N are of the
late C14 and were built for the Sandfords. The tower was
tunnel-vaulted at ground level, and partly still is. It has a
double-chamfered doorway from the N which is now inside
the house, and one ogee-headed window to the W. The s front
of the tower was very handsomely remodelled about 1685–90
with five bays and two and a half storeys, the windows all with
mullion and transom crosses, the doorway with an open segmental pediment and some rustication. The top battlements
restored and the raised corners Victorian. (On an upper floor
is an impressive fireplace with a lintel with joggled joints.)
In the former hall area N of the tower is now the stately late
C17 staircase with strong twisted balusters. The N wing
remains, though altered. It must have housed the offices, as
the doorways from the hall survive. The rest is mostly Late
Elizabethan with a variety of windows. The entrance arch to
the courtyard from the W has a rope-moulded label with knots
as label-stops.

The VILLAGE is of the North Riding type, with a wide expanse
of grass between the long road and the cottages l. and r.*

COP STONE. This standing stone, 4¾ ft high, originally formed
one element in a stone circle enclosed in a stone bank, traces of
which are still visible in the vicinity of the stone.

CAIRN, 400 yds NW. The cairn is now represented by a low
mound of stones, 40 ft in diameter, from which the slabs of
the revetment kerb project. In the C19 a cremation burial
accompanied by a Food Vessel was found beneath the
mound.

Other small CAIRNS exist on Moor Divock. Some of these were
opened in the C19 and found to cover cremations.

---

* The MHLG lists many small houses and cottages with date stones.

SKIRSGILL HILL SETTLEMENTS. Two roughly oval embanked enclosures occur on the hill, some 250 yards apart. Each contains hut circles and internal banks.

AUGILL CASTLE see BROUGH

BAMPTON

5010

ST PATRICK. 1726–8; restored 1885. The Georgian church has its W tower with a very slender doorway with broken segmental pediment and its still C17-looking bell-openings. Also of 1726 the seven bays of rather thin arched side windows of the church and the wooden columns inside. They carry arches, 98 and also cross-arches to the outer walls. This and the upper parts of the nave are of 1885, as is the chancel. – PULPIT. Also probably of c.1726. With slender blank arches and slender angle colonnettes, still derived, though distantly, from the Jacobean type. – COMMUNION RAIL. C18. – FONT. Plain, square, with a round arch on each side. Probably C12, but dated 1662.* – PLATE. Two Chalices, Newcastle, 1748; Paten, London, 1813. – MONUMENT. William Noble † 1823. By *Regnart*. Grecian, with lush leaves.

THORNTHWAITE HALL, 1¼ m. SW. L-shaped, with one wing a former pele tower. Mullioned windows. The house went from the Curwens to Lord William Howard (see Naworth).‡

CASTLE CRAG FORT. This is a tiny oval fort with a maximum diameter of 150 ft, defined by a single rampart traceable on the S, E, and W. Excavation on the N located the rampart at this point, where it had a well-built outer face, 10 ft high, and an imprecisely defined inner limit. A number of hut floors were found in the interior of the fort.

CAIRNS AND STANDING STONES. On Four Stones Hill are a pair of standing stones and three round cairns, the largest 36 ft in diameter and 4 ft high.

BARBON

6080

ST BARTHOLOMEW. By *Paley & Austin*, 1893. An excellent work in a freely treated Perp style with a crossing tower with stressed staircase turret. The tower is a little wider than nave

---

* The Rev. G. de Burgh Thomas mentions two PAINTINGS, Bishop Gibson by *Vanderbank* and John Boustead by *James Ward*, 1833.

(‡ HIGH ROUGH HILL has a Later Georgian plaster ceiling, a rarity in this area. MHLG) and transept, a subtlety which makes all the difference. The composition of the s side, with gabled porch, gabled transept, and an aisle between which starts only some way E of the porch, is subtle too. This arrangement of the aisles is also effective inside. The arcades are of two bays, the piers an elongated octagon, with the arches dying against them. The crossing tower is open at the top of its lower stage, with pairs of windows to N and s. This also makes for fine views. The whole interior is ashlar-faced.

BARBON MANOR, up the long drive in serpentines to the house, which is wonderfully sited but architecturally disappointing. It is by *E. M. Barry*, 1862–3, and is no more than an Italianate villa in a town street might be. Basement and two storeys, three-bay front, but to the other side, thanks to a big bow, four bays. Above the ground floor a balcony of iron.

WHELPRIGG, ¾ m. SE. 1834, according to Burke's *Seats*. Tudor, with smallish gables beset with finials. The use of stepped mullioned windows shows that the architect knew local motifs.

BARTON

4020

ST MICHAEL. The focal point of the church is the low central tower. This is Norman, and was originally not hidden on the N and s sides. Inside the s aisle is one Norman window of the tower. The w and E arches are also original, with little in the way of moulding. They were strengthened in the late C13 or early C14 by lower bridge-arches or strainer-arches. The tower has inside, quite high up, a transverse tunnel-vault, a highly exceptional, decidedly northern feature. The N aisle has a doorway also Norman, with one continuous roll-moulding. The s doorway must be just a little later; round arch with fillet on the roll. Two orders of shafts with high, simply moulded capitals. The porch in which the doorway is must be the work of the C17. Most of the windows of the church are Late Perp, but the chancel E window of three stepped lancet lights is late C13. The problem of the church is the arcades. The N arcade still shows clearly, at the w and E ends, where the wall of the aisleless Norman church had been. The N arcade is of three bays and quite straightforward. Quatrefoil piers, the foils more than semicircular and with fillets; double-chamfered arches. That may be mid C13. But the s arcade with octagonal piers, plainly moulded capitals, and also double-chamfered arches could be earlier or later.

The s chapel of one bay is dated by the RCHM C14, yet seems Late Perp, as is the s doorway to it. The corbels with a figure and a shield really exclude the C14. – FONT. The C14-looking font is not ancient, though the base seems to be. – COMMUNION RAIL. The strong balusters indicate the mid C17. – PLATE. Cup of 1632.

(BARTON HALL. 1710 and 1868. The early part is of five bays. The doorway has a broken curved pediment. The windows still have stone crosses. MHLG)

BARTON CHURCH FARM. L-shaped, partly C16, partly of 1628. In one room on the first floor a handsome plaster ceiling.

THE COCKPIT, 1½ m. SE of Pooley Bridge, on the N slope of Barton Fell. This is a large ring cairn, 120 ft in diameter, with a bank 6 ft thick with inner and outer facing-stones.

BARWISE HALL
6010

2¼ m. SW of Appleby

Two dates are inscribed: 1579 and 1676. The dumb-bell balusters of the staircase are of course 1676, but what is 1579? Not, on Yorkshire evidence, the lintel, with its decoration by a figure 3 lying prostrate. This suits 1676 much better. And can the mullioned windows with the hood-moulds connected into a continuous band, always rising above the windows, be of 1579? Surely they also make better sense in 1676.

BEETHAM
4070

ST MICHAEL. The thin, unbuttressed w tower is of the late C12, as the slightly pointed and slightly chamfered arch to the nave proves. The corbelled-out bell-stage with straight-headed three-light bell-openings is early C16. The body of the church is low and partly embattled. The windows are varied, but all Perp. The earliest is in the s (Beetham) chapel. The s arcade of four bays is also late C12. The w and E imposts are still many-scalloped. The piers are round, with shallow plain capitals and square abaci. The arches are round and slightly chamfered. The N arcade and N chapel arcade are C15 and have standard elements treated coarsely. The s chapel arcade has the same elements. Between it and the s arcade a piece of the C12 wall remains. – In the chapel a Beetham MONUMENT of the early C15. Two effigies, severely damaged, on a tomb-chest with shields and a large, rude head in quatrefoils. – Several

8—C.W.

good tablets, and also a free-standing black urn to William
Hutton † 1810 (s aisle). – FONT COVER. 1636. Octagonal,
steeply spire-shaped. – STAINED GLASS. In the s chapel C15
fragments including the figure of a king. – In the s aisle a
two-light window, signed *A.B.* 1852 (TK: *Burrow* of Milnthorpe). – Better the w window in the tower. This has genuine
C15 figures, well set off by the dark mid C19 glass. – PLATE.
Cup of 1692.

Immediately N of the churchyard PARSONAGE FARM. The
blocked doorway towards the churchyard proves that it is a
medieval building. It was called The College. Immediately s
of the churchyard two Early Georgian houses of three bays
each, with fine doorways, characteristic of their date. Both
have segmental pediments, and one also has a frieze rising in
the middle in a typical way.

About 100 yds s of the church is ASHTON HOUSE, Georgian, of
five bays and three storeys with a pedimented doorway. Lower
Later Georgian one-bay wings with tripartite windows. In the
garden an embattled GAZEBO dated 1791.

BEETHAM HOUSE is NE of the church, just across and above the
river Beela. It has a date 1772 and is also of five bays and has
low one-bay wings. A partly embattled BARN behind.

BEETHAM HALL, ⅜ m. s. The house is dated 1693 (1653 ?) on a
lintel of typical West Riding details, but it stands on part of
the site of an interesting early or mid C14 fortified manor
house. Quite a portion of the curtain wall survives, and in
addition the hall with the solar wing continued by the chapel.
Of the service wing only little remains, except a staircase in the
thickness of the wall immediately next to the hall doorway.
The hall has three original windows, one to each side of two
lights, straight-headed, the third larger, of three lights, with a
reticulation unit. This belonged probably to the high-table
end. The chapel still has its piscina and its E (actually s) window of three lights, straight-headed. The rere-arches of the
chapel windows are not arches but shouldered lintels, a C13
motif which survived long in castle architecture.

BELLE ISLE *see* BOWNESS-ON-WINDERMERE

BENTS HILL *see* CROSBY GARRETT

BEWLEY CASTLE *see* BOLTON

BIRKRIGG PARK *see* PRESTON PATRICK

BIRKS *see* WARCOP

BLEASE HALL *see* OLD HUTTON

BOLTON

6020

ALL SAINTS. The N and S doorways are Norman. They have
one order of columns. In one capital a figure holding two
staves(?). Saltire crosses chip-carved in the abaci. One
hood-mould with billet, the other with rosettes. Above the N
doorway a small, very remarkable relief of two Knights on
horse-back fighting. This also is Norman.* The chancel windows are lancets but have round arches to the inside. So that
will be late C12. There was once a W tower, but its E wall has
been taken out, so that only the thickness of the wall tells of
it. A bell-turret was built in, probably in the C17. With its
saddle-back roof, it helps the skyline. The nave N windows
were re-done in the C18. – FONT COVER. 1687. Of plain
spire shape. – SCREEN. With bold, large, and successful Dec
tracery. Probably of the restoration of 1848 or even a little
later. – MONUMENT. Effigy of a praying Lady, outside the
church, weathered and enframed by ivy. Is she C14?
BEWLEY CASTLE, 1¼ m. S. In ruins. Oblong, with a projecting
tower at the S end towards the E. This is vaulted at ground
level. So is the N end of the oblong range, which therefore
was probably also a tower.

BORROWDALE HEAD *see* FAWCETT FOREST

BOWNESS-ON-WINDERMERE

4090

The character of Bowness itself is mid C19, houses and hotels
from the Italianate villa type with asymmetrical tower to the
type with bargeboarded gables. Of the biggest hotels the
BELSFIELD HOTEL is Italianate, though not in the villa way,
the OLD ENGLAND HOTEL is gabled. ‡ Outside and higher
up are also private houses of *c*.1830, not spectacular, e.g.
BELFIELD, FERNEY GREEN, and MATSON GROUND.§

* A similar relief is at Fordington, Dorset. This the RCHM dates *c*.1100.
‡ The oldest part of this is of 1859, the W extension of 1879, the S extension
of 1926.
§ On this *see* below. Ferney Green has three wide bays with bow windows
and seems to date from *c*.1810–20 (*see* NMR). Belfield was built as a private
house in 1840.

St Martin. Perp (consecrated 1483) and of the restoration of 1870. To this belong the E end and the tower top with its saddleback roof. The clerestory looks a C16 addition or alteration. The interior is a strange sight. The arcade piers are square and chamfered, and the walls and all the rest are white and decorated with typically High Victorian spiky linear painted decoration, verses and their surrounds. The verses of the spandrels of the arcades alone are older – of c.1600. – FONT. Octagonal, with tiny C12-looking heads at four corners. – SCULPTURE. Well-carved wooden group of St Martin and the Beggar. The RCHM calls it probably C17 and foreign. It looks considerably re-carved c.1850. – STAINED GLASS. The E window is of the late C15, with the Crucifixion and assistant figures. It may come from Furness or from Cartmel. In the tracery centre fragments, e.g. an early C14 Virgin. – PLATE. Cup and Cover Paten, 1682. – MONUMENTS. Richard Bishop of Llandaff † 1816. By Flaxman. Tablet with mitre, books, and crozier. The crozier sticks out oddly, far below the tablet. – Fletcher Raincock † 1809. Tablet with bust in recess.

St John Evangelist. See Windermere.

Carver Memorial Congregational Church. See Windermere.

Royal Windermere Yacht Club. By Gill & Rhodes, 1964–5. Timber-framed, but with two heavy stone screen or baffle walls. The building is quite small and has an odd sawtooth roof, one set of teeth pointing downward, another in a syncopated order upward.

Belle Isle. Belle Isle is the appropriate name for this house on an island in the lake, accessible only by boat. The house makes the isle belle; for it was the first mansion in the Lake District decided upon for picturesque reasons. It was built for a Mr English in 1774, to the designs of John Plaw. In 1781 it changed hands. It was bought by Mrs Curwen of Workington Hall, and she and her husband J. C. Curwen landscaped the isle (gardener: Thomas White). It has remained in the possession of Curwens ever since. The house is highly unusual, if not unique, in that it is cylindrical. Ickworth in Suffolk, the better known cylindrical mansion of the Earl of Bristol, Bishop of Derry, was begun only in 1791, and the same erratic patron's Ballyscullion, also circular, in 1787. So Plaw and Mr English have the prévenir. The house has a dome with a lantern and, to the E, a portico of four slender unfluted Ionic columns. The capitals are, oddly enough, of wood. The frieze is pulvinated, and there is a pediment at the top. A curved two-arm staircase rises inside the portico. The body of the house has three Venetian windows in the other three main directions. Their middle arch is set in a blank arch. The offices are in the basement – excavated square, not round. The ground floor has a vestibule, then in the middle of the cylinder the staircase with an apsed end, but overhead an oblong with two semicircles, and three living rooms and cabinets. The principal W room has a groin-vaulted centre, two apses, and a shallow curved projection for the Venetian window. In the principal S room is an Adamesque stucco ceiling. Bedrooms on the first and second floors, servants' rooms in an attic hidden in the dome. In the lantern the flues run up. The picturesque setting has grown too high and spreads too fully. Originally the view from the portico towards Bowness and Windermere was free.

STORRS HALL, 1¾ m. SSW. Storrs Hall is largely of 1808–11 and by *Gandy*, but at the back a core of *c*.1790 is visible, with a canted bay window. The window surrounds are here all unmoulded. The wings as well as the veranda belong to the second phase. The climax of this is the front of the house, of three bays recessed between short wings and with a five-bay Doric porch, the columns of the Samian type with only the upper parts of the shaft fluted. In the wing ends three-light windows with pediment on thick corbels. These and other equally thick details, e.g. the fleshy leaves, are characteristic of Gandy. Entrance hall with circular skylight, staircase also with such a skylight. On the l. of the staircase a screen of two columns. In the main W room a good chimneypiece.

By the lake, and in fact pushed forward into it, an octagonal GARDEN HOUSE with four arched openings and four tablets. This dates from 1804 and was erected in honour of Admirals Duncan, St Vincent, Howe, and Nelson. House and temple were built for Sir John Legard. Gandy worked for the next owner: Col. John Bolten.

BLACKWELL SCHOOL, Blackwell. On the upper road to Newby Bridge. 1900 by *Baillie Scott* for Sir Edward Holt. Much influenced by Voysey – cf. e.g. the window shapes and details – but less disciplined in outline, with several gables, a more complicated plan, and such imitative Tudor motifs as the heads of the doorways. The interior is purest Baillie Scott, especially the hall with its peacock frieze, its ingle-nook, its 99

half-timber areas, and the over-rich leaf decoration. The
finest room is the drawing room, with the square bay or oriel
to the lake. There are also plenty of characteristic fireplaces
with exceedingly thin mantelshelves and plenty of good Art
Nouveau stained glass, all purely ornamental. A particularly
odd motif is thin iron shafts carrying burgeoning-out leaf
capitals.

BROADLEYS (Motor Boat Club) of 1898, *Voysey*'s masterpiece,
is just across the Lancashire border. So is Voysey's MOOR
CRAG, also of 1898.

MATSON GROUND, Langdales, 1 m. w. In the grounds of the
house which looks *c.*1830 a modern house was built in 1961
by *Basil Ward*. It is quite on its own and enjoys splendid
views. It is large, and in its surfeit of motifs – glass, timber-
boarding, a chimneystack of slate, monopitch roofs, and even
sloping walls – a little too reminiscent of the villas of Cortina.

BRATHAY HOW see GREAT LANGDALE

BRAVONIACUM see KIRKBY THORE

BROUGH

Brough is a village along the A 66 with very little to report, and a
village by the castle and the church. The latter, Church
Brough, is a planned settlement, though very minor, with an
oblong green and houses on two sides. In the road village,
Market Brough, the meeting with the road to church and
castle is marked by the CLOCK TOWER, dated 1911, but
crowned by an over-tapered Tuscan column and finial, which
look C17 rather than C20. Can the omnipresent Lady Anne
Clifford have been responsible? At the same crossing the
CASTLE INN, five bays, three storeys, with a Tuscan porch.

ST MICHAEL. A typical North Country exterior, extremely long
and low, with plain parapets and a broad, low w tower. The
tower dates from 1513, the rest mostly from the Perp centuries from the late C14 to the early C16. The windows tell of
this, all straight-headed. Those of the chancel come last. They
are long and have depressed-rounded tops to the lights, and
the E window is indeed so curious in its entirely uncusped
tracery that again one might be tempted to believe in a remodelling by the Lady Anne. If one looks carefully, one can
see that the body of the church is much older. There is plenty

of Norman masonry on the S side, and in any case the S
doorway is Norman. It has one order of columns, the abaci
decorated with little lozenges, the inner order with big human
beakhead faces, the outer order with zigzag at r. angles to the
wall. W of the doorway is a Norman window too. Inside there
is the tower arch of three continuous chamfers, and the N
arcade, seven bays long, of standard elements, though with
one pier a re-used replacement. In the S wall is a tomb
recess. – PULPIT. Of stone, completely undecorated, but on a
moulded corbel. The date 1624 is surprising. – COMMUNION
RAIL. Later C17. – STAINED GLASS. Some C15 bits in a N
window. – PLATE. Pair of Chalices, Newcastle, 1724. –
MONUMENT. A tablet with a Greek, though Runic-looking,
inscription.

BROUGH CASTLE. Brough started as one of William Rufus's
royal castles about 1095. This castle was largely destroyed by
William the Lion of Scotland in 1174. It was rebuilt after. In
1204 it was granted to Robert de Vipont, and his progeny,
the Lords Clifford, held it still when Lady Anne Clifford did
restorations. The castle stands in a dominant position above
the steep bank of the Swindale Beck. It occupies the N third
of the Roman fort of Verterae.* The moats are well preserved,
and the ruin is a majestic, moving sight from a distance. The
oldest surviving masonry, of c.1095 indeed, is parts of the
curtain wall. NNE of the gatehouse very coarse herringbone
masonry is a sign of that date. The keep was rebuilt after
William the Lion. It stands up high, though gutted. Its top
storey is a heightening, probably decided upon soon after
building, and it is easily visible from the roof-line of the first
roof. Only one Norman upper window survives – in the W
wall. It has a shaft between two lights, the shaft having in
section two semicircles and a spur between. The windows to
the N belong to Lady Anne's restoration. Almost entirely
Lady Anne's is the fine rounded tower at the SE corner,
though the base courses are assigned to the early C14. Lady
Anne's masonry and square mullioned windows are a fine job.
Between this tower and the gatehouse was the hall range. The
hall was on the first floor, and its high two-light windows with
a reticulation unit date it to the C14. Below are undercrofts,
all tunnel-vaulted. The vaults are Lady Anne's, but very
probably they replaced C14 ones (cf. e.g. Bolton Castle in the

* VERTERAE was a 3-acre Roman fort, the platform and ditch of which can
still be recognized.

North Riding). The rooms in front of the hall range are an infilling of Lady Anne's. Hers also is the staircase, of which the
lowest steps remain.* The gatehouse also dates from the C14.
It has two outer buttresses with triangular ends and was
originally tunnel-vaulted with big, broad, single-chamfered
transverse arches. In the C13 part of the N curtain wall is a
well-preserved garderobe.

(HILLBECK HALL. The house stands in a dominant position
on the fellside, above the A66 road. Georgian Gothic. Two
storeys. The centre is of five bays, with ogee-headed windows. Lower two-storey wings with pavilion roofs. MHLG)

AUGILL CASTLE, ¾ m. E. A fine essay in Early Victorian castle
building, still Late Georgian in its symmetry. A central gatehouse, as it were, with round turrets and a porch, and gabled
and castellated side pieces also ending in round turrets.
Castellated stables on the l. Nice wooden Dec tracery. The
house was built in 1842.

In the same year SOUTH STAINMORE CHAPEL, 3 m. ESE, was
built. Three-bay nave and chancel with projecting square bell-
turret and lancets. Flat ceiling inside, i.e. this also still in the
older tradition. The three-bay attachment behind may be the
SCHOOL built in 1699.

MAIDEN CASTLE, 5 m. SE, is a small, ¼-acre fortlet, surrounded by a defensive stone wall 6 ft thick. It was built in the
C2 and occupied until the late C4. The site commands a
splendid view of the descent to the Eden valley and lies at a
natural stopping-place for convoys.

ROPER CASTLE, 1½ m. SW of Maiden Castle. A small Roman
Earthwork, 60 ft by 46 ft, surrounded by a single ditch
entered through the S side. Its position – in sight of Maiden
Castle and Bowes Moor in the North Riding – suggests that
it served as a signal station.

REY CROSS. See The Buildings of England: Yorkshire: North
Riding.

BROUGHAM

BROUGHAM CASTLE. The Roman fort lies SE of the castle,
at the junction of the road from York and the Lancashire
coast road.

The medieval story starts at the time of Henry II. Under
John the castle went to the Vipont family, and from them in

* Evidence for a C13 hall running S–N cannot here be discussed.

the third quarter of the C13 by marriage to the Cliffords. It remained with them to the death of Lady Anne Clifford, Countess of Pembroke, in 1676. The castle is chiefly *temp*. Henry II and late C13 to early C14. A little is of the early C13. As Brougham Castle is very unusual in plan, it is best described as it is seen.

One enters by an outer and an inner gatehouse with a small courtyard between. The OUTER GATEHOUSE is of *c*.1300–30. It is of three storeys and has windows, some with reticulation units. The inscription referring to Lady Anne's restoration in the years 1651 and 1652, 'after it had layen ruinous ever since about August 1617', is re-set. The Lady Anne's romantic passion for castles appears in several places in Westmorland (cf. Introduction, pp. 28–9). The gatehouse has a portcullis groove, a pointed tunnel-vault, and a porter's room on the r. with a garderobe in the big NE angle-buttress. This feature repeats on the second upper floor.

In the courtyard the N side of the Norman keep is exposed. The upper windows are large and shafted. On the third floor, however, they are different and later. All this will be discussed in detail presently.

The INNER GATEHOUSE is of the late C13. A two-light window has pointed-trefoiled lights and a pointed quatrefoil over, i.e. pre-ogee motifs. There is again a portcullis groove. Two-bay rib-vault with single-chamfered transverse arches and ribs. In the N wall is an L-shaped passage leading to an arrow-slit. More wall-passages on the first and second floors.

Through the inner gatehouse one enters the INNER COURT. This is roughly L-shaped. Along the W side was a range of buildings not now exposed. In the SW corner is a tower of *c*.1300 with fireplaces on all floors and garderobes on two. The S wall and range are late C13, but with alterations (*see* below).

The KEEP can be seen from the court in its W and S sides 78 and also, as one can now pass through it, its E side. The N side has already been mentioned. The W side has upper windows like the N side. On the S side the top storey is partly corbelled out on two faces, and further to the r. there is more corbelling for a garderobe. On the E side was the forebuilding. The main entry was originally on the second floor. This is badly preserved: one jamb-shaft; arch with a keeled roll and hollows, i.e. *c*.1175. The ground floor, inside, has an inserted rib-vault of the C13, with single-chamfered ribs on a middle pier. The blank arcading on the second floor (see N wall, W part) is also

C13. Looking at the top floor now from inside it is at once recognizable that this is an addition of *c.*1300. The room has chamfered corners and squinches. The window to the E is of two lights with a circle over, i.e. a late C13 form. In the SE corner, the part corbelled out outside contains a tiny semi-octagonal chapel with seven radial single-chamfered ribs. Boss with two heads. In the E window N jamb two small figures. Doorway with an inner and an outer cusped arch. The mouldings are typical of the late C13. In the S wall two recesses, one with a trefoiled arch. Two more such recesses in the N wall. PISCINA in the SE wall.

The keep was pierced about 1300 to create a passage, a strange thing to do. It is strange also that the late C13 and early C14 gatehouses should have been built so close to the keep. Stranger still, however, is that, according to the RCHM in the early C13, the GREAT CHAMBER should have been built E of the keep, i.e. flanking the approach to the (later) gatehouses. There is very little preserved of this, but the clasping SE buttress shows the date. S of the Great Chamber was the GREAT HALL, of the early C14. It was on the first floor and was moderate in size. Small outer two-light windows with ogee-headed lights to the E. To the N one jamb of the doorway to the Great Chamber. The KITCHEN lay S of the hall, also on the first floor. Fireplace in the S wall.

N of the kitchen was the S range. It consisted of two separate buildings of *c.*1300, one with a square projection, and the CHAPEL set between late in the C14. Of the chapel the SEDILIA and PISCINA survive, and two single-light S windows.

ST NINIAN (NINEKIRK), 1⅝ m. NE of the castle, above the river Eamont. The church was rebuilt completely by the Lady Anne in 1660 and is an eminently interesting example of Gothic Survival. It is also almost completely furnished as it was in the Lady Anne's time. The windows are of single lights, round-headed and uncusped, with hood-moulds. Nave and chancel are in one, and it is only the evenness of the whole and the two windows E and two windows W which betray the century. The porch is of 1841. Roof with collar-beams on long arched braces. In the E wall a wreath with the initials A.P. (Anne Pembroke) and the date 1660. – FONT. 1662, plain, octagonal. – SCREEN, FAMILY PEWS, and BENCHES are all preserved, one bench with the date 1661. The screen and family pews have balusters still in the Jacobean tradition. –

The balusters of the COMMUNION RAIL on the other hand are on the way to the dumb-bell form of the later C17. – PULPIT. The sounding board has little pendants. – POOR BOX. Dated 1666. – CUPBOARDS (S wall). They are made up of woodwork brought in, probably in the 1840s (cf. St Wilfrid's Chapel). – PLATE. Secular Cup, made at Nuremberg in the C17.

ST WILFRID'S CHAPEL, SW of the castle and connected by a bridge across the road with the high walls and turrets of the boundary of BROUGHAM HALL, built largely in c.1830–40 and demolished in 1934. The chapel is also entirely due to the Lady Anne, and it is also a low, long rectangle with windows of one light only with hood-moulds. The lights, however, are pointed. The chapel was built in 1658.* It suffered at the hands of Lord Brougham and Vaux in the 1840s. He normanized the internal appearance of the windows and added the W rose window. But he also filled the chapel with a profusion of woodwork from Continental sources. It would require the space of a learned paper to sort out what is what. Here only this can be said: FONT. C17 bowl; the stem, with zigzag and eight sides all coming out triangularly, is said by the RCHM to be C19, but could well be c.1660. – SCREEN. The screen is even more puzzling. It is called by the RCHM French c.1500 but is undeniably reminiscent of the Preston Screen at Cartmel and of Bishop Cosin's medieval revival work of c.1660 in County Durham. The screen has very closely set strong round uprights, decorated in patterns as similar to the piers of Durham Cathedral as to Early Tudor chimney-shafts. The uprights are connected by highly stilted little cusped arches. – The STALLS or seats are arranged college-wise and have panelling with Flamboyant tracery said to be French. Much of it could come from chests. – PULPIT. Placed in the middle of one long side, in a typical Commonwealth way. Enriched with bits of C17 woodwork. – SCULPTURE. Large parts of a Flemish triptych of c.1520. – Two wings of a South German early C16 altarpiece with religious scenes in relief. – LECTERN. Big, of bronze, on four animals as feet. With the Brougham arms. Made to look convincingly late medieval. – More PANELLING with reliefs against the W wall. – STAINED

* But the Rev. T. E. T. Burbury assumes from masons' marks and consecration crosses that the building is of the C14. He also denies that the chapel was ever Lady Anne's property.

GLASS. Badly preserved pieces of the C14 and later. – PLATE. German C17 Paten; Paten, London, 1716.

EAMONT BRIDGE, across the Eamont, the boundary to Cumberland. C16. Of three segmental arches with triangular cutwaters. Very similar to Warcop Bridge.

MANSION HOUSE, 200 yds s of the bridge. 1686, and well preserved. Five bays and two and a half storeys. The windows of the façade are now sashed, but no doubt had mullion and transom crosses, as they still have round the corner. Formerly also there was probably an outer staircase in the middle of the façade leading up to what is now the central first-floor doorway to a balcony. The doorway has a scrolly open pediment. Staircase with twisted balusters.

MAYBURGH HENGE MONUMENT, ¼ m. SW of Eamont Bridge. *See* Yanwath.

(HORNBY HALL, ⅝ m. E. C16, still with arched lights to several windows. In the W wall a doorway with a lintel dated 1602 and already provided with a simple crenellation motif – the earliest of the decorated C17 lintels so frequent in Westmorland and the West Riding. Inside a little original plasterwork. RCHM)

COUNTESS PILLAR, 2 m. ESE of the castle. Erected in 1656 by the Lady Anne to commemorate her last farewell from her mother forty years before. It is an octagonal pillar with a cubic top, a truncated pyramid roof, and a finial. On the cube shields, a sundial, and the commemorative inscription.

STONE CIRCLE, Leacet Plantation. *See* Clifton.

BURNESIDE

ST OSWALD. 1880–1 by *Ferguson*. Dec, with a SW steeple. Quite a big church. Nave and chancel in one; aisles. – PLATE. Paten, London, 1716.

BURNESIDE HALL. Hall-house of the C14 with a long s wing and a shorter, but also oblong N wing which is in fact a pele tower. It is odd in plan. Two tunnel-vaulted chambers at ground level separated by a narrow tunnel-vaulted passage without direct doorways to the chambers (cf. Preston Patrick). The hall has to the W near the s end a doorway and a small two-light window over, and then N of this two three-light windows with transoms and cusped lights. In the s wing on the upper floor a room with a fine stucco ceiling of about 1600: quatrefoils with patterns of tendrils in them and in the spaces between them.

(HOLLINS, Strickland Ketel, 500 yds SSW. The house has a cruck-truss in the W wing and in one room an overmantel panel of plaster with close and intricate leaves. This is dated 1687. RCHM)

TOLSON HALL, ½ m. WSW. Large house of 1638, but no external features of interest of that date. Nice early C19 bargeboarded gables. Inside on the first floor some coarse plasterwork above two fireplaces, dated 1638 and 1639. Of the same date panelling and a wooden overmantel on the ground floor.

OBELISK, ⅜ m. SSE of Tolson Hall. Put up in 1814 by James Bateman of Tolson Hall to celebrate William Pitt 'the Pilot that weathered the storm'.

LOW BRUNDRIGG, 1½ m. WSW. A room on the first floor has long settles along part of the walls and a pretty overmantel and frieze of stucco with stylized grapes. What can the settles have been for?

GODMOND HALL, 1¼ m. N. Late C17 five-bay house; attached a pele tower, with no notable features.

BURTON HALL see WARCOP

BURTON-IN-KENDALE

5070

ST JAMES. The lower part of the low and broad W tower is Norman, cf. the unmoulded arch towards the nave and the reveals of the W window filled with Dec tracery. Norman also the NW corner of the former aisleless nave. Next in date is the E window of the N chapel, with intersecting tracery, i.e. c.1300, and the slightly later re-set E window of the S chapel, with cusped intersecting tracery. The rest is Perp, the windows straight-headed, the arcade of standard elements, the N later and more primitive than the S. – PULPIT. Jacobean, with intricate patterns including the usual low blank arches. – SCULPTURE. Fragments of a CROSS SHAFT. One has figure subjects (Christ standing, and, above him, two small standing figures l. and r. of a cross) and plenty of scrolls and interlace, a very late derivative from the Anglian past, 'in its final stage of disintegration' (Kendrick). Another smaller fragment has zigzag, and yet another a defaced figure and also a wheelhead. – PLATE. Cup of 1634 (York) and Cover Paten of 1633.

The village is chiefly one long MAIN STREET. It widens midway to E and W into THE SQUARE. Modest Georgian houses on both sides. On the W side an even, three-storeyed block of ten bays. Further S a house on the E side with a doorway with pulvinated frieze and pediment. Then a former CHAPEL, Italianate, of six bays with double entrance and double windows over. Opposite MARTINS BANK with an apsed hood on excellent carved brackets. On the same side a house with a doorway with Tuscan columns, and then, again on the E side, a house of 1707, but all the details late C18, i.e. flat windowframes and flatly framed Venetian windows.

Then BURTON HOUSE, later C18, and quite splendid. It lies back, and has a centre of three generously spaced bays and two and a half storeys with the main windows pedimented. Low two-bay links, recessed quite a distance, connect the centre with low, one-bay pedimental pavilions. The house at present has two doorways in the links and the main doorway, of the Venetian type, in the side wall of the centre. Was it originally in the middle? As it is, it leads straight into the staircase hall. This represents one of the three centre bays. The other two are the apsed drawing room, with a fine Adamish ceiling. Another is on the first floor. The house has the offices and kitchen in the basement. The back towards the garden has tripartite windows with flat raised frames, a homelier motif than the display on the front.

DALTON HALL, 1 m. SE. Early C19 and 1859. The older part is probably represented by the plain five-bay centre of the S front, 1859 by the added bays l. and r. and the veranda. 1859 is no doubt the porte-cochère on the W side. Inside, the grand staircase is typical of 1859, i.e. the thick ornamental motifs of the staircase balustrade and balcony or gallery balustrade. The staircase rises in one flight and returns in two. The skylight also is Victorian. The passage between the old house and the staircase hall on the other hand, with two Roman Doric columns carrying an arch, is clearly early C19.

CALGARTH see WINDERMERE

CASTERTON

HOLY TRINITY. Built for the school in 1831–3 and paid for by the Rev. William Carus Wilson. Grey stone, with W tower, lancets, a wide nave, and originally (as a school chapel) with no chancel. The short chancel was added c.1860. – WALL PAINTINGS. By *James Clarke*, c.1905–10. Biblical stories, painted in an all-too-easy idealizing realism. Everybody looks real but specially noble. This won't do, if the job of such paintings is considered to be the rousing of emotions which go deep. – The wall paintings in the chancel by *Henry Holiday*, of 1894, suffer from the same sentimentality, but they are composed by a competent artist who knew his Burne-Jones as well as his Leighton. The picture above the s windows is the most attractively arranged. Holiday painted the pictures in his studio, and they were then cemented to the walls. – By *Holiday* also the STAINED GLASS in the chancel and the w lancets; 1894–7. The influence of Morris glass is obvious, but Holiday is again a little less exacting. – MONUMENT. Rev. William Carus Wilson † 1859. Gothic tablet.

CASTERTON SCHOOL. Founded for clergy daughters in 1823 and moved to Casterton in 1833. No early architecture of interest. A three-storeyed dormitory block with steep gable, rather grim. On it the initials of William Carus Wilson. The block was built in his memory. The headmistress's house is gabled like a villa at Bowness.

CASTERTON HALL. Early C19, of three bays, ashlar-faced, with a semicircular porch of Tuscan columns. Round the corner a façade with a big bow and l. and r. blank niches. Entrance hall with a shallow segmental vault. Staircase hall with oval skylight.*

CASTERTON OLD HALL, W of the church. C17, with mullioned and transomed windows. One overmantel has re-set wooden panels of c.1530–40.

STONE CIRCLE, 200 yds SE of Langthwaite Gill Plantation. The circle stands on a flattened mound, and now consists of twenty small stones with a diameter of 60 ft. No stone projects more than 1½ ft above the turf, and they may in fact be the kerbstones of a vanished cairn rather than a free-standing circle.

CASTLE CRAG FORT *see* BAMPTON

CHALLON HALL *see* PRESTON PATRICK

CHAPEL STILE *see* GREAT LANGDALE

CHURCH BROUGH *see* BROUGH

CHURCH TOWN *see* CROSTHWAITE

* The house is very similar to Leck Hall, Lancs. The early C19 date is confirmed by a date 1811 inside on a memorable door-post.

CLAPPERSGATE see AMBLESIDE

1020

CLIBURN

ST CUTHBERT. The masonry of nave and chancel is Norman. In the chancel just one N window is preserved, in the nave the S doorway with a lintel (at whose ends stand two small figures) and a blank tympanum. Zigzag arch. Most of the windows of the church are of 1886–7. The chancel arch may be basically Norman, but is completely re-done. – FONT. The shaft is round and Norman. Shallow zigzag pattern. – PLATE. Cup of *c.*1565; Cross of olive wood with ebony and mother of pearl said to come from Vallombrosa.

CLIBURN HALL. Over the doorway is an inscription with the date 1567. The interesting thing is that not only is the inscription still in black-letter, but also all the windows are in the Henry VIII tradition of straight tops and round-arched lights without cusping and little pairs of sunk triangles in the 83 spandrels. The side opposite that of the doorway is specially impressive in its fenestration.

CROSSRIGG HALL, 1¼ m. ESE. Large, Victorian Tudor, with battlements and mullioned and transomed windows, very varied in outline.

1020

CLIFTON

ST CUTHBERT. Norman nave – cf. the S doorway with un-decorated tympanum. C13 chancel, rebuilt in 1846 but with original materials. Lancet windows, in the E wall three, widely spaced and stepped. The S doorway has a shouldered lintel. Windowless C17(?) N aisle, but with a medieval doorway. Instead of a chancel arch a screen of two columns and three arches, put up in 1846, when the chancel was lengthened (Rev. T. E. T. Burbury). – PULPIT. Made up of old wood-work. – STAINED GLASS. In the E window small Virgin and small St John; C15. – PLATE. Cup, London, 1703; Cup and Paten, 1706; Paten, Newcastle, 1743. – MONUMENT. Bronze urn on a square base, in the churchyard. It commemorates the Rev. William Hogarth † 1816.

CLIFTON HALL. The pele tower of *c.*1500 alone survives, but the two doorways in its S wall show where the hall range was. The tower has to the E large C18 windows in three tiers. The battlements were stepped up at the corners (cf. Yanwath Hall).

STONE CIRCLE, in Leacet Plantation, 2¼ m. S of Brougham church. All that remains of this site is an arc of seven stones giving a diameter of approximately 38 ft. Excavation in the C19 revealed a central pit containing a cremation. Further cremations in Early Bronze Age collared urns were found at the bases of a number of the stones.

THE COCKPIT see BARTON

COLBY HALL 6020

Dated 1685, yet still entirely with mullioned windows – a remarkably retardataire attitude, considering that Crackenthorpe, only a few miles away, is wholly William-and-Mary in style. Colby Hall has windows of three lights, except for the hall window, which is still emphasized by having four lights. The doorway, though it already has a bolection moulding, is still in the medieval, non-central position.

COP STONE see ASKHAM

COUNTESS PILLAR see BROUGHAM

COWMIRE HALL see CROSTHWAITE

CRACKENTHORPE HALL 6020

The pre-C19 part of the house is a handsome five-bay range with a pedimented three-bay centre. The pediment has plenty of square modillions. The doorway has a pediment too, and all the windows have stone crosses. Staircase with twisted balusters. All these features look c.1680–90, and 1685 is indeed recorded. In the hall a chimneypiece made up of divers C17 pieces. The large addition to the house, dated by the RCHM 1880, is remarkably faithful to the style of 1685, a style not at all popular before about 1890.

The site of a much-ploughed ROMAN CAMP, 1,000 ft square, lies 1½ m. NW, beneath the modern York–Carlisle road at the point where the road to Long Marton branches off. What little remains of the original gates suggests that the original camp was very similar to that at Rey Cross (see *The Buildings of England: Yorkshire: North Riding*).

CRAKE TREES see CROSBY RAVENSWORTH

CROGLAM CASTLE see KIRKBY STEPHEN

CROOK

ST CATHERINE. 1887 by *Stephen Shaw*. Plain, roughcast, with an unbuttressed W tower. Wide nave and aisles. The style is Late Perp.

The tower of the OLD CHURCH remains, ¼ m. S. It is supposed to date from *c.*1620. The bell-openings and parapet indeed look Jacobean. No buttresses.

HOLLIN HOW, 1 m. NE. Attached to the house is a pele tower of the C15. The gable is stepped. Round chimney-shafts, tunnel-vault at ground level.

CROOK OF LUNE *see* DILLICAR

CROSBY GARRETT

ST ANDREW. Splendidly placed on a steep hill, with views over the fells to N, E, and S, i.e. in the Cumberland, the West Riding, and the Baughfell and Whernside directions. The church is interesting to study. The chancel arch has, visible from the E, a blocked narrow arch above, and this is in all probability Anglo-Saxon. The church which belonged to it was widened and provided with a N aisle about 1175. The N arcade has three bays with round piers carrying flat, square capitals, and abaci with odd and characteristic fleshy leaves similar to one group at Lowther. The arches are round and single-stepped. The W front of the church has a projecting square bell-turret on corbels, and that seems to be a C13 piece. The chancel was rebuilt in the C14 and is Dec, and the N aisle is of 1866 (by *E. Johnson* of Liverpool; GS). – COMMUNION RAIL. C17. – MONUMENT. Matthew Thompson † 1871, yet still entirely Georgian, with a kneeling woman bent over an urn. By *Gaffin* of 63 Regent Street.

(RECTORY. Dated 1719. Five bays, sash windows. MHLG)

CAIRNS, on Irton Hill, 1½ m. W of the church. The N of the two cairns is 45 ft in diameter and 3 ft high. The second site lies 150 ft S and is 30 ft in diameter and 1 ft high. Both have the remains of boulder kerbs set around their perimeters. One or other of the cairns was excavated in the C19, when a male inhumation was found.

CAIRN, on Bents Hill, 2¼ m. SW of the church. The cairn is 35 ft in diameter and 4 ft high. It was opened in the C19, when a number of fragmentary and disjointed human bones were found in the mound but no intact primary burial. 1 ft below the top of the cairn and at the centre was a secondary cremation accompanied by an iron knife, shears, buckle, and a bridle bit – presumably a post-Roman deposit.

RAYSEAT PIKE LONG CAIRN, on the SW border of the parish. The cairn is now badly damaged. It has a maximum length of 180 ft and is 60 ft wide at its broader, SE end. The site was partially excavated in the C19, but the account of the work is very confused. A cremation trench containing a few small fragments of burnt bone was located beneath the SE end and set transversely to the long axis of the mound. From the inner end of this feature, and running along the axis of the mound to a large standing stone, 6 ft high, buried beneath the cairn, were six unaccompanied cremated remains which had apparently been burnt *in situ*. The description of this feature suggests some form of mortuary building such as have been noted beneath a number of Neolithic long barrows in southern Britain. Further burials, which the excavator regarded as secondary, were found in the body of the mound.

CAIRNS, Gaythorn Plain. *See* Great Asby.

CROSBY RAVENSWORTH

6010

ST LAWRENCE. A fine sight, with the splendid old trees around, and a church of great architectural interest. The story begins with the crossing. This must be c.1190–1200. The piers are tripartite to each crossing arch, with the big middle shaft keeled (cf. Lanercost and Cartmel). The capitals are very crude, the arches triple-chamfered. The E arch is missing, as the chancel is Victorian E.E. (of 1875, by *J. S. Crowther* of Manchester). But the responds were apparently re-used between N aisle and N transept. The nave arcades followed soon after the crossing. They have quatrefoil piers with short diagonals between the foils and double-chamfered arches. The S side has a little nailhead and leaf paterae as label-stops. The arch from S aisle to S transept is double-chamfered and steep. E.E. also is the S doorway, quite a fine piece, with two orders of colonnettes and much dog-tooth. The exterior of all these parts was made resolutely E.E., also by Crowther. He worked at the church from the 1850s. His are e.g. the transept fronts with their rose windows and the quatrefoil windows of the clerestory. The Perp contribution is the W tower, original except for the top, with its higher stair-turret. The N chapel is Dec – cf. the E window, now inside the church – but the extremely wide arch to the chancel must be of the time of the Reformation, or even *c.*1550. Finally, in 1809–11 *Robert Smirke* (who was building Lowther Castle) rebuilt parts of the church. Of his work remain the s porch front and the s priest's doorway, both fancy-Gothic, in a way closer to Strawberry Hill than to Rickman. – FONT. Completely plain octagonal bowl, dated 1662. – MONUMENTS. Under the wide arch of the N chapel big anonymous tomb-chest with odd vertical fluting. The RCHM suggests the date 1512, but *c.*1550 is more likely. – George Gibson (who was responsible for Smirke's activity) † 1835. Tablet of black and white marble. Gothic architectural setting and white marble statuettes of Faith, Hope, and Charity. By *Dunbar* of Newcastle. At the foot a musical still-life.

CRAKE TREES, ½ m. NW. In ruins. The s wing was the pele tower and has the usual tunnel-vaulted ground level. In the house itself one ogee-headed window to the E, with, in the tympanum a leopard rampant.

MEABURN HALL, Maulds Meaburn, 1⅜ m. N. Quite a stately house. Built in 1610 – see the date above the two segmental arches of the door lintel. The main (E) front has two projecting wings. Unfortunately the l. half of the centre has been replaced by some very humble quarters. But l. and r. there are still three-light mullioned and mullioned-and-transomed windows. The s front was altered in 1676. It is symmetrical now l. and r. of a chimneybreast. Behind is the staircase with dumb-bell balusters and coarse leaf garlands on the newel posts. Is this 1676 too? In front of the s façade was a walled garden. At the corners two C18 SUMMER HOUSES survive.

(HOLEFOOT. Centre with a Greek Doric porch. Low flanking wings with niches. MHLG)

(FLASS HOUSE. Victorian. Asymmetrical front with tower and Tuscan porch. Symmetrical garden side with broken pediments and Venetian windows. Iron and glass CONSERVATORY.*)

(REAGILL GRANGE. Main block late C16 with massive round chimneys and two-storeyed porch. The back wing is dated 1700. MHLG)

EWE LOCK SETTLEMENT, 1½ m. SSW of the church. This is a group of small conjoined rectangular enclosures linked to a

* I owe the details about this house to Mrs Davies, and Mr Geoffrey Spain tells me that in *The Builder* the house is credited to *G. J. J. Mair.*

large sub-rectangular enclosure to the s. Limited excavations on the site failed to produce evidence of its date.

CROSSCRAKE
5080

ST THOMAS. 1875 by *Paley & Austin*. Small, of square slate blocks. Nave and chancel and transepts. Lancet windows and one with geometrical tracery. Central space inside with arches to the w, E, and N. The style inside is late c12 to early c13, including even two round arches. A civilized handling of period material, and not at all in a fashion current about 1875.

SELLET HALL, 1 m. SE. A c17 front of three bays on the way to symmetry. All windows mullioned and transomed except the one l. of the entrance, which has mullions only, expressing probably the service part. Staircase with elaborate vertically symmetrical balusters. Is the house really late c16, as the RCHM suggests, and not rather after 1630?

CROSSRIGG HALL *see* CLIBURN

CROSTHWAITE
4090

ST MARY, Church Town. 1878. Rock-faced, with a w tower, an aisleless nave, and a shallow apse. Perp in style. – PLATE. Cup and Cover Paten, 1567 (York). – MONUMENT. William Pearson † 1856. Free-standing bust.

COWMIRE HALL, 2 m. SW. Plain late c17 house of six bays with a doorway protected by a semicircular hood. The house is attached to a pele tower probably of the early c16. A straight-headed three-light window with arched lights. The ground level of the tower is tunnel-vaulted. In the house a chimney-piece with c17 decoration.

SOUTH HOUSE, Pool Bank, ½ m. s of the above. The house has a Yorkshire lintel dated 1693, and at the back mullioned and transomed windows and a wooden spinning gallery.

CURWEN WOODS *see* HOLME

DALE END *see* GRASMERE

DALLAM TOWER *see* MILNTHORPE

DALTON HALL *see* BURTON-IN-KENDALE

6090   ## DILLICAR

(CROOK OF LUNE BRIDGE. C16 or earlier. Two semicircular
arches. 'Extremely picturesque and elegant'; MHLG.)

DRYBECK HALL see ORMSIDE

6020   ## DUFTON

ST CUTHBERT. Nave and chancel of old masonry. But the w
tower is of 1784, and that could also be the date of the windows, with their Y- and intersecting tracery. The ceiling is
canted and has thin stucco panelling. – SCULPTURE. In the
chancel s wall a small panel with a figure in a sunk field, badly
preserved. Could it be Anglo-Saxon? – STAINED GLASS.
Lozenges in strong, primary colours, probably also *c*.1784.
The glass is by *Faucet* of Appleby (TK). – PLATE. Cup,
Newcastle, 1724.

The village has an oblong GREEN with trees.

FORT, on Castle Hill. The site consists of a roughly circular
area covering 1 acre enclosed by a ditch and external bank
broken by entrance gaps on the NE and NW. Within the
earthworks are a number of hut circles and a square enclosure
on the SW.

EAMONT BRIDGE see BROUGHAM

EWE LOCK SETTLEMENT see
CROSBY RAVENSWORTH

5000   ## FAWCETT FOREST

BORROWDALE HEAD. C17. Inside, a plaster panel of a stylized
branch with boughs and leaves.

6090   ## FIRBANK

ST JOHN EVANGELIST. 1842 by *Bateman* of Dent(?). Bell-
turret, lancet windows, short chancel, flat ceiling with one
stucco roundel. – PLATE. Cup, London, 1722.

Two fine sandstone RAILWAY VIADUCTS are near Firbank, the
LOW GILL VIADUCT of eleven arches (1858–61), and
another s of Firbank of three stone arches l., three r., and an
iron centre part with panel tracery.

FOUR STONES HILL *see* BAMPTON

GAYTHORNE HALL *see* GREAT ASBY

GILTHWAITERIGG *see* SKELSMERGH

GODMOND HALL *see* BURNESIDE

GRANGE HALL *see* GREAT ASBY

GRASMERE

3000

ST OSWALD. The exterior is so thickly encrusted with pebble-dash that no dating is possible. The tower has a batter one would call Voyseyish; but it is medieval. The E side has three windows, the top one C14, the others Late Perp, as are the side windows. There is no documentary certainty, which is a great pity, as the interior is both highly puzzling and visually exciting. It is divided longitudinally by a wall which forms a roughly pointed arcade, and above it an upper segment-headed arcade with the openings above the spandrels of the lower one. The wall does not touch the ridge of the roof, but reaches only to the collar-beam. Below this the roof divides 87 into two, one for each nave (or one for the nave and one for the N aisle), and both have kingposts, the N one with fourway struts, the S one with raking queenposts. It is a fascinating structure. The RCHM dates the nave and tower C14, the arcade *c.*1562,* the upper arcade and roof C17. – POOR BOX. Dated 1648. – SCULPTURE. Part of a slim shaft with rounded corners, about 5–6 in. across. On two sides foliage, on one a stylized beast, on the fourth an upright figure. He and the whole fragment look C12. – STAINED GLASS. Two N windows by *Holiday*, *c.*1891. – PLATE. Two Cups of 1714; Alms-dish, inscribed 1729; Paten on feet, London, 1731. – MONU-MENTS. Daniel Fleming † 1701. – Wordsworth † 1850. By *Thomas Woolner*. With a profile medallion. – Is the profile medallion to Elizabeth Fletcher † 1858 by him as well ?

(DALE END, ¾ m. S. The core of the house is a farmhouse of 1661. One fireplace and the roof structure remain. The bow window of the drawing room must be of *c.*1800, but most of what makes the house prominent is of shortly after 1893.)

---

* Will of John Benson. He left money 'so that the Roofe be taken down and maide oop again'.

5090

GRAYRIGG

St John. 1837. Lancets and a flat ceiling. The w tower is of 1869. – plate. Cup, London, 1709.

6010

GREAT ASBY

The village has a long green up both grassy banks of a beck. The church is on an island site in the green.

St Peter. 1866 by Messrs *Hay*. Of grey stone. Some geometrical tracery and some single-light windows with pointed-trefoiled heads. Ornate s porch. Spacious interior. – stained glass. The e window initialled by *Burrow*. – plate. Early c17 Cup. – Several tablets, e.g. one, † 1812, by *Webster* of Kendal.

Rectory, s of the church. One wing, really the pele tower of the house, dates from the early c14 and has a large, transomed two-light window. Round the corner later c17 fenestration. The doorway to the tower is single-chamfered and has a hood-mould. It is now inside the house. In the house also a c14 window-head from the medieval predecessor of the present church.

Settlement, ¾ m. s of the church, on Holborn Hill. The site consists of a stone bank enclosing a roughly oval area with a maximum diameter of 150 yds. Inside this bank are further grass-grown banks, forming internal divisions. The site has been badly damaged, particularly on the n. It is unexcavated, but is probably Iron Age or native Roman.

Settlement, 1½ m. ssw of the church. This is a group of small rectangular and oval enclosures defined by a stone bank. Undated, but again presumably Iron Age or native Roman.

Grange Hall, 1½ m. s. The c15 part of the house has in one end wall a handsome oriel, of five sides of a decagon, with cusped window lights and a big moulded corbel as a support. Also one window with two ogee-headed lights.

Cairn, 500 yards ne of Grange Hall. The cairn is some 40 ft in diameter and 5 ft high. A central depression marks the position of an excavation in the c18, when an unaccompanied inhumation burial was found.

Gaythorne Hall, 2 m. w, off the Orton Road. A very interesting, probably Jacobean house. Its interest is its plan. The windows are of the standard mullioned and transomed kind, and a Jacobean date is probable. The house is a square,

with four projections in the middles of the sides. Two, N and
S, are staircases with square, solid masonry cores; the other
two are porches, and consequently smaller. The E part of the
house was rebuilt in 1702, but without change of plan. The
general features of the plan are very similar to Kiplin Hall in
the North Riding of Yorkshire, a house of c.1625. For the
duplication of porches and staircases the only reason can be
that this was a house for two brothers, or in any case two
families. Inside the house, in one room, is a Jacobean stucco
frieze.

CAIRNS, on Gaythorn Plain, 2½ m. SE of Crosby Garrett church.
The W of these two cairns has a diameter of 34 ft and is 3 ft
high; the second, 100 yds SSW, is 25 ft in diameter and 2 ft
high. Both were opened in the C19, when inhumation burials
without grave goods were found in each. In the W cairn a
secondary cremation in an Early Bronze Age collared urn was
also found.

HOLLIN STUMP CAIRN, 2 m. WSW of the church. The cairn is
70 ft in diameter and 5 ft high. A stone cist containing an unaccompanied inhumation was found beneath the mound in
the C19.

SETTLEMENT, 3 m. SW of the church, on Great Asby Scar. This
triangular enclosure covers an area of 1¼ acres. Within the
stone bank and abutting on its internal face are a series of hut
circles. A gap on the S probably marks the original entrance
to the settlement.

GREAT LANGDALE

3000

HOLY TRINITY, Chapel Stile. 1857 by *John A. Cory*. Quite a
sizeable church. S tower, nave, chancel, and N aisle. The style
is late C13 to early C14. – PLATE. Cup of 1571.

BRATHAY HOW. Large, Voyseyish gabled house of c.1913. Is it
by *Mawson*?

GREAT MUSGRAVE *see* MUSGRAVE

GREAT ORMSIDE *see* ORMSIDE

GREAT STRICKLAND

5020

ST BARNABAS. 1872. Lancet windows, and a fanciful wooden
bell-turret on the E wall of the nave.

GUNNERKELD BOTTOM *see* SHAP

HACKTHORPE HALL *see* LOWTHER

HALLBECK *see* KILLINGTON

7000
HARTLEY CASTLE

(The house is Gothic, C18 and later. A fragment of the medieval castle wall is in the farmyard. MHLG)

HARTSOP HALL *see* PATTERDALE

4070
HAZELSLACK TOWER

1¼ m. E of Arnside

A pele tower, built probably in the late C14. Originally a building was attached to it on the E side. On the same side is a small original doorway, with a pointed head and unchamfered. The building was originally divided into a S and a N half. The latter had a tunnel-vaulted ground floor. The staircase was in the S half.

HEAVES *see* LEVENS

HELM HILL *see* NATLAND

4080
HELSINGTON

ST JOHN. The masonry of the (roughcast) church is supposed to date from 1726. What one sees now must be mainly of the restorations of 1898 or 1910. Nave and chancel in one and bellcote. The side windows are pairs, with shouldered lintels. The E and W windows have intersecting tracery instead, i.e. a re-creation of late C13 details.

HELSINGTON LATHES. *See* Kendal, p. 259.
SIZERGH CASTLE. *See* p. 289.

4080
HEVERSHAM

ST PETER. Mighty Victorian W tower in the E.E. style (1869–70 by *Paley & Austin*). The rest externally all Perp. The S aisle windows come first, with two-centred arches and (renewed) panel tracery. The rest is straight-headed, except for the large five-light E window and one window in the NE chapel which has intersecting tracery but is yet considered early C16 by the RCHM. The lancet windows of the clerestory are of course

Victorian too. The interior strikes one as Victorian also, but the s arcade has one complete pier of the late C12 with a waterleaf capital, the shaft of a second pier, and the E respond with crockets and rather more fluted or streaked leaves. This must be late C12 and may derive from Lowther. The N chapel arcade is primitively Late Perp. – SCREEN. To the N chapel, with balusters of 1605. – SOUTH DOOR. With C13 ironwork. – SCULPTURE. Part of a late C9 CROSS SHAFT with scrolls, 74 grapes, and birds and beasts in pairs. The type is still that of Rothwell and Bewcastle, but the motifs are bigger and coarser. – STAINED GLASS. The E window by *Warrington* (TK). – PLATE. Cup, London, 1655; Cover Paten, probably 1655; Paten on foot and two Flagons, London, 1673; Paten on foot, London, 1713. – MONUMENT. Anna Preston † 1767 by *I. Stewart*, Dublin. Classical urn in a shallow recess.

HEVERSHAM HALL, ¼ m. w. The house is of the C14, but in-complete. On the ground floor (the upper-floor windows are Elizabethan or later) the N front has a doorway and to its l. one, to its r. two windows of two lights with pointed-trefoiled heads and a transom. In the opposite wall (s) the hall also has two such windows. In the hall a small doorway to the former solar stairs. In the E wall one original two-light window.

PLUMTREE HALL, 300 yards N. Three-bay house of c.1800 with a porch with Adamish Ionic columns.

ROWELL, 1¼ m. SE. The house has a panel with the date 1719. Yet all the windows are mullioned, and the doorway has a four-centred head. So the date probably does not apply.

HINCASTER HALL, 1 m. NE. Symmetrical front of three bays with mullioned windows, except that the hall window is distinguished by having seven lights. Round chimneys. What date does that represent? The RCHM says late C16. Inside is a wooden panel with the date 1660.

HILLBECK HALL see BROUGH

HILL TOP see NEW HUTTON

HINCASTER HALL see HEVERSHAM

HOLBORN HILL see GREAT ASBY

HOLLIN HOW see CROOK

HOLLIN STUMP CAIRN see GREAT ASBY

5970

HOLME

HOLY TRINITY. 1839, with lancets and an awkward w tower.
CURWEN WOODS, ⅝ m. SE. Probably of *c.*1830–40. With a
recessed centre and a loggia which has in the middle a pair of
square pillars.

HORNBY HALL *see* BROUGHAM

HOWGILL CASTLE *see* MILBURN

4000

HUGILL or INGS

ST ANNE. Built in 1743 at the expense of Robert Bateman, a
child of the parish who, as Wordsworth wrote, 'grew wondrous
rich'. He was a merchant at Leghorn and has his funerary
monument there. The church consists of unbuttressed w
tower, nave and chancel in one, and a N attachment of 1878–9,
done extremely well. The E window of the church is of the
Venetian type, but has a broken pediment into which the
arched part of the window reaches up. The side windows are
arched, with blocky imposts and keystones. Only the tower
details are old-fashioned and look more C17 than C18. Pedimented w doorway. The coved ceiling of the church is
probably of 1878–9, and not so well done. The PAVING is of
marble sent by Bateman from Leghorn, and the ALTAR top
has inlay also of marble.* – FONT. Square, bulgy baluster and
bowl with four over-big cherubs' heads. – WOODWORK in
the tower arch, with pilasters. It must have been interfered
with. – PLATE. Cup and Cover Paten, London, 1634.

RESTON HALL, ¾ m. E. Dated 1743 on a rainwater head. This
was Robert Bateman's house. Plain seven-bay front. Inside, a
fine arch with pilasters connects entrance hall and staircase
hall. The staircase has slim balusters. In an adjoining room an
equally fine cupboard with pilasters.

ASHES, 1 m. S. This house also has a big cupboard with pilasters,
and in the same room a surprisingly refined and ornate stone
chimneypiece of *c.* 1730. It is said to have been at Rayrigg
Hall, Windermere.

5070

HUTTON ROOF

ST JOHN. 1881–2 by *Paley & Austin*, a good, honest job. Perp,
not large, with a S porch tower and a N aisle. The style is Perp.

* Information from the Rev. E. B. Kitts.

(In the vicarage garden the re-erected bellcote of the predecessor of the church, i.e. of 1757. RCHM)

SETTLEMENT, 1¾ m. W of Kirkby Lonsdale church. This is a small, oval, embanked enclosure, 70 yds in maximum diameter, with an entrance on the SE. Within the main enclosure bank, which is some 7 ft in width, are further partitioning banks and at least one hut circle. The site has been partially excavated, but no datable finds were recovered.

INGS see HUGILL

IRTON HILL see CROSBY GARRETT

KELD CHAPEL see SHAP

KENDAL

5090

Kendal is the largest town in Westmorland. It was a weaving town at least from the C14. Incorporation took place in 1575, and prosperity did not decline in the C17 and C18. The layout of the town is characterized by the narrow lanes or yards branching off the main street at r. angles. The general view from any distance suffered badly in the C19 and C20 – by two mistaken structures, the gasometer and a new insurance headquarters no less wrong in scale.

CHURCHES

HOLY TRINITY. Externally a typical prosperous Perp town church, a perfect rectangle with double aisles, no projection even for the chancel, and also the W tower embraced by the aisles. Internally the church is more varied. The exterior and the interior were considerably affected by a drastic restoration which took place in 1850–2. The E view of the church, i.e. the view towards the river Kent, is quite splendid, but it is, except for the walling of the inner aisles, entirely Victorian. All the external details are (or represent) the Late Perp, from the mid C15 to the early C16. The W porch is Victorian. Inside, the story is this. The nave arcades are clearly divided into three E bays of the C13 (round piers, round or octagonal abaci, double-chamfered arches), and the W bay plus the tower bay of the Perp period. The E piers of the tower are of colossal girth. They and the arcade W piers have no capitals, nor has the pair of piers where a chancel arch must once have been. E of this, the chancel chapels again have C13 arcades, but these are completely Victorian. Were they restored correctly? They have octagonal alternating with round piers and occasional bits of nailhead. The arcades of the outer aisles run through unbroken from E to W and are very different in all their details. Those of the N arcade are normal Perp standard, but those on the S side have capitals so elementary that they at first seem to be early C13 material re-used. However, in the early C16 masons up here returned to this simplicity. The outer NE chapel (Bellingham Chapel) has a charming ribbed ceiling of the C19, incorporating genuine bosses.

FURNISHINGS. FONT. Large octagonal bowl of black marble with concave sides and plain shields. A type which recurs in the North Riding of Yorkshire in the late C15. – SCREEN. To the inner S chapel, with some genuine Flamboyant, i.e. North Country early C16, tracery. – SEATING. Four re-used bench ends with poppy-heads, quite nice (outer N aisle). – Stalls with carved arms (W wall). – More stalls with plainer and probably later poppy-heads (outer S aisle). – SCULPTURE. Fragment of an Anglo-Saxon cross-shaft with scrolls with grapes and leaves; C9. – STAINED GLASS. In the inner S chapel head of a King, C15. – The E window is by *O'Connor*, 1855 (TK), and not good. – PLATE. Small Cup and Cover Paten, Chester, 1728. – MONUMENTS. In the Bellingham Chapel coffin lid with a foliated cross, sword, and shield; late C13. – In the same chapel tomb-chest with brasses of Sir Roger Bellingham † 1533 and wife. Good effigies, 36 in. long, with nice decoration round the heads. – Brass of Alan Bellingham † 1577 (20 in.). – Zachary Hubbersty of London † 1787. By *Flaxman*. In the tympanum of the tablet the disconsolate family and an angel hovering over them. – In the S chapel plain tomb-chest with just a few shields; early C16. – Walter Strickland † 1656. Table-tomb on Tuscan column supports. Below, the damaged effigy. – In the outer S chapel another plain early C16 tomb-chest with just shields. – In nave and aisles many tablets. – Against the W wall George Romney, the painter, a Kendal boy who died at Kendal in 1802. Black classical urn in relief. – John James of London † 1823. Grecian tablet.

ST GEORGE, Castle Street. 1839–41 by *G. Webster*, the chancel 1910–11 by *Austin & Paley*. The old part, which cost £4,242 (GS), has the typical thin lancets and thin buttresses, but the

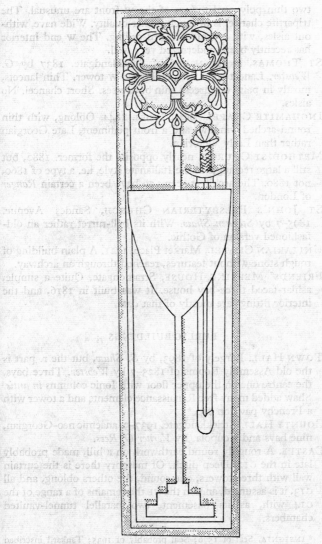

Kendal church, coffin lid, late thirteenth century

two thin polygonal towers of the w front are unusual. The tripartite chancel is of much higher quality. Wide nave, without aisles, with a canted ribbed ceiling. The w end interior has recently been modernized very well.

ST THOMAS, at the N end of Stricklandgate. 1837 by *G. Webster*. Lancet style with embraced w tower. Thin lancets, mostly in pairs or threes; thin buttresses. Short chancel. No aisles.

INGHAMITE CHAPEL, Beast Banks. 1844. Oblong, with thin round-arched windows and a front pediment, Late Georgian rather than Early Victorian.

METHODIST CHURCH, nearly opposite the former. 1882, but still a large rectangle in the Italianate style, i.e. a type of 1860, not 1880. The architect seems to have been a certain *Ranger* of London.

ST JOHN'S PRESBYTERIAN CHURCH, Sandes Avenue. 1895–7 by *Stephen Shaw*. With its bell-turret rather an old-fashioned version of Gothic.

UNITARIAN CHAPEL, Market Place. 1721. A plain building of rough stone without features, reached through an archway.

FRIENDS' MEETING HOUSE, Stramongate. Quite a simple, ashlar-faced three-bay house. It was built in 1816, and the interior fittings are mostly of that date.

PUBLIC BUILDINGS

TOWN HALL. Largely of 1893, by *S. Shaw*, but the r. part is the old Assembly Rooms of 1825–7 by *Webster*. Three bays, the centre one on the upper floor with Ionic columns *in antis*. Shaw added many free Renaissance elements and a tower with a Frenchy pavilion cap.*

COUNTY HALL, Stricklandgate. 1937–9, anaemic neo-Georgian, nine bays and a cupola. By *Verner O. Rees*.

CASTLE. A roughly round earthwork on a hill, made probably late in the C12. Deep ditch. Of masonry there is the curtain wall with three towers, one round, the others oblong, and all C13, it is assumed, and on the NE the remains of a range of the C14 with, as its basement, two parallel tunnel-vaulted chambers.

* INSIGNIA. Seal of 1576; Seal probably of 1635; Tankard inscribed 1629; pair of Maces, London, 1648; Loving Cup of 1667, remodelled in the late C17; Sword, *temp*. Charles II or a little later; large Tankard, London, 1681.

ABBOT HALL (Art Gallery), N of the church. Built as a private house by *John Carr* in 1759.* The house is approached through an archway in the middle of the stables. They have blank arches towards the house. The house is built of rough, squared and coursed stone. The entrance side has a centre of three widely spaced bays and slightly lower, very bare, projecting wings. The doorway is pedimented and reached by an outer staircase. Towards the river the house has two canted bays, a middle doorway, and lower wings with a Venetian window set in a blank arch. The doorway has the same motif. Plain parapets, and indeed a becoming masculine plainness all round. The entrance hall has a screen of two Roman Doric columns. To the l. the dining room doorway with pulvinated frieze and pediment. Staircase with umbrella balusters.

CARNEGIE LIBRARY, Stricklandgate. 1908 by *T. F. Pennington*. Red sandstone in a free Baroque with Gibbs motifs.

STATION. Probably of 1847. With half-hipped gables; quite picturesque.

GASWORKS, Parkside Road. They incorporate the older building inscribed 'Kendal Undertaking, 1825' and also 'Ex fumo lucem'. It is a little building with a little classical front, two angle pillars, two Tuscan columns, and a pediment.

PERAMBULATION

It is hardly necessary, or indeed possible, to perambulate consistently. From the church N in KIRKLAND at its N end the Late Georgian QUEEN'S HOTEL, facing down HIGHGATE. These two streets, and Stricklandgate, the N continuation of Highgate, are the spine of the town. They run S-N, never quite straight. There are no specially good houses, but no damaging ones either. Houses are of exposed stone or rendered. In Kirkland Nos 26–42 are a good group (No. 28 has internal crucks; MHLG). In Highgate Nos 134–6 (W) are handsome Late Georgian, six bays, ashlar. The BREWERY HOUSE, No. 118 (W), is of three bays with a nice doorway. It is of 1757, and the brewery itself is attached to it. Opposite the town hall a street runs W and leads to the hospital and close to it on CASTLE HOWE the OBELISK, erected in 1788

* The client was Col. George Wilson of Dallam Tower, and the cost was £8,000.

and dedicated to liberty.* Back into Highgate. The KENDAL
HOTEL (E) is probably c.1840, in a Latest Classical with
pedimented first-floor windows. Then on the same side NEW
BANK YARD (No. 17), an attractive group. At the corner of
the Market Place the former MOOT HALL, with a corner
tower or eminence with lantern and a Venetian window towards Highgate. It was built in 1759. In STRICKLANDGATE
on the W side No. 13 has a seven-bay late C18 front. Doorway
with columns and a pediment. No. 92, the RURAL DISTRICT
OFFICES, is also late C18, also of seven bays. Doorway with
Corinthian columns and pediment. No. 95 (Y.W.C.A.) is a
plain five-bay house. The date 1724 is on a rainwater head.

From a little SE of the Market Place to the NE runs STRAMON-
GATE. Here, at the corner of New Road, the PROVINCIAL
INSURANCE. The part towards New Road is of c.1830, with
a Doric porch in antis. The part towards Stramongate is an
addition of c.1920, well done. On the new building behind
comment has already been made. The continuation of
Stramongate is STRAMONGATE BRIDGE of 1794, with four
segmental arches and arched recesses in the piers. Then
WILDMAN STREET with, on the N side, CASTLE DAIRY, a
hall-house of the C14. In the hall a three-light window with
trefoiled heads and the original doorway. Rounded chimneys.
Inside, the hall beams are early C16. The wings project to
one side only (not H-wise). They have kingpost roofs. From
the SW end of Stramongate Kent Street runs to the river and
across it at the end of BRIDGE STREET is a strategically
placed early C19 three-bay house. From here NW in AYNAM
ROAD Messrs Goodacres' factory, apparently Early Victorian.
The continuation of Aynam Road is THORNEY HILLS,
with a few good Late Georgian houses, especially No. 4 with
wreaths in the friezes. S of Bridge Street the road runs along
the river and is tree-planted, a rare case in England of such a
promenade.

Four individual outer items. No. 103 SEDBERGH ROAD is
Voysey's LITTLE HOLME, 1908, small, but treated with all
the care Voysey was capable of. Just an oblong with a hipped
roof and one chimney. Entrance recessed under a big plain
arch, a motif repeated by innumerable spec builders. The
porch is sheltered by a big canopy of substantial timbers. The
staircase window is typical Voysey (three lights, two tran-

* Castle Howe is a MOTTE AND BAILEY CASTLE, 3½ acres in size. The
motte rises 25 ft above the bailey.

soms, no mouldings whatever), as are the other windows with their flat mullions and quoining. It is all inspired by rural Tudor, yet in its plainness and flushness on the way to the new style of the C20.

s of the town to the E of MILNTHORPE ROAD is WATTS FIELD, late C17, with a segmental pediment over the doorway and in the pediment a cherub's head. A little further s, to the W, along COLLIN ROAD, is COLLINFIELD, with a plaster panel of 1674 over the fireplace. Lady Anne Clifford's secretary retired to this house in 1668. Yet further s is HELSINGTON LATHES, partly pre-Reformation with a three-light window with uncusped ogee-heads, partly late C16 or early C17 with some plasterwork. The E front must be late C17, because of its symmetry.

At WATERCROOK, I m. S, within a U-bend of the river Kent, is the site of a ROMAN FORT, represented now by a raised platform about 3 acres in extent. A civil settlement is known to have extended down to the river, and on the landward side the site of a bath house is known. Occupation began in the Flavian period.

KENTMERE

4000

ST CUTHBERT. The roof-beams are C16; all the rest is 1866, with alterations in the 1950s. Nave and chancel in one, and W tower. Norman windows in groups of three, a singular rhythm. – BERNARD GILPIN MEMORIAL. 1901, by the *Keswick School of Industrial Arts*. Bronze tablet with a frame of trees with intricate roots and branches. Arts and Crafts, almost Art Nouveau.

KENTMERE HALL, ¾ m. w. Ruinous pele tower of the C14, tunnel-vaulted at ground level. Staircase in one corner. Part of the parapet with machicolations. To the s one two-light window with ogee-headed lights. A C15 house attached to the E, with hall and shallow cross-wing at the E end. The hall has the screens passage with stone walls both sides.

KILLINGTON

6080

ALL SAINTS. Nave and chancel in one; bell-turret. The N windows are C14 or C15, the s windows C17. – PLATE. Cup, London, 1722. – TABLETS. One, † 1771, is all of black marble and has no effigy or other figures.

KILLINGTON HALL. The l. part is the oldest and is in ruins. It seems C15 and has to the front a four-light, and above it a three-light window, the lights all cusped. There may have been battlements too. The rest is dated 1640 and has in its two gables stepped three-light windows. But the doorway and the adjoining ogee-headed window are of 1803 (inscription). Round chimneys.

LOW HALL, Hallbeck, ½ m. SE. Dated 1684, yet still with irregularly placed mullioned windows. The doorway is specially typical of 1680–90 in Westmorland farmhouses. It has pilasters, but they have the oddest sunk moulding. It has capitals, but they are almost Anglo-Saxon in their incorrectness. And it has a lintel with simple geometrical decoration and a pediment minus its base.

KING ARTHUR'S ROUND TABLE see

YANWATH

KIRKBY LONSDALE

ST MARY. The church lies hidden behind Market Street and reveals itself only from Fairbank, i.e. the W. It is approached from Market Street by iron GATES with an iron arch dated 1823. From the churchyard one has marvellous views into the fells to the N and E, and for that reason a GAZEBO was built inside the churchyard in the C18 or early C19. It is octagonal, with four arched openings in the main directions. Ruskin wrote of the Lune valley at Kirkby Lonsdale that it is 'one of the loveliest scenes in England – therefore in the world'.

The church exhibits an interesting and promisingly mixed exterior. The W tower is embraced by the aisles. Its upper parts have windows of C15 and early C16 character, but there was some rebuilding in 1705. However, at the foot of the tower is a sumptuous Late Norman portal of two orders of shafts with reeded capitals and additional inner mouldings. One arch order has panels basically each a saltire cross, but with decoration inserted. The outer order has a long, thin archer(?), a dragon etc. The aisles end to the W in one round-headed and one pointed lancet, indicating the narrowness of the aisles at that time. If one makes this assumption, then the Late Norman N aisle W doorway (one continuous chamfer) must be re-set. The N side of the church has an outer in addition to the inner aisle. The aisles are embattled on N and S and have C15 to early C16 windows with straight tops. The E view of the church reveals a yet more complex story; for the chancel E end has three, only slightly stepped lancets of c.1200, and the S and the inner N aisle have Dec E windows with reticulated tracery. The S priest's doorway of c.1200 with a round arch is again re-used, as the interior will show. Re-used also is the zigzag and the thick roll hood-mould above the S doorway. The S porch is of 1866.

This is a complex enough story, but the interior has yet a further surprise in store and faces us with the most powerful Early Norman display in Westmorland (or Cumberland). It is only a fragment, but it will not be forgotten. It is a fragment of an interior of arcades of seven bays flanking, without any 75 intervening chancel arch, an oppressively narrow nave. The aisles are wider than the nave, and then there is a further seven-bay arcade between inner and outer aisle. The oppressiveness is entirely due to the massiveness of the NW respond and the three very closely spaced N piers. They can hardly be later than about 1115 and deserve detailed description. The respond and the second pier are of the compound kind, with triple shafts to the arch openings. The respond capitals are the earliest, with primitive volutes and crude interlaced bands; the compound pier has a scalloped capital. But pier one and pier three are round, and they have the boldly incised or carved-in trellis of Durham Cathedral, taken no doubt direct from there. The first pier has a trellis of three parallel lines of incisions, the third one of deep and quite broad grooves. The first pier has a square abacus and a capital of four big scallops. The first arch has three parallel fat rolls, the second one step and one chamfer, the third a moulding of a half-roll framed by two half-hollows, again taken from Durham. The fourth pier is later, as it has an octagonal capital.

The church thus begun must have been intended to have a wider nave and altogether a different scale. It may have been started with a view to vaulting – cf. the shaft of the compound pier, clearly meant to be continued upward. This however was not done. Also, as one capital of this early work was left unfinished, we may assume a break in operations. The work of c.1115 was no doubt built far W of a smaller preceding church. Then came a reduction, and, later in the C12, the S arcade was started. The first pier still has a square abacus. The capital is flat and has scallops, but the arches have two slight chamfers, and the next pier has the round capital of c.1200. When the new church had reached that far, i.e. when not much upper wall and no roof were yet done, the lodge must have received a new impetus. The old church was pulled down, and work proceeded apace. The E bays on both sides have slender alternating round and octagonal piers and double-chamfered arches, and the beautiful E lancets terminated the work. They were elegantly shafted inside, with boldly detached shafts with one shaft-ring, and this arcading continued for the E windows of the aisles (windows now, as we have seen, Dec). Some of the capitals of the shafts at the E end have waterleaf and some have crocket capitals. That also indicates that the end of the work was about 1200. The late C12 piers were higher than the old, and so the W bays were rebuilt on high, square bases. The W tower was begun at the time of the S arcade, as the tower arch and the W portal show.

The outer aisle arcade is Late Perp, as are the N windows. The piers are round – still, or again – and the capitals as plain and simply moulded as to make them quite similar to early C13 capitals. Only the chapel piers are octagonal.

FURNISHINGS. PULPIT. 1619. With closely ornamented panels in two tiers, the upper with the usual short, broad, blank arches. – SCREENS. The iron screens round the choir are Victorian and probably of c.1866. – Tracery heads of a Perp screen in the S aisle at the E end. – CUPBOARD. A splendid cupboard in the N aisle at the W end. Flamboyant and Jacobean motifs. Is this re-used material, or Flamboyant Revival like the Preston Screen at Cartmel? – STAINED GLASS. Faith, Charity, and Hope (S aisle), no doubt by *Powell*. Date commemorated 1878. – PLATE. Cup and Cover Paten, London, 1571; Cup and Cover Paten, London, 1633; Cup and Cover Paten, Chester, 1736. – MONUMENTS. Quite a number of Georgian tablets, and one bigger standing monument, black, just with a big urn. This is to Hugh Ashton † 1749 and many others. – Janet Webster † 1805 has the urn in an unusual place, John Wilson † 1792 an elegant large urn in a grey recess.

(MOTTE AND BAILEY CASTLE. N of the vicarage, on the W bank of the Lune. Curwen)

PERAMBULATION. Kirkby Lonsdale is a town of dark grey stone houses, enjoyable to wander through, and indeed nowhere not enjoyable. The best start is the MARKET SQUARE. The CROSS and shelter, octagonal, in the Tudor style, looks 1845 and is of 1905. At the far end is the SAVINGS BANK, of *c.*1840, on the strength of the double round-arched window on the first floor. Otherwise all is still classical. Three bays, porch with two pairs of Doric pilasters and a balcony. Open turret. Opposite and thus really in Main Street is the ROYAL HOTEL, C18, ashlar-faced, with a ground floor in smooth rustication. Porch of unfluted Ionic columns, pulvinated frieze and pediment. Parapet at the top of the building. On the N side not a house to deserve notice, on the S side two handsome shop-fronts, one bowed, the other with Roman Doric columns. Off the Market Square to the E, at the end of JINGLING LANE is PROSPECT HOUSE, well named. It is ashlar-faced, of three bays, with a broad flat band round the arched doorway.

S along the narrow, not strictly straight MAIN STREET not much of note, though several acceptable doorways. No. 9 juts forward, with its gable treated as a pediment and pierced by an arched window. The front is to the S, i.e. looking at it from the S, blocking part of the view. There is here a large round-headed middle window and a larger archway to the stables. Then on the W side TOWN END HOUSE with a Tuscan porch. Main Street is continued in Bridge Brow, where *Waterhouse*'s LUNEFIELD of 1870 has alas been pulled down, and so to the famous DEVIL'S BRIDGE, now replaced by a new one. The old is of the C15 and has three splendid round arches, triple-chamfered and on the underside with ribs. Triangular cut-waters with, on top, polygonal balconies.

Back to the Market Square and now to the N along MAIN STREET. The DISTRICT BANK, an Early Victorian ashlar front of projection and recession, asymmetrical, with one gable but with restrained details, seems to date from *c.*1855 (lease of premises by the bank). On the opposite side of the street several Early Victorian shop-fronts. At the end of Main Street turn E into MILL BROW. A little square on the l. has the former MARKET CROSS, a C17(?) column with an octagonal cap and a ball finial. Behind it an over-restored C16 house. Steeply down the lane, with the view to the fells, crushingly Victorianly caught up at the end by a gasometer. The farthest house on the S side, the five-bay MANOR HOUSE, is the best at Kirkby Lonsdale. It is of *c.*1700, with the windows still with stone crosses, but the doorway with a segmental pediment.

Now from the end of Main Street W, down MARKET STREET. At the corner is the MARKET HOUSE of 1854, a successfully rounded corner, with rustication below, round-headed windows above, no Victorian enrichments yet. The SUN INN has its front on three C17 pillars. Opposite, the KING'S ARMS and the adjoining house have twin Georgian façades, with a tripartite window and in the gable a tripartite lunette window. (Inside the King's Arms a C17 plaster ceiling. RCHM) The end of the street is closed by FOUNTAIN HOUSE, Georgian, of five bays. The doorway has unfluted Ionic columns, a pulvinated frieze, and a pediment. Nice lamp overthrow. To the l. of Fountain House, at r. angles, another five-bay house, this one probably early C19. W of the church FAIRBANK starts. At the start, facing the church a nice group of houses, including the METHODIST CHAPEL of 1834 behind trees. Lancet windows in the front.

Up MITCHELGATE, to end the perambulation at ABBOTS HALL, a C16 and C17 house, not in its original state, as the porch is now at one end of the front. Mullioned windows, in the l. half on the ground floor under one continuous string-course, which is a later C17 motif. (The MHLG also dates the staircase late C17.)

TEARNSIDE HALL, 1½ m. W. Dated 1686. Two-storeyed, with a two-storeyed porch. Mullioned windows of two lights. Continuous string-courses. A very typical doorway with oddly moulded pilasters and capitals almost Anglo-Saxon in their accumulation of thin slabs (cf. Low Hall, Hallbeck). The lintel has an elementary leaf-pattern. A second doorway has a lintel with the motif of the printer's bracket.

UNDERLEY HALL. See p. 295.

SETTLEMENT. See Hutton Roof.

KIRKBY STEPHEN

ST STEPHEN. A long, red town church with an impressive Perp W tower. It has a W doorway with shields in the spandrels, a three-light W window, diagonal buttresses, and bell-openings of two pairs of tall lights under ogee gables. The arch towards the nave is the highest in the county. The tower can be dated c.1506. As for the rest of the church, the external details are nearly all the restorers'. Only on the N side, and especially at the NW corner, is there early masonry, including the original roof-line. Actually, the N transept is E.E. and the two W lancets are in order, and the S aisle is Perp and at least partly in order. The chancel and its chapels date from 1847 and are by *Carpenter*, and so are the N aisle and the clerestory. Inside, however, the arcades are of the early C13, with round piers, waterholding bases, octagonal abaci, and double-chamfered arches. The transept arch on the S side is of the same date. It is triple, and the middle member is filleted. The wide arch from the S aisle to the transept is Perp. Perp also a reredos niche in the N transept E wall. In the chancel Carpenter re-used the very fine, steeply trefoil-pointed SEDILIA and PISCINA. They must be late C13. The capitals have awkward upright leaves. In the S chapel, re-set, is a C13 corbel, with a motif of zigzag consisting of lanceolate leaves. – But the oldest architectural member of the church is a very beautiful Norman CAPITAL, lying loose by the tower arch. It has leaves, including an almost Grecian honeysuckle motif. The abacus is square. So it must be *c.*1175 at the latest (cf. Lowther). – SCREEN. Parts of a made-up screen in the N transept, with early C17 balusters, Flamboyant tracery, and Early Renaissance friezes. – PULPIT. Probably *c.*1872. Sumptuous, of red and green marbles; round. – SCULPTURE. Fragment of an Anglo-Danish cross-shaft, with interlace and the so-called Bound Devil, a bearded figure, bound indeed. The fragment is in the Jellinge style, i.e. of the C10, and similar to one of the Penrith crosses. Other, smaller fragments by the tower arch. – STAINED GLASS, S aisle W. The drawings, much better than the glass, are displayed close by. They are signed J.C. 1903. This means no doubt *James Clarke* of Casterton. – PLATE. Cup with baluster stem, London, 1656; Cup, Newcastle, late C17. – MONUMENTS. Hogback gravestone with 'tiled' roof (N aisle W). – Tomb-chest with effigy of a Knight, early C15, probably a Musgrave (S chapel). – Tomb-chest in a recess with a coarsely foliated gable. To Richard Musgrave † 1464 (also S chapel). – Low tomb recess in the N aisle. – Thomas, first Lord Wharton, † 1568. Stone effigies of him and two wives; very bad. Tomb-chest with kneeling family and at the corners detached balusters (N chapel).

HOLY FAMILY (R.C.). 1864, built as the Congregational Chapel. With a SW turret with spire and flowing tracery.

METHODIST CHAPEL. 1839, and no longer really Georgian. It is the two arched doorways under one pediment which indicate the moment of disintegration of the Georgian pattern-book discipline. The fancy angle *tourelles* are even more telling.

TEMPERANCE HALL. 1856. Debased Classical, with a statue of Temperance and very large Grotesque lettering.

THE CLOISTERS. Built in 1810 by *George Gibson* as a screen between Market Place and churchyard. Eight Tuscan columns arranged so that four project in front of the others. Triglyph frieze and pediment with bellcote.

The best individual building at Kirkby Stephen is MARTINS BANK, given its present façade in 1903 by *John F. Curwen*. It is a lively, quite asymmetrical, but resourcefully composed, gabled façade. A high chimney separates the two gables, which are not in line.

A few Georgian five-bay houses, one E of the church, one in the Market Place, and one, with a pedimented doorway, in a position reached by turning s of Martins Bank up a long four-foot-wide alley between walls.

WINTON MANOR HOUSE, 1½ m. NE, is a six-bay house of three storeys, dated 1726. It has a doorway with bolection moulding and segmental pediment.

STOBARS HALL, ½ m. W. A Late Georgian front with a Tuscan porch and tripartite ground-floor windows, but the parapet embattled. At the back in the middle an apparently later embattled tower, and a second for the stables. There are dates 1695 and 1866, but neither fits.

CROGLAM CASTLE, ¾ m. SSW of the church. This is an oval enclosure of 1½ acres defined by a ditch with external bank. An entrance gap occurs on the NE. No hut foundations or other features are visible in the interior.

ROUND BARROW, 1½ m. SW of the church, on Wiseber Hill. The site is now only 28 ft in diameter and 1½ ft high. Excavation in the C19 revealed an inhumation in a tree-trunk coffin accompanied by a bronze bowl and a glass bead. This deposit had cut through an earlier interment by cremation, with which was found a leaf-shaped flint arrowhead of Neolithic type.

SMARDALE HALL, 2½ m. WSW. Assigned to the late C16 by the RCHM. An exceedingly odd plan: an oblong, 86 by only 27 ft, and with four round corner towers with conical roofs. A similar house in the North Riding of Yorkshire is Allerthorpe Hall of 1608. The elements are Scottish more than English.[*]

---

[*] A propos such connexion with Scotland, it is worth pointing out that a Warcop girl, i.e. one of the Smardale family, married Sir John Dalston of Dalston Hall, another Scottish rather than English house.

Of original details or even masonry surface, very little is preserved at Smardale Hall.

SETTLEMENT, SE of Smardale Hall. This is a group of enclosures disposed on the E and W slopes of the ridge and covering about 1 acre. A number of circular hut sites are visible within the enclosures.

WHARTON HALL, 1¾ m. S. An irregular house round a courtyard, partly in ruins. It was the original home of the Whartons. One approaches it through a gatehouse of 1559, with segmental arches. It was originally three storeys high. Opposite is the oldest part of the house, a hall of the C15 with solar and service wings. The S (service) part is tunnel-vaulted beneath. So is the porch adjoining it. This led into the hall, which has its projecting chimneybreast. S of this range the first Lord Wharton in 1540 built a new hall, 68 by 27 ft in size. Of this only the fireplace is recognizable, but it was followed by the best part of the house, the Great Kitchen, with an undercroft and the kitchen proper above. This has to the courtyard two grand transomed three-light windows, with uncusped depressed-arch heads to the lights below and above the transom. The windows in the hall range also have arched (uncusped) heads to the lights, and so have those of the N range running E–W. The details differ, but nothing seems earlier than the late C15.

KIRKBY THORE 6020

ST MICHAEL. The W tower has Dec bell-openings, but the imposts of the (widened) chancel arch are Norman. The chancel windows are Dec too, but the N window is set in a Norman arch. The two-bay N arcade has quatrefoil piers with the foils more than circular in section, and capitals typical of the late C13. The aisle windows, however, are Dec. – FONT. 1688. Plain octagonal bowl with a coat of arms. Short baluster stem. – PULPIT. Dated 1631. With caryatids at the corners and arabesque as well as blank-arched panels. – COMMUNION RAIL. With twisted balusters, dated A. R. Caroli II 35. That must mean 1649 + 35 = 1684. – PLATE. Cup and Cover Paten, London, 1633.

KIRKBY THORE HALL. The hall range has masonry attributed by the RCHM to the C14, but the mullioned windows and the bay with its mullioned and transomed windows are Elizabethan or Jacobean. The service wing on the l. has disappeared, but the solar wing remains, and has in its gable-end a two-light window with a transom. The tracery is of an arch upon the two arched heads of the two lights and a pointed quatrefoil in the upper arch, i.e. a form of *c*.1300 or a little later.

Kirkby Thore is the site of the ROMAN FORT of BRAVONIA-CUM.

LADY'S PILLAR see MALLERSTANG

LAMMERSIDE CASTLE see MALLERSTANG

LANGDALE CHACE see WINDERMERE

LANGDALES see BOWNESS-ON-WINDERMERE

LANGDALES see GREAT LANGDALE

LANGTHWAITE see CASTERTON

4080

LEVENS

ST JOHN EVANGELIST. 1828. Nave and chancel; lancet windows. Bell-turret with octagonal top and spire. Inside, the bell-turret stands on two buttresses, and a WEST GALLERY is divided into three parts by them. Wide nave, and roof with scissor bracing. – PLATE. Set presented 1828.

LEVENS HALL. Levens Hall is by far the largest Elizabethan house in Westmorland or Cumberland, but as it is in all its façades entirely informal, it has managed to preserve an intimate scale. The term Elizabethan house is correct for most of the features one sees now, but it is very likely that some of the masonry is considerably older. As one approaches from the N the impression is at once the familiar one in these counties of a pele tower and an attached hall range. Indeed the tower has a spiral stair inside, and in the basement a doorway with a hollow-chamfered pointed arch. Recently two more such doorways have been discovered immediately next to it, so that it looks as if a medieval hall adjoined the tower at that level and had its entries here into kitchen, pantry, and buttery.* The tower however is not vaulted, as one would expect. On the other hand to the E of what one assumes to have been the medieval hall is an area which is tunnel-vaulted and has three doorways in different directions, all with shouldered

---

* This description is partly based on information given me by Mrs and Mr R. Bagot.

lintels. So one may even believe that the house had two towers like Bewley Castle, Bolton.

The de Redman family held Levens from c.1225 to 1578. Then James Bellingham followed. He built most of what makes the house memorable and died in 1641. In 1688 the house was sold to James Graham. Later by marriage the Howards, Earls of Suffolk, had the house.

The N front has the big embattled tower and to its r. one gabled bay, to its l. two. The windows are mullioned and transomed. The main doorway (with ears) looks c.1690 (rain-water heads, 1691, 1692). On its l. is the hall bay window with six lights to the front and two to the doorway. The E side towards the garden with its marvellous topiary is as asymmetrical: one canted bay window, one square projection, and then a recessed part continued along the S side, but interrupted by the Howard Tower, begun in 1807. It has a higher stair-turret. The S side is in its present form regular. With its mullion-and-transom cross windows it must be c.1700, i.e. of James Graham's years. The rainwater heads say 1788, the clock face of the turret 1773, but the bell inside 1707. The masonry is presumably older, and this applies also to the end block, at the SW corner. However, the one-step four-light window in its gable is as a rule a sign of the late C17.

The HALL is Elizabethan, but in the medieval position. Until the time of James Graham it had its screens passage, and still has a plaster ceiling with interlocked quatrefoils and a plaster frieze with short pilasters and coats of arms. The bay window corresponds of course to the high-table end. What is however bewildering is that the present doorway leads, not into a presumed screens-passage place, but into the middle of the room. That can't have been so (in spite of the one and only case: Sutton Park). On the other hand, how did one come in? Through the tower? The GRAND STAIRCASE behind the hall, with three rather heavy balusters to the tread, is obviously Graham. E of the hall is the DRAWING ROOM, with a ceiling 85 with eight-pointed stars formed of ribs of quite some depth of relief and with little pendants. The chimneypiece is dated 1595. It is specially illuminating to consider that work in the adjoining mansion of Sizergh was complete by c.1575, whereas it seems to have started at Levens after 1578. So the only ceiling at Sizergh similar to this one is the latest there. The chimneypiece is very grand, with short columns and pairs of short columns in two tiers in the overmantel, but

fluted pilasters l. and r. of the opening. The columns mostly
frame coats of arms. In the adjoining SOUTH DRAWING
ROOM is a simpler ceiling, but an exceptionally interesting
chimneypiece with Samson and Hercules l. and r. of the opening, figures of Touch, Smell, and Taste standing above, and
Hearing and Sight reclining on the open pediment above.
Also carved panels of the four Elements and the four Seasons –
a whole panoply of uncomplicated allegory. The wall panelling has lozenges (as at Sizergh). The DINING ROOM E of the
hall has a chimneypiece dated 1586 and a stucco ceiling whose
chief motifs are apsidally-ended Greek crosses. The SMOKING
ROOM behind the dining room has puzzling panelling, obviously not Elizabethan, but equally obviously intended to
look Elizabethan. It was put in c.1810. More of the same
panelling in the other rooms. On the first floor above the hall
was originally a LONG GALLERY. In the S range is a room
with typical late C17 panelling and a staircase with equally
typical twisted balusters.

The TOPIARY of the garden is the most famous feature of
Levens. It was made for James Graham by Monsieur *Beaumont* about 1700.*

NETHER LEVENS, W of Levens Hall. The centre of the house is
the hall, dating probably from the early C16. It has a four-
light window with four-centred heads to the lights, a big plain
fireplace, and a large, elliptical chimney-shaft. To the N the
hall range continues with a slightly later range, also with such
chimneys. To the S was a long cross-wing of the same date as
the hall. This is in ruins. On the E side is an addition of 1594
with mullioned and transomed windows.

HEAVES, 1 m. N of Levens Hall. Late Georgian, of three widely
spaced bays. The l. and r. ground-floor windows are tripartite.
Porch of four unfluted Ionic columns. Fine Soanian entrance
hall with rounded corners and a shallow vault. Staircase
spacious and with a chastely Grecian iron handrail.‡

SETTLEMENT, on Sizergh Fell. *See* Sizergh Castle.

LITTLE STRICKLAND

ST MARY. 1814. Lancets with Y-tracery. – PLATE. Set, London,
1810.

---

* A lead cistern has the date 1704. M. Beaumont, so Mrs Bagot tells me,
also designed the gardens of Edenhall.
‡ Also some C16 remains reported.

Low Hall. L-shaped. In one range mullioned windows, in the other mullioned and transomed windows. (In a room on the first floor a plaster ceiling with close octagons, crosses, etc., and the panels filled in with roses, scrolls, etc. It is of c.1600.)

(High Hall. Mullioned windows and a date 1600 on a huge fireplace. MHLG)

LONG MARTON

6020

St Margaret and St James. A very interesting church, essentially CII and CI2. The masonry with the enormous quoin stones of the nave indicates the CII, and to this may well belong the S doorway with its forceful and barbaric tympanum of a quadruped with wings, a big dragon with a 76 twisted tail, and a winged sword and shield(?). The W doorway now leads into the tower, but the tower is a slightly later addition. The proportions of this are characteristically Saxon, and the tympanum with a beast and a bird at the top goes with the other tympanum. The chip-carved saltire crosses below and the trellis of the lintel on the other hand are familiar Norman motifs. The N doorway is definitely Norman, i.e. CI2, but the smaller N window might be either CII or CI2. Again without a doubt CI2 is the W tower. Its bell-openings, though much renewed, represent a date late in the century. It originally had a W doorway. The chancel E end also belongs to the CI2, cf. the splays of the former E windows. Otherwise the chancel is Dec – see the E window, S doorway and windows, SEDILIA and PISCINA. Dec also the S transept. – PLATE. Elizabethan Cup.

(Brampton Tower. Three-storeyed Victorian tower of red sandstone with lower wings, stepped gable, and corner turret.*)

LONG SLEDDALE

5000

Church. 1863. Nave and chancel and bellcote. Lancet windows, mostly small. – PLATE. Cup and Cover Paten, London, 1571.

Yewbarrow Hall, ¼ m. SE. Pele tower tunnel-vaulted at ground level, and attached cottage.

LOUGHRIGG BROW see AMBLESIDE

LOW BORROW BRIDGE see TEBAY

* Information received from Mrs Davies.

LOW BRIDGE HALL *see* SELSIDE

LOW BRUNDRIGG *see* BURNESIDE

LOWTHER

LOWTHER CASTLE. The first Lowther to be knighted was Sir
John in 1640. His grandson died in 1700. He was made Viscount Lonsdale in 1694. It was he who built the church,
and also Lowther Castle, as it was illustrated in the second
volume of *Vitruvius Britannicus*. The house was mostly burnt
in 1720. *Robert Adam* in 1767 made plans for a castellated
mansion, but when the great mansion, of which now only the
shell remains, was finally built, the architect was *Smirke*, then
aged only twenty-five, and just returned from Italy and Greece.
Lowther was his first job. He had been recommended by
Dance and Dance's patron Sir George Beaumont. Building
began in 1806 and finished in 1811. It is regrettable, though
understandable, that the house was abandoned. Yet what pain
must it be to the owners to live so near this memorial of past
glories. The shell must be safeguarded. The county can ill
afford to lose so spectacular a ruin. The N front is 420 ft long,
symmetrical, turreted and embattled. The skyline is varied.
The nine-bay centre has a raised centre behind which a yet
higher, square, keep-like tower appears. Then there are low
links and angle pavilions, higher than the links, but lower than
96　　the centre. The s façade is more varied, with two round
towers, sharp pinnacles, a central Perp porch, and a large Perp
window over. To the l. of the s façade in a separate wing is the
equally Gothic Sculpture Gallery. Neale tells of the size of
the main rooms: hall 60 by 30 ft, staircase 60 by 60 ft (in the
'keep'), saloon 60 by 30 ft, dining room 45 by 26 ft, etc. In
front of the N front, at some distance, is a gatehouse with
battered walls and altogether appearing very fortified. Thick
sham machicolations. The curtain walling has turrets too.

PENRITH LODGE. Castellated, with an asymmetrical tower.

TRIMBY LODGE. Large; Tudor.

ST MICHAEL, N of the castle. A strange, baffling exterior. Nave
and aisles, a high central tower, a low s transept, and a chancel.
The high tower has groups of three lancets as bell-openings
and also for the stage below, and that is clearly Victorian. It
dates in fact from 1856. But to the s the lower tier is replaced
by a rectangular window with a moulded frame, and the aisles

and clerestory have the same windows. They are unexpected
in a church, and represent an almost total rebuilding by Sir
John Lowther in 1686. His is the s transept as well with its
steep pediment, and also allegedly the tall round-arched windows at the W and E ends. He finished the tower with a dome
and lantern. A pity they are not preserved. The interior after
all this is a complete surprise. One sees at once that this is a
medieval church. The N arcade must be of c.1165–75. It has
round piers with square abaci and single-stepped arches. One
capital is multi-scalloped, the others have free plays of foliage
with little heads, unfortunately totally re-tooled, towards the
nave. The foliage capitals are of two types: those with the
heads are earlier in style (though not in date); the others, e.g.
the NW respond, look more Transitional. One pier and the E
respond have base spurs. The s arcade is a little later, say
c.1200. The piers are now octagonal and the arches, still
round, have two slight chamfers. The arches from the aisles
to the transepts look early C13. That is also the date of the
central tower. The responds on all four sides are triple, with
the big middle shaft keeled. That suggests the early C13. Only
the intermediate columns in the N and s arches are C19.

FURNISHINGS. PULPIT. C18. – FONT. A baluster. –
COMMUNION RAIL. With twisted balusters, c.1690. – PLATE.
Paten on foot 1682(?); Flagon 1685 (York); Cup and Cover
Paten 1686; Cup c.1685. – MONUMENTS. Hogback coffins in
the porch. – In the s transept Sir Richard Lowther † 1608.
Alabaster effigy. – John Viscount Lonsdale † 1700. By *William* 92
Stanton. Excellent semi-reclining figure against a reredos
background with open segmental pediment. – Sir John
Lowther Sen. and Jun. † 1637 and 1675. Made about the
latter date. Two white busts against black drapery. Between
the two a skull on a black cushion. At the foot garlands and a
cartouche. – In the N transept: James Viscount Lonsdale.
Made in 1805 by 'Messrs *Fishers* of York'. Tablet with
sarcophagus. – Richard Viscount Lonsdale † 1751, made by
the same at about the same time. The sarcophagus here has a
background of scythe, hourglass, caduceus, etc. – William
Earl of Lonsdale † 1844. Free-standing marble tomb-chest. –
LOWTHER MAUSOLEUM. In the churchyard. Built in 1857
to the design of *B. Band* of London. It is a strange building
with solid side-walls of three panels with triangular heads and
the jambs sloping forward as they go downward. Corner turrets. Inside, all white and all alone, the seated earl, a picture

of loneliness. The figure is by *E. B. Stephens*, 1863. Mausoleum and churchyard are beautifully placed above the river Lowther.

Sir John Lowther pulled down the old village of Lowther when he built his new church and built a new village called LOWTHER NEW TOWN. As he had bought the estate in 1682, the new village must have been started *c*.1683–4. It was intended as a replacement of the then existing village. It lies just E of the lawn and avenue between castle and church. The houses are mostly of five bays and two storeys with plain window and door surrounds. The roofs are hipped. The houses stand single or semi-detached. At the N end is the estate office, now mostly Early Victorian, but built in 1709 (according to the RCHM) as the COLLEGE. It was not used as such, and became Sir John's carpet manufactory. ½ m. SE is

93   another so-called village, LOWTHER VILLAGE. This seems to have been begun *c*.1765 and built on intensively till 1773 and after that more spasmodically. The architect was probably *James Adam*. It consists of two closes, both ending on the N side with a seven-bay, two-storey house with a three-bay centre and a hipped roof. The side ranges of the W close are twenty-one bays long and articulated in height and roofs. The second close has as its side pieces single-storey terraces with S returns running E and W. Finally the E end of the composition is a crescent open to the E and broken by the road in the middle. Beginning and end of either half are marked by a higher square pavilion with a pyramid roof. The original plan provided for four, not two ranges, i.e. a complete circus.*

HACKTHORPE HALL, 1½ m. SE. A Jacobean house with four-light mullioned and transomed windows.

1080   # LUPTON

ALL SAINTS. 1867, yet neo-Norman. Small; nave, chancel, and apse. – FONT. From Kirkby Lonsdale church. The RCHM says that a date 1686 is assigned to it. However, it does not look that period.

MAIDEN CASTLE *see* BROUGH

* For information on Lowther Village I have to thank Mr B. C. Jones and Mr Brunskill.

MALLERSTANG

ST MARY, Outhgill. C17, C18, and C20. Of 1663, i.e. the time
of the Lady Anne Clifford, the N windows and the S doorway,
of 1768 the S windows, of the C20 the E window. The Lady
Anne's work is recorded in an inscription over the S porch.
It is in Roman capitals of typical C17 character.

(LADY'S PILLAR, 2¼ m. ESE. Of the pillar erected by the Lady
Anne in 1664 nothing of any shape remains.)

PENDRAGON CASTLE, ¾ m. N. This is important as a Late
Norman pele tower, built apparently to stand on its own. Not
much can be recognized, very much less than at Buck's time,
i.e. in the mid C18. In the walls some vaulted mural chambers.
Lady Anne restored the castle in 1660, after it had been burnt
by the Scots in 1541.

LAMMERSIDE CASTLE, 1⅜ m. NW, but across the Eden – no
path leads to the ruin – is an oblong C14 pele tower, divided
by a cross wall. At the lowest level the rooms were all tunnel-
vaulted, and a corridor ran across from N to S (cf. Burneside
Hall and Preston Patrick Hall).

MANSERGH

ST PETER. 1880 by *Paley & Austin.* Late Perp style, treated
freely, with a W tower with saddleback roof. Paley & Austin
are never slipshod. Pleasant interior with a semicircular
plastered wagon roof. – FONT. A Georgian baluster with a
small urn with a lid instead of a bowl. – MONUMENT.
Christopher Wilson † 1845. Large, very Gothic tablet with a
nodding-ogee canopy.

RIGMADEN PARK, Christopher Wilson's house, is in ruins.
It was built in 1825 and had a splendid view to the E. The
front has a large middle bow and l. and r. one tripartite window with pediment. At the back giant pilasters and a porte-
cochère.

MARDALE

HOLY TRINITY. The church has disappeared in Haweswater,
the Manchester reservoir.

MARKET BROUGH see BROUGH

4010

MARTINDALE

St Peter, sw of the houses, up steep serpentines. 1880–2 by *J. A. Cory*. Nave and chancel, lancet windows, slate and red sandstone. – PLATE. Cup, London, 1834.

St Martin, ¾ m. s of the former. Built in 1633. Nave and chancel in one. Plain bellcote. Oblong windows. – LECTERN. Jacobean, 1634, with simple patterns on the panels. – BENCHES. The ends of a plain, but unusual design. – PANELLING. Probably also of *c*.1633–4.

MATSON GROUND see
BOWNESS-ON-WINDERMERE

MAULDS MEABURN see CROSBY RAVENSWORTH

MAYBURGH see YANWATH

4080

MEATHOP

Meathop Hall. Late c17, with a typical Yorkshire lintel and at the top three equally typical stepped three-light windows. The gables above them have early c19 bargeboards.

6080

MIDDLETON

Holy Ghost. 1878–9 by *C. J. Ferguson*. Nave and chancel and bellcote. Perp in style. – PLATE. Cup, London, 1722.

Middleton Hall, ⅞ m. NNE. An H-shaped c15 house. The house is approached through a high wall by a gate-arch formerly the w side of a gatehouse. The arch is segmental, and there are two cusped single-light windows above. A stable range was on the l. In front the c14 hall range. Entry and exit are preserved, and the three doorways formerly from the screens passage to buttery, kitchen, and pantry. The entry has two sunk quadrant mouldings, but the three service doorways are simply single-chamfered. The hall has its fireplace against the screens passage, but that is an Elizabethan insertion. The hall windows are not large and date from the c15. Two have Perp panel tracery under their straight heads. (In the s wing a good mid c16 fireplace, illustrated by the RCHM.)

MILBURN

6020

The village is obviously made and not grown. It has an oblong green with houses, mostly not detached, on all four sides. Streets enter at the four corners, and the approach roads are managed so as to make that possible. At the top of the Green set into it the SCHOOL of 1851.

ST CUTHBERT. Nave with bellcote, chancel, and s aisle. The s doorway is Late Norman (one order of columns), in the w wall is a short re-set Norman piece with chip-carved saltire crosses (cf. Long Marton), and the chancel masonry is probably Norman too. But the s arcade of two bays is early C14, modelled on Appleby. Quatrefoil pier with fillets on the foils, double-chamfered arches. – PANELLING. Behind the altar; C17. – STAINED GLASS, s aisle E, 1935, in the Expressionist mood. – PLATE. Cup and Cover Paten, 1633.

HOWGILL CASTLE. It looks like a house in the Wren tradition, H-shaped, with sash windows. They date from 1733. But the masonry is C14, and both wings are tunnel-vaulted on the ground floor. The vaults are elliptical. Projecting from the middle wing at the back is a later C17 staircase with dumbbell balusters. (One chimneypiece has garlands on the posts, but also still slight Jacobean echoes; NMR. It is probably later C17 too.)

MILNTHORPE

4080

ST THOMAS. 1837 except for the chancel, which is of 1883. W tower, lancet windows in pairs, thin buttresses – i.e. the Commissioners' type. No aisles of course, but a w gallery with iron posts and thin iron geometrical tracery. – STAINED GLASS. In the E window by *Frederick Barrow* of Sandside; 1872; bad.

The church lies on the Green, and w of this is the market area with the C18 MARKET CROSS, a column with a ball finial.

To the NE of the church is HARMONY HALL, three bays, early C19, with an Ionic doorway with pediment. Further out along this road the Gothic KITCHING ALMSHOUSES of 1881 and then the former WORKHOUSE, built in 1813: four bays, a canted centre, and another four bays. To the N of the almshouses a round TOWER, built, it is said, c.1838 as a summer house.

DALLAM TOWER, ⅞ m. WSW. A substantial, regular house of seven bays with attachments to both sides. The house itself is typical of the date 1720–2 given it by the RCHM, i.e. it has tall, slender windows and the middle three bays singled out by strips of rustication of even length. Originally the house was not rendered but had its brick walling exposed. Also the doorway has the unmistakable frieze curving up in the centre. All this is in perfect order on the garden side, but on the entrance side the centre is hidden by a deep porch with four Tuscan columns. This dates from 1826, as do the side pavilions. The architect was *H. E. Kendall Sen.* Inside a fine staircase with four slender balusters to each tread, a room of *c.*1720–5 with pilasters and panelling, all very beautifully detailed, and another room with enriched panelling of *c.*1730–50. The first floor has a cross-corridor reached from the staircase by two arches. This is typical of *c.*1720–5 again. Behind the house is a CONSERVATORY, vaulted in the way which just came in about 1825–30. It is quite a rare pre-Paxton survival. The kitchen-garden has a GATEWAY, dated 1683. It is still in the impure (and jolly) classical of the mid C17. In the park a DEER SHELTER with, as the MHLG says, 'rough stone quasi-Doric columns'.

MOOR DIVOCK see ASKHAM

5020

MORLAND

ST LAURENCE. Morland church has the only Anglo-Saxon W tower in Westmorland or Cumberland. It is at once recognizable by the bell-openings with mid-wall shaft and by the narrow and high doorway to the nave. The top storey is a C17 addition. Yet later pretty lead spire. The Saxon work is of the C11. The church belonging to this tower is unknown to us; but zigzag lengths above a transept N and the N aisle W window may well have belonged to a Norman chancel arch. This church was extended by aisles in the late C12. The S arcade has round piers with octagonal abaci and double-chamfered pointed arches. The N arcade is the same but has one octagonal pier with a scalloped capital, and also the W respond with such a capital. So this probably came first. The E responds are quite different (triple, with a fillet on the middle shaft), and they were only provided when *c.*1225 transepts were decided on. The transepts have fine double-chamfered lancets and strange stop-chamfered buttresses. The S transept S windows at the lower level have dog-tooth in the hood-mould. The S doorway with shafts and several rolls goes with the transepts. The s aisle roof-line of the late C12 is still visible at the w end. What the chancel was originally like, we do not know. It is now Late Perp, with unmistakable windows. The chancel arch is obviously altered. The l. respond is late C12 (waterleaf), the r. respond just a little later (plain moulded capital), and both were interfered with when the arch was widened. There is a one-bay N chapel whose standard details point to the C13. Such a chapel existed also E of the s transept. The w arch is blocked. It must have been pulled down before the Late Perp chancel windows were made. The s porch entrance of two continuous chamfers is *ex situ*. Finally the N aisle, which has Georgian arched windows with keystones and dates from 1758. – FONT. 1662. Small, octagonal bowl. – Contemporary FONT COVER with inscriptions. – PULPIT. Early Georgian. – SCREEN. Top rail of a late C14 or C15 screen with nine male heads and an angel bust; very pretty. – COMMUNION RAIL. Probably mid C17. – BENCHES with knobs at the junction of back and arm and PANELLING against the w wall. – PLATE. Paten on foot, 1706 (London); Tankard, 1712 (London); Cup, given in 1705, but remodelled 1793 or 1817 (Newcastle). – MONUMENT. Brass to John Blyth † 1562, palimpsest of an early C16 brass with an 11 in. figure of a Knight. – Specially handsome C13 coffin lid with foliated cross; late C13 (s transept E).

MURTON 7020

St JOHN. 1856 by *G. Robinson*. Nave with bellcote and chancel in one. Lancets. – Inside, near the middle of the N side, a three-decker PULPIT, an amazing thing in a church of 1856.

MURTON HALL. An interesting house. It has, used as a doorhead, a Dec window-head of three ogee arches under a stepped hood-mould, and on the opposite side of the house in a garden wall the head of a two-light window, also Dec. The rest of this wing of the house is mid C17 or a little later, with mullioned and mullioned-and-transomed windows. The position of the hall is easily recognizable. On the upper floor one round window. (Also one octagonal C14 chimney with a gabled top. RCHM)

MUSGRAVE 7010

St THEOBALD. 1845 by *G. R. Appleby*. Reached by a footpath down to the Eden. Thin w tower, nave and chancel in one, lancets. – PLATE. Cup, made in Newcastle, 1705; Set given in

1809. – MONUMENTS. Coffin lid, late C13. Foliated cross, the head encircled, sprigs emanating from the stem. To the r. of the stem a sword (cf. Warcop). – Brass to a Priest, c.1500, 13½ in. figure, an inscription across his chest. – CURIOSUM. Fifteen Maiden Garlands (cf. Warcop).

NATLAND

5080

ST MARK. 1909–10 by *Paley & Austin,* and as good as any of the churches by the best church architects of those years, say Temple Moore. The style is Perp with slight touches of Arts and Crafts. Substantial W tower with higher stair-turret. Inside, the E wall of the tower rests on mighty round piers with arches dying into them. The arcades are more conventional, but the chancel again has two-bay arcades without any capitals, and instead of a chancel arch again sturdy round piers without capitals. The roof is segmental, and plastered, but has tie-beams and curved queenposts. It is a resourceful and strong interior, not at all mannered or pedantic.

SEDGEWICK HOUSE, 1½ m. SW. 1868–9 by *Paley & Austin.* Perp, with tower and attached porte-cochère. Rather dull.

(TOP OF THE HILL, in Sedgewick Village, has a plaster panel with vine and foliage and the date 1694. RCHM)

HILLFORT, on Helm Hill, SE of the village. This is a small oval fort defended by a ditch and two banks best preserved on the N and S. To the E the ground slopes steeply away from the hilltop, and no artificial features are visible at this point.

NETHER STAVELEY see STAVELEY

NEWBIGGIN

6020

ST EDMUND. Norman masonry, especially the flat W buttress. Dec nave and chancel windows, the E window reticulated. Late Perp N chapel. – STAINED GLASS. In the E window C14 and C15 fragments. – PLATE. Cup, Newcastle, 1778.

NEWBIGGIN HALL. Of the Crackenthorpe family. An inscription of 1533 in a part mostly Victorian. Victorian also, and inscribed 1844, the tower at the other end. A three-bay Georgian stretch has the date 1759.

NEW HUTTON

5090

ST STEPHEN. 1828–9 by *George Webster.* Lancet-style, with an awkward W tower. – PLATE. Cup, inscribed 1814. – MONU-

MENT. Ralph Fisher † 1837. Also by *Webster*. With a Grecian sarcophagus. – The CHURCHYARD GATES have on the piers two hounds, and another such pair of piers is to the SE of the church. They must have led to a house no longer in existence.

(STRAWBERRY BANK, ⅜ m. SW. In a room over the fireplace a very fine stucco panel of the early C17 with a close pattern of leaves and grapes, probably by the artist of the ceiling at Blease Hall, Old Hutton.)

HILL TOP, 1 m. W. The S front symmetrical, of the early C19, with a wooden Tuscan porch, but the doorway and the hexagonal entrance hall, and probably more, earlier Georgian.

NINEKIRK see BROUGHAM

OLD HUTTON
5080

ST JOHN BAPTIST. 1873 by *Brade & Smales*. Small, with an apse and an asymmetrical bell-turret. Plate tracery. How wilful and irresponsible compared with the neighbouring churches by Paley & Austin! – ALMSBOX. Late C17; a strong, classical baluster and a small bowl with lid on top. – PLATE. Chalice; the oldest piece of plate in the county. It is of *c.*1500 and has the Crucifixus engraved on the foot.

BLEASE HALL, ¾ m. NW. The house is of *c.*1600. It has large mullioned and transomed windows, including a straight-sided bay with, in front, three plus three lights and one each round the corners (cf. Levens Hall). Inside, a fragmentary plaster ceiling, the best in the county. It has a large spiral with grapes 86 and leaves, and had more of them.

ORMSIDE
7010

ST JAMES, on a hill above the hall. Low W tower with only small windows, lancets and square-headed, and no doorway, i.e. suited for defence. Nave and chancel, the chancel on the S side wider than the nave and early C16 at the earliest. The one window with the ogee lights above the doorway must be re-set. As one gets ready to enter, there is a S doorway, clearly C11, i.e. very narrow, of very raw masonry and with an enormous lintel and a blank tympanum. Moreover, the tower arch is of the same proportions. It has a thickening to the W which must have been made for a bellcote. So the W tower was an addition, still of the late C12. It has an upper doorway into the church. Earlier than this but later than the S doorway

– say of *c.*1140–50, as it depends on Carlisle – is the two-bay N arcade. The arch has one step only, the round pier has a square abacus. The capitals have scallops. – PLATE. Cup, Newcastle, *c.*1672; Paten on foot, Newcastle, 1707. – In the churchyard in the early C19 the ORMSIDE BOWL was found which is now in the York Museum. It is the richest and most Carolingian piece of Anglo-Saxon metalwork, and in its own, more fantastical, way up to the standard of the Ruthwell and Bewcastle Crosses. It dates from the C9.

ORMSIDE HALL, by the church. C14 or C15 SW tower wing. On the first and second floors two-light windows with cusped lights. (Inside a room with a C17 plaster frieze. RCHM)

VIADUCT of the Settle–Carlisle Railway. The engineer was *J. C. Crossley*. It was built in 1870–5, is of stone, and has ten arches.

(DRYBECK HALL, 2¼ m. SW. Dated 1679. Mullioned windows of two and three lights. Asymmetrically placed doorway with battlement decoration in the lintel.*)

6000

ORTON

ALL SAINTS. The church started cruciform in the early C13, and of that time is the arch to the S transept (tripartite with the centre part keeled) and the trefoiled S transept PISCINA. The W arch of the crossing is represented only by the lowest part of the S jamb, with two nook-shafts. There is also a base in the same pier indicating that a S aisle existed. The crossing probably carried a tower, and this may have collapsed or become insecure. So the Perp W tower was built, with its diagonal buttresses with many set-offs. The N aisle belongs to the same period, or at least was built so as not to take the former N transept into consideration at all. The S aisle is also Late Perp. – FONT. Dated 1662, and very characteristic of those years. Octagonal, with the date, initials, some stylized flowers, and the blank head of a Perp window. – COMMUNION RAIL. Parts of the former communion rail are preserved. They are Jacobean. – PLATE. Pair of Cups, London, 1721.

ORTON HALL. A Georgian house with curved walls extending the three-bay façade towards one-bay pavilions with broken pediments and one ogee-headed window. The centre also has a broken pediment. There is a Venetian window below it. The

---

* Mrs Davies suggested that I should include Drybeck Hall.

doorway looks Early Victorian. This may be part of the work of *c*.1836 by *G. H. Smith* (Colvin). Behind the house a large neo-Elizabethan extension dated 1900.

ORTON OLD HALL. In the village street. Dated 1604, with irregularly placed two- and three-light windows.

OUTHGILL see MALLERSTANG

OVER STAVELEY see STAVELEY

PATTERDALE

3010

ST PATRICK. 1853 by *Salvin*. Small, with a NE tower with saddleback roof. Geometrical tracery, with some rather fanciful motifs. – TAPESTRY. Panels by *Ann Macbeth*, probably of about the 1940s. – PLATE. Cup by *Gabriel Sleath*, London, 1714.

PATTERDALE HALL. Fragments of the C17, called 'lately rebuilt' about 1800. Richard Holden, travelling in 1808, wrote: 'The King of Patterdale has modernized his house or built a new one.' The Mounseys were known as kings of Patterdale, and the house was known as the Palace. In 1824 John Mounsey sold the house to William Marshall of Leeds, owner of the Marshall Mills. Due to him probably are the additions by *Salvin*, 1845–50 (GS). The impression is irregular and classical, and the only decidedly Victorian feature is the clock tower.*

HARTSOP HALL, 2¾ m. S. With two C16 windows with uncusped arched light-heads.

SETTLEMENT, ½ m. S of Brothers Water. The roughly oval enclosure of 1¼ acres is defined by a turf-covered bank within which are a series of hut circles and lesser enclosures. The site is unexcavated, but is presumably Iron Age or native Roman.

PATTON

5090

(SHAW END. Early C19. Seven bays, two storeys, rendered. Porch of four Doric columns with pediment. Entrance hall with columns. MHLG)

PENDRAGON CASTLE see MALLERSTANG

POOL BANK see CROSTHWAITE

* I owe the information on the Mounseys and Marshall to Mr D.F. James.

4020

POOLEY BRIDGE

ST PAUL. By *Cory & Ferguson*, 1868. Small, with lancet windows and a small bell-turret with spire, standing inside on two octagonal piers.

WATERFOOT, ¾ m. W, in Cumberland. A fine house of about 1800, ashlar-faced. To Ullswater seven bays, the centre one a large blank arch with a Venetian window with Ionic columns set in. The other ground-floor windows are arched, and the window above the Venetian one is tripartite. The entrance side has a shallow bow, and attached to this is the Ionic porch. The entrance hall is circular. The house was built for Mr Clarkson (said Richard Holden in 1808).

DUNMALLET HILLFORT, ¼ m. W, also in Cumberland. This is a small and undistinguished hillfort of univallate construction. The defences enclose a roughly oval area of 1 acre. A gap on the SW probably marks the original entrance.

THE COCKPIT, *see* Barton.

5080

PRESTON PATRICK

ST GREGORY. 1852 by *Sharpe & Paley*, and the chancel 1892. Handsomely isolated on a hill. Rock-faced; Perp NW tower with higher stair-turret. In it one original Perp window. Original Perp also the two canopied niches l. and r. of the E window. – PLATE. Large Cup, London, 1832; Paten, London, 1836.

FRIENDS' MEETING HOUSE. 1691 originally. Of that date only the stables and coach-house with upper class-rooms and an outer staircase.

PRESTON PATRICK HALL. Hall-house of the C14, with the most prominent windows (including one now in the barn) a renewal of *c.*1500. The old windows have ogee-headed lights, the later ones straight heads, panel tracery, and unusual details: elongated trefoils with prominent cusps. The original doorways have shouldered lintels, including the two leading into the E wing, which has two tunnel-vaulted chambers separated by a tunnel-vaulted passage not originally connected with them, exactly as at Burneside Hall. The whole is proof of a former pele tower. Instead there is now, above, the Court Room with the later windows. In the W wing on the first floor is a mighty fireplace with lintel on corbels. Good kingpost roofs in both wings.

CHALLON HALL, ¾ m. NE. Rebuilt in 1760. The details are characteristic, i.e. five bays, flat frames to doorway and windows, and flat string-courses. Only one detail seems to be in contradiction, the big door lintel with two large broadly curved shapes, i.e. a Yorkshire lintel of C17 character. Can it really be so late?

BIRKRIGG PARK, 2¼ m. N, is dated 1742 and has the same flat window frames.

RAVENSTONEDALE   7000

ST OSWALD. W tower of 1738, the rest of 1744, i.e. a Georgian church throughout. The quoins and the long row of seven windows convince, but the bell-openings and the details of the porches look C17, and the S porch entrance seems a re-used piece of c.1200. The chancel arch moreover is clearly C13. The interior has kept its Georgian (Protestant) arrangement of three-decker PULPIT (with sounding board) and BOX PEWS. The pulpit is in the middle of the N side, the pews are arranged college-wise. – WEST GALLERY. – The TEN COMMANDMENTS are held by the painted figures of Moses and Aaron. – COMMUNION RAIL. C18; it curves forward. – SCULPTURE. On a window sill a big Norman beakhead. – PLATE. Cup, London, 1664; Flagon, London, 1706; Cup and Cover, London, 1743; Salver, silver-gilt, London, 1792.

N of the church excavations in 1927–8 have exposed the foundations of what was probably the premises of the GILBERTINE CELL from Watton which existed at Ravenstonedale. They are not very telling.

(THE LANE COTTAGE. A fantastic cottage orné, dated 1887 and 1892, inscribed 'T. Hewitson del., W. Hodgson sculp.'. Crenellation, intersecting tracery, quatrefoils, and also volutes. MHLG)

(TARN HOUSE, 1¾ m. ESE. Built in 1664. With a porch and mullioned windows set so that those on the first correspond to those on the ground floor. The hood-moulds are extended to form a continuous band rising above each window. The band starts with a hefty scroll. RCHM)

RAYRIGG HALL see WINDERMERE

RAYSEAT PIKE see CROSBY GARRETT

RESTON HALL see HUGILL

ROPER CASTLE see BROUGH

ROTHAY HOLME see AMBLESIDE

ROWELL see HEVERSHAM

3000
RYDAL

ST MARY. 1824. Typical w tower with low bays l. and r. Nave and chancel with free Perp tracery (of 1884). Flat ceiling. – STAINED GLASS. One s window by *Holiday*, 1891. The commemorative brass tablet which goes with it is a good Arts and Crafts specimen. – PLATE. Cup, finely chased, London, c.1670–90.

RYDAL HALL. The wide s front Early Victorian with a central bow, all rendered. Behind this a C17 house, cf. the staircase.

SEDGEWICK see NATLAND

SELLET HALL see CROSSCRAKE

5090
SELSIDE

ST THOMAS. 1838, with a tower of 1894. The tower is oddly broad and entirely open to the old nave. The nave has the lancet windows typical of its date. – FONT. C18 marble bowl on a foot of 1894. – PLATE. Cup and Paten on foot, 1708.

SELSIDE HALL, sw of the church. C14 hall-house with N and s wings. The s wing has two tunnel-vaulted chambers at ground level and on the first floor a transomed two-light window. The solar was here, and probably a second living room. In the N wing a smaller two-light window. The hall had its fireplace against the wall towards the screens passage.

LOW BRIDGE HALL, 1¼ m. N. Built in 1837. Large and asymmetrical, with bargeboarded gables.

5010
SHAP

ST MICHAEL. Unbuttressed w tower of 1828. Miscellaneous windows, mostly Victorian. Chancel of 1898–9. But the s arcade c.1200, four bays, round piers with the simplest round capitals, round abaci, and double-chamfered round arches. – PLATE. Cup, London, 1629; Cup of 1754.

MARKET HOUSE. In the village street, halfway down. The

market was granted in 1687. So the building will be of *c*.1690. Three by three bays. Round arches on short, stubby columns. Small round-arched windows on the upper floor, now blocked. All rather miniature.

KELD CHAPEL, 1 m. SW. Plain and oblong, probably C16. That at any rate seems the date of the three-light E window.

SHAP ABBEY, 1¼ m. W, buried in the valley of the river Low-ther. The abbey was founded for Premonstratensian canons at Preston-in-Kendale late in the C12, and before 1201 moved to its present site. But nothing so early survives. In fact not very much survives altogether, and the only really imposing piece is the W tower, the last of the buildings before the Reformation. It must be of the early C16, had a vast W win-dow, and still has its three-light bell-openings. The church itself must have been rebuilt from the early to the later C13, and rebuilding as usual started from the E. The straight-ended E half of the chancel is a C15 lengthening, but the W half is early C13. The difference in the base mouldings is striking. The base of the original E wall is now the first step of the two in the chancel. The crossing piers can still be guessed in their bases. They are so strong that in all pro-bability they carried a tower. The transepts had an E aisle. In the S transept the foundation of the canons' night stair is preserved. A doorway leads into the cloister, a second from near the E end of the nave, a third from the nave further W. The nave has only a N aisle. There must have been a break in building operations halfway down the nave. It is clearly visible in the masonry of the S wall, and also in the bases of the arcade piers. Those further W with their thin mouldings are C14 rather than C13. The piers were quatrefoil, with fillets and slim shafts in the diagonals as well. The E bay is blocked by a wall put up probably because the crossing tower gave trouble. That would also explain the encasing of the NW pier in simple canted masonry. The W bay is partly blocked by the C19 or C20 E buttress of the tower, but the springer of the W arcade arch appears to the N of the buttress. The W side of the tower shows the original roof-line and a second Perp one of flatter pitch allowing for clerestory windows. This change must of course post-date the tower.

The monastic parts are – like the church – relatively small. They are also congested towards the river, because there was no more space. The various elements are easily recognized: the sacristy S of the S transept, the chapter house projecting further E and with three early C13 columns no doubt carrying rib-vaulting. There are also two wall-shafts halfway down. S of the chapter house a vaulted room, characterized by the fireplace as the warming house. It has three octagonal piers. In the S range came first the usual passage and then the usual refectory. It was on the upper floor. The undercroft had a row of piers along its middle. Of the W range two tunnel-vaulted stores are preserved, built into the C13 walls in the C14. The dormitory above the E range was, again in the customary fashion, continued E from its S end by the reredorter or lavatories. Several drains survive here. S of the reredorter was the infirmary, of irregular plan and not in axis with the other buildings. Of the abbot's quarters nothing is left at all.

STONE CIRCLE, 1¼ m. NNE of the church, on Gunnerkeld Bottom. Only three of the stones of this circle remain standing, although further recumbent examples lie half buried beneath the turf. The circle has a diameter of 105 ft and encloses a low cairn surrounded by a stone kerb 52 ft in diameter. The cairn has a central depression which was produced when this area was opened in the C19 and a stone cist discovered.

STONE CIRCLE AND AVENUE, 1¼ m. SSE of the church. In the C18 much more of this ceremonial site was visible than is preserved today. The circle now consists of six large granite boulders indicating a circle 80 ft in diameter. It is partly covered by the railway embankment. All that remains of the avenue of standing stones which ran from the circle for a distance of ¾ m. NW are nine irregularly spaced stones, two bearing cup marks. The avenue terminated at the Thunder Stone, a great recumbent granite boulder 8 ft high.

SHAP WELLS

3½ m. SSE of Shap

A chemical analysis of the waters was made in 1828. After that the Earl of Lonsdale had the HOTEL built. It was in existence by 1850, but has since been altered.

QUEEN VICTORIA MONUMENT. By *Mr Mawson* of Lowther, 1842. Column with figure of Britannia on the top. Against the base relief of a libation. An old man holds up a shallow bowl and a young girl pours water into it. Another relief of a lion, a third of a laurel wreath. The sculptural work is by *Thomas Bland* of Reagill, a self-taught artist.

SHAW END *see* PATTON

SIZERGH CASTLE   4080

Sizergh is the most impressive house in Westmorland of the type
consisting of pele tower, hall range, and later enlargements.
It has belonged to the Strickland family ever since 1239, but
nothing as old as this is preserved. The tower, on the strength
of heraldry, can be dated to about 1340, though the upper
windows preserved belong to the C15. Between the three- and
the two-light windows on the N side is a recess with a coat of
arms. It is one of the largest of the pele towers (60 by 40 ft)
and has the usual tunnel-vaulted basement. What distinguishes it visually from most others is the spacious attachment
on the W side which rises higher than the tower itself and
originally served as garderobes, and the staircase turret, also
rising higher. The walls of the pele are $9\frac{3}{4}$ ft at the foot,
tapering to $5\frac{1}{2}$ ft at the top. On the s side the tower has a
Venetian window, part of the alterations done *c.*1770 by
Cecilia Towneley, wife of Charles Strickland. The four-light
C15 window above it is original.* So much of the exterior of the
tower.

The adjoining hall range is most probably C14 or C15 in
some of its masonry, but no features are there to corroborate
such a date. The features are of the mid C16 and later. To the
N, i.e. the entrance side, the porch is fairly recent. So are the
mullioned and transomed windows l. and r. The sash windows, and especially the main first-floor window with its ogee
head, are of *c.*1770. Top battlements. On the garden side the
pointed first-floor windows are of course also *c.*1770. One
more bay follows, gabled to N as well as S, and this has
Elizabethan mullioned and transomed windows and to the s
a second Venetian window, where Cecilia Towneley had
intended to put a second tower to match the pele. To this
house, in the middle or the later C16, wings were added projecting to the N and not strictly parallel. They have mullioned
and transomed windows so far as they are original. Those of
the W wing are placed towards the forecourt in a regular
manner. In the E wing there are now only two on the ground
floor giving light to the Elizabethan kitchen and two further
N on the upper floor.

* It appears at any rate in the Buckler engraving of 1822.

10+C.W.

As one enters the house, one is at once faced with a wooden screen carrying the date 1555. It is not *in situ*, but it was a felicitous idea of the present owner to put it here; for it introduces the main theme of the interior of Sizergh. No other house in England has such a wealth of Early Elizabethan woodwork of high quality. Moreover, it was one carver or one group of carvers that must have been at work over twenty years. They may of course have been English, but their source of inspiration was the Netherlands and France, and so they may well have come from the Netherlands. But the earliest woodwork is definitely English. It is benches, and though *The Buildings of England* do not usually take notice of movable furniture, these must be mentioned. The oldest piece, a two-seater, is undated, but as it combines little buttresses with some minor Early Renaissance scrolls, *c.*1530 may be the right date. Others are dated 1562, 1570, and 1571. But the climax of Sizergh is the chimneypieces. There are five in various rooms, dating from 1563 (Morning Room), 1564 (Dining Room), 1569 (Queen's Room), and 1575 (Inlaid Chamber, Boynton Room).* They are characterized by very lush acanthus and similar scrolls, swamping the coats of arms, by little children frolicking among them, by balusters to flank the fireplaces and frame parts of the overmantel, and by pediments, with or without a head in them. One of the pediments (1569) is of the then quite exceptional kind consisting of two shallow s-curves. Balusters instead of columns or pilasters are an Early Renaissance sign, and their use up at Sizergh shows a certain conservatism. But the chimneypiece of 1564 has indeed no balusters, but four columns, and also two caryatids, and l. and r. of the fireplace two atlantes, and one of the two chimneypieces of 1575 turns to fluted pilasters. The carving has passages of outstanding quality. There is absolutely nothing here of that grossness and grotesqueness which mars so much Elizabethan woodwork (e.g. at Levens). The panelling also is excellent. The oldest here is linenfold (in the anteroom to the Morning Room), but much is of the most attractive type with lozenges set in oblong panels (Morning Room, i.e. 1563; Boynton Room, i.e. 1575). The specially fine inlaid panels of the Inlaid Chamber and the bed, dated 1568 and

_____

* The Queen's Room and Dining Room are in the tower on the first floor, the Morning Room is in the hall range on the same floor, the Inlaid Chamber is in the tower on the second floor, the Boynton Room and the Bindloss Room in the hall range on the same.

having in the bedhead again a pediment, are now at the Victoria and Albert Museum. So is a specially ornate lobby.

The ceiling, however, remained. It is of *c*.1575 (chimney-piece!) and is the only one in the house of the type which became current in the later Elizabethan houses, i.e. of stucco, with intricate rib patterns, pendants, and floral etc. motifs in the interstices. The other ceilings at Sizergh have wooden ribs in much more modest – i.e. again Early Elizabethan – patterns: eight-pointed stars with small pendants (Dining Room), octagons and Greek crosses (Queen's Room), lozenges and elongated rectangles connected by short straight pieces (Morning Room).

Of additional details of interest at Sizergh, it may be mentioned that not only the ground floor of the pele tower is tunnel-vaulted but also the Muniment Room on the ground floor of the gabled projection E of the hall. That looks as if indeed a second tower had been planned here, such as Cecilia Towneley intended to build so much later. The Stone Parlour above has the only Georgian stucco ceiling in the house. It looks *c*.1730. The kitchen lies at the S end of the projecting E wing. It has a fireplace 13½ ft long in its E wall. This, as has only recently come out, had been in the N wall, probably until the wing was lengthened and the fireplace turned out to be an obstacle. So perhaps the kitchen was a short attachment to the hall range originally. On top of the pele tower is the so-called Banqueting Hall, now open through two floors. It has splendidly moulded beams of the C15 or early C16, i.e. corresponding in date with the upper windows. In the Bindloss Room is a bed made up of parts of the Strickland family pew once in Kendal church. Square panels, each with a mask.

SETTLEMENT, on Sizergh Fell, 1 m. NNE of Levens church. This is an oval embanked enclosure covering ½ acre with secondary enclosures to the S. Hollows in the interior may indicate the sites of buildings. On the hilltop is a small round CAIRN, 24 ft in diameter. A Bronze Age urn was found beneath it. 150 yards E is another small round cairn, 30 ft in diameter and 3 ft high, which covered five unaccompanied inhumation burials.

SKELSMERGH

5090

ST JOHN BAPTIST. 1871 by *Joseph Birtley* of Kendal. Nave and chancel; bellcote; E.E. Fine view to the W. – PAINTING. Virgin by *Cignani*, from Lowther Castle.

SKELSMERGH HALL. One wing is a pele tower. The date is probably the C15. Tunnel-vaulted lowest level. The attached house is Jacobean and has mullioned and transomed windows. Garderobe with a slit window.

GILTHWAITERIGG, ½ m. wsw. Hall-house of the C15. In the w wing two windows with cusped heads to the two lights.

SKIRSGILL HILL see ASKHAM

SMARDALE HALL see KIRKBY STEPHEN

5020

SOCKBRIDGE
1¼ m. NE of Barton

SOCKBRIDGE HALL. Two ranges at r. angles to each other. One has on one side regularly placed mullioned and transomed windows, on the opposite side one Henry VIII window, i.e. with uncusped, round-arched lights. The other range also has mullioned and transomed windows, but a stepped gable.

(WORDSWORTH HOUSE. Dated 1699. The windows are of the cross type; the staircase has twisted balusters.*)

7010

SOULBY

ST LUKE. Nave and chancel in one. The round-headed s doorway with its vaguely Perp moulding and the bell-turret indicate the C17, and the church was indeed built by Sir Philip Musgrave in 1662-3. The Musgraves owned Hartley Castle near Kirkby Stephen, and also Edenhall, Bewley Castle, and large properties in Cumberland. The patently Victorian features are of 1873.

SOUTH STAINMORE see BROUGH

STAINMORE see BROUGH

4090

STAVELEY

ST MARGARET. The tower is all that remains. It is supposed to have been built in 1388, and the one three-light window with cusped lights suits that date. But there must also be other pieces of other dates set in at random. Two tiny windows have

* Included at the suggestion of Mrs Davies.

moulded arches almost as if they were Anglo-Saxon, and the
bell-openings cannot be earlier than the C17.

ST JAMES, ½ m. NW. 1864–5 by *J. S. Crowther*. Nave and chancel
and a bell-turret with spirelet on an overpowering W buttress.
Lancet windows, making quite a fine show inside. – STAINED
GLASS. Small C15 fragments in a N lancet. – The three E
lancets have very beautiful glass by *Burne-Jones*, made by
Morris & Co. The date of death commemorated is 1874. In
the centre-light Crucifixus and above Ascension with many
angels. In the side lights three tiers each of single angels.
The figures all against a background of dark blue with stars.

STOBARS HALL *see* KIRKBY STEPHEN

STORRS HALL *see* BOWNESS-ON-WINDERMERE

STRICKLAND KETEL *see* BURNESIDE

TARN HOUSE *see* RAVENSTONEDALE

TEARNSIDE HALL *see* KIRKBY LONSDALE

TEBAY
6000

ST JAMES. 1880 by *C. J. Ferguson*. Paid for by the railway companies and railway workers. A building on a falling site, not
without interest. It is rock-faced (of Shap granite) and has a W
baptistery in the form of a big apse and next to it a round
turret with a conical spire. The porch is immediately E of this.
The interior is brick-faced, yellow with red bands.

Tebay is a railway village, with terraces of workers' housing.
The railway came in 1846, but it was only in 1861 that Tebay
became a junction.

CASTLE HOWE, ¼ m. NNW. A motte-and-bailey castle, just
under 2 acres in size.

LOW BORROW BRIDGE, 2 m. S. The platform of a 3-acre
ROMAN FORT survives at this bridge at the confluence of the
rivers Lune and Borrow; its W side is limited by the railway.
The fort lies on the main Roman west-coast road, leading to
Carlisle. Little is known of its internal arrangements.

TEMPLE SOWERBY
6020

ST JAMES. Built in 1754 and enlarged by an aisle in 1770. The
W tower, however, with its round-arched W window and its

ogee-arched bell-openings is, according to records, of 1807–8
(Rev. H. Prince). The nave and s aisle have lancet windows
probably of the early C19. The chancel details must belong to
the restoration of 1873. But inside, entirely unexpected, is an
arcade with round piers, scalloped capitals, and square abaci.
This is also of 1873. – PLATE. Paten, London, 1771; Cup and
Paten, Newcastle, 1778.

ACORN BANK, ¾ m. NW. The house has a long three-storey s
front of nine bays with a doorway with segmental pediment.
This is probably c.1730–50. There are lower wings ending in
Venetian windows. There is also a fine fireplace of c.1760 with
putto atlantes set in profile. But the centre and the w wing of
the house are in fact of c.1600, with the large hall fireplace
and the large kitchen fireplace preserved. There are also two
panelled rooms upstairs.

THORNTHWAITE HALL see BAMPTON

5030

TIRRIL

(Former FRIENDS' MEETING HOUSE. Dated 1733. A plain
cottage, single-storeyed. MHLG)

TOLSON HALL see BURNESIDE

TOWN END see TROUTBECK

4000

TROUTBECK

JESUS CHAPEL. The w tower is of 1736, but in its fenestration
still looks C17. Nave and chancel in one and lancet windows.
They may be 1828 (date of repairs), but there is also a date
1879. – STALLS and COMMUNION RAIL. The panelling came
from Calgarth Hall, Windermere, i.e. it is Jacobean. The usual
blank arches and lozenges in them. – (COLLECTING SHOVELS.
Two, dated 1692.) – STAINED GLASS. The E window is by
Morris & Co., 1873, i.e. by *Burne-Jones*, *Morris* (Annunciation, Baptism), and *F. M. Brown* (the two bottom r. hand
stories). Brown's figures are more agitated than Burne-
Jones's, and he uses more perspective too.* – PLATE. Cup,
probably of 1584; Cup of 1679.

TOWN END, ½ m. SW. With mullioned windows and typical
chimneys. Probably of 1626.

* I am grateful to Mr Sewter for these details.

STONE CIRCLE, W of Troutbeck Park, in Hird Wood. Only one stone of this circle remains standing, but three other fallen stones indicate a diameter of 38 ft.

ROMAN FORT AND CAMPS. About 2½ m. W of the station, a small Roman fort and two temporary camps are known, on the N side of the Roman road leading from Penrith to the SW. The fort, 280 ft square, has two gates, each with an external *clavicula*. ¼ m. to the W, lying partly beneath the modern road, is a Roman camp nearly 700 by 600 ft. Four gates with internal *claviculae* can be seen, one in each rampart. To the E of this camp is another, about four times the size.

UNDERBARROW

4090

ALL SAINTS. 1869, and a naughty design, with a spirelet on the s porch turret and a polygonal apse with a gable to each side. – PLATE. Cup, London, 1609; Flagon, London, 1742.

UNDERLEY HALL

6080

1 m. N of Kirkby Lonsdale

By *Webster* of Kendal, 1825 – an amazingly early date for a mansion in the Jacobean style. Both main fronts are strictly symmetrical. The entrance side has two angle turrets with caps, two bay windows, and a frontispiece of pairs of columns in two tiers. Parapet with openwork Jacobean decoration. Round the corner two turrets, two canted bays, and a porch of four enriched Doric columns. The large extension with the tower continuing this façade is of 1873. Underley Hall is now St Michael's College, and as such has added in 1964–5 a CHAPEL which is easily the best recent ecclesiastical building in the county. It is built of small stones not only of brick-size but also of gault-brick colour, so that the effect at a distance is – perhaps unfortunately – of brick. The building seems at first not to have any windows. Apart from the lantern-lighting above the altar there are only high slit windows between projecting, completely sheer blocks of various shape and height – a very impressive, severe, and exacting design. The chapel is by *William White* and *John Sheridon* (of *Building Design Partnership*).

WARCOP

7010

ST COLUMBA. The N wall of the nave is Norman, cf. a blocked doorway concealed by the boiler-house. Otherwise E.E. and

Perp is the general impression, if one counts the long chancel with its beautiful lancet windows as E.E., though it was rebuilt in 1855. Apart from the chancel the N transept is E.E., but the two E lancets are again not physically ancient. A very fine interior space. The chancel arch is C13, and the transept arches are C13 too. The two-bay S arcade, however, is Perp, as are the nave and S aisle windows. – MONUMENTS. (Coffin lids with ornamental crosses, altogether eight. All late C13 or early C14. One has sprigs emanating from the stem – cf. Musgrave. RCHM) – Defaced C14 effigy of a Lady (S transept; floor). – CURIOSA. Many Maidens' Garlands (cf. Musgrave). – (In the churchyard two re-erected fragments from BURTON HALL, which was demolished in 1957. They belonged to a C15 or C16 doorway and a C13 window-head.)

WARCOP HALL. The l. part of the front is Elizabethan, with mullioned windows and one mullioned and transomed. Then follows an excellent Georgian stretch, dated 1746 by Kelly. It is of six bays, and the doorway has Ionic pilasters and a pediment. The r. end of the house is Victorian. Inside, one unexpectedly splendid room of c.1746, with stucco ceiling, a doorway with a curly open pediment on pilasters, and, against the wall, six Corinthian columns. It is odd as the decoration of a room, and is probably *ex situ*.

WARCOP BRIDGE. C16. Three segmental arches, and cutwaters. One of the finest in the county. It is very similar to the Eamont Bridge (cf. p. 236).

BIRKS, 1¾ m. WNW. About 300 yds N of the farm is a barn which was in the late C18 a Sandemanian chapel (Sandeman had died in Connecticut in 1771).

SETTLEMENT, 2¼ m. NNE of the church, at a height of 1,100 ft above sea level. This is a roughly rectangular embanked enclosure of ¾ acre at the centre of which is a square earthwork 40 ft long. Hut circles occur immediately within the main enclosure on the N and NE. Access to the settlement was by means of a clearly defined entrance gap on the W side.

WATERCROOK see KENDAL

WATERFOOT see POOLEY BRIDGE

WHARTON HALL see KIRKBY STEPHEN

WHELPRIGG see BARBON

WINDERMERE

4090

ST MARY, Ambleside Road. A complicated history. Of the original chapel of 1848 hardly anything remains. A s aisle with round arches was added in 1852, a N aisle with pointed arches (by *Crowther*) in 1857, a nave W extension in 1861, a N transept (by *Crowther*) in 1871, and finally the chancel, the tower, and the W end by *Paley & Austin* in 1881–2. The final result looks strange. Central space with tower, two bays deep. The arcade with no capitals, and two tall two-light windows over. The nave N arcade has round piers and normal details, the s arcade round piers, far-projecting, deliberately primitive capitals, and round arches. Short chancel.

ST JOHN EVANGELIST, Lake Road. 1886 by *Joseph Pattinson* of Bowness. Large, without a tower. Cruciform and aisleless. The style is of *c.*1300. – SCREEN. Intricate Arts and Crafts carving, done by the then vicar, *E. S. Robertson*, and his parishioners from 1896 onwards. – STAINED GLASS. The W and NW windows of the N aisle by *Holiday*, 1905–8, quite good in a belated Pre-Raphaelite way.

ST HERBERT (R.C.), Prince's Road. 1884 by *Robert Walker*, with lancets and a SW spirelet. Now replaced by

OUR LADY OF WINDERMERE AND ST HERBERT (R.C.), Lake Road. By *Sandy, Norris & Partners*; recent.

CARVER MEMORIAL CONGREGATIONAL CHURCH, Lake Road. 1880 by *Robert Walker*. Large, churchish, with a SW steeple. Geometrical tracery.

THE PRIORY, close to St Mary. Splendidly Gothic, with a tower and turret. Architect and dates could not be traced.

RAYRIGG HALL, ¾ m. SW of St Mary. The entrance side looks *c.*1700 or a little earlier, the side at r. angles to it, with two bow windows, *c.*1790. (Elizabethan panelling inside.)

CALGARTH HALL, 1 m. NW. Externally nothing outstanding. Two mullioned and transomed windows to the lake. Inside, a very jolly Jacobean plaster ceiling on the first floor, with thick trails, comic lions, and eagles and pendants. Also an equally crude and enjoyable plaster panel over a fireplace on the ground floor.

CALGARTH PARK, ¼ m. NW of the former. Now a hospital. Apparently early C19. With a semicircular columned porch.

LANGDALE CHACE HOTEL, 2 m. SE of Ambleside. Large, Elizabethan and gabled. 1891 by *J. L. Ball, J. T. Lee & Pattinson* of Manchester.

10*

HILLFORT, crowning Allen Knott, 1½ m. N of St Mary. Much of the site has been destroyed by quarrying, and only the NW stretch of the rampart, some 7 ft high, can now be traced. The fort was of roughly rectangular plan.

WINSTER

2½ m. SE of Bowness

4090

HOLY TRINITY. 1875. Low; nave and chancel in one and a bellcote on a mid-buttress. – STAINED GLASS. In the E window good glass of *c.*1875; large figures.

WINTON *see* KIRKBY STEPHEN

WISEBER HILL *see* KIRKBY STEPHEN

WITHERSLACK

4080

ST PAUL. Built about 1669 under the will of John Barwick, Dean of St Paul's, and his brother, physician to Charles II, both natives of Witherslack. It is an almost perfect example of a plain Gothic church of that date, honest and unpretentious. It is moreover in a beautiful position. It consists of W tower and nave and chancel in one. The only important later change is that the nave and chancel were heightened in 1768. The side windows originally had no transom and consisted only of the present lower part. Three lights and arched heads to the lights. The nave is wide, and must have appeared more so when it was lower. The roof pitch of the S porch perhaps gives an indication of how one should reconstruct it in one's mind. The E window of five stepped lights under a segmental arch is probably original. Plain, unbuttressed W tower. Inscription in a cartouche over the subsidiary S doorway. Peaceful interior. The coved ceiling and the screen of two Ionic columns to separate the altar space are of 1768. – PULPIT. Made up in 1880 out of parts of the three-decker of *c.*1670, though the carving still looks Jacobean. The sounding board is a renewal of *c.*1768. – LECTERN. Also with panels of *c.*1665–70. – STAINED GLASS. Heraldic glass of *c.*1670 attributed by Mr Kenneth Harrison to *Henry Giles* of York. – PLATE. Flagon, London, 1720; Cup, London, 1749; Paten, Newcastle, 1749. – MONUMENT. Geoffrey Stanley † 1871. Small boy, asleep. The pattern for this type of monument is Thomas Banks's Penelope Boothby of 1793 and Chantrey's Robinson Children of 1817.

WITHERSLACK HALL (Sandford School), 1½ m. N. 1874. Red and grey stone, large, asymmetrical, with a tower and many gables. Mullioned and transomed windows.

YANWATH

YANWATH HALL. A splendidly preserved low C14 pele tower and a C15 hall and kitchen make up the S front. The tower has a tunnel-vaulted ground floor, at the top battlements stepped up at the corners, and on the first floor Elizabethan five-light mullioned and transomed windows. Inside at this level is a room with the Royal Arms over the fireplace and a modest plaster ceiling with an openwork pendant at the intersection of the beams. The hall is distinguished near its high-table end by a bay window with a front of three lights. The window has a transom and rather coarse cusping of the arches of the lights at the top of the lower and the upper part. Small similar windows in the hall to the S as well as the N. On the N this window is placed between two buttresses. The hall roof is preserved, with collar-beams on arched braces and cusped brackets from the principals to the purlins above and below them. But this roof is now only visible from the upper floor, as the hall was horizontally subdivided in the later C16. At the same time the large fireplace was put into the wall between hall and screens passage. Entrance and exit of the passage are both still there, and both are round-arched.

MAYBURGH HENGE MONUMENT, ¼ m. SW of Eamont Bridge, on a slight rise. The site consists of a roughly circular bank, 8–15 ft high, enclosing some 1½ acres. A single stone, 9 ft high, stands in the centre of the site. In the C19 there were three further stones in the central area and two pairs flanking the entrance on the E. The site is unusual among British henge monuments in that it lacks a ditch. The bank in the present site is composed of pebbles from the neighbouring rivers which made the digging of an internal quarry ditch unnecessary.

KING ARTHUR'S ROUND TABLE, ¼ m. E. This is a second henge, 300 ft in diameter, with an external bank, 5 ft high, enclosing the quarry ditch. The site was considerably disturbed in the C19, and the low mound in the centre of the site is modern. In the C17 two standing stones were recorded outside the N entrance; both the stones have gone, and only the S entrance is now visible. Excavations revealed a cremation trench containing human bones at the centre of the monument, and the excavator believed that some form of stone setting had originally stood in this area, although modern disturbance made interpretation difficult.

YEWBARROW HALL *see* LONG SLEDDALE

GLOSSARY

Abacus: flat slab on the top of a capital (q.v.).

ABUTMENT: solid masonry placed to resist the lateral pressure of a vault.

ACANTHUS: plant with thick fleshy and scalloped leaves used as part of the decoration of a Corinthian capital (q.v.) and in some types of leaf carving.

ACHIEVEMENT OF ARMS: in heraldry, a complete display of armorial bearings.

ACROTERION: foliage-carved block on the end or top of a classical pediment.

ADDORSED: two human figures, animals, or birds, etc., placed symmetrically so that they turn their backs to each other.

AEDICULE, AEDICULA: framing of a window or door by columns and a pediment (q.v.).

AFFRONTED: two human figures, animals, or birds, etc., placed symmetrically so that they face each other.

AGGER: Latin term for the built-up foundations of Roman roads; also sometimes applied to the banks of hill-forts or other earthworks.

AMBULATORY: semicircular or polygonal aisle enclosing an apse (q.v.).

ANNULET: see Shaft-ring.

ANSE DE PANIER: see Arch, Basket.

ANTEPENDIUM: covering of the front of an altar, usually by textiles or metalwork.

ANTIS, IN: see Portico.

APSE: vaulted semicircular or polygonal end of a chancel or a chapel.

ARABESQUE: light and fanciful surface decoration using combinations of flowing lines, tendrils, etc., interspersed with vases, animals, etc.

ARCADE: range of arches supported on piers or columns, free-standing: or, BLIND ARCADE, the same attached to a wall.

ARCH: round-headed, i.e. semicircular; pointed, i.e. consisting of two curves, each drawn from one centre, and meeting in a point at the top; segmental, i.e. in the form of a segment;

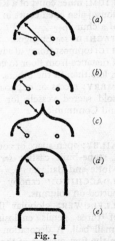

Fig. 1

pointed; four-centred (a Late Medieval form), see Fig. 1(a); Tudor (also a Late Medieval form), *see* Fig. 1(*b*); Ogee (introduced *c.*1300 and specially popular in the C14), *see* Fig. 1(*c*); Stilted, *see* Fig. 1(*d*); Basket, with lintel connected to the jambs by concave quadrant curves, *see* Fig. 1(*e*) for one example; Diaphragm, a transverse arch with solid spandrels carrying not a vault but a principal beam of a timber roof.

ARCHITRAVE: lowest of the three main parts of the entablature (q.v.) of an order (q.v.) (*see* Fig. 12).

ARCHIVOLT: under-surface of an arch (also called Soffit).

ARRIS: sharp edge at the meeting of two surfaces.

ASHLAR: masonry of large blocks wrought to even faces and square edges.

ATLANTES: male counterparts of caryatids (q.v.).

ATRIUM: inner court of a Roman house, also open court in front of a church.

ATTACHED: *see* Engaged.

ATTIC: topmost storey of a house, if distance from floor to ceiling is less than in the others.

AUMBRY: recess or cupboard to hold sacred vessels for Mass and Communion.

BAILEY: open space or court of a stone-built castle; *see* also Motte-and-Bailey.

BALDACCHINO: canopy supported on columns.

BALLFLOWER: globular flower of three petals enclosing a small ball. A decoration used in the first quarter of the C14.

BALUSTER: small pillar or column of fanciful outline.

BALUSTRADE: series of balusters supporting a handrail or coping (q.v.).

BARBICAN: outwork defending the entrance to a castle.

BARGEBOARDS: projecting decorated boards placed against the incline of the gable of a building and hiding the horizontal roof timbers.

BARROW: *see* Bell, Bowl, Disc, Long, *and* Pond Barrow.

BASILICA: in medieval architecture an aisled church with a clerestory.

BASKET ARCH: *see* Arch (Fig. 1e).

BASTION: projection at the angle of a fortification.

BATTER: inclined face of a wall.

BATTLEMENT: parapet with a series of indentations or embrasures with raised portions or merlons between (also called Crenellation).

BAYS: internal compartments of a building; each divided from the other not by solid walls but by divisions only marked in the side walls (columns, pilasters, etc.) or the ceiling (beams, etc.). Also external divisions of a building by fenestration.

BAY-WINDOW: angular or curved projection of a house front with ample fenestration. If curved, also called bow-window: if on an upper floor only, also called oriel or oriel window.

BEAKER FOLK: Late New Stone Age warrior invaders from the Continent who buried their dead in round barrows and introduced the first metal tools and weapons to Britain.

BEAKHEAD: Norman ornamental motif consisting of a row of bird or beast heads with beaks biting usually into a roll moulding.

BELFRY: turret on a roof to hang bells in.

BELGAE: Aristocratic warrior bands who settled in Britain in two main waves in the CI B.C. In Britain their culture is termed Iron Age C.

BELL BARROW: Early Bronze Age round barrow in which the mound is separated from its encircling ditch by a flat platform or berm (q.v.).

BELLCOTE: framework on a roof to hang bells from.

BERM: level area separating ditch from bank on a hill-fort or barrow.

BILLET FRIEZE: Norman ornamental motif made up of short raised rectangles placed at regular intervals.

BIVALLATE: Of a hill-fort: defended by two concentric banks and ditches.

BLOCK CAPITAL: Romanesque capital cut from a cube by hav-

Fig. 2

ing the lower angles rounded off to the circular shaft below (also called Cushion Capital) (Fig. 2).

BOND, ENGLISH or FLEMISH: see Brickwork.

BOSS: knob or projection usually placed to cover the intersection of ribs in a vault.

BOWL BARROW: round barrow surrounded by a quarry ditch. Introduced in Late Neolithic

times, the form continued until the Saxon period.

BOW-WINDOW: see Bay-Window.

BOX: A small country house, e.g. a shooting box. A convenient term to describe a compact minor dwelling, e.g. a rectory.

BOX PEW: pew with a high wooden enclosure.

BRACES: see Roof.

BRACKET: small supporting piece of stone, etc., to carry a projecting horizontal.

BRESSUMER: beam in a timber-framed building to support the, usually projecting, superstructure.

BRICKWORK: *Header:* brick laid so that the end only appears on the face of the wall. *Stretcher:* brick laid so that the side only appears on the face of the wall. *English Bond:* method of laying bricks so that alternate courses or layers on the face of the wall are composed of headers or stretchers only (Fig. 3*a*). *Flemish Bond:* method of laying

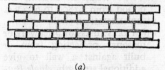

(a)

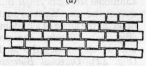

(b)

Fig. 3

bricks so that alternate headers and stretchers appear in each course on the face of the wall (Fig. 3*b*).

BROACH: see Spire.

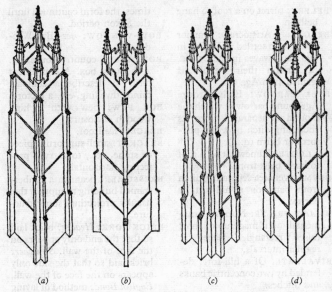

(a)   *(b)*   *(c)*   *(d)*

Fig. 4

BROKEN PEDIMENT: *see* Pediment.

BRONZE AGE: In Britain, the period from *c.*1800 to 600 B.C.

BUCRANIUM: ox skull.

BUTTRESS: mass of brickwork or masonry projecting from or built against a wall to give additional strength. *Angle Buttresses:* two meeting at an angle of 90° at the angle of a building (Fig. 4*a*). *Clasping Buttress:* one which encases the angle (Fig. 4*d*). *Diagonal Buttress:* one placed against the right angle formed by two walls, and more or less equiangular with both (Fig. 4*b*). *Flying Buttress:* arch or half arch transmitting the thrust of a vault or roof from the upper part of a wall to an outer support or buttress. *Setback Buttress:* angle buttress set slightly back from the angle (Fig. 4*c*).

CABLE MOULDING: Norman moulding imitating a twisted cord.

CAIRN: a mound of stones usually covering a burial.

CAMBER: slight rise or upward curve of an otherwise horizontal structure.

CAMPANILE: isolated bell tower.

CANOPY: projection or hood over an altar, pulpit, niche, statue, etc.

CAP: in a windmill the crowning feature.

CAPITAL: head or top part of a column.

CARTOUCHE: tablet with an ornate frame, usually enclosing an inscription.

CARYATID: whole female figure supporting an entablature or other similar member. *Termini Caryatids:* female busts or demi-figures or three-quarter figures supporting an entablature or other similar member and placed at the top of termini pilasters (q.v.). Cf. Atlantes.

CASTELLATED: decorated with battlements.

CELURE: panelled and adorned part of a wagon-roof above the rood or the altar.

CENSER: vessel for the burning of incense.

CENTERING: wooden framework used in arch and vault construction and removed when the mortar has set.

CHALICE: cup used in the Communion service or at Mass. *See also* Recusant Chalice.

CHAMBERED TOMB: burial mound of the New Stone Age having a stone-built chamber and entrance passage covered by an earthen barrow or stone cairn. The form was introduced to Britain from the Mediterranean.

CHAMFER: surface made by cutting across the square angle of a stone block, piece of wood, etc., usually at an angle of 45° to the other two surfaces.

CHANCEL: that part of the E end of a church in which the altar is placed, usually applied to the whole continuation of the nave E of the crossing.

CHANCEL ARCH: arch at the W end of the chancel.

CHANTRY CHAPEL: chapel attached to, or inside, a church, endowed for the saying of Masses for the soul of the founder or some other individual.

CHEVET: French term for the E end of a church (chancel, ambulatory, and radiating chapels).

CHEVRON: Norman moulding forming a zigzag.

CHOIR: that part of the church where divine service is sung.

CIBORIUM: a baldacchino.

CINQUEFOIL: *see* Foil.

CIST: stone-lined or slab-built grave. First appears in Late Neolithic times. It continued to be used in the Early Christian period.

CLAPPER BRIDGE: bridge made of large slabs of stone, some built up to make rough piers and other longer ones laid on top to make the roadway.

CLASSIC: here used to mean the moment of highest achievement of a style.

CLASSICAL: here used as the term for Greek and Roman architecture and any subsequent styles inspired by it.

CLERESTORY: upper storey of the nave walls of a church, pierced by windows.

COADE STONE: artificial (cast) stone made in the late C18 and the early C19 by Coade and Sealy in London.

COB: walling material made of mixed clay and straw.

COFFERING: decorating a ceiling with sunk square or polygonal ornamental panels.

COLLAR-BEAM: *see* Roof.

COLONNADE: range of columns.

COLONNETTE: small column.

COLUMNA ROSTRATA: column decorated with carved prows of ships to celebrate a naval victory.

COMPOSITE: *see* Order.

CONSOLE: bracket (q.v.) with a compound curved outline.

COPING: capping or covering to a wall.

CORBEL: block of stone projecting from a wall, supporting some feature on its horizontal top surface.

CORBEL TABLE: series of corbels, occurring just below the roof eaves externally or internally, often seen in Norman buildings.

CORINTHIAN: *see* Order.

CORNICE: in classical architecture the top section of the entablature (q.v.). Also for a projecting decorative feature along the top of a wall, arch, etc.

CORRIDOR VILLA: *see* Villa.

COUNTERSCARP BANK: small bank on the down-hill or outer side of a hill-fort ditch.

COURTYARD VILLA: *see* Villa.

COVE, COVING: concave undersurface in the nature of a hollow moulding but on a larger scale.

COVER PATEN: cover to a Communion cup, suitable for use as a paten or plate for the consecrated bread.

CRADLE ROOF: *see* Wagon roof.

CRENELLATION: *see* Battlement.

CREST, CRESTING: ornamental finish along the top of a screen, etc.

CRINKLE-CRANKLE WALL: undulating wall.

CROCKET, CROCKETING: decorative features placed on the sloping sides of spires, pinnacles, gables, etc., in Gothic architecture, carved in various leaf shapes and placed at regular intervals.

CROCKET CAPITAL: *see* Fig. 5. An Early Gothic form.

CROMLECH: word of Celtic origin still occasionally used of single free-standing stones ascribed to the Neolithic or Bronze Age periods.

Fig. 5

CROSSING: space at the intersection of nave, chancel, and transepts.

CROSS-WINDOWS: windows with one mullion and one transom.

CRUCK: big curved beam supporting both walls and roof of a cottage.

CRYPT: underground room usually below the E end of a church.

CUPOLA: small polygonal or circular domed turret crowning a roof.

CURTAIN WALL: connecting wall between the towers of a castle.

CUSHION CAPITAL: *see* Block Capital.

CUSP: projecting point between the foils in a foiled Gothic arch.

DADO: decorative covering of the lower part of a wall.

DAGGER: tracery motif of the Dec style. It is a lancet shape rounded or pointed at the head, pointed at the foot, and cusped inside (*see* Fig. 6).

Fig. 6

DAIS: raised platform at one end of a room.

DEC ('DECORATED'): historical division of English Gothic architecture covering the period from c.1290 to c.1350.

DEMI-COLUMNS: columns half sunk into a wall.

DIAPER WORK: surface decoration composed of square or lozenge shapes.

DIAPHRAGM ARCH: *see* Arch.

DISC BARROW: Bronze Age round barrow with inconspicuous central mound surrounded by bank and ditch.

DOGTOOTH: typical E.E. ornament consisting of a series of four-cornered stars placed diagonally and raised pyramidally (Fig. 7).

Fig. 7

DOMICAL VAULT: *see* Vault.

DONJON: *see* Keep.

DORIC: *see* Order.

DORMER (WINDOW): window placed vertically in the sloping plane of a roof.

DRIPSTONE: *see* Hood-mould.

DRUM: circular or polygonal vertical wall of a dome or cupola.

E.E. ('EARLY ENGLISH'): historical division of English Gothic architecture roughly covering the C13.

EASTER SEPULCHRE: recess with tomb-chest, usually in the wall of a chancel, the tomb-chest to receive an effigy of Christ for Easter celebrations.

EAVES: underpart of a sloping roof overhanging a wall.

EAVES CORNICE: cornice below the eaves of a roof.

ECHINUS: Convex or projecting moulding supporting the abacus of a Greek Doric capital, sometimes bearing an egg and dart pattern.

EMBATTLED: *see* Battlement.

EMBRASURE: small opening in the wall or parapet of a fortified building, usually splayed on the inside.

ENCAUSTIC TILES: earthenware glazed and decorated tiles used for paving.

ENGAGED COLUMNS: columns attached to, or partly sunk into, a wall.

ENGLISH BOND: *see* Brickwork.

ENTABLATURE: in classical architecture the whole of the horizontal members above a column (that is architrave, frieze, and cornice) (*see* Fig. 12).

ENTASIS: very slight convex deviation from a straight line; used on Greek columns and sometimes on spires to prevent an optical illusion of concavity.

ENTRESOL: *see* Mezzanine.

EPITAPH: hanging wall monument.

ESCUTCHEON: shield for armorial bearings.

EXEDRA: the apsidal end of a room. *See* Apse.

FAN-VAULT: *see* Vault.

FERETORY: place behind the

high altar where the chief shrine of a church is kept.

FESTOON: carved garland of flowers and fruit suspended at both ends.

FILLET: narrow flat band running down a shaft or along a roll moulding.

FINIAL: top of a canopy, gable, pinnacle.

FLAGON: vessel for the wine used in the Communion service.

FLAMBOYANT: properly the latest phase of French Gothic architecture where the window tracery takes on wavy undulating lines.

FLÈCHE: slender wooden spire on the centre of a roof (also called Spirelet).

FLEMISH BOND: see Brickwork.

FLEURON: decorative carved flower or leaf.

FLUSHWORK: decorative use of flint in conjunction with dressed stone so as to form patterns: tracery, initials, etc.

FLUTING: vertical channelling in the shaft of a column.

FLYING BUTTRESS: see Buttress.

FOIL: lobe formed by the cusping (q.v.) of a circle or an arch. Trefoil, quatrefoil, cinquefoil, multifoil, express the number of leaf shapes to be seen.

FOLIATED: carved with leaf shapes.

FOSSE: ditch.

FOUR-CENTRED ARCH: see Arch.

FRATER: refectory or dining hall of a monastery.

FRESCO: wall painting on wet plaster.

FRIEZE: middle division of a classical entablature (q.v.) (see Fig. 12).

FRONTAL: covering for the front of an altar.

GABLE: *Dutch gable:* A gable with curved sides crowned by a pediment, characteristic of c.1630–50 (Fig. 8a). *Shaped gable:* A gable with multi-curved sides characteristic of c.1600–50 (Fig. 8b).

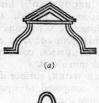

(a)

(b)

Fig. 8

GADROONED: enriched with a series of convex ridges, the opposite of fluting.

GALILEE: chapel or vestibule usually at the W end of a church enclosing the porch. Also called Narthex (q.v.).

GALLERY: in church architecture upper storey above an aisle, opened in arches to the nave. Also called Tribune and often erroneously Triforium (q.v.).

GALLERY GRAVE: chambered tomb (q.v.) in which there is little or no differentiation between the entrance passage and the actual burial chamber(s).

GARDEROBE: lavatory or privy in a medieval building.

GARGOYLE: water spout projecting from the parapet of a wall or tower; carved into a human or animal shape.

GAZEBO: lookout tower or raised

summer house in a picturesque garden.

'GEOMETRICAL': *see* Tracery.

'GIBBS SURROUND': of a doorway or window. An C18 motif consisting of a surround with alternating larger and smaller blocks of stone, quoin-wise, or intermittent large blocks, sometimes with a narrow raised band connecting them up the verticals and along the face of the arch (Fig. 9).

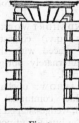

Fig. 9

GROIN: sharp edge at the meeting of two cells of a cross-vault.

GROIN-VAULT: *see* Vault.

GROTESQUE: fanciful ornamental decoration: *see* also Arabesque.

HAGIOSCOPE: *see* Squint.

HALF-TIMBERING: *see* Timber-Framing.

HALL CHURCH: church in which nave and aisles are of equal height or approximately so.

HAMMERBEAM: *see* Roof.

HANAP: large metal cup, generally made for domestic use, standing on an elaborate base and stem; with a very ornate cover frequently crowned with a little steeple.

HEADERS: *see* Brickwork.

HERRINGBONE WORK: brick, stone, or tile construction where the component blocks are laid diagonally instead of flat. Alternate courses lie in opposing directions to make a zigzag pattern up the face of the wall.

HEXASTYLE: having six detached columns.

HILL-FORT: Iron Age earthwork enclosed by a ditch and bank system; in the later part of the period the defences multiplied in size and complexity. They vary from about an acre to over 30 acres in area, and are usually built with careful regard to natural elevations or promontories.

HIPPED ROOF: *see* Roof.

HOOD-MOULD: projecting moulding above an arch or a lintel to throw off water (also called Dripstone or Label).

ICONOGRAPHY: the science of the subject matter of works of the visual arts.

IMPOST: bracket in a wall, usually formed of mouldings, on which the ends of an arch rest.

INDENT: shape chiselled out in a stone slab to receive a brass.

INGLENOOK: bench or seat built in beside a fireplace, sometimes covered by the chimneybreast, occasionally lit by small windows on each side of the fire.

INTERCOLUMNIATION: the space between columns.

IONIC: *see* Order (Fig. 12).

IRON AGE: in Britain the period from *c.* 600 B.C. to the coming of the Romans. The term is

also used for those un-Roman-
ized native communities which
survived until the Saxon incur-
sions.

JAMB: straight side of an archway, doorway, or window.

KEEL MOULDING: moulding
whose outline is in section like
that of the keel of a ship.

KEEP: massive tower of a Norman castle.

KEYSTONE: middle stone in an
arch or a rib-vault.

KING-POST: see Roof (Fig. 14).

KNEELER: horizontal decorative
projection at the base of a
gable.

KNOP: a knob-like thickening in
the stem of a chalice.

LABEL: see Hood-mould.

LABEL STOP: ornamental boss
at the end of a hood-mould
(q.v.).

LACED WINDOWS: windows
pulled visually together by
strips, usually in brick of a
different colour, which continue vertically the lines of the
vertical parts of the window
surrounds. The motif is typical
of c. 1720.

LANCET WINDOW: slender
pointed-arched window.

LANTERN: in architecture, a
small circular or polygonal
turret with windows all round
crowning a roof (see Cupola) or
a dome.

LANTERN CROSS: churchyard
cross with lantern-shaped top
usually with sculptured representations on the sides of the
top.

LEAN-TO ROOF: roof with one
slope only, built against a
higher wall.

LESENE or PILASTER STRIP:
pilaster without base or capital.

LIERNE: see Vault (Fig. 21).

LINENFOLD: Tudor panelling
ornamented with a conven-
tional representation of a piece
of linen laid in vertical folds.
The piece is repeated in each
panel.

LINTEL: horizontal beam or
stone bridging an opening.

LOGGIA: recessed colonnade
(q.v.).

LONG AND SHORT WORK: Saxon
quoins (q.v.) consisting of
stones placed with the long
sides alternately upright and
horizontal.

LONG BARROW: unchambered
Neolithic communal burial
mound, wedge-shaped in plan,
with the burial and occasional
other structures massed at the
broader end, from which the
mound itself tapers in height;
quarry ditches flank the
mound.

LOUVRE: opening, often with
lantern (q.v.) over, in the roof
of a room to let the smoke from
a central hearth escape.

LOWER PALAEOLITHIC: see
Palaeolithic.

LOZENGE: diamond shape.

LUCARNE: small opening to let
light in.

LUNETTE: tympanum (q.v.) or
semicircular opening.

LYCH GATE: wooden gate structure with a roof and open sides
placed at the entrance to a
churchyard to provide space
for the reception of a coffin.
The word *lych* is Saxon and
means a corpse.

LYNCHET: long terraced strip of soil accumulating on the downward side of prehistoric and medieval fields due to soil creep from continuous ploughing along the contours.

MACHICOLATION: projecting gallery on brackets constructed on the outside of castle towers or walls. The gallery has holes in the floor to drop missiles through.

MAJOLICA: ornamented glazed earthenware.

MANSARD: see Roof.

MATHEMATICAL TILES: Small facing tiles the size of brick headers, applied to timber-framed walls to make them appear brick-built.

MEGALITHIC TOMB: stone-built burial chamber of the New Stone Age covered by an earth or stone mound. The form was introduced to Britain from the Mediterranean area.

MERLON: see Battlement.

MESOLITHIC: 'Middle Stone' Age; the post-glacial period of hunting and fishing communities dating in Britain from c. 8000 B.C. to the arrival of Neolithic communities, with which they must have considerably overlapped.

METOPE: in classical architecture of the Doric order (q.v.) the space in the frieze between the triglyphs (Fig. 12).

MEZZANINE: low storey placed between two higher ones.

MISERERE: see Misericord.

MISERICORD: bracket placed on the underside of a hinged choir stall seat which, when turned up, provided the occupant of the seat with a support during long periods of standing (also called Miserere).

MODILLION: small bracket of which large numbers (modillion frieze) are often placed below a cornice (q.v.) in classical architecture.

MOTTE: steep mound forming the main feature of C11 and C12 castles.

MOTTE-AND-BAILEY: post-Roman and Norman defence system consisting of an earthen mound (the motte) topped with a wooden tower eccentrically placed within a bailey (q.v.), with enclosure ditch and palisade, and with the rare addition of an internal bank.

MOUCHETTE: tracery motif in curvilinear tracery, a curved dagger (q.v.), specially popular in the early C14 (Fig. 10).

Fig. 10

MULLIONS: vertical posts or uprights dividing a window into 'lights'.

MULTIVALLATE: Of a hill-fort: defended by three or more concentric banks and ditches.

MUNTIN: post as a rule moulded and part of a screen.

NAIL-HEAD: E.E. ornamental motif, consisting of small pyramids regularly repeated (Fig. 11).

Fig. 11

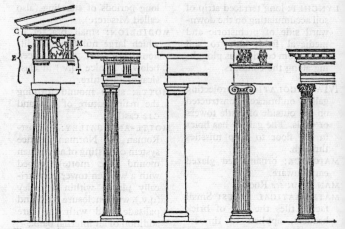

Fig. 12. Orders of Columns (Greek Doric, Roman Doric, Tuscan Doric, Ionic, Corinthian) E, Entablature; C, Cornice; F, Frieze; A, Architrave; M, Metope; T, Triglyph.

NARTHEX: enclosed vestibule or covered porch at the main entrance to a church (see Galilee).

NEOLITHIC: 'New Stone' Age, dating in Britain from the appearance from the Continent of the first settled farming communities c. 3500 B.C. until the introduction of the Bronze Age.

NEWEL: central post in a circular or winding staircase; also the principal post when a flight of stairs meets a landing.

NOOK-SHAFT: shaft set in the angle of a pier or respond or wall, or the angle of the jamb of a window or doorway.

NUTMEG MOULDING: consisting of a chain of tiny triangles placed obliquely.

OBELISK: lofty pillar of square section tapering at the top and ending pyramidally.

OGEE: see Arch (Fig. 1c).

ORATORY: small private chapel in a house.

ORDER: (1) of a doorway or window: series of concentric steps receding towards the opening; (2) in classical architecture: column with base, shaft, capital, and entablature (q.v.) according to one of the following styles: Greek Doric, Roman Doric, Tuscan Doric, Ionic, Corinthian, Composite. The established details are very elaborate, and some specialist architectural work should be consulted for further guidance (see Fig. 12).

ORIEL: see Bay-Window.

OVERHANG: projection of the upper storey of a house.

OVERSAILING COURSES: series of stone or brick courses, each one projecting beyond the one below it.

OVOLO: convex moulding.

PALAEOLITHIC: 'Old Stone' Age; the first period of human culture, commencing in the

Ice Age and immediately prior to the Mesolithic; the Lower Palaeolithic is the older phase, the Upper Palaeolithic the later.

PALIMPSEST: (1) *of a brass:* where a metal plate has been re-used by turning over and engraving on the back; (2) *of a wall painting:* where one overlaps and partly obscures an earlier one.

PALLADIAN: architecture following the ideas and principles of Andrea Palladio, 1518–80.

PANTILE: tile of curved S-shaped section.

PARAPET: low wall placed to protect any spot where there is a sudden drop, for example on a bridge, quay, hillside, housetop, etc.

PARGETTING: plaster work with patterns and ornaments either in relief or engraved on it.

PARVIS: term wrongly applied to a room over a church porch. These rooms were often used as a schoolroom or as a store room.

PATEN: plate to hold the bread at Communion or Mass.

PATERA: small flat circular or oval ornament in classical architecture.

PEDIMENT: low-pitched gable used in classical, Renaissance, and neo-classical architecture above a portico and above doors, windows, etc. It may be straight-sided or curved segmentally. *Broken Pediment:* one where the centre portion of the base is left open. *Open Pediment:* one where the centre portion of the sloping sides is left out.

PENDANT: boss (q.v.) elongated so that it seems to hang down.

II—C.W.

PENDENTIF: concave triangular spandrel used to lead from the angle of two walls to the base of a circular dome. It is constructed as part of the hemisphere over a diameter the size of the diagonal of the basic square (Fig. 13).

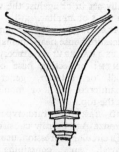

Fig. 13

PERP (PERPENDICULAR): historical division of English Gothic architecture covering the period from *c.*1335–50 to *c.*1530.

PIANO NOBILE: principal storey of a house with the reception rooms; usually the first floor.

PIAZZA: open space surrounded by buildings; in C17 and C18 England sometimes used to mean a long colonnade or loggia.

PIER: strong, solid support, frequently square in section or of composite section (compound pier).

PIETRA DURA: ornamental or scenic inlay by means of thin slabs of stone.

PILASTER: shallow pier attached to a wall. *Termini Pilasters:* pilasters with sides tapering downwards.

PILLAR PISCINA: free-standing piscina on a pillar.

PINNACLE: ornamental form crowning a spire, tower, buttress, etc., usually of steep pyramidal, conical, or some similar shape.

PISCINA: basin for washing the Communion or Mass vessels, provided with a drain. Generally set in or against the wall to the S of an altar.

PLAISANCE: summer-house, pleasure house near a mansion.

PLATE TRACERY: *see* Tracery.

PLINTH: projecting base of a wall or column, generally chamfered (q.v.) or moulded at the top.

POND BARROW: rare type of Bronze Age barrow consisting of a circular depression, usually paved, and containing a number of cremation burials.

POPPYHEAD: ornament of leaf and flower type used to decorate the tops of bench- or stall-ends.

PORTCULLIS: gate constructed to rise and fall in vertical grooves; used in gateways of castles.

PORTE COCHÈRE: porch large enough to admit wheeled vehicles.

PORTICO: centre-piece of a house or a church with classical detached or attached columns and a pediment. A portico is called *prostyle* or *in antis* according to whether it projects from or recedes into a building. In a portico *in antis* the columns range with the side walls.

POSTERN: small gateway at the back of a building.

PREDELLA: in an altarpiece the horizontal strip below the main representation, often used for a number of subsidiary representations in a row.

PRESBYTERY: the part of the church lying E of the choir. It is the part where the altar is placed.

PRINCIPAL: *see* Roof (Fig. 14).

PRIORY: monastic house whose head is a prior or prioress, not an abbot or abbess.

PROSTYLE: with free-standing columns in a row.

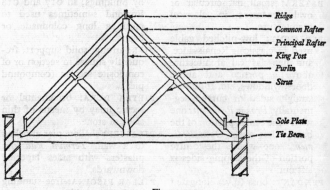

Ridge
Common Rafter
Principal Rafter
King Post
Purlin
Strut
Sole Plate
Tie Beam

Fig. 14

PULPITUM: stone screen in a major church provided to shut off the choir from the nave and also as a backing for the return choir stalls.

PULVINATED FRIEZE: frieze with a bold convex moulding.

PURLIN: see Roof (Figs. 14, 15).

PUTHOLE or PUTLOCK HOLE: putlocks are the short horizontal timbers on which during construction the boards of scaffolding rest. Putholes or putlock holes are the holes in the wall for putlocks, which often are not filled in after construction is complete.

PUTTO: small naked boy.

QUADRANGLE: inner courtyard in a large building.

QUARRY: in stained-glass work, a small diamond- or square-shaped piece of glass set diagonally.

QUATREFOIL: see Foil.

QUEEN-POSTS: see Roof (Fig. 15).

QUOINS: dressed stones at the angles of a building. Sometimes all the stones are of the same size; more often they are alternately large and small.

RADIATING CHAPELS: chapels projecting radially from an ambulatory or an apse.

RAFTER: see Roof.

RAMPART: stone wall or wall of earth surrounding a castle, fortress, or fortified city.

RAMPART-WALK: path along the inner face of a rampart.

REBATE: continuous rectangular notch cut on an edge.

REBUS: pun, a play on words. The literal translation and illustration of a name for artistic and heraldic purposes (Belton = bell, tun).

RECUSANT CHALICE: chalice made after the Reformation and before Catholic Emancipation for Roman Catholic use.

REEDING: decoration with parallel convex mouldings touching one another.

REFECTORY: dining hall; see Frater.

RENDERING: plastering of an outer wall.

REPOUSSÉ: decoration of metal work by relief designs, formed by beating the metal from the back.

REREDOS: structure behind and above an altar.

RESPOND: half-pier bonded into a wall and carrying one end of an arch.

RETABLE: altarpiece, a picture or piece of carving, standing behind and attached to an altar.

RETICULATION: see Tracery (Fig. 20e).

REVEAL: that part of a jamb (q.v.) which lies between the glass or door and the outer surface of the wall.

RIB-VAULT: see Vault.

ROCOCO: latest phase of the Baroque style, current in most Continental countries between c.1720 and c.1760.

ROLL MOULDING: moulding of semicircular or more than semicircular section.

ROMANESQUE: that style in architecture which was current in the C11 and C12 and preceded the Gothic style (in England often called Norman). (Some scholars extend the use of the term Romanesque back to the C10 or C9.)

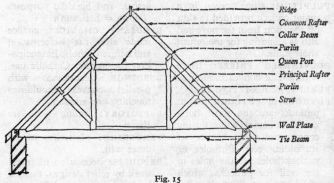

Ridge
Common Rafter
Collar Beam
Purlin
Queen Post
Principal Rafter
Purlin
Strut
Wall Plate
Tie Beam

Fig. 15

ROMANO-BRITISH: A somewhat vague term applied to the period and cultural features of Britain affected by the Roman occupation of the C1–5 A.D.

ROOD: cross or crucifix.

ROOD LOFT: singing gallery on the top of the rood screen, often supported by a coving.

ROOD SCREEN: *see* Screen.

ROOD STAIRS: stairs to give access to the rood loft.

ROOF: *Single-framed:* if consisting entirely of transverse members (such as rafters with or without braces, collars, tie-beams, king-posts or queen-posts, etc.) not tied together longitudinally. *Double-framed:* if longitudinal members (such as a ridge beam and purlins) are employed. As a rule in such cases the rafters are divided into stronger principals and weaker subsidiary rafters. *Hipped:* roof with sloped instead of vertical ends. *Mansard:* roof with a double slope, the

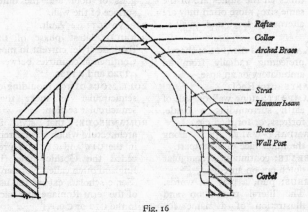

Rafter
Collar
Arched Braces
Strut
Hammer beam
Brace
Wall Post
Corbel

Fig. 16

lower slope being larger and steeper than the upper. *Saddleback:* tower roof shaped like an ordinary gabled timber roof. The following members have special names: *Rafter:* roof-timber sloping up from the wall plate to the ridge. *Principal:* principal rafter, usually corresponding to the main bay divisions of the nave or chancel below. *Wall Plate:* timber laid longitudinally on the top of a wall. *Purlin:* longitudinal member laid parallel with wall plate and ridge beam some way up the slope of the roof. *Tie-beam:* beam connecting the two slopes of a roof across at its foot, usually at the height of the wall plate, to prevent the roof from spreading. *Collar-beam:* tie-beam applied higher up the slope of the roof. *Strut:* upright timber connecting the tie-beam with the rafter above it. *King-post:* upright timber connecting a tie-beam and collar-beam with the ridge beam. *Queen-posts:* two struts placed symmetrically on a tie-beam or collar-beam. *Braces:* inclined timbers inserted to strengthen others. Usually braces connect a collar-beam with the rafters below or a tie-beam with the wall below. Braces can be straight or curved (also called arched). *Hammer-beam:* beam projecting at right angles, usually from the top of a wall, to carry arched braces or struts and arched braces. (*See* Figs. 14, 15, 16.)

ROSE WINDOW (or WHEEL WINDOW): circular window with patterned tracery arranged to radiate from the centre.

ROTUNDA: building circular in plan.

RUBBLE: building stones, not square or hewn, nor laid in regular courses.

RUSTICATION: *rock-faced* if the surfaces of large blocks of ashlar stone are left rough like rock; *smooth* if the ashlar blocks are smooth and separated by V-joints; *banded* if the separation by V-joints applies only to the horizontals.

SADDLEBACK: *see* Roof.

SALTIRE CROSS: equal-limbed cross placed diagonally.

SANCTUARY: (1) area around the main altar of a church (*see* Presbytery); (2) sacred site consisting of wood or stone uprights enclosed by a circular bank and ditch. Beginning in the Neolithic, they were elaborated in the succeeding Bronze Age. The best known examples are Stonehenge and Avebury.

SARCOPHAGUS: elaborately carved coffin.

SCAGLIOLA: material composed of cement and colouring matter to imitate marble.

SCALLOPED CAPITAL: development of the block capital (q.v.) in which the single semi-circular surface is elaborated into a series of truncated cones (Fig. 17).

Fig. 17

SCARP: artificial cutting away of the ground to form a steep slope.

SCREEN: *Parclose screen:* screen separating a chapel from the rest of a church. *Rood screen:* screen below the rood (q.v.), usually at the W end of a chancel.

SCREENS PASSAGE: passage between the entrances to kitchen, buttery, etc., and the screen behind which lies the hall of a medieval house.

SEDILIA: seats for the priests (usually three) on the S side of the chancel of a church.

SEGMENTAL ARCH: *see* Arch.

SET-OFF: *see* Weathering.

SEXPARTITE: *see* Vault.

SGRAFFITO: pattern incised into plaster so as to expose a dark surface underneath.

SHAFT-RING: motif of the C12 and C13 consisting of a ring round a circular pier or a shaft attached to a pier.

SHEILA-NA-GIG: fertility figure, usually with legs wide open.

SILL: lower horizontal part of the frame of a window.

SLATEHANGING: the covering of walls by overlapping rows of slates, on a timber substructure.

SOFFIT: underside of an arch, lintel, etc.

SOLAR: upper living-room of a medieval house.

SOPRAPORTE: painting above the door of a room, usual in the C17 and C18.

SOUNDING BOARD: horizontal board or canopy over a pulpit. Also called Tester.

SPANDREL: triangular surface between one side of an arch, the horizontal drawn from its apex, and the vertical drawn from its springer; also the surface between two arches.

SPERE-TRUSS: roof truss on two free-standing posts to mask the division between screens passage and hall. The screen itself, where a spere-truss exists, was originally movable.

SPIRE: tall pyramidal or conical pointed erection often built on top of a tower, turret, etc. *Broach Spire:* a broach is a sloping half-pyramid of masonry or wood introduced at the base of each of the four oblique faces of a tapering octagonal spire with the object of effecting the transition from the square to the octagon. The *splayed foot spire* is a variation of the broach form found principally in the south-eastern counties. In this form the four cardinal faces are splayed out near their base, to cover the corners, while the oblique (or intermediate) faces taper away to a point. *Needle Spire:* thin spire rising from the centre of a tower roof, well inside the parapet.

SPIRELET: *see* Flèche.

SPLAY: chamfer, usually of the jamb of a window.

SPRINGING: level at which an arch rises from its supports.

SQUINCH: arch or system of concentric arches thrown across the angle between two walls to support a superstructure, for example a dome (Fig. 18).

SQUINT: a hole cut in a wall or through a pier to allow a view of the main altar of a church from places whence it could not otherwise be seen (also called Hagioscope).

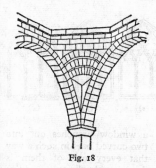

Fig. 18

STALL: carved seat, one of a row, made of wood or stone.

STAUNCHION: upright iron or steel member.

STEEPLE: the tower of a church together with a spire, cupola, etc.

STIFF-LEAF: E.E. type of foliage of many-lobed shapes (Fig. 19).

Fig. 19

STILTED: see Arch.

STOREY-POSTS: the principal posts of a timber-framed wall.

STOUP: vessel for the reception of holy water, usually placed near a door.

STRAINER ARCH: arch inserted across a room to prevent the walls from leaning.

STRAPWORK: C16 decoration consisting of interlaced bands, and forms similar to fretwork or cut and bent leather.

STRETCHER: see Brickwork.

STRING COURSE: projecting horizontal band or moulding set in the surface of a wall.

STRUT: see Roof.

STUCCO: plaster work.

STUDS: the subsidiary vertical timber members of a timber-framed wall.

SWAG: festoon formed by a carved piece of cloth suspended from both ends.

TABERNACLE: richly ornamented niche or free-standing canopy. Usually contains the Holy Sacrament.

TARSIA: inlay in various woods.

TAZZA: shallow bowl on a foot.

TERMINAL FIGURES (TERMS, TERMINI): upper part of a human figure growing out of a pier, pilaster, etc., which tapers towards the base. See also Caryatid, Pilaster.

TERRACOTTA: burnt clay, unglazed.

TESSELLATED PAVEMENT: mosaic flooring, particularly Roman, consisting of small 'tesserae' or cubes of glass, stone, or brick.

TESSERAE: see Tessellated Pavement.

TESTER: see Sounding Board.

TETRASTYLE: having four detached columns.

THREE-DECKER PULPIT: pulpit with Clerk's Stall below and Reading Desk below the Clerk's Stall.

TIE-BEAM: see Roof (Figs. 14, 15).

TIERCERON: see Vault (Fig. 21).

TILEHANGING: see Slatehanging.

TIMBER-FRAMING: method of construction where walls are built of timber framework with the spaces filled in by plaster

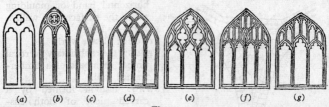

(a)   (b)   (c)   (d)   (e)   (f)   (g)

Fig. 20

or brickwork. Sometimes the timber is covered over with plaster or boarding laid horizontally.

TOMB-CHEST: chest-shaped stone coffin, the most usual medieval form of funeral monument.

TOUCH: soft black marble quarried near Tournai.

TOURELLE: turret corbelled out from the wall.

TRACERY: intersecting ribwork in the upper part of a window, or used decoratively in blank arches, on vaults, etc. *Plate tracery: see* Fig. 20(a). Early form of tracery where decoratively shaped openings are cut through the solid stone infilling in a window head. *Bar tracery:* a form introduced into England *c.*1250. Intersecting ribwork made up of slender shafts, continuing the lines of the mullions of windows up to a decorative mesh in the head of the window. *Geometrical tracery: see* Fig. 20(b). Tracery characteristic of *c.* 1250–1310 consisting chiefly of circles or foiled circles. *Y-tracery: see* Fig. 20(c). Tracery consisting of a mullion which branches into two forming a Y shape; typical of *c.* 1300. *Intersecting tracery: see* Fig. 20(d). Tracery in which each mullion of

a window branches out into two curved bars in such a way that every one of them is drawn with the same radius from a different centre. The result is that every light of the window is a lancet and every two, three, four, etc., lights together form a pointed arch. This treatment also is typical of *c.* 1300. *Reticulated tracery: see* Fig. 20(e). Tracery typical of the early C14 consisting entirely of circles drawn at top and bottom into ogee shapes so that a net-like appearance results. *Panel tracery: see* Fig. 20(f) and (g). Perp tracery, which is formed of upright straight-sided panels above lights of a window.

TRANSEPT: transverse portion of a cross-shaped church.

TRANSOM: horizontal bar across the openings of a window.

TRANSVERSE ARCH: *see* Vault.

TRIBUNE: *see* Gallery.

TRICIPUT, SIGNUM TRICIPUT: sign of the Trinity expressed by three faces belonging to one head.

TRIFORIUM: arcaded wall passage or blank arcading facing the nave at the height of the aisle roof and below the clerestory (q.v.) windows. (*See* Gallery.)

TRIGLYPHS: blocks with vertical

grooves separating the metopes (q.v.) in the Doric frieze (Fig. 12).

TROPHY: sculptured group of arms or armour, used as a memorial of victory.

TRUMEAU: stone mullion (q.v.) supporting the tympanum (q.v.) of a wide doorway.

TUMULUS: *see* Barrow.

TURRET: very small tower, round or polygonal in plan.

TUSCAN: *see* Order.

TYMPANUM: space between the lintel of a doorway and the arch above it.

UNDERCROFT: vaulted room, sometimes underground, below a church or chapel.

UNIVALLATE: of a hill-fort: defended by a single bank and ditch.

UPPER PALAEOLITHIC: *see* Palaeolithic.

VAULT: *Barrel-vault:* see Tunnel-vault. *Cross-vault:* see Groin-vault. *Domical vault:* square or polygonal dome rising direct on a square or polygonal bay, the curved surfaces separated by groins (q.v.). *Fan-vault:* late medieval vault where all ribs springing from one springer are of the same length, the same distance from the next, and the same curvature. *Groin-vault* or *Cross-vault:* vault of two tunnel-vaults of identical shape intersecting each other at r. angles. Chiefly Norman and Renaissance. *Lierne:* tertiary rib, that is, rib which does not spring either from one of the main springers or from the central

boss. Introduced in the C14, continues to the C16. *Quadripartite vault:* one wherein one bay of vaulting is divided into four parts. *Rib-vault:* vault with diagonal ribs projecting along the groins. *Ridge-rib:* rib along the longitudinal or transverse ridge of a vault. Introduced in the early C13. *Sexpartite vault:* one wherein one bay of quadripartite vaulting is divided into two parts transversely so that each bay of vaulting has six parts. *Tierceron:* secondary rib, that is, rib which issues from one of the main springers or the central boss and leads to a place on a ridge-rib. Introduced in the early C13. *Transverse arch:* arch separating one bay of a vault from the next. *Tunnel-vault* or *Barrel-vault:* vault of semicircular or pointed section. Chiefly Norman and Renaissance. (*See* Fig. 21.)

VAULTING SHAFT: vertical member leading to the springer of a vault.

VENETIAN WINDOW: window with three openings, the central one arched and wider than the outside ones. Current in England chiefly in the C17–18.

VERANDA: open gallery or balcony with a roof on light, usually metal, supports.

VESICA: oval with pointed head and foot.

VESTIBULE: anteroom or entrance hall.

VILLA: (1) according to Gwilt (1842) 'a country house for the residence of opulent persons'; (2) Romano-British country houses cum farms, to which the description given in (1)

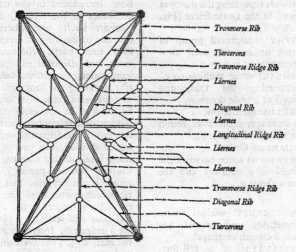

Transverse Rib
Tiercerons
Transverse Ridge Rib
Liernes
Diagonal Rib
Liernes
Longitudinal Ridge Rib
Liernes
Liernes
Transverse Ridge Rib
Diagonal Rib
Tiercerons

Fig. 21

more or less applies. They developed with the growth of urbanization. The basic type is the simple corridor pattern with rooms opening off a single passage; the next stage is the addition of wings. The courtyard villa fills a square plan with subsidiary buildings and an enclosure wall with a gate facing the main corridor block.

VITRIFIED: made similar to glass.

VITRUVIAN OPENING: A door or window which diminishes towards the top, as advocated by Vitruvius, bk. IV, chapter VI.

VOLUTE: spiral scroll, one of the component parts of an Ionic column (see Order).

VOUSSOIR: wedge-shaped stone used in arch construction.

WAGON ROOF: roof in which by closely set rafters with arched braces the appearance of the inside of a canvas tilt over a wagon is achieved. Wagon roofs can be panelled or plastered (ceiled) or left uncovered.

WAINSCOT: timber lining to walls.

WALL PLATE: see Roof.

WATERLEAF: leaf shape used in later C12 capitals. The waterleaf is a broad, unribbed, tapering leaf curving up towards the angle of the abacus and turned in at the top (Fig. 22).

Fig. 22

WEALDEN HOUSE: timber-framed house with the hall in the centre and wings projecting only slightly and only on the jutting upper floor. The roof, however, runs through without a break between wings and hall, and the eaves of the hall part are therefore exceptionally deep. They are supported by diagonal, usually curved, braces starting from the short inner sides of the overhanging wings and rising parallel with the front wall of the hall towards the centre of the eaves.

WEATHERBOARDING: overlapping horizontal boards, covering a timber-framed wall.

WEATHERING: sloped horizontal surface on sills, buttresses, etc., to throw off water.

WEEPERS: small figures placed in niches along the sides of some medieval tombs (also called Mourners).

WHEEL WINDOW: *see* Rose Window.

INDEX OF PLATES

INDEX OF ARTISTS

INDEX OF PLACES